South Wales

South Wales

Ruth Thomas

John Bartholomew & Son Limited
Edinburgh and London

Other Titles in this Series:

Available in 1977:
Cumbria JOHN PARKER
Devon & Cornwall DENYS KAY-ROBINSON
The Scottish Highlands JOHN A. LISTER

In preparation:
South-East England OLIVER MASON
North Yorkshire CHRISTOPHER STAFFORD

First published in Great Britain 1977 by
JOHN BARTHOLOMEW & SON LIMITED
12 Duncan Street, Edinburgh EH9 1TA
And 216 High Street, Bromley BR1 1PW

ISBN 0 7028 1024 X

All maps © John Bartholomew & Son Limited

Book and jacket design: Susan Waywell

Printed in Great Britain by
Hazell Watson & Viney Limited,
Aylesbury, Buckinghamshire

Colour sections printed in Great Britain by
John Bartholomew & Son Limited, Edinburgh

Contents

* The map section at the end of the book is numbered separately, in bold type.

Regional Map

Showing the Area Covered by this Guide

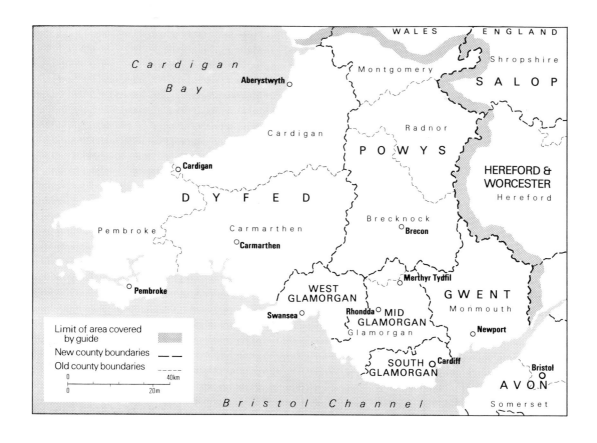

Acknowledgements

I should like to thank the following authors and publishers for their permission to quote from copyright material: J. M. Dent and Sons Ltd for the extract from Daniel Defoe's *Tour through England and Wales*, in the Everyman edition; Jonathan Cape Ltd and Mr F. R. Fletcher for extracts from *Kilvert's Diary*, edited by William Plomer; J. M. Dent and Sons Ltd and the Trustees for the Copyrights of the late Dylan Thomas for extracts from 'A Visit to Grandpa's', in *Portrait of the Artist as a Young Dog* (1940), 'Reminiscences of Childhood', 'Laugharne', and 'Welsh Poets', in *Quite Early One Morning* (1954; Aldine Paperback 1967); R. S. Thomas for lines from his poem 'Where to Go', published in *Welsh Voices* (Dent, 1967); the *New Statesman* for the extract from 'What's wrong with South Wales?' by Dr Thomas Jones, which I found in Professor Brinley Thomas's article 'The growth of industrial towns', *Wales through the Ages*, ed. A. J. Roderick, Christopher Davies Ltd, Swansea, 1960, Vol. II. The extract from William Williams's elegy on the death of Daniel Rowland is quoted from the essay by E. D. Jones, 'The Methodist Revival', in the same collection.

I am very grateful to those who courteously answered my queries or sent materials: to Mr A. V. Babbidge of the Pontypool Museum, Hilary Bulmer of the Brecknock Museum, the Curator of the Museum at Tre'r Ddol, the Vicar of St Nicholas, Montgomery, and Mr E. D. Williams of the Traffic Assistants Office, British Rail, Aberystwyth. I am particularly indebted to Elizabeth M. Davies of the Wales Tourist Board, who undertook the onerous task of reading through the whole of the gazetteer, making a number of useful corrections and suggestions. On a personal note, I would like to record my special thanks to all my relatives – Welsh, English, and Irish – for their practical help, encouragement, and forbearance.

Finally I must make a general acknowledgement to all those writers of local guides, histories, and specialized studies of Welsh life and landscape, to whom this book is indebted.

Ruth Thomas
York
June 1976

Publishers' Note
The publishers of this guide are always pleased to acknowledge any corrections brought to their notice by readers. Correspondence should be addressed to the Guide-book Editor, John Bartholomew & Son Limited, 216 High Street, Bromley BR1 1 PW.

Introduction

Landscape and Nature

South Wales has some of the oldest and hardest rocks in Britain. Folded and pleated by movements of the earth's surface, eroded by rivers or by submergence in the sea, blanketed by sediments and blown sands, carved by the passage of glaciers, these resistant rocks form, none the less, the underlying structure of the landscape. What lies in layers under one's feet – the vertical structure, or the geology – bears a complex relationship to what appears around one: the horizontal structure, or the geography that is, for example, the height of the land, the shape of the coastline, the direction of rivers and the distances between their courses. And while these raw materials help to determine the activities of man in the landscape – his farming, mining, the placing of castles, towns, or sea-ports – man himself has been a constant factor in the changing appearance of the countryside. Landscape is a compromise between man and nature, a struggle, a co-operation, and a set of mutual constraints.

The centre of Wales is a high plateau, a complex area geologically, whose uniform surface has been produced by erosion. Plynlimon (Pumlumon) is its highest point, and from this flattish head rising above other flat-topped hills can be seen a vast expanse of brown, heathery uplands. Snowdon and Cadair Idris lie to the north, much higher; Cardigan Bay is to the west, and in the south the escarpment of the Brecon Beacons. A number of rivers and their headwaters cut valleys in this huge tract of uninhabited moorland: the Rheidol, for example, which rises in the cwm-lake directly beneath the north face of Plynlimon, the Wye, the Severn, the Towy, and the Teifi. In the higher land their valleys are wide and gentle, merging into the rounded surface of the plateau; on the borders of the upland, however, they become steep gorges such as that of the Rheidol at Devil's Bridge. On the high plateau proper there are almost no villages, and until recently there were few roads. Settlements are found only in the river valleys; their isolation, and the barrenness of the surrounding countryside, have kept them from growth. On the south-east edge of the central plateau anticlinal folding has brought to the surface volcanic, Ordovician rocks, which remain deeply buried elsewhere in mid Wales. This gives a varied, rugged appearance to the scenery around Builth, Llandrindod, and Llanwrtyd Wells.

To the west of these central mountains, Cardigan Bay has its own coastal plateau of about 180m., clearly recognizable to anyone travelling the main coast road between Cardigan and Aberystwyth. This plateau meets the sea in a series of high cliffs, which are much less indented than those of Pembrokeshire or Gower. Narrow, often forested valleys have cut deeply into the uplands: the Teifi below Llandysul, for example, with its falls at Cenarth and its steep wooded gorge at Cilgerran. Smaller valleys reach the sea through clefts in the plateau; small sandy beaches, such as Llangranog, have formed at the rivers' mouths.

On the geological map, south-west Dyfed, or Pembrokeshire, shows as an area of considerable complexity; these are the oldest rocks in all South Wales. In contrast to the smooth sweep of Cardigan Bay, the coast here is deeply embayed and indented, with greater variety of rock types and more dramatic evidence of deposit, erosion, and folding.

Between Strumble Head and Ramsey Island, for example, hard igneous rocks stand out as headlands between bays formed by the erosion of softer, sedimentary rocks. Stacks and islands – Skomer, Skokholm, Elegug Stacks – are also the product of wave erosion. From Tenby round to Angle folded Mountain Limestone and Old Red Sandstone give magnificently varied coastal scenery: Lydstep with its steep limestone cliffs and caverns, Manorbier with its reddish rocks, and red and blue beach pebbles. At St Bride's Bay, south of Newgale, and at Saundersfoot (where a geological anticline is clearly visible on the beach itself), the Coal Measures meet the sea, forming dark cliffs. The results of volcanic activity can be seen in the accumulation of lavas near Skomer, Treffgarne (at the quarries), and at Strumble Head, where the deposits are hundreds of metres thick. In a number of places – Caldy Island, for example – a raised beach occurs, a little above the present high-water mark, while elsewhere – Amroth, Manorbier, Lydstep – the rise in sea-level after the melting of the last ice has left drowned peats and other sediments, and, below the sands, the remnants of forests.

Behind the shore a level plateau, 60m.–90m. high, is also the result of marine erosion. Indeed, the whole surface of Pembrokeshire with its gentle, rounded hills was probably once a sea floor; no other agent, it is thought, could have reduced so complex an underlying structure to so uniform a plateau. However, the scenery is far from monotonous. The plateau itself rises in steps from about 60m. near the coast to nearly 180m. north-east of Newport. The Ridgeway behind Tenby and the hills of Carn Llidi and Penberi near St David's are isolated relics of higher platforms. The Preseli Hills themselves, Ordovician rocks with volcanic outcrops, rise above the plateau; the dolerites of this area, with their pink and white spots of quartz, provided the famous 'bluestones' of Stonehenge. On the lower ground of south Pembrokeshire huge boulders have been deposited by a moving ice-sheet: one from Scotland stands at Bosherston, another, from North Wales, at St Govan's Head. And if the variety of underlying rock is not reflected in the accidents of the terrain, it can be seen in the older buildings of the peninsula: St David's Cathedral in purple Cambrian sandstone, Pembroke town and castle in grey Mountain Limestone. In the south of the peninsula the scenery is further varied by the forked complex of rivers known as the Cleddau, which meet the sea at Milford Haven, itself a *ria* or drowned valley.

Between this peninsula and the borders of the South Wales coal-field the Towy River flows along the fold of the Towy anticline, a long inlier of Ordovician rocks that runs from west Carmarthenshire deep into Powys near Rhayader and Llandrindod. (The mid-Wales railway from Shrewsbury follows this line for much of its course.) In the broad, fertile valley with alluvial meadows are small but significant market-towns: Llandovery, Llandeilo, and Carmarthen. Carmarthen Bay itself, into which flow the Towy, Taf, and Gwendraeth rivers, is eroded partly in Upper Carboniferous shales and partly in Old Red Sandstone; the character of its coastline has been much affected by blown sand. Inland, and to the north-east, the Black Mountain is a bleak moorland of Millstone Grit with a thin northern border of Carboniferous Limestone, on an outlier of which stands, notably, the castle of Carreg Cennen. The Black Mountain reaches a peak in the Carmarthen Van (790m.), where the Usk rises, and the Tawe has its source in Llyn-y-fan fawr, a moraine-dammed lake beneath a dramatic escarpment. From here a continuous expanse of mountain, mainly Old Red Sandstone, stretches through Fforest Fawr and the Brecon Beacons as far as the low-lying borderland of northern Gwent.

Industrial South Wales is largely confined, for obvious reasons, to the coal-field. South of this area, however, and totally unlike it, are two regions that are almost un-spoilt. The Gower Peninsula, designated an Area of Outstanding Natural Beauty, lies south and west of Swansea, where the Coal Measures end. Like the peninsula of south-west Dyfed, Gower consists mainly of Old Red Sandstone and Mountain or Carboni-ferous Limestone, sharply folded on an east–west plane, but with a low plateau surface formed, here again, by the erosion of waves. That Gower once lay beneath the sea ac-counts for its flat-topped headlands and level farming country. The underlying Old Red Sandstone comes to the surface in the narrow ridge of Cefn Bryn, a sharp anticline, which reaches 180m. This backbone of Gower has resisted denudation because of the presence in its rocks of hard quartz conglomerates. Llanmadog Hill and Rhosili Down are residuals of the same Old Red Sandstone, and reach similar heights above the plateau. Over much of inland Gower the basic limestone has a blanket of boulder clay, which makes fertile agricultural land. The southern coast, however, has splendidly varied limestone cliffs, and deep bays, which occur at faultlines or which conform, as at Port Einon and Oxwich, to synclines in the Millstone Grit. Raised beaches can be recog-nized, from the presence of shells in the compressed shingle, at a number of places along this coast, and the bone caves, Paviland for example, where remains of prehistoric animals and men have been discovered, often open onto this earlier beach platform. At Bishopston, in the limestone, the Pennard stream runs underground, forming a 'dry valley'. The north Gower coast has an entirely different character, for the limestone cliffs (where they occur) now stand some distance inland, while the shoreline itself has been built up by sand blown by the prevailing south-westerlies.

Between the southern rim of the coal-field and the sea, the Vale of Glamorgan is another lowland, agricultural region, which is more fertile and less isolated than Gower. The Vale is not a valley but rather a plateau drained by a number of small rivers. At the coast it meets the sea in a series of almost vertical cliffs, which are kept steep and sharp by constant rock-falls. A low platform of rock often lies beneath these cliffs, which are frequently complex in their strata and rich in fossils. Penarth Head, for example, has horizontal beds of red marls, green marls, black shales, and blue and yellow limestones. Near Lavernock the beds are undulating, so that in places blue lias limestone is found at sea-level. Barry has its own peculiarities in cliffs: at Cold Knap grey Mountain Lime-stone, steeply inclined, is capped by horizontal rocks of New Red Sandstone lying un-conformably on the slanting, older rocks. Here the basic rock 'floor' of the Vale – lias limestone and New Red Sandstone – occurs above sea-level, exposing the more disturbed formations beneath. Mountain Limestone reappears at Witches Point (Southerndown) and at Porthcawl, and inland east of Ogmore, where newer beds have been removed by denudation.

The coal-field is a large basin stretching from Kidwelly and Ammanford in the west to Merthyr Tydfil and Pontypool, and back round to Llantrisant and Swansea. South of the Old Red Sandstone escarpment of the Brecon Beacons are further high scarps of Carboniferous Limestone and Millstone Grit, which dip southwards under the softer shales of the Coal Measures. In turn, these shales dip beneath the Pennant Sandstone, which reaches nearly 600m. at Craig-y-llyn (at the head of the Rhondda) and which forms an undulating plateau of high, flat-topped hills within the coalfield. Beneath this layer of dull greyish-green sandstone (which provided much of the material for early house building in this area) the Coal Measures lie in a saucer-shaped stratum, the deeper seams giving, in general, the better coal. Where the shales of the Coal Measures come to the surface, on the borders of the coal-field, as for example at Merthyr Tydfil or Caerphilly, the valleys are wider and settlements much less constricted; however, the seams have been more quickly exhausted, and many collieries have now closed. Further in, the plateau is cut by deep, parallel valleys – Taff, Ebbw, Rhymney, Rhondda, and so on – that run north-west to south-east without relation to the present underlying geological structure. It seems likely that some earlier cover of rock, now eroded away, at one time determined the course of these rivers. Exceptions are, near the western edge, the Neath and Tawe valleys, which follow 'disturbances', that is, valleys formed by belts of crushed and weakened rocks. While these two rivers have thus been able to erode their valleys into broader trenches than those of east Glamorgan and Gwent, their small tributaries, running over much harder rock, have carved out narrow gorges: the waterfalls of the lower Neath Valley are good examples. At the top of the same valley the head-streams of the Neath River cross the belts of Mountain Limestone and Millstone Grit that border the coal-field, and the result is a magnificent series of limestone caverns, chasms, and falls.

To the north of the coal-field the Carmarthenshire Black Mountain, Fforest Fawr, the Brecon Beacons, and the Black Mountains of Powys and Gwent are a huge uplifted and south-tilting mass of Devonian Old Red Sandstone. Layers of resistant Brownstones over 240m. thick are the predominant element; above these, plateau beds of conglomerates and sandstones give these mountains their characteristic table-tops. There are dramatic escarpments, all of which face north or north-west, and which reach their highest point in Pen-y-fan (872m.). Beneath the Black Mountain scarp, Llyn-y-fan fach and Llyn-y-fan fawr are two cwm-lakes formed in glaciated hollows (where the sun could not melt the ice) and dammed up behind moraines. Elsewhere, corrie lakes have been reduced to boggy hollows or to small head-streams such as the Taf Fechan. Glaciation has also been responsible for a number of other scenic features in the Brecon Beacons National Park: the morainic mounds near Storey Arms, for example, the 'glaciated pavement' in the Millstone Grit surfaces near Ystradfellte, and the long snow scree at the foot of Fan Hir in the Black Mountain.

Between the Beacons and the coal-field thin belts of Carboniferous Limestone and of Millstone Grit come to the surface. The spectacular scenery of the upper Neath Valley near Ystradfellte has already been mentioned. The presence of limestone also produces the swallow- or sink-holes that are particularly frequent in the Brecon Beacons National Park. These small pits are formed by solution of the rock by rainwater or streams, and by the collapse of the Basal Grit into caverns in the limestone below. Porth-yr-ogof, through which the Mellte flows, is the best known of the caverns. Elsewhere are limestone cliffs with their characteristic flora, as at Craig-y-ciliau; Pen Cerrig Calch (*calch* = chalk) is an isolated limestone outlier north of the Usk. Millstone Grit can be seen at Garreg Lwyd ('grey rock'), in the western scarp of the Black Mountain, and at the opposite end of the region, on the slopes of Blorenge and Gilwern Hill near Abergavenny.

The Borderland is an area of special geological interest, for here two types of countryside, upland and lowland, meet. This transitional zone is, however, a wide one, and no clear geological boundary may be drawn between Wales and England, except perhaps in the south-east, where the margin of the coal-field, between Newport and Abergavenny, is strongly marked by escarpment. (This does not, of course, coincide with the 'political' border.) In the north-east of our region the border runs to the west of the line where the upland plateau meets the English plain. From Montgomery Castle, for instance, one can look out east towards Corndon Hill (505m.), the Stiperstones, the Long Mynd, and the Clee Hills, all outcrops of Wales inside Shropshire. The Kerry Hills, south of Newtown, are part of the same folding that produced the Long Mountain syncline. Further south the border follows the course of the Teme, which rises in Clun Forest, another 'English' extension of the mid-Wales upland plateau.

South of Ludlow an extensive area of Old Red Sandstone stretches southwards to Monmouth and meets the Bristol Channel coast near Newport. On the east, where the softer marls form the surface, the country is undulating and fertile, with reddish fields; it is crossed by the broad plain of the Wye and its tributaries, the Lugg and the Monnow. To the south-west the Black Mountains are a high plateau of harder rock that forms a scarp above the Wye and is dissected by deep valleys such as those of the Honddu and the Grwyne Fawr. The chalk cliffs on which Chepstow Castle is built are part of a basin of Carboniferous Limestone in whose north-east outcrop lies the small Forest of Dean coal-field.

The Wye itself is a sort of geological curiosity, for below Ross its valley cuts deeply into the Old Red Sandstone, avoiding the easier path a little further west. The river's course is thus determined neither by the present relief nor by the underlying structure of rock. Its valley may, like those of the South Wales coal-field, have been developed on a gently inclined layer of newer rocks, which have since disappeared through erosion and the continual staggered uplift of the mass of Wales. The meanders are particularly remarkable, for they normally occur in wide alluvial plains rather than in deeply-incised gorges. The most notable loops of the Wye are those at Symonds Yat and, further downstream, at Tintern and Wynd Cliff, where precipitous crags of limestone overhang the water. At Redbrook on the English bank is an abandoned meander, partly dry and partly occupied by tributaries. Newland village, near Redbrook, stands in a hanging valley where the river clearly flowed, at some distant time, in a bed nearly 120m. above the present channel. At St Briavel's a semicircular amphitheatre of limestone must also once have been the river's gorge.

South Wales, then, is a mountainous country, with a long coastline facing south and west into the prevailing Atlantic gales. Behind the shore is a coastal plain or plateau of varying width, and this, with a few broad river valleys, provides the only good agricultural land. These, too, until the nineteenth-century development of the coal-field, were the natural areas for human settlement: the uplands, still thinly peopled, are suitable only for sheep and conifers. Upland and lowland has been a traditional contrast of life in Wales, though in fact much of the country seems to straddle the two; there are not many places in South Wales from which one cannot, at least in fine weather, see a mountain. But towns and villages have, for obvious reasons, stuck to the lower ground; higher up are mainly scattered farmsteads with the occasional chapel or church, serving a huge parish, and seemingly miles from anywhere. Indeed, until comparatively recent times, the practice of transhumance meant that the higher pastures were used mainly in the warmer months: the flocks would be driven up from the *hendre* or 'winter residence' to the mountain sheep-walks. *Hafod*, 'summer dwelling', is still a popular name for Welsh houses.

It is, too, a peculiarly watery country. Winters are mild, windy, and wet, the mountains often disappearing for weeks into a fine veil of mist. (Summers are on the whole no wetter than in other parts of western Britain.) Every inland town has its river, and often an ancient bridge as part of its townscape. Freshwater lakes are rare, but small streams are everywhere, running as boggy flushes over the high moorlands, falling over mossy ledges into larger streams, joining up to form the major river systems: Usk, Wye, or Towy. The only sizeable towns of central Wales lie along the river valleys, which have provided routes out of, and into, Wales from England. All the major coastal towns stand at river mouths. And while there are six words in Welsh to denote different varieties of valley, the prevalence in place-names of *aber* (mouth of a river, or confluence of a smaller with a larger water-course, is also a clue to the importance of running water.

The simple geographical facts of South Wales explain more than its scenery or the differences in its farming. The mass of mountains in its centre, for example, divides North from South Wales and much of South Wales from itself, so that the country is difficult to unite politically. Small communities in these uplands remained traditional in life-style, self-sufficient but neighbourly amongst themselves, hospitable to travellers but slow to accept new settlers. Railways and good roads are, after all, only a hundred years or so old, and for centuries before that travel by sea was the quickest and most convenient form of transport. In early times the sea acted as link rather than as division, joining South Wales to the other Celtic countries of the west: Ireland, Scotland, Brittany. (Early Celtic literature is full of sea voyages.) Later settlers, when they did not use the southern coastal plain, also came by sea, bringing English and Flemish elements into Pembrokeshire and Gower. Sea-trade from the western South Wales ports was once an important part of the economy, while the south-coast ports from Pembrey east were a decisive factor in the development of the coal-field. And the sea-coast, which by its nature looks outward, has helped counteract the introspectiveness of the upland communities.

Until 1974 the administrative divisions of South Wales – the shires, or counties, that is – dated back to the Act of Union with England under Henry VIII, and, in some cases, even earlier. Reorganization was unpopular, for generations of Welshmen had been accustomed to thinking of their country in terms of these traditional units. Each county had its own mental contours of landscape and character, often partaking of folk-lore (the myth, for example, that the 'Cardy', or Cardiganshire man, is a miser, the Scotsman of Wales), but none the less deeply cherished and with more than a grain of truth. Welshmen are likely for quite some time to go on thinking of their own bit of land as Pembrokeshire or Carmarthenshire and so on, and older maps and books will of course still contain the terms; it is worthwhile, then, examining them in a little detail.

The new county of Gwent, now officially part of Wales, largely coincides with the former county of Monmouthshire, itself created in 1536 out of the Norman lordships that had usurped the ancient Welsh kingdom of Gwent. (This circular motion of names and boundaries will be observed again later.) Monmouthshire had been for centuries unsure of where its allegiance lay, and today, with its Welsh-speaking population reduced to the tiniest minority, its inclusion in Wales still seems to some people debatable. In the east of the county there may well appear to be no difference between the two banks of the Wye or the Monnow, which are the boundary with England. Yet in the industrial valleys of the west, towns such as Ebbw Vale, Pontypool, or Abertillery may not be Welsh in language but are unmistakably Welsh in flavour.

Glamorgan (the name is from Morgannwg, the eighth-century Welsh kingdom) remains almost exactly as it was, though divided now into West, Mid, and South for reasons of population density. Its southern, lowland portion (the Norman lordship) and the hilly Welsh country of the interior were fused into a shire at the 1536 Act of Union. Indeed, this contrast of Bro Morgannwg and Blaenau Morgannwg, vale and uplands, agriculture and mining (in simple terms), gives the county its particular strength and character. The Gower Peninsula, a separate lordship under the Normans, is a sort of misfit; joined onto Glamorgan in 1536 and retained by inertia ever since, its real historical links are with Deheubarth, the medieval Welsh kingdom of the south-west.

Powys, too, was an ancient Welsh kingdom, of fluctuating extent, and is now an enormous new county, which has gobbled up Breconshire, Radnorshire, and much of Montgomeryshire. All three creations of the Act of Union, Breconshire included the once independent territory of Brycheiniog (named after an early ruler, Brychan), while Radnorshire and Montgomery were parts and offshoots of Powys, which had like the rest of the Marches fallen into Norman hands. Breconshire and Radnorshire, pierced as they are by the long valleys of the Usk and the upper Wye, have in spite of their forbidding mountains been receptive to English influences; Montgomery, further north, less so.

Of the three shires that have been amalgamated to form the new county of Dyfed, Cardiganshire and Carmarthenshire were created as early as 1284 after Edward I had confiscated the Welsh territories of his adversary Llywellyn ap Gruffydd. 'Cardigan', which stretched from the Teifi to the Dovey, is an English version of Ceredigion, land of Ceredig, the son of the semi-legendary fifth-century Celtic king Cunedda. Carmarthenshire, named after its chief town (itself named somewhat poetically after the enchanter Merlin), was an addition of the royal county and lordship of Carmarthen and, inland, the territory on each side of the Towy River. The third, Pembrokeshire, dated from 1536, and was a fusion of a number of separate lordships, from Tenby and Pembroke in the south to Cemais and Cilgerran in the north. This latter, with its Norman settlements the most Anglicized of the south-western shires, is also the only one to fall firmly within the boundaries of the historical Welsh kingdom of Dyfed. (Dimetia was, however, in Roman times, the larger territory of the tribe of the Demetae.) The confusion of these three counties into one is a peculiarly hard concept for the Welsh mind to swallow; there was, it seemed, something more homely, Welsh, and austere in Cardiganshire, something more fertile, green, and open in Carmarthenshire, something more mysterious, bluish-grey, foreign about Pembrokeshire, which, thrown into a melting-pot, will not emerge as the character of 'Dyfed'. But however regrettable the anomalies created by the administrative boundary revisions of 1974, they – of course – impinge not at all on the natural life of Wales: other, more fundamental, influences affect the flora and fauna.

Three-quarters of the land-mass of South Wales was once, like much of Britain, covered in deciduous forest. Five thousand years of grazing herds, 4,000 years of ploughing, have made gradual inroads, a steady process of attrition that in the last two centuries, with their insatiable demand for timber as fuel and building material, has become a galloping consumption. Huge numbers of trees disappeared into the early charcoal furnaces, and, later, into the mines as pitprops. In the south-east the fumes from metal-working destroyed vast areas of vegetation; elsewhere, farming meant drainage and hedges, the loss of some habitats and the appearance of new ones. Fortunately for the natural life of South Wales, population and industry have been largely concentrated in one corner of the region, while much of the rest, though it has lost its forests, has otherwise remained relatively unspoilt. At present the risks are as great as ever: the pollution of the shore by oil and refuse, the sprawl of towns, the widespread use of chemicals in farming are serious threats. At the same time, however, concern and conservancy are on a wider and more public scale. The Forestry Commission has, since 1919, replanted huge areas of woodland (though not with the indigenous oak). Reservoirs, which destroy valleys, have also provided new breeding-grounds for waterfowl. South Wales has two extensive National Parks and an increasing number of Nature Reserves. Every county now has its signposted Nature Trails, often with leaflet and information kiosk to explain the life of the countryside. Meanwhile, individuals who dislike this somewhat museum-like approach to nature (essential though it is if we are not to kill the very thing we love) still have plenty of space. There remains a prodigious amount of unspoilt coastline, from rocky cliffs and islands to dunes and estuaries; bare, grassy uplands, heaths and moors; peat-bogs, river valleys, and freshwater pools; farmland and forest. Detailed information on any particular locality can be obtained from the National Park information centres, or from the County Naturalists' Trusts (one each for Gwent, Glamorgan, Brecknock, Hereford with Radnor, plus the West Wales Naturalists' Trust, which covers the present county of Dyfed).

Gwent is an excellent example of the variety of habitat that can be found within a small area in South Wales. It lacks, of course, the dramatic coast-line of the more westerly parts of the region, but the flat, muddy shores of the Severn Estuary, protected along much of its length by sea walls and drained by a mesh of ditches or 'reens', provide haunts and breeding-places for large numbers of wildfowl. Access to the 24ha. Nature Reserve south of Magor is limited, but many other stretches of this strange coast, near Caldicot, Undy, Goldcliff, and Peterstone Wentloog, for example, can be reached by minor roads and trackways. Common waders here include snipe, curlew, and sand-piper; there are a small herd of mute swans (and visiting whooper swans) and a large flock of wintering teal at Nedern Brook (near Caldicot). Peregrine, long-tailed skua, and razorbill have been observed at Goldcliff. Gwent County Council are planning to establish a walk along the Severn shore from Newport to Chepstow.

Inland, the county's eastern border is the deep wooded gorge of the Wye, with Tintern Forest now mainly coniferous. In the Wye Valley (a scheduled Area of Outstanding Natural Beauty) a Nature Trail runs through the Wynd Cliff National Nature Reserve, whose deciduous mixed woodland provides habitat for a rich flora: the rare Martagon Lily, for example, and the Tintern Spurge (*Euphorbia stricta*), which is found only in these limestone woods. Grey herons and cormorants fish the river below. Between the Wye and the edge of the coal-field near Pontypool much of eastern Gwent is undulating agricultural country. North-east of Newport, Wentwood, once a royal chase and heavily forested, now has conifers and a small reservoir. A number of nature walks start there, with views out to the Bristol Channel and the chance to see kingfisher, dipper, buzzard, nightjar, and woodpecker. Golden orioles have occasionally been seen, while a variety of waterfowl winter on the reservoir. To the north, Gwent's uplands shade into the Black Mountains and the Brecon Beacons; to the west is the characteristic scenery of the industrial valleys, with their newly-established forests and bare, heathery upland plateaus. There are Forestry Commission walks near Abercarn in the Ebbw Valley, while the moorlands on Blorenge Mountain near Abergavenny have indigenous red grouse, merlin, ring ouzel, wheatear, and meadow pipit. Around Caerwent and Caerleon botanists might look for the poisonous Meadow Saffron (*Colchicum autumnale*, sometimes known as Naked Ladies), and the glossy-leaved Alexanders (*Smyrnium olusatrum*) once eaten like celery, which are both thought to have been introduced into Britain by the Romans.

Glamorgan is the county most heavily scarred by industry in South Wales. Yet more than half its area remains unspoiled: the extensive tract of mountain and acid moorland that separates the valleys, plus the farmlands of the Vale of Glamorgan and of Gower. Between Cardiff and Swansea large stretches of coastline have been preempted by industrial and urban development; for example, a long belt of sand-dunes once rich in bird and plant life now lies under the Margam steelworks. There remains only a small but still fascinating area around the freshwater Kenfig Pool, with its rare Welsh Mudwort (*Limosella subulata*) and Fen Orchid. Further east, however, between Porthcawl and Penarth, a rocky and dangerous coast has largely resisted such inroads. Penarth and Lavernock Point are good places for observing the migrations of birds in spring and autumn: unusual sightings include Bonelli's warbler, the red-backed shrike, waxwing, shearwater, and Arctic skua, while the limestone cliffs themselves yield interesting flora and fossils.

Glamorgan's town dwellers are, in fact, well served by nature walks. Even in Cardiff the City Council has recently prepared a whole range of trails and rambles using the city's numerous parks and commons, and the newly-reclaimed Glamorgan Canal. There are Country Parks at Aberdare, Afan Argoed (north of Port Talbot), and Margam; a series of trails runs through deciduous forests of oak, alder, larch, birch, and beech, while Margam has, as legacy from its 'castle', a large herd of fallow deer. But anyone familiar with the county will know how close the iron and coal towns always were to the open countryside, often high above them, with its persistent flora: sessile oak, mountain ash, gorse, broom, heather, bracken, whinberry, bluebell, and foxglove. Larks, lapwings, meadow pipits nest on the upland plateau; on the higher reaches, above Blaen Rhondda, for example, buzzard, kestrel, the occasional sparrowhawk, and even the snow bunting, appear. There are moles, rabbits, foxes, and a variety of moths and butterflies.

While industry sprawls out westwards to Llanelli and Burry Port, the small peninsula of the Gower has, through its lack of exploitable resources, remained untouched; the only serious threat to the area is the increasing numbers of summer tourists. Here in a few square km. are farmlands, heathland, oakwoods, salt-marshes, dunes, limestone cliffs and the grasslands on their tops. Broad Pool, at Cillibion, on Cefn Bryn, is a small freshwater lake, now a Nature Reserve (public access), where lapwing, snipe, curlew, and redshank can be observed among the yellow Fringed Water-lily; Bewick's swan has been seen here in winter. Elsewhere, the coast, never far away in Gower, is the best place for birdwatching. Oxwich, a National Nature Reserve, has a variety of habitat: woodland, marsh, dune, and foreshore; it is the most westerly breeding site for the reed warbler. Port Einon has large numbers of waders on its tidal rocks, and ravens, stonechats, and linnets breed on and around the limestone cliffs. At Rhosili, also a Nature Reserve, Worms Head is accessible at low tide, with its colonies of razorbill, guillemot, kittiwake, and the occasional puffin. On the north coast cliffs give way to the extensive sand-dunes and saltmarshes of the Burry Estuary. Enormous flocks of oystercatcher, knot, and dunlin can be seen from the Reserve at Whiteford Burrows, with wintering divers and grebes, a resident flock of eider duck, and a few nesting red-breasted merganser.

Gower with its limestone is exceptionally rich in wild flowers, some of them rare. Yellow Whitlow-grass (*Draba aizoides*) found in the Alps and Pyrenees grows near Pennard and nowhere else in Britain. Fen orchid, Marsh orchid, and Marsh Helleborine grow in the dunes, and the pink flowers of Marsh Mallow on Llanrhidian marshes. On the southern cliffs grow Bloody Cranesbill with its large purple petals, and the blue spikes of Spring Squill. Gower is the only Welsh locality for the Isle of Man Cabbage, usually a more northerly plant; other rare or scarce species include Goldilocks, Hoary Rock-rose, Purple Gromwell, and Small Rest-harrow.

The whole of south-west Wales is now one huge maritime county, Dyfed. Seals, porpoises, and visiting sharks can be spotted near its rocky shores, while its estuaries and offshore islands provide varied sanctuary for seabirds. Even semi-industrial areas like Pembrey and Burry Port on the Carmarthen Bay coast have unusual birds of passage – the occasional roseate tern, the eider duck, the great crested grebe, for example – and at Laugharne the Taf Estuary is a mass of waders, which feed on the cockle-beds. Laugharne Burrows is a military firing-range, but Witchett Pool, within this, a small freshwater lake among dunes and reedbeds, with a wide population of waterbirds, can be visited in winter by organized parties. Talley Lakes, north of Llandeilo, are a breeding-place for grebe, mallard, and coot; wild swan, goosander, and goldeneye visit in winter. On Cardigan Bay is Bird Rock (near New Quay) with its huge colonies of kittiwake and guillemot, and Cardigan Island, a Nature Reserve that has lost its puffins but still has its gulls (including the great and the lesser black-backed), fulmars, shags, oystercatchers, and a pair or two of ravens. Perhaps the most important site for ornithologists on this Cardigan Bay coast is the Dovey Estuary, where nearly 1,500ha. of marsh and foreshore have been set aside as a Nature Reserve and Wildfowl Refuge. An enormous variety of birds breed or visit, and there is an established heronry. Ynys-hir, near the head of the estuary, where farm and woodland meet the marshes, is a reserve of the RSPB, open to the public several days a week in summer.

The soils of Cardiganshire and Carmarthenshire are predominantly acid, and there is increasing plantation of conifers. The Rheidol Valley near Devil's Bridge has, however, retained some magnificent oakwoods, while on the bare tops of Pumlumon (watch for red kite and buzzard) can be found some unusual club-mosses. Two fine examples of peat-bog, between Tregaron and the Dovey, are of special interest to naturalists. Cors Goch Glan Teifi or the 'Red Bog' of Tregaron is the result of ancient and gradual drainage of a moraine-dammed lake. Its otters and polecats, butterflies, moths, resident and visiting birds (including white stork and purple heron), rare mosses and bog-plants are now protected by a 300ha. National Nature Reserve. Cors Fochno, near Borth, is a similar but smaller area shading into the sand-dunes of Ynys-las.

In the extreme south-west of Dyfed, a line drawn from the Teifi near Cardigan to a point not far north of Tenby was the boundary of the former county of Pembroke. The entire coastline of this mild and windy peninsula, together with the upper reaches of the Cleddau and the Preseli Hills, is now a National Park; elsewhere in Pembrokeshire are sheep-grazed uplands, and, in the south, extensive dairy farming. Most of the offshore islands (Caldy is a notable exception) are Nature Reserves; the whole county is rich in plant and bird life (and not badly stocked with naturalists). Both the gentle countryside of the south and the wilder, more rugged moorlands of the north are worth exploring. In the Gwaun Valley inland from Fishguard, for example, steeply hanging oakwoods shelter primrose, bluebell, wood anemone, and a variety of birds, from buzzard, owl, and raven to grey wagtail, wood warbler, dipper, and kingfisher.

The charm of the interior, however, cannot compete with the constant surprises of the coastline. With Ramsey Island, Skomer, and the rocky mainland cliffs, Pembrokeshire produces more grey-seal pups than anywhere in Britain south of Northumberland. Porpoises, dolphins, even whales, have been seen offshore. Grassholm Island, 19km. out, has the fourth largest gannet colony in the North Atlantic. Landing there is difficult, but Skomer is more accessible: it has large flocks of guillemot, kittiwake, and razorbill, puffins (which sit on the Warden's roof) and the nocturnal Manx shearwater, plus its own species of common bank vole. Skokholm is the oldest bird observatory in the British Isles, and is especially good for bird migration; there is a colony of storm-petrel or Mother Carey's chicken. On the mainland precipitous cliff formations protect vast numbers of seabirds, while along the coastal footpath buzzards and the rare chough and peregrine falcon may occasionally be seen.

In spring the cliffs and headlands are a blaze of flowers: gorse, pink Thrift, bluebell, kidney vetch, cowslip, white Scurvy-grass, and Sea Campion. Tree Mallow, with large pink flowers, has colonized many of the offshore stacks. Some of the Pembrokeshire plants are rare, and confined to small areas: the long-trumpeted Tenby daffodil, for example, the Perennial Centaury, two kinds of dwarf Rock Sea-lavender, and the prostrate broom. On the boggy parts of the Preseli Hills grow cranberry, Bog Orchid, long-leaved Sundew; on the moorlands further south, near St David's, several varieties of orchid, and some unusual species – Waved St John's wort (*Hypericum undulatum*) and the small Slender Yellow Centaury (*Cicendia filiformis*).

Powys, with the Brecon Beacons National Park in its southern portion, is an immense and thinly populated upland county that stretches, at Machynlleth, across the whole width of Wales. It has no sea coast, but its high plateaus are dissected by a large number of river valleys, of which Usk, Wye, Severn, Irfon and Ithon, Lugg, Teme, and Arrow are only the best known. Farmland in the valleys, sheep-grazed moorland and coniferous forest above, share out the terrain. Here and there are the remains of the indigenous oakwoods: a fine one at Nant Irfon, above Llanwrtyd Wells, now forms part of a Nature Reserve. In certain lights these short trees, their twisted trunks grey with lichen, seem the Welsh translation of the Mediterranean olive-grove. The Forestry Plantations, darker and more regimented, are also poorer as habitat, though certain species of animal – the polecat, the tiny goldcrest – prefer their cover. Freshwater lakes are relatively few, but great crested grebe breed at Glan Llyn near Rhayader, and grebe and tufted duck at Llan Bwch-llyn on Llandeilo Hill near Aberedw. Llyn Mawr, north-west of Caersŵs, high in the moorlands, is an 8ha. Nature Reserve rich in water-plants. Its breeding birds include heron, mallard, teal, snipe, curlew, and the great crested grebe; wigeon, pochard, goldeneye, and a small flock of white-fronted geese can be seen in winter. The man-made reservoirs of the Elan Valley and Llyn Clywedog near Llanidloes provide new habitats for waterfowl; on the moorlands are buzzards and kestrels, the merlin and the golden plover, voles, lizards, and butterflies.

Brecon Beacons is a convenient name for the National Park, though in fact its 1,344 sq. km. stretch from the gentle slopes of the Towy Valley eastwards across the Carmarthenshire Black Mountain, Fforest Fawr, and the Beacons proper to the Black Mountains and the English border. In the north, around Brecon, is lowland farming; in the south, the edges of the coal-field and the caves and waterfalls of the upper Neath and Tawe valleys. Most of the park lies above the 300m. mark, mountains and open moorland grazed by the sheep and ponies, which far outnumber the human inhabitants. There is deciduous and coniferous woodland, much of it replanted after centuries of neglect, fine natural lakes (Llangorse, and the two Llyn-y-fans), and man-made reservoirs. The park is large enough to absorb huge numbers of summer visitors, but the western sections are perhaps least likely to be crowded. From Brecon, a primary base for the park, eight short walks have been organized; varying between 2 and 10km., these include the woodland of Priory Groves, the canal towpath, the summit of Pen-y-crug, and the Ffrwdgrech Falls. Around Abergavenny, in the Gwent section of the park, there are thirty signposted walks, of distances up to 18km.: Blorenge, the Sugar Loaf, Skirrid Fawr (all mountains), and the Usk and Honddu valleys (the latter with Llanthony Priory) are all within reach. These walks are especially valuable where enclosed farmland separates the walker's town base from the open hills.

Empty for much of the year, the moorland, forests, valleys, and fresh water of the park provide varied shelter for birds and mammals. Polecat, fox, and badger breed; grey squirrel and field vole can be destructive inhabitants. Marten have (very rarely) been seen, and, on a few occasions, the stoat has been known to change its winter fur to white, an unusual occurrence in the south of Britain. In the woodlands are goldcrest, woodpecker, stock dove, treecreeper, redstart; on the hills and moors curlew, snipe, buzzard, and the occasional kite. Around Blaenavon, in the south-east corner of the park, are the most southerly indigenous red grouse in Britain. At Llangorse Lake, the largest natural freshwater lake in South Wales, waterfowl breed and visit, though their peace is increasingly disturbed by the presence of campers and sportsmen. The courtship display of the great crested grebe can be watched here; tufted duck and mute swan breed; and sedge warblers and reed buntings are to be seen on the lake's fringes. Migrating in late summer, ringed plover, sandpiper, greenshank, spotted redshank, sanderling, and ruff have made visits. Talybont Reservoir, further south, has wintering goosander, shoveler, and goldeneye, and passing waders and terns; Llwyn-onn Reservoir above Merthyr Tydfil has a heronry. In the Carmarthenshire Black Mountain, at 500m., Llyn-y-fan fach is a small natural lake lying in the shadow of great cliffs of Old Red Sandstone; waterfowl here are less persistent than the upland birds, buzzard, merlin, ring ouzel, red grouse, and golden plover.

Much of the National Park is acid moorland: heather and bilberry moor in the drier, eastern mountains, and purplegrass moor in the wetter regions of the west. In boggy areas and around the numerous small water-courses grow bog-mosses and lichens, Butterwort, Bog asphodel, and the insectivorous Sundew. Of the open water, Llangorse Lake has the richest flora: reeds and aquatic plants (including the Fringed Waterlily), yellow flags, and, on the damp meadows nearby, the creamy-yellow Meadowrue and the Great Spearwort. The special botanical interest of the park, however, lies in its limestone outcrops. At Craig-y-Ciliau near Llangattock, in the beechwoods of Cwm Clydach, and in the Taf Fawr Valley, occur rare Whitebeams (*Sorbus leyana*, *S. minima*, and *S. leptophylla*), which grow nowhere else in the world (all three areas are Nature Reserves). The cliffs of Craig-y-Ciliau protect an exceptionally fine limestone flora from the cropping of sheep. Further north, Craig Cerrig Gleisiad near Brecon is one of the richest sites for arctic-alpine plants, some of which reach their southernmost point in Britain in the Brecon Beacons. Green Spleenwort, Least Willow, Northern Bedstraw, and Purple Saxifrage survive here on the high ledges.

Crickhowell (Powys), have only one ring of ramparts. Later ones, Pen-y-crug above Brecon, and Llanmelin at Chepstow, for example, have multiple defences and elaborate entrance arrangements. Some of these 'forts' seem to have been used as permanent tribal or family homes by men who cultivated the land below and grazed their herds on the upland pastures. Moel Drygarn (Dyfed) clearly housed a large population. Others may have served mainly as places of refuge from raiders in search of slaves and cattle. Carn Alw and Craig Gwrtheyrn in Dyfed are unusual in that, like Iberian fortified camps and some Irish ones, they make use of *chevaux-de-frise*: flat, pointed stones set at an angle into the surrounding hillside and providing a serious obstacle to any attacker on foot or horse.

The hill and promontory forts are not always easily traced at ground level. Many of them, indeed, have only been discovered by aerial photography, for their huts and ramparts have been reduced to faint grassy circles. However, they are often magnificently sited, and the views from hill or cliff-top compensate for the muddle on the ground. Pen-y-crug above Brecon, Pen Dinas above Aberystwyth, Carn Goch at Llangadog, Moel Drygarn and the coastal 'castles' of south-west Dyfed, and Gateholm Island off Marloes, where the hut settlement was undefended, are for this reason alone well worth a visit.

It was these mainly pastoral peoples with their circular fortresses that the Romans found when they arrived in Britain in 55 BC. The conquest of Wales, under the governor Ostorius Scapula, began nearly a hundred years later, in about AD 47. Wales was hostile, and the Roman advance was met by fierce resistance from the Silures of south-east Wales and the Ordovices of the north and central uplands. Not until *c.* 80, after Caractacus had been defeated (in 51), the Druids of Anglesey massacred (in 60), and the Silures subdued by Julius Frontinus (after 74), was the conquest complete. Even then, Wales remained largely a military zone, right up until the legions departed in the late fourth century.

Experts disagree as to how far the Roman invasion affected life in Wales. Evidence of the Romanization of lowland South Wales has been growing steadily, in the form of newly discovered villas and forts; however, large tracts of upland presumably remained untouched, while the Celtic hill-forts went on being inhabited until well after the conquest. On the landscape, as a whole, the Romans' effect was negligible. For the visitor, however, South Wales has a few outstanding Roman sites, and several lesser ones of some interest.

The Romans had established a line of fortresses along the Welsh border from the Dee to the Usk. From their major bases at Chester (Deva) in the north and Caerleon (Isca) in the south, and from smaller camps such as Usk (Burrium) and Abergavenny (Gobannium), they penetrated along the coastal plain and the lines of the river-valleys. Caerleon, the key to the military subjection of south-east Wales, is also one of the best-preserved Roman sites in the country, with the extensive remains of a large fortress, plus the only fully excavated amphitheatre in Britain. At Cardiff the Roman walls are clearly visible at the base of the curtain-wall of the later, Norman castle. Brecon Gaer, near Aberyscir, also has the remains of fort walls, over 3m. high in places, and the foundations of gateways. At Gelligaer in Glamorgan (note here again the place-name element *caer* = Latin *castrum*, a fort) only the outline of the ramparts has survived. There are good remains of marching camps at Y Pigwn near Trecastle, and feeble but extensive traces of practice-camps near Llandrindod Wells.

The most westerly Roman fort in South Wales is thought to have been Carmarthen

(Moridunum) in the territory of the Demetae (Dyfed). This tribe, it is suggested, may have accepted Roman rule peacefully and in preference to that of their neighbours, the Silures; certainly there are no military sites known in the extreme west. Recent excavations show Moridunum to have been the cantonal capital of the tribe. Town and amphitheatre date from the late second century, and the arena walls have now been partly reconstructed.

Though a number of Roman villas or Romanized farmsteads have been discovered along the south coast of Wales (Ely, near Cardiff, Llantwit Major, and Oystermouth, near Swansea, for example), and in the more fertile inland areas (Llanfrynach, near Brecon, and Llys Brychan, near Llangadog), none of these is presently on view to the public. Nor are there any remains of the rural temples thought to have stood at Wynd Cliff above the Wye and at St Donat's in South Glamorgan. The only significant relic in our region of civilian life under the Romans is the town of Caerwent (Venta Silurum), where extensive remains of the town walls, with their towers, and the foundations of a temple, house, and shops can be visited. Caerwent town makes an interesting contrast to the Iron Age hill-fort at Llanmelin Wood, only 2km. north-west, where members of the Silures lived up to and possibly after the Roman invasion.

At the height of Roman power in Wales a network of maybe 560km. of Roman road joined forts and auxiliary forts. At Aberyscir or Brecon Gaer three major highways crossed; another ran along the southern coastal plain from Caerleon to Loughor and Carmarthen. Roman roads tended to avoid the valleys, which were often marshy or heavily wooded. Their upland course can sometimes still be traced with the help of a large-scale map. A good stretch can be walked from Coelbren on the borders of West Glamorgan and Powys north-east across Fforest Fawr. In Wales Roman roads are often marked 'Sarn Helen', 'Helen's causeway', after the Welsh wife of the Emperor Magnus Maximus (the Macsen Wledig of Welsh legend). Such at any rate is the most attractive explanation; others invoke the Welsh for 'angle', *elin*, or for 'legion', *lleng*.

The road west from Brecon Gaer through Llandovery led to Pumsaint and the Dolaucothi gold-mines, which may have been an important justification for the Roman penetration of upland Wales. The site is the only known Roman gold-mine in Britain (and one of only a few in the whole of the Empire); there are the remains of an impressive aqueduct and reservoir system. A small fort has been excavated close by, a reminder that gold-mining was under strict military control. Later workings have somewhat obscured the Roman remains, at least for the non-specialist visitor, but the mine is worth seeing if only for its rarity value. The rural setting is peaceful and attractive, on National Trust land.

By the late fourth century most Roman forces had left Britain, forced to withdraw by the Barbarian invasions that threatened to destroy the Empire. In Wales the period of nearly seven centuries between the departure of the legions and the coming of the Normans, sometimes conveniently but misleadingly known as the Dark Ages, saw in fact a revival of native Celtic culture. The Irish Sea and the western sea-routes to France and Scotland became once more major highways, uniting rather than dividing the societies on their shores. The Romans had brought Christianity to Britain; in Wales, Scotland, and Ireland this now flourished in its own special form, producing saints, missionaries, and scholars who moved with ease from one province to another. A peaceful Celtic colonization of Brittany, from southern and eastern Wales, Devon, and Cornwall, took place in the fifth and sixth centuries, led by princes and clerics working together. Once there, they did valuable land clearance and established powerful religious centres. Not all cultural contacts were peaceful ones: Irish raids on the Welsh coast had been known and feared since the third century, before the Romans left. In the fifth, Irishmen from Leinster conquered Dyfed, establishing a dynasty that lasted four centuries and more. Brycheiniog (Brecon) in mid Wales also had a ruling house whose ancestors included an Irish prince; it is thought he may have come from the Irish colony in Pembrokeshire, or, perhaps more likely, on a separate invasion along the line of the Usk.

Politically, the centuries after the Roman withdrawal show the gradual emergence in Wales (as in England) of a number of small kingdoms whose boundaries vary with the strength of each ruler. North and South, separated by mountains, tend to develop into distinct regions, though the kingdom of Powys stretched at one time from the Dee to the upper Wye. Dyfed (smaller than its present area), Gwent, Morgannwg (Glamorgan), and a number of smaller unities each had its own ruling house. These kingdoms and those of the North were briefly brought together under the rule of Rhodri the Great (d. 878), who fought against the invading Danes and Saxons, and under his grandson Hywel the Good (d. *c.* 950), who codified the Welsh laws and followed a pragmatic policy of cooperation with the English king Athelstan.

One of the most lasting, yet intangible, monuments left by the Celtic Dark Ages on the modern map is the Welsh place-name. Some names are content to describe their locality – Aberaeron, 'mouth of the Aeron', Pontrhydygroes, 'bridge of the ford of the Cross', and so on. Others, however, reflect events that happened perhaps as long as fifteen centuries ago and have otherwise left little trace. *Llan*, for example, often roughly translated as 'church', means, more precisely, the enclosure within which a Celtic monk and his followers lived in religious community. In South Wales the chief of these were Llanilltud (Llantwit Major), where St Illtud set up a monastic school, Llancarfan, a site founded by St Cadoc but, unusually, named after its brook, and Llanbadarn Fawr (at Aberystwyth), a foundation of St Padarn or Paternus. During the fifth and sixth centuries an enormous missionary effort took flower in the Celtic lands. In Wales itself the 'saints', often members of royal houses, worked within their own homelands, as well as travelling to Cornwall or Brittany. Thus one can trace on the present map, and merely by studying the place-names, the spheres of influence of the different saints: Teilo (Llandeilo, Llantilio), Cadoc (Llangattock, Llangadog, Llangatwg, Cadoxton), David or Dewi (Llanddewi, Llanddew). Later on these major monastic churches became collegiate churches, ruled by a community of canons under an abbot or bishop. The name for these 'mother-churches' is *clas*, reflected in place-names such as Glascwm and Glasbury (Powys).

Anyone interested in the way such names provide keys to local history must also notice the prevalence, along the south coast of Wales, of place-names of Scandinavian origin. These, too, date from the Dark Ages: islands especially (Caldy, Skomer, Grassholm, Flatholm) and early harbours (Milford, Swansea, which is Sweyn's *ey* or island) were named by the Vikings who raided and settled on the land's edges in the last two centuries before the Norman Conquest. Even some Cardiff street-names – Gollgate, Womanby Street – reflect this same phenomenon.

Unfortunately, no church or monastic building has survived from the Celtic 'Age of Saints' in Wales. We have, however, a large number of inscribed gravestones and memorial-stones and several impressive high crosses. Apart from the museums at Cardiff and Carmarthen, there are special collections of early stones and crosses at Margam and in the church at Llantwit Major. Inscriptions, which commemorate priests and rulers, are usually in Latin, but in the south-west, and occasionally in Glamorgan and southern Powys (Breconshire), the Ogham alphabet is used. Ogham is an Irish form of writing – Irish influence was, as we have seen, strong in those parts of Wales – that consists of long and short strokes cut across or on one side of a line or edge. Some stones, the Voteporix stone at Carmarthen, for example, and the Sagranus stone at St Dogmaels, have bilingual texts. A number of memorials and grave-slabs carry crosses or incised ornaments, but the finest examples of Celtic religious sculpture in South Wales are the standing crosses, richly carved with intricate geometrical designs. The best examples are at Nevern, Carew, Penally (all in Dyfed), and Margam (West Glamorgan). Most of these differ from the Irish crosses of the same period, for their ornament is usually entirely abstract; the Penally cross, however, with its vine-scrolls and animal motifs, shows the influence of Northumbrian art.

The only other major relic of pre-Norman times is Offa's Dyke, the huge earthwork constructed by King Offa of Mercia in the late eighth century to provide a frontier and a line of defence between his kingdom and those of Wales. A number of short dykes had already been made, with the aim of protecting Mercian farmers on the edges of the Welsh uplands: Wat's Dyke, for instance, in the north, and Wantyn's Dyke in the Kerry Hills near Newtown. Offa's Dyke, however, superseded all these; running from Prestatyn in the north to the mouth of the Wye, it was a spectacular achievement. The dyke consisted of a high earthen bank, still 2m. high in places, and a ditch, usually on the western or Welsh side, with an average width of about 20m. across the two. Breaks in the dyke coincided with natural obstacles that rendered its continuation unnecessary – the Wye, for example, or heavy forest. That the frontier was agreed on by both sides seems clear from its course, for it left the Welsh the Severn crossing and their traffic on the lower Wye. However, it also denied them access to the rich lands of Hereford and Shropshire. Good stretches of the dyke can be seen near Montgomery and Knighton, and a long-distance footpath running along its length was opened in 1971.

Irish raids and settlements, Viking attacks on the south coast, powerful Saxon kingdoms to the east, none of these had fundamentally disrupted the Celtic culture of Wales. But in 1066 the most efficient fighting force in Europe succeeded in invading England; a few years later Wales was to feel the blow. The Normans proceeded to change Welsh life and the Welsh landscape on a scale that probably remained unequalled until the Industrial Revolution. Less thorough than in lowland England, for it could not of course subdue the most mountainous regions, the Norman Conquest brought both new political structures (the lordships, with their stone castles and walled towns) and a new agricultural system (the manor, with its open fields and strip-farming). The Church was reorganized, and new forms of monasticism were introduced from France. Most of South Wales' finest buildings date from this period of foreign occupation, while the majority of its older towns, in the lowlands and in the river valleys, have their origin in early Norman boroughs.

The conquest of Wales was not a concerted invasion. It happened, rather, piecemeal, as powerful Norman families pushed in as the occasion arose. The first to cross into what is now South Wales was William FitzOsbern, the recently created Earl of Hereford and one of the Conqueror's strongest knights. FitzOsbern moved down into Gwent, established the lordship of Strigoil and fortified Chepstow and Monmouth. By the time of his death in 1071 he had reached the Usk. In mid Wales, in the late 1080s, Bernard of Newmarch moved from Hay-on-Wye into the Welsh kingdom of Brycheiniog, building castles as he went. From Brecon Newmarch and his knights followed the Usk Valley southeast to Abergavenny, where Hamelin de Balun set up a castle and a Marcher lordship. About this same time, 1090 perhaps, Philip de Breos took Radnor and proceeded westwards towards Builth. In 1090–1 Robert FitzHamon overran Glamorgan from his base at Gloucester; his new castle was built at Cardiff, on the site of the old Roman fort. In the south-west the tide had been stemmed for a while by a strong Welsh ruler, Rhys ap Tewdwr, who retained his kingdom by swearing allegiance to William I. But after his death in 1093 the invasion ran riot. Roger of Montgomery, Earl of Shrewsbury, swept down from the Severn Valley through Cardiganshire and into Pembroke. Fierce if sporadic resistance from the Welsh delayed the completion of the conquest, and it was not until the reign of Henry I (1100–35) that some balance of power in South Wales was finally achieved.

It is important, however, not to overestimate the extent of Norman influence in South Wales. The fertile, low-lying lands of Glamorgan and Gwent were of course particularly susceptible to the new order. South Pembrokeshire, around Haverfordwest and the Cleddau rivers, where Henry I is said to have installed colonies of Flemings, was also much affected. But in upland west Wales, 'Deheubarth' as it was known then, large tracts of country were reconquered by the Welsh in the eleventh century and remained in their hands until the Wars of Independence two centuries later. Even in the Norman lordships of the south-east the territory was often divided into the 'Englishry' and the 'Welshry', the latter lying above the 120m. mark. In these upland areas Welsh laws and customs and Welsh agricultural practices survived. For several centuries, too, Wales was torn by sporadic revolts against the conquerors. Those of Llewellyn the Great and Llewellyn the Last in the thirteenth century (followed by the reconquest of the country by Edward I) and that of Owain Glyndwr around 1400 are the most significant, but many smaller, local insurrections took place. Meanwhile both Norman and Welsh ruling houses used strategic intermarriage to consolidate their power.

The very number and strength of the castles that survive in varying states of ruin in the South Wales countryside today testify to the difficulty with which the Normans imposed their rule – and the fear with which they regarded the native population. Not all, of course, are strictly 'Norman'. While the majority perhaps were built or at least founded by the Normans along their lines of advance or at the centres of the new lordships, others were erected by the Welsh, who were quick to use the Normans' own techniques against them. Yet others, though not so many in South Wales, were built by Edward I in the late thirteenth century as part of an ambitious and largely successful attempt to subdue the whole country once and for all.

In its earliest version the castle was a simple structure that could be rapidly constructed in the course of a military campaign. The central feature of the defence was a high flat-topped mound of earth, natural or artificial, known as the *motte*, surrounded by a ditch and crowned by a timber fence or palisade enclosing timber buildings. Below and beyond the motte was the *bailey*, a courtyard or series of courtyards each with its own ditch and timber defences. Wales and the borderlands are studded with these early motte-and-bailey castles, built as the Normans moved in along the river valleys and the coastal plain. Many remain as isolated grassy mounds; others have been incorporated into the plan of a later castle. The motte can be clearly seen at Cardiff Castle, at Llandovery, at Skenfrith, and many others. At Tretower the softness of the soil meant that the motte had to be given a revetment of stone.

Timber defences were especially easy to burn down, as can be seen from some of the dramatic scenes depicted in the Bayeux Tapestry. Stone began to be used, where available, soon after the Conquest. At Chepstow (Gwent), one of the earliest points of Norman penetration into Wales, parts of the Great Tower, built in stone by William FitzOsbern before 1071, are still visible in the lower storeys. In the following century, and as the Normans settled down in their new lands, construction in stone became increasingly common. Many of the old motte-and-bailey castles were now abandoned as the Norman lord concentrated his attention on fewer and better defences. The timber buildings on top of the motte began to be replaced by square or rectangular keeps, not, however, positioned on the mound itself, for they were too heavy. In the Vale of Glamorgan Ogmore Castle has an early-twelfth-century rectangular stone keep (though here there had apparently never been an elevated mound but a 'ring-motte' or circular enclosure within an earthen rampart). Newcastle (Bridgend) and Coity in the same area have late-twelfth-century stone curtain walls and square keeps. Elsewhere the motte itself might be given a stone curtain wall to protect its buildings: a fine example of such a 'shell-keep' can be seen at Cardiff Castle.

The evolution or development of the medieval castle can be seen as a sort of spiral, an 'arms race' of the period in which improvements in methods of siege and attack lead to improvements in fortifications and *vice versa*. In the twelfth century the early Crusaders came back from the East where they had seen immense fortresses of stone capable of resisting the usual attack by fire and sword. Complicated 'engines' began to be built, some designed to hurl large stones against or over castle walls, others capable of battering down the walls with huge wooden 'rams'. High towers on wheels came into use, to help with the scaling of high walls, while from underneath sappers mined the foundations to bring whole towers tumbling to the ground (a procedure not without danger for the attackers). To counteract such methods castles developed even higher walls, with wide moats, and projecting towers from which fire could be directed at the adversary directly beneath.

One of the most notable of these developments was the change from square to round towers for keeps, wall-turrets, and gateways. In a square or rectangular tower the most vulnerable points are the angles, which fall easily when mined; the circular tower is thus a much stronger structure. Circular wall- and gate-towers are common in all castles from the thirteenth century. Circular keeps are less frequent, for by the time they were invented the main focus of defence had shifted away from the centre of the castle to the curtain wall and entrance. Perhaps the finest example of the round keep in the whole of Britain is at Pembroke Castle, where the 22m.-high tower (*c.* 1200) had five storeys, a first-floor entrance, and an unusual domed roof of stone. In the Borders and mid Wales there are smaller round keeps or donjons at Skenfrith, Bronllys, and Tretower.

In the thirteenth century the tendency was more and more to make the castle into a series of separate compartments so that no attacker could be sure of success until he had gained the whole. Each wall-tower became a small fort in its own right, sometimes with no access from the ground floor to the floors above. Gateway defences were particularly elaborate: these can be well seen at Carreg Cennen with its ditches, ramps, and barbican, and at Pembroke and Llansteffan.

Castle-building in Britain reached its peak of efficiency, and indeed a sort of perfection, in the late thirteenth century with the Edwardian reconquest of Wales. Edward I's great castles – Caernarvon, Conwy, Beaumaris, and so on – are, alas, almost all in North Wales; there is little left at Aberystwyth. In the South, however, Kidwelly and Caerphilly, built by Marcher lords in the same period, are excellent examples of the concentric, 'Edwardian' castle; Caerphilly, indeed, has been called the finest castle in Britain. At Caerphilly there is no longer any keep as such; the great hall and other domestic buildings stand within a strong inner ward with its own gatehouses, curtain wall, and projecting towers. Surrounding this is the outer ward, itself protected by a completely encircling system of moats and lakes. Beyond this again are defensive outworks, the south platform, and the horn-work.

One of the fascinations of medieval castles is that no two are alike. For one thing, no site is the same, so that we have hill-top castles like Carreg Cennen, Dryslwyn, and Dinefwr, castles built on precipitous gorges such as Cilgerran, castles on sea-cliffs like St Donat's, Llansteffan, Manorbier, and castles like Caerphilly where flat marshy ground has been exploited to make lakes and moats. All castles need a supply of fresh water, from well or river; most command long views over the approaches and the surrounding countryside. And each castle is a unique mixture of centuries of building, in which each period pulled down, improved, or reconstructed what the previous one had left it. To decipher the various layers of the structure, from the early motte-and-bailey, if there was one, to the later, concentric fortress, can be confusing but it is worth the trouble. Two of the most interesting castles in South Wales are, indeed, Carew and Raglan, where the layers extend beyond the Middle Ages. These show, in their different ways, the transition from the medieval castle, built for defence, to the new, still fortified, aristocratic residence where considerations of elegance, comfort, and social status have taken pride of place. By Tudor times many of the castles were falling into disrepair, no longer needed in a more peaceful age; several of the Welsh castles were, however, revived like old soldiers to serve in the Civil War of the seventeenth century, and this too is an interesting part of their story.

Impressive in both number and quality, the castles are now a source of compelling interest. Even if one has no historical imagination, it is still possible to enjoy them, from the outside as an immense spectacle, and from the inside as a kind of enormous sculpture in which angles, curves, masses, the trick of the light from window or doorway create an endless succession of pleasures. The 'rooms' within the castle can be vast, small, round, square, deep in cavernous bowels, three-storeys high, lit by slit-like apertures that give the most panoramic of views: a variety of spatial experience unknown to modern house-dwellers. Otherwise, one can reconstruct in one's mind the cramped, smelly, blood-thirsty life of the inhabitants, or figure out the workings of the defences and the possible ways of outwitting them; one can meditate on the strategy of the castle's position – on hill-top, ford, inlet of the sea – or imagine instead the effect on the Welsh peasantry as they watched from a safe distance the construction of something, in size and technique, unusual and remote.

The castles follow the lines of the Norman invasion: from Chepstow to Cardiff and the south coast; from Montgomery through mid Wales to Pembroke; to Brecon via the Usk and the Talgarth gap. On the coastal plain a line of castles controlled the entries to the valleys; at estuaries and inlets castles are clustered, as in Pembrokeshire around the Cleddau. Following the castles came the towns, a radical change in both Welsh life and landscape. Towns played no part in pre-Norman Wales: there were the 'royal villages', centres of local government set around a prince's hall, but these were small and the rural economy had no need of larger settlements. In Europe towns had begun to reemerge at the end of the Dark Ages, in response both to a need for protection and a revival of trade. Rulers next began to use the castle-town as a weapon of conquest, 'planting' colonists and establishing markets. In England the Norman William FitzOsbern gave Hereford a town charter based on that of Breteuil, a small bastide or fortified township in his Norman territories. Its burgesses received exclusive trading rights and a limited amount of self-government. In the Welsh boroughs terms were harsher: in, for example, Chepstow, Monmouth, Cardiff, Brecon, and Haverfordwest only Englishmen were given full status, and in some places the Welsh were not even allowed to settle within the walls.

For the Normans towns had a dual purpose. Walled, gated, usually in the shadow of the lord's castle, they controlled trade, holding markets and levying tolls within a specific area. At the same time they were islands of support in an alien and frequently hostile countryside. Like the castles, they were an essentially lowland phenomenon; most lie below the 200m. mark, in valleys or on the coastal plain. They helped to create the contrast between the uplands and the lowlands, town and country, that still exists, though much tempered, in present-day Wales.

Most of the pre-industrial South Wales towns have their origins in a Norman borough. In some cases, Aberavon (Port Talbot) for example, all physical traces have now disappeared. In other places, outside the industrial south, one can find the remains of medieval fortifications and street-patterns. Tenby, in spite of its later development as a seaside resort, has retained stretches of town walls and a well-preserved five-arched gateway (c. 1300), remains that are more impressive than the castle itself. Pembroke and Chepstow, with their first-rate castles, also have considerable relics of thirteenth-century town walls. At Cowbridge in the Vale of Glamorgan there are part of a fourteenth-century town wall and one gateway; this town was unusual in that its castle appears to have stood some distance away at Llanblethian. At Haverfordwest the town walls are much reduced, but the medieval pattern of streets on the hill around the castle is still very much in evidence, while at New Radnor (Powys) the thirteenth-century 'town' has failed to develop into anything more than a village, leaving the original chequer-board plan clearly visible. Apart from Tenby, the most striking relic of the medieval town in South Wales is the Monnow Gate at Monmouth, a rare example of the fortified bridge-gate.

Not content with ousting the Welsh from their lands, and planting castles and fortified townships, the Normans also proceeded to reorganize the Celtic Church. The latter had grown independently during the Dark Ages and had recognized the authority of Rome only very late in those pre-Norman centuries. The invaders, moved by a mixture of pragmatism and spiritual concern, imposed on the Celtic Church a new, land-based system, in which the whole territory was divided up into dioceses and parishes. In the South Normans were now appointed as bishops, at St David's in 1115 and at Llandaff a year later; both acknowledged the superior authority of the Archbishop of Canterbury and introduced all the practices and ritual of the Roman Church.

Where the Celtic churchman had been solely a spiritual leader, often a scholar, hermit, or missionary, the Norman bishop, who was frequently an aristocrat, became a great landowner, deriving enormous revenues from his estates. The Bishop of St David's was especially wealthy and powerful: a Marcher lord in his own right, he owed secular allegiance to none but the King, and had an income equal to that of the three other Welsh bishops combined. At St David's itself, the elaborate and beautiful Bishop's Palace is the work of these powerful prelates – Bishop Bek and Bishop Henry Gower, in particular – in the thirteenth and fourteenth centuries. At Lamphey, near Pembroke, are the remains of another, smaller, seat built for the bishops. Llawhaden Castle, near Narberth, a third residence, was heavily fortified in the twelfth century and again in the fourteenth, a reminder of the continuing hostility of the native population.

At the same time the Normans introduced a new form of monasticism that entirely displaced the old, Celtic kind. In fifth-century Italy St Benedict had drawn up a 'rule' or code of conduct for the religious life, which was adopted as a model by monastic communities on the Continent. When in the centuries following standards declined from the original purity and austerity set by its founder, reformed orders arose: Cluniacs (910), Carthusians (1086), Cistercians (1098). In the mid eleventh century the Augustinian or Black Canons were formed, with the intention of providing a preaching fraternity for the parish churches. The White Canons were a reformed offshoot of the Augustinians; they were also known as Premonstratensians, after their house at Prémontré in France. In the early thirteenth century came the Friars – Black Friars (Dominicans), Grey Friars (Franciscans), White Friars (Carmelites), and Austin Friars – who lived in communities but spent their time preaching among the people.

The Benedictine Order was the first to be established in Wales as the early Norman conquerors seized land and handed it over, free of all dues and services, to French and English abbeys. Chepstow was the earliest, founded by William FitzOsbern as a daughter-house of the abbey of Cormeilles in Normandy. Abergavenny, Monmouth, Pembroke, and Brecon followed. The Benedictines, as a result of this close connexion with the Conquest, suffered from the hostility of the Welsh and were never fully accepted by them. Benedictine houses usually stand within safe distance of a Norman town and castle. At Ewenny Priory, with no castle near, the monastery itself was, if not fortified, at least intended to look embattled. Ewenny is one of several fine Benedictine churches that have survived for parish use; unlike the Cistercians, this order allowed part of the nave of the monastery church to be used for lay worship. Brecon Cathedral and St Mary's, Abergavenny, were also once parts of monasteries.

Most other orders had fewer houses in South Wales. There were three foundations of Augustinian Canons, at Carmarthen, Haverfordwest, and Llanthony, and only the latter has significant remains. Cluny had at least two houses: Malpas (Gwent), and St Clears (Dyfed), where the parish church is a survival. Talley Abbey, probably the only Premonstratensian house, was founded in the late twelfth century by the Welsh ruler Rhys ap Gruffydd. The order that had most success in Wales was undoubtedly the Cistercian. Their earliest houses were, like the Benedictines', Norman foundations: Tintern (1131), Margam (1147), Neath (1130; transferred from the Savignac Order in 1147). Welsh rulers, however, soon began to emulate the Norman system of patronage. In west Wales, by 1151, Cistercians were established at Whitland, the site of a Welsh royal palace, and daughter-houses sprang up at Abbey Cwmhir, Strata Florida, and

Strata Marcella. Llantarnam, near Caerleon, an offshoot of Strata Florida, was founded in 1179 by Hywel ab Iorwerth.

The Cistercian Order had been founded at Cîteaux in France in 1098, in an attempt to reestablish the original simplicity of the monastic rule. It laid stress not only on devotions and worship but on manual labour, a simple diet, and the lack of worldly possessions. Houses were to be sited in wild, remote areas, far from all human habitation. But in Wales, as elsewhere, the Cistercians were unable to retreat so completely from the world. On the contrary, while often remaining centres of spirituality and learning, they became great land-owners, and an influential force in medieval agriculture, industry, and trade. Generous grants of land from their founders and, later, patrons gave them huge estates, while their emphasis on manual work, their powers of organization, and their abundant supply of cheap labour in the lay-brethren they employed enabled them to exploit their opportunities to the full. That they were never as rich as the English Benedictine monasteries was partly due to the nature of the land, much of which was in hill-country, and partly to the constant disruptions caused by revolts and reconquest in Wales.

The Benedictines, whose houses lay in lowland areas, often on the outskirts of a town, practised mainly arable farming. The Cistercians, on the other hand, had huge tracts of pastureland on which they raised great flocks of sheep and cattle. Wool production, for sale and export, was one of their major sources of revenue. Their estates, which were widely dispersed over an often difficult terrain, were managed by means of 'granges': chapel, barn, mill, accommodation for lay-brothers and stock, lying at the limit of a day's journey. The monks cleared woodlands, erected defences against encroaching sea or sand. They held fairs and markets, brewed and sold their own beer, owned ships and harbours, weirs and fishing-rights. Not only farmers, they had extensive property in towns such as Cardiff and Bristol; they collected tithes, enjoyed exemption from duty and tolls. They mined coal at Neath, coal, lead, and iron-ore at Margam, lead at Strata Florida, and iron-ore at rural Tintern. Though saints and scholars must have been among their numbers, the Cistercians must also have had their fair share of hardheaded businessmen.

The monasteries suffered throughout their four centuries of existence both from natural disasters and from the continual violent skirmishing between the Welsh and their overlords. The Glyndwr rebellion of the early fifteenth century caused enormous damage to Strata Florida, Talley, Margam, and others. Tintern alone, nearer to England, escaped the worst of these troubles. At the Dissolution, 1534–9, the monasteries of South Wales met a variety of fates. The Benedictine monastic churches, used for parish worship, often survived, as we have seen. The Cistercian churches, which were divided between monks and lay-brothers, with a separate chapel for the parish, were usually despoiled, Margam Abbey church being a rare and fine survival. Llantarnam, Neath, and Ewenny were bought by royal servants and adapted for private residence; Neath, later, became the site of an iron foundry.

Of the ruined abbeys of South Wales, Tintern is certainly the most impressive, with extensive remains of church and claustral buildings in a magnificent setting beside the Wye. The Augustinian priory of Llanthony, in the Black Mountains, might come second in these ratings. Llantarnam and Whitland have virtually disappeared. Caldy and Neath are curiosities: Caldy because it is still in use (though there are modern buildings), and Neath because of its industrial connexions. Margam has a splendid church, but the monastic buildings, which include a fine ruined chapter-house, are not normally open to view. Strata Florida and Talley have scanty remains but their settings are peaceful and remote, and their atmosphere in some undefinable way peculiarly Welsh. Abbey Cwmhir is best treated as an agreeable expedition into the country. Those houses that do have substantial remains show in their buildings the increasing wealth of the monastic orders and the move away from simplicity and austerity towards a more comfortable and elegant style of life.

If Welsh monks were poorer than their English counterparts, so too were Welsh parish churches. Most of the many hundred churches built in Wales in the Norman and later-medieval period were small, simple in both plan and construction, austere. Often the work of local craftsmen using local materials (including wood), they contrast with the rich churches of lowland England and of northern France. Early Welsh churches were usually rectangular, a simple nave and chancel; they often retain their Celtic dedication. Norman churches sometimes have transepts (for the tomb of the lord of the manor) and are dedicated to saints of the Latin Church or to the Virgin Mary. (At St David's the Normans changed the dedication to Andrew, but the old name persisted.) In the areas most heavily Normanized – the Vale of Glamorgan, Breconshire, south Carmarthenshire, and south Pembrokeshire, to use the old, convenient names – churches tend to have square towers, which are usually fortified. The picture is complicated by the fact that in the fifteenth and sixteenth centuries many churches were enlarged or elaborated, often acquiring Perpendicular detail on an earlier, simple plan.

Nor can the two great medieval cathedrals of South Wales, St David's and Llandaff, compare in size or magnificence with the Gothic splendours of York, Lincoln, Chartres, or Notre-Dame. (Brecon, Newport, and Swansea attained cathedral status only in recent times.) Smaller in scale, less profuse of ornament, St David's and Llandaff have, none the less, their own particular beauty. Indeed, this principle seems to hold true for most of the churches in South Wales. While there are fine parish churches that should not be missed (at Abergavenny, Haverfordwest, Tenby, for example), more moving are the smaller and more primitive buildings that fit into a wilder setting. The tiny white-washed church almost on the beach at Mwnt (Dyfed), the squat grey churches of Gower, the hidden churches of Powys (Llananno, Patrishow) with their amazing rood-screens, which somehow survived the Reformation, these seem more in tune with the character of the Welsh countryside. Like the latter, they have an austerity that does not exclude warmth and a sort of simplicity that does not degenerate into the plain or the foolish. And perhaps because of the frequent presence of ancient crosses or inscribed stones, and the circular, raised churchyards, which denote the re-use of a much earlier, even pagan, religious site, there is in Welsh churches a sense of continuity sometimes absent from the well-fed churches of the English plain.

Wales has never been a rich country, and if I have devoted some space and attention to her medieval castles and abbeys, it is partly in deference to those experts who claim that her architecture reflects her poverty and that after the castles and abbeys nothing much of note was ever built there again. Certainly it is true that in comparison with England, Scotland, and Ireland South Wales is not rich in great country houses, which were the castles' natural successors.

With the relative peace and prosperity of the Tudor age, the need for fortified dwellings gradually vanished; comfort and elegance replaced security as the primary functions of the noble house. In Wales the accession of a Welshman, Henry Tudor, to the English throne (in 1485) meant a corresponding rise in the fortunes of the Welsh gentry. Indeed, the more ambitious followed the new king to London, taking up office there, and abandoning their Welsh estates to the more stay-at-home branches of the family. In the following reign the Act of Union of England and Wales abolished the Marcher lordships and divided Wales into shires on the English model; this, with the Dissolution of the Monasteries, gave new powers and property to the gentry in Wales. It has been calculated that there were over 600 'country seats' in South Wales in the seventeenth century. But, unlike England, Wales saw no great burst of country-house building in the eighteenth and early nineteenth centuries. For whatever reasons, there is little in Wales to compare in scale or splendour with Woburn or Blenheim.

Poverty is certainly one of those reasons: many Welsh 'gentry' lived in houses no grander than a large farmhouse. 'A Knight of Wales, / A gentleman of Cales, / A Laird of the North Countree– / A Yeoman of Kent / Sitting on his penny rent / Can buy them out all three', went an old rhyme pointing the fact. Another was the sheer inaccessibility of the Welsh countryside in the centuries before the building of modern roads and railways. Not only were the roads in Wales atrocious, but the countryside long remained uninviting to the English eye. Daniel Defoe's tour of Great Britain in 1724–6 is revealing in this respect. Defoe had travelled widely in Europe and elsewhere, yet he found the mountains of Brecknockshire in some places more 'horrid and frightful' than the Alps or the Andes, for the latter rose gradually one behind the other, while the mountains of Wales often rose directly from the valley floor. Snowdon he refers to as a 'monstrous height'; in Montgomeryshire he became very 'tired with rocks and mountains'. It was not only in North Wales that the terrain proved tiresome. Entering Glamorganshire from the north, Defoe complained, 'we were saluted with Monuchdenny-Hill on our left, and the Black-Mountain on the right, and all a ridge of horrid rocks and precipices between, over which, if we had not had trusty guides, we should never have found our way; and indeed, we began to repent our curiosity, as not having met with any thing worth the trouble; and a country looking so full of horror, that we thought to have given over the enterprise, and have left Wales out of our circuit'. Only much later in the eighteenth century did mountains become picturesque, romantic, objects of awe and delight rather than frightful and tedious obstacles to the traveller. Yet country seats remained confined to the more populous southern plain, and the wide, fertile valleys of the Usk and the Wye.

Like England in one respect, Wales has lost many of her country houses through calamity, neglect, or sheer lack of income. In the last hundred years alone, according to a recent calculation, nearly thirty country houses in South Wales have been demolished or have fallen into ruin. These include Hafod House (near Pontrhydygroes, Dyfed), the lavish, Gothic home of the reforming land-owner Colonel Johnes; Middleton Hall (Dyfed), a neo-Classical mansion built by S. P. Cockerell in the 1790s for the Mayor of Carmarthen, Sir William Paxton (whose 'folly' still stands); Derry Ormond House (Dyfed), also by Cockerell; Ruperra Castle (Glam.), an early-seventeenth-century house possibly by Inigo Jones. Aberglasney House, near Llangathen (Dyfed), the home of the minor poet and painter John Dyer, is also in ruins. Of those still standing, some are still in private hands, but others have been turned into hotels, schools, conference centres, or acquired by local authorities for public use. St Fagan's, near Cardiff, is the central core of the National Museum of Wales' folk-life collections, and Cyfarthfa Castle at Merthyr Tydfil also houses a museum. Of the remaining 'great houses', Cardiff Castle and Castell Coch near Tongwynlais are masterpieces of Victorian fantasy, the product of the wealth and genius of the architect William Burges and his eccentric patron Lord Bute. Nanteos, near Aberystwyth, is advertised as the 'Welsh stately home', and this very label seems to indicate the extreme rarity of the species in Wales. Deprived of what the butler saw, we can turn instead to the ordinary farmhouse and cottage.

In Wales – a predominantly rural country until fairly recent times – relief, soils, and climate have determined a pattern of settlement that lasted almost unchanged for centuries. In the wider valleys and on the coastal plains, where the Normans moved in, there is mixed farming, and villages of the English type, centred around a church or even a village green, are to be found. In the uplands and much of the south-west, life for the Welsh remained largely what it had been before the Conquest, living in scattered farmsteads, raising sheep and cattle on inhospitable moors. The villages are disappointing to the visitor, for they often turn out to be no more than a crossroads, an inn, or a wind-bitten chapel. Even the church often stands isolated on a hillside, its parish covering large tracts of empty landscape. And in the industrial valleys this pattern has persisted: the nineteenth-century terraces peter out as they climb the hillsides, and, on the bare tops, small farms and old mountain churches (Llangynwyd, Llanwonno) have remained unengulfed. The lowland villages of Glamorgan and south-west Dyfed, lying below the 100m. mark, were mostly established by the twelfth century; names ending in -ton (Wiston, Picton, in south-west Dyfed, Laleston, Flemingston, in the Vale of Glamorgan) reveal their Norman origin. In the uplands some settlements grew at those points along the 'drovers' roads' where the herds of Welsh cattle were assembled and shod for the long journey to London; Llangurig and Abergwesyn, to take two examples, are, however, still little more than villages.

The farmhouses and cottages of South Wales are often of uncertain antiquity, their shapes, sizes, and materials reflecting regional distinctions and the accretions of changing tastes. In the Welsh Marches timber-framed and cruck-built houses are not uncommon (cruck-building uses a curved treetrunk, split in two, to provide an arched framework or truss), and some flamboyant half-timbering can be seen in the Vale of Severn. As one approaches the main watershed of Wales, however, this kind of building vanishes, for the sessile oak of these parts is unsuitable for such construction. Stone is a common material in the west, its rugosities and natural colour often hidden under coats of wash. Roofs are frequently of slate; thatch, once common, is much rarer now. Corrugated iron is, unfortunately, replacing both these in the less wealthy areas.

Cottages are often surprisingly small, one or two rooms, with, in earlier times, a loft for sleeping, warmed by the main chimney and reached by a ladder from the kitchen or by an outside stair. The smallest cottages may perhaps be relics of the traditional Welsh *ty unnos*, 'house of one night': according to this custom, if a squatter could erect a dwelling overnight, and have the chimney smoking by morning, the house was his, and the land within one axe-throw in every direction. (The cottage could be built very quickly of turf, and the walls then strengthened later, at leisure.) Occasionally, one sees examples of the 'long-house', a one-storey building, which originally housed the farm family at one end and the cattle at the other. Inside, a door led directly from the kitchen into the byre, and the main fireplace often separated, and warmed, the two. Such houses needed to be built on a slope so that the animals' urine could drain away from the living quarters. In south-west Dyfed (Pembrokeshire) tall chimneys are especially interesting, linking domestic architecture to medieval castle-building. Of these so-called 'Flemish' chimneys, the cylindrical ones are found in 'gentry' houses, while the conical ones tend to be used in farmhouses. Round chimneys like this are also found on the other side of the Bristol Channel, in the West Country. Pembrokeshire also has huge square chimneys attached to unusually large ovens, which seem to have been tacked onto the house; in such cases the chimney seems to dominate the whole construction.

Fine examples of various types of Welsh cottages and farmhouses can be seen in the Welsh Folk-Museum at St Fagan's near Cardiff. In the countryside it is difficult to pinpoint examples: each generation adds a porch, renews the windows, or sells the place as a holiday cottage; it may then acquire louvred shutters, cart-wheels, bottle-glass, bow-windows. Or the whole thing may be engulfed in a plantation of conifers. Many of the old cottages were poky, damp, and uncomfortable; many had, none the less, a sense of belonging to the often harsh landscape that surrounded them.

Towns, as we have seen, were not a Celtic phenomenon, and it is tempting, though oversimplified and nostalgic, to think of the countryside as the 'real' Wales. Yet by 1851 well over half the working population of the country were employed in non-agricultural occupations, and this proportion has not ceased to go on growing. Indeed, with the amalgamation of small uneconomical farms, the use of huge tracts of land for re-afforestation, and the reluctance of many young people to take on the old farms, the countryside is perhaps emptier than it ever was. And no influx of holidaymakers, however respectful of the land, can make up this balance.

The defensive settlements by the Normans in the lee of their castle walls were encouraged, by privileges and charters, to become trading and market centres. When the castle finally became redundant, at the end of the Middle Ages, or at the latest after the Civil War, the town needed some positive economic function to survive at all. Many of the Norman boroughs grew, slowly, into the market-towns of modern times: Brecon, Carmarthen, Haverfordwest, for example. Others, for a variety of reasons, decayed or almost vanished: New Radnor, overshadowed by the proximity of Presteigne; Aber-avon, its narrow coastal plain lacking good land, only revived by the Industrial Revolution; Kidwelly, its harbour silted up; Kenfig, overwhelmed by blown sand. The better the agricultural land, the bigger and more prosperous the town, in the pre-industrial period. Brecon and Carmarthen, chosen as local 'capitals' under the terms of the Acts of Union of 1536 and 1542, were both surrounded by wide tracts of good farming country. Both, too, were easily accessible, another vital factor, while Carmarthen, which remained until 1831 the largest town in Wales, had the added advantage of a flourishing sea-trade.

In the sixteenth and seventeenth centuries a number of other Norman boroughs, smaller than Brecon or Carmarthen, had become major market-centres. Cardiff was 'a propper fine towne (as townes goe in this country) and a very commodious haven'; Haverfordwest 'a good town, wealthie and well governed'; Swansea 'a pretie town and good. Much frequented by shipping'; Abergavenny 'a fine walled town, neately welle inhabited'. (The writers are Camden, George Owen, and Leland.) By 1835, before the full effects of the Industrial Revolution had really been felt, a natural distribution of towns in South Wales could be seen to have emerged, governed by the nature of the countryside, its economy, the inherited traditions and privileges of the various towns, and their distance one from the other. Brecon, Cardiff, Carmarthen (the 'Emporium of South Wales'), Swansea, Haverfordwest, and Abergavenny are still in the first rank; Newport, which had badly declined since Norman times, has begun its industrial growth, while Aberystwyth has flourished at the expense of Cardigan. Monmouth, Pembroke, Chepstow, and Llandovery are smaller market-towns, of Norman origin; Neath, Newtown, Merthyr Tydfil, and Pontypool are growing industrial centres.

Of the larger pre-industrial towns of South Wales, only Brecon was not a sea- or river-port. In early times the whole coast of our region was, in spite of its dangers to shipping, studded with small ports and harbours. In the south-east not only Cardiff, Barry, Neath, and Swansea, but Caerleon, Goldcliff, Aberthaw, Ogmore, among others, carried on a trade by sea with Bristol and the west of England; in some cases this dated back to before the Normans. Kidwelly and Carmarthen were both ancient ports, though both eventually lost their maritime importance because of the silting up of their rivers. (In the days of piracy it had of course been an advantage for a port to lie a little way inland from the open sea.) Further west, Pembrokeshire had its creeks and harbours: Tenby, Pembroke, and Haverfordwest, Solva, Porthgain, and Fishguard. On Cardigan Bay small but once flourishing sea-ports have turned into summer resorts for Sunday yachtsmen, but the retired sea-captains and master mariners dreaming in New Quay cottages of a wider world than west Wales are no figments of a Dylan Thomas's imagination.

A few but significant South Wales towns developed in the pre-industrial period out of a new search for health and leisure. First came the small spas or 'wells' of mid Wales: Llanwrtyd, discovered in about 1732, Llandegley, Builth, Llangammarch, Llandrindod. Their mineral springs and their remote and beautiful settings in the wooded Welsh valleys made them for a time the miniature rivals of Bath and the Continental spas, in a century – the eighteenth – when travel had become easier, and wealth (and over-eating and dyspepsia) more common. But after the decline of the 'waters' only Builth and Llandrindod grew into commercial and market centres. The others have remained villages, sometimes with a railway station to mark a popularity that persisted into the nineteenth century. Their Pump House Hotels have now become centres for golfing, fishing, or walking holidays.

Brecon and Abergavenny also became for a time popular inland resorts with the discerning English traveller, anxious to sample the wild Welsh scenery now that mountains had become 'romantic' and 'picturesque'. In 1870 the Revd Francis Kilvert records in his diary his horror and rage at finding tourists at Llanthony, 'one of them of course discoursing learnedly to his gaping companion and pointing out objects of interest with his stick. . . . Of all noxious animals too the most noxious is a tourist. And of all tourists the most vulgar, illbred, offensive and loathsome is the British tourist'.

After the spas came the seaside resorts. Aberystwyth and Tenby both began to develop in the latter years of the eighteenth century; both have elegant Georgian and Regency houses, and Tenby a seawater Bathhouse dating from 1811. The railways (which reached Aberystwyth in 1864) brought more and different visitors; at Aberystwyth the old College building on the sea-front started life as a fantastic hotel, begun in the 1860s to accommodate the new, railway tourist. Promenade piers were built at Tenby and Aberystwyth, Mumbles (Swansea) and Penarth, in imitation of the one that, finished in 1823, had so contributed to the popular attractions of Brighton. Porthcawl,

Barry, and Aberavon developed much later, in response to the needs of the huge new population of the South Wales coal-field.

Towns are more interesting if we can piece together something of their development and history. The central core may be medieval in pattern, with fragments of castle or town wall and narrow streets unsuitable for modern traffic. Outside this may come older houses, possibly Georgian, often of local stone. The railway, when it came, changed more than merely the seaside resort: it brought a new uniformity of building materials and styles. From the post-railway age date the stone terraces with red-brick window surrounds and the bow-fronted villas with silvered iron railings and front gate.

Most towns in South Wales grew up totally unplanned, changing as population levels, economic needs, tastes, and styles also changed. However, as Fleure and Davies put it in their *Natural History of Man in Britain*, English urban planning of the late eighteenth century 'ran as a spent wave across Wales, and on its western limits left a feeble, though interesting, small imprint on the early nineteenth century core of Milford Haven . . . and the small port of Aberaeron'. This latter was planned as a commercial venture, by a local clergyman, in 1807; sober, well-proportioned, and attractive, it did not, however, develop into a modern port, for it lacked the deep natural harbour that made the fortunes of Milford. Morriston, near Swansea, is a rare example of planned housing of the early industrial age.

South Wales in 1750: a rural landscape, with a few small ports and market-towns, and, here and there, the scattered blotches of what was soon to burst in a long, black explosion over the one, large, south-eastern corner. The Industrial Revolution scarred the face of the countryside more deeply than any other event in Welsh history. And precisely because of the extraordinary and lasting ugliness of it, and the inhuman conditions of life it required, it is not easy even now to approach the subject dispassionately. Yet given the narrow, grey towns, the denuded hillsides, the streams choked with the filth of decades, the murderous slag-heaps – and these have not been easy things to live with, to put it at its mildest – one must still say that without coal and iron South Wales might have faced the fate of nineteenth-century Ireland: a depressed and depopulated countryside, mass emigration to England and America, the impoverishment of her native language and culture.

Mining in Wales dates back at least to the Romans, who found gold and lead, while in medieval times Cistercian monks and Norman land-owners extracted coal, lead, and iron, by primitive methods, from outcrops lying at or near the surface. Over the following centuries industry developed slowly, piecemeal, and in a variety of areas. In Henry VIII's reign the rise of the new bourgeoisie and the new legal protection offered by the 1536 Act of Union combined with the King's need for brass and iron for military matters to produce a distinct burst of industrial activity. From 1565 iron-works were set up at Coity, Pontypool, and the northern rim of the South Wales coal-field. Copper-smelting had an early but unsuccessful start at Neath, from 1582 to the end of the century, reviving again later. A brass and wire factory and an iron-works opened at Tintern in 1570. Lead was mined extensively in the north-Cardiganshire valleys, and Sir Hugh Middleton made a fortune, which he proceeded to lose on other ventures before his death in 1631. Coal was only just coming into general use as a fuel; it was already being mined, however, at Llanelli and Kidwelly in 1536. By 1600 coal was being exported from Cardiff, Neath, and Swansea to the West Country, Ireland, the Channel Islands, and France.

The Industrial Revolution proper began in the mid eighteenth century with the sudden development of the iron industry. From Hirwaun to Blaenavon in south-east Wales a belt of limestone country provided, it was found, all the materials required to produce iron: the iron-stone itself, coal (now replacing charcoal for smelting), limestone, and water. English entrepreneurs – the great ironmasters such as Guest, Bacon, Crawshay – moved in, setting up furnaces in the areas around Merthyr, Hirwaun, and Ebbw Vale. A rapid population growth in Britain generally, in the late eighteenth century, and an agricultural depression following the Napoleonic Wars, sent a plentiful supply of labour to the new industry from the farms of England and west Wales. Roads, canals, tramroads, and railways connected the valleys with the coastal ports; the railways not only facilitated transport, but themselves created a huge new demand for steel and iron.

The coal boom came later, from about 1850 to 1921; steam replaced sail at sea, and new techniques of mining enabled the deeper, better seams to be worked. Industrialization now spread into valleys such as the Rhondda, hitherto relatively unspoiled. On the south coast the ports, too, saw their best years of prosperity. Newport handled iron, and the bituminous Gwent coal used for locomotives; Cardiff, Penarth, and Barry exported 'Best Admiralty', the almost smokeless fuel used by the Royal Navy exclusively after 1872. The anthracite coal of the western coal-field was shipped from Port Talbot, Neath, Swansea, and Llanelli, and there, on the coastal plateau, copper, nickel, and tin-plate provided more diversified development. As local supplies of iron-ore became too difficult to extract, the iron industry, also, from the late nineteenth century on, tended to relocate itself at the coast, nearer to the point of import. Ebbw Vale remains, a steel town in the Valleys, an artificial relic created by well-meaning social policy.

The coal-field, coast and valleys, contained some of the finest and most dramatic scenery in the whole of southern Britain, and the impact of nineteenth-century industry was all the more devastating. Early travellers' accounts of the sylvan beauties of the Rhondda or Neath valleys make poignant reading for those who know them now. 'Nothing can surpass the beauty of this sequestered spot . . . the atmosphere is mild and temperate, and the air soft and salubrious: the arbutus, the myrtle, the magnolia, and other exotics grow luxuriantly in the open air', writes Samuel Lewis in 1848 of Briton Ferry, a small township on the coast between Neath and Port Talbot; metallurgical and chemical works, ship-breaking yards, modern highways, railways, and houses of no distinction have since flourished where the magnolias grew. At Swansea, to the east of the river-mouth, a huge stretch of land was made waste, and fumes from copper-smelting destroyed all vegetation on the nearby hills.

Perhaps only an eccentric – or a man with a strong taste for social history – would spend time, without family or business reasons, in the towns of the South Wales coal-field. Yet most of them lie near either to sea or mountains, and, climbing up past the terraces onto the sheep-tracked higher ground, one can look down on their curious and characteristic urban scenery. And if one can do without the Gothic churches, Tudor half-timbering (with tea-shoppes), Georgian crescents, and all those other creamy delights the tourist expects from his towns, these places provide their own, peculiar, stark interest.

Where no previous village or centre of settlement existed the new industrial towns developed brutally; Mumford's 'the non-plan of the non-city' means exactly this haphazard spread of primitive working-class housing in the immediate vicinity of mine or works. In the valley towns river, railway, colliery, and main street compete for the long ribbon of the valley floor; terraces of small, neat houses run parallel where they can, or straggle up the hillsides. Where the valley is particularly narrow slag-heaps and spoil-tips formerly loomed above the houses; it took the tragedy of Aberfan for many of these to be removed. Punctuating the terraces are larger buildings, the pubs, the Working Men's Clubs, the ubiquitous chapels (for by 1851 nearly 80 per cent of the Welsh population was Nonconformist). The boom years of industrial South Wales saw the great age of chapel-building, in town and countryside; rectangular in shape, and of local stone, the early valley chapels often resemble the colliery winding-houses and lamp-rooms, which were their neighbours. The Anglican churches were slower to respond to the new populations: their Victorian Gothic contrasts with the often Classical architecture of the Nonconformist chapel.

Quite a lot has changed in the coal-field since the end of the boom years. Between 1921 and 1931 alone a quarter of a million people left South Wales to find employment in England or abroad. This exodus has continued. Ammanford, a typical mining town, declined in population by nearly 12 per cent between 1931 and 1951 and by nearly 5 per cent in the following decade. All the industrial towns have lost population through emigration, except the sea-ports (Cardiff, Swansea, Newport, Port Talbot), for major industries have increasingly moved to the coast. Many collieries have closed, steel has moved out of the valleys (except for Ebbw Vale), and a major new industry – oil – has shifted development away from its traditional nineteenth-century cradle. There are huge refineries and harbours not only at Llandarcy near Swansea, but in the rural south-west, at Pembroke and Milford Haven, where care has, however, been taken to reduce the impact on the landscape. Meanwhile, attempts continue to be made to attract new investment to keep the valleys alive. And the scars of mining and metal-working are gradually being healed, waste land reclaimed, slag-heaps removed, new forests planted. Old towns have built themselves modern centres, and at Cwmbran (Gwent) a New Town is being developed. The first in Wales, Cwmbran is designed eventually to house 55,000 people; here, at least one tree is planted for every new dwelling.

Despite their enormous economic difficulties the South Wales industrial towns have shown considerable will to survive. Indeed, a sort of natural dignity, pride even, noted by English travellers in the Welsh miner and metalworker, is now being reinforced by the new interest in industrial archaeology and new emphases in history itself. Strange as it may seem, the common man has only fairly recently become the object of the historian's scrutiny, while archaeologists for years refused to acknowledge the existence of anything much after 1500. The process of redressing the balance is not without danger, of course, and we may be tempted to romanticize the Industrial Age just as we have already romanticized Merrie England and the countryside before 1800. None the less, any attempt to focus on the social, political, and aesthetic effects of industrialization and to throw away the outdated notion of history as made only by kings and generals cannot but be a healthy one.

In the valleys themselves there is increasing recognition of the potential interest of early industrial buildings, machinery, and transport systems such as canals and tram-roads. At Pontypool an ambitious scheme is under way that will turn almost a whole valley into a 'history trail'. At Cardiff a new Industrial and Maritime Museum is being constructed on the site of one of the old Bute docks. Elsewhere, outside the coal-field, there are the desolate remains of the mid-Wales lead-mines (which went out of business in the nineteenth century), visible near the foot of the Clywedog Dam, for example, and in the Ystwyth Valley. A silver-mine can be visited at Llywernog, near Ponterwyd. At Furnace (Dyfed) there is a well-preserved charcoal-powered furnace where iron was made in the late eighteenth century; here, early industry can be seen in its authentic rural setting.

Much of the impact of the present century on the South Wales landscape has been a continuation of and an adaptation to the conditions of the last. Industries decline, are removed elsewhere, are replaced by new ones. Canals, tramroads, and small railway lines have become derelict or have been turned into tourist attractions, but transport systems continue to develop; the South Wales motorway, the Severn Bridge, and the Heads of the Valleys road have changed both physical and psychological contours for the traveller. In rural mid Wales new reservoirs and forests have transformed great tracts of country-side, opening them up with new access roads, sometimes closing them in again as the growing conifers obscure the view. Tourism itself, a new high-growth industry, is in danger of spoiling the countryside for the very people it wants to attract: caravans and chalets, car parks and picnic sites must not be allowed to disfigure and denature the land.

The Culture of Wales

Wales is the nearest foreign country to England. Wales is no more different from the rest of England than Yorkshire or the West Country. Which of these is true? Has Wales any claim to be regarded as a separate nation and a distinctive culture? Who are the Welsh, anyway? Are they merely a shorter, more musical variety of Englishman? Since tents and caravans have no national characteristics, and hotels are getting to be the same everywhere (motels even more so), it is perfectly possible for the casual visitor to be almost unaware of having crossed the Welsh 'border', to receive no culture shock. (One can, likewise, eat fish and chips, washed down by pale ale, on the Costa Brava.) Deeper in, on a farmhouse holiday, perhaps, or out of season, or merely away from the more crowded of beaches, one probably becomes aware of a tangible, if not easily defined, sense of difference.

Like England and everywhere else, Wales can make no claims to racial purity. Successive waves of immigration have left a mixture, though it is not quite the same mixture as in England. Prehistoric settlers, Celts, Romans, Irish, Vikings, Normans, Flemish, and 'English' of every period have all contributed to the size, shape, colouring of the Welsh physique. Outside the industrial cities – where Italian, Polish, Chinese, Irish, English, and Commonwealth immigrants have added new ingredients, thereby improving both Welsh ice-cream and Welsh cricket – certain physical types seem, however, remarkably persistent. In the uplands there is the short, dark-haired, dark-eyed, long-headed Welshman, whom some anthropologists have claimed as the direct descendant of the Neolithic inhabitants of Wales. Near the coast there may be a taller, fair-haired Welshman, whose ancestor may have been a Viking, a Norman, or an Iron Age Celt. There is, too, a short, fair-haired, fair-skinned Welshman with light-blue eyes, whose 'relatives' may be seen in northern Brittany. And there are also red-headed Welshmen, and Welshmen with dark hair and light eyes, types that appear more commonly, however, in Ireland.

A Welshman will most often describe himself as a Celt. This, being translated, can mean simply, 'I am fiery, quick-witted, eloquent, poetic, oppressed, and much more interesting than any ordinary English person'. But leaving aside this natural desire to don a more interesting identity, there is some truth in the Celtic label. For one thing, Welsh, like Irish, Scots Gaelic, Manx, and Breton, is a Celtic language, and it has survived better than any of these the inroads and onslaughts of other tongues and groups. For another, the geographical entity now called Wales was predominantly Celtic for a large, if indefinite, number of formative centuries. Conservative (in the strictly non-political sense) like any peasant society, Wales preserved for many hundreds of years some distinctive patterns of the Celtic character.

The Celts first appear in prehistoric Europe as a small, dynamic tribe, living in the Bavaria–Bohemia–Rhine region. From there they migrated outwards in all directions. By 300 BC their territories stretched from Galatia in Asia Minor to Ireland, a peak of power and influence from which they have, ever since, declined. To the Greeks, in whose writings we first meet them, the Celts were Barbarians, but their culture was not uncivilized. Its two major Continental flowerings, the Halstatt culture (*c.* 800 to *c.* 450 BC) and the La Tène (from *c.* 450 BC), the latter in particular, produced beautiful and distinctive works of art. As a tribal group their character formed a contrast to the temperate Greeks; Myles Dillon and Nora Chadwick describe it as 'marked by extremes of luxury and asceticism, of exultation and despair, by lack of discipline and by the gift for organising secular affairs, by delight in natural beauty and in tales of mystery and imagination, by an artistic sense that prefers decoration and pattern to mere representation' (*The Celtic Realms*, 1973, p. 12). Classical writers describe the Celts of western Europe as brave and warlike, honouring bards, priests, and philosophers, boastful, vain, speaking in riddles, quick to learn, 'much given to religion'.

Exactly when the Celts first came to these islands is a matter for controversy among scholars. According to some the Celts are the same as the Bell-Beaker people who arrived in about 2000 BC, and whose Bronze Age society is known as the Wessex Culture (*c.* 1500 BC). For others the first Celtic immigration was that of the Early Iron Age, about 600 BC, and certainly from then until the invasions of the (part-Celtic?) Belgae in the first century BC there were successive waves of Celts. In either case, when the Romans came they found the island largely occupied by Celtic tribes, speaking varieties of Celtic languages, and living in separate, often warring, kingdoms.

The Romans imposed their model of civil life and government on lowland, southern Britain, but in the uplands of the north and west the Celtic patterns remained largely unchanged. Then, after the Celtic expansion, and the Roman Empire, it was the turn of the Teutonic peoples of northern Europe to explode outwards over the Continent. In the fifth and sixth centuries Saxons, Angles, and Jutes poured into an eastern England left vulnerable by the departure of the legions; the Celts were pushed back into the mountainous north and west. They left in southern Britain the Celtic place-names given to mountains, forests, and rivers; in the west they formed, on the very edge of Europe, a fringe of Celtic provinces – Wales, Cornwall, Man, Cumbria, Scotland, and Ireland – around the Celtic pond, the Irish Sea.

Politically disunited, often hostile to one another, the Celtic lands shared, none the less, in trade, religion, learning, literature, and mythology. In Wales this state of affairs lasted until late into the so-called Dark Ages. By the mid ninth century, still and unavoidably disunited, the Welsh had, however, come to think of themselves as a distinct entity, *Cymry*, 'compatriots'. About this time, too, they began to turn away from the Celtic west and towards Anglo-Saxon England and the (Latin) Continent.

Early Celtic life in Britain, and Wales in particular, has to be pieced together from the evidence of archaeology, of poetry, myth, and law, and from the observations of travellers and conquerors. What emerges is fascinating, not only in its own right, but for the threads of continuity, some stronger than others, that are still traceable in the values, social patterns, and behaviour of Welshmen today.

The most obvious point is of course that society was essentially rural: towns, as we have seen, were unknown, and villages, where they existed, were small and undeveloped. In the uplands scattered holdings were the rule, and the practice of transhumance (moving flocks from lower, winter pastures to high ground in summer) survived from the Celtic period until the late eighteenth century. Money was little used, for wealth was reckoned in cows, and trade carried on by barter of livestock. Fines were payable in the same way: for example, in the laws of the tenth-century king Hywel Dda, 'Howell the

Good', the penalty for killing the cat that guards the King's barn is estimated by holding the corpse head down towards the floor, and pouring wheat grains over it until the very tip of the tail is hidden.

Society was strongly hierarchical, and for the farmers and the warrior nobility, which constituted its upper classes, kinship was all important. For the princes this meant ancestry, a pedigree, often fanciful by modern standards, that established their descent from the kings and heroes of the past. But in the middle ranks, too (there were bondsmen and slaves beneath this), it was the family that gave a man his essential identity, enabled him to inherit land, protected or avenged him against murder. The 'family', as also in early Ireland, seems to have been reckoned as a four-generation group, that is, it was composed of all those descended from a common great-grandfather. In the early eighteenth century Daniel Defoe noted the Welshman's pride in his ancestry, while in much of Wales today who a person's grandfather was, and who his second cousins, is still a matter of interest and importance.

Somewhere between princes and herdsmen, the bards were a separate and honoured class in Celtic society. This is not uncommon in what is called a 'heroic age', when a man's status depends on others being well informed of his warlike deeds and character. Praise of the hero, accounts of his battles, his ancestry, the wealth of his court, laments for his death, these were the functions of the poet, who received, in return, food and lodging at the prince's hall. Since illiteracy was the rule, poetry and learning were handed down orally; poets were men of good memory, and the more eloquent and highly patterned the verse, the more easily could it be memorized. Welsh literature we will examine briefly later; at present what concerns us is the extraordinary persistence of certain basic traits. Other cultures have come to distrust the persuasive tongue: Yorkshire is a good example, where blunt speaking is preferred to rhetoric. In modern Wales, on the contrary, the man of words is still admired, and the legendary Welsh preachers of the religious revivals were in a sense the inheritors of the ancient bardic tradition.

Another trait of early Welsh culture, and one more open to speculation, is the status of women. By historic times Celtic rulers, warriors, priests, and land-owners were men, though women were by no means without rights. But there is some evidence to suggest that, much earlier, Celtic society had been matriarchal. It is known, for example, that among the Picts of Scotland, a partly Celtic people, succession was through the female line, right up until the ninth century AD; noble Pictish women took fathers for their children from unrelated clans, and even from visiting foreign princes. The dynastic marriages of the early-medieval Welsh ruling houses also suggest the importance of the female line (and one wonders therefore in what light the Welsh viewed the marriage of their princesses with the Norman barons, after 1066). In Celtic religion the 'cult of the Mothers' – the Earth, that is, in triple form, worshipped as a source of fertility – was one of the oldest and most powerful of the images. In Celtic myth, Irish and Welsh, great warrior queens rule the land, and women with supernatural powers teach the heroes both spiritual wisdom and feats of arms. In history, too, the Romans' fiercest British adversaries were the Celtic queens Boudicca (Boadicea) and Cartimandua, while Ammianus Marcellinus, writing in the fourth century AD, describes the warlike Celtic women of Gaul:

> A whole troop of foreigners would not be able to withstand a single Gaul if he
> called his wife to his assistance, who is usually very strong, and with blue eyes;

especially when, swelling her neck, gnashing her teeth, and brandishing her sallow arms of enormous size, she begins to strike blows mingled with kicks, as if they were so many missiles sent from the string of a catapult.

Christianity took over aspects of Celtic religion: the water-gods of river, stream, and source were translated into the medieval holy wells, and the Cult of the Virgin Mary drew strength from this earlier Celtic tradition of mother-goddesses and strong queens. In the Celtic lands the prestige of women remained high: the Welsh or the Irish mother dominate the home, which has, after all, only been a narrow sphere since the Industrial Revolution. In the industrial valleys, until fairly recent times, it was common practice for the collier to hand over his entire wage-packet to his wife, and receive back only his pocket-money.

The most tangible survival of the Celtic past is, of course, the Welsh language, that strange tongue that seems to intrigue and infuriate the English visitor, and that BBC news-readers, who pride themselves on their elegant French and Italian, can rarely be bothered to get right. Were it not for the Anglo-Saxon invasions, however, the whole of Britain might well be speaking a form of Welsh today.

Welsh and English both belong to the large family of languages known as Indo-European, which include some Eastern languages such as Hindu, and almost all the languages of Europe (Basque and Finnish are the only exceptions, and their origins are a continuing puzzle to philologists). Within this family English, with German, Dutch, and Flemish, is a Germanic language; Welsh, Irish, Scots Gaelic, Manx, Breton, and Cornish are Celtic. Within Celtic itself are two further subdivisions: Welsh and Breton (and Cornish, now virtually extinct) are Brythonic, while Irish, Scots Gaelic, and Manx are Goidelic. These two branches are sometimes called 'P-Celtic' and 'Q-Celtic', for what changed very early into a 'P' sound in the one group has remained as a 'K' sound in the other. (Thus the Welsh for 'four' is *pedwar*, the Irish *cethir* – and the Latin *quattuor*.)

Languages, like races, do not remain 'pure'; so long as they can escape being swamped by foreign invasion they can grow and flourish by borrowing words from others. This sort of linguistic inter-marriage with settlers and neighbours brings a wider vocabulary, new concepts and fields of meaning to deal with new conditions of life. From the Romans, for example, Welsh took, or was given, Latin words, some connected with the military occupation of the country (*castellum*, Welsh *castell*, a fort; *fenestra*, Welsh *ffenestr*, a window). From the Latin of the medieval church Welsh acquired *eglwys*, Latin *ecclesia*, a church; *ysgol*, *schola*, a school, and so on. Early Irish settlements and trading contacts left a few everyday words (*brechtán*, Welsh *brechdan*, a slice of bread and butter), Old English, from east of Offa's Dyke, left others (*bāt*, Welsh *bad*, a boat). From Anglo-Norman or from medieval French Welsh gained *twr* (*tour*, a tower), *siambr* (*chambre*, a room).

Clearly, however, English has been the most frequent and obvious source of Welsh loan-words for the last ten centuries or so. *Ystryd*, a street, was borrowed early; others, less acclimatized, but in frequent use, are much more recent: *bws*, a bus, *ambiwlans*, an ambulance, *plismon*, a policeman, *sigaret*, a cigarette. When one remembers that the Welsh contribution to English is confined to a few curiosities such as 'flannel', and 'flummery' (fl being the Anglo-Saxon tongue's attempt at a Welsh ll), it becomes apparent that this traffic has been travelling a one-way street. Too much borrowing can imperil the health of a language, and even the French have recently passed a law ban-ning, in official publications, the use of English words when a French one will do. Of the many minority languages in Europe, Welsh has survived relatively well, and, of the Celtic languages of the British Isles, it has survived the best; it is, however, by no means out of danger.

It was, ironically, a monarch from a Welsh dynasty – the Tudors – who first passed a law making Welsh the inferior tongue in Wales. But before this inroads had already been made. Along the borders, naturally, the linguistic frontier tended to be a fluid one; Offa's Dyke, in the eighth century, did not prevent Welsh being spoken in what became Hereford, Gloucestershire, Shropshire, nor Anglo-Saxon in the Lugg or Arrow valleys. In south-west Dyfed, Gower, and South Glamorgan English and Flemish settlers had by the sixteenth century ousted Welsh speech from large stretches of the coastal plain. The Norman kings were not concerned with the status of the languages – their own tongue was, after all, French, and they had equal contempt for both Saxon and Welsh. However, the Norman boroughs, where only Englishmen enjoyed the full privileges of citizenship, helped to establish English as the major language of trade and commerce in Wales.

Henry VIII's Acts of Union in 1536 and 1542 gave Wales and England equal rights under the Crown, but with one important proviso: that 'henceforth no Person or Persons that use the Welsh Speech or Language shall have or enjoy any Manner of Office or Fees within this Realm of England, Wales, or other of the King's Dominion, upon Pain of forfeiting the same Offices or Fees, unless he or they use and exercise the English Speech or Language'. English now became the official language, not only of commerce, but of administration and the law; in the new grammar schools the medium was Latin, but when this declined it was English, not Welsh, that took its place.

It would be naïve to blame Henry VIII for this act of cultural imperialism. The whole trend of political thought and statescraft in Renaissance Europe was towards the enlargement and the clearer definition of the autonomous nation-state, and such a state clearly needed one, national language. Two other, equally international, movements of ideas helped, at this same time, to preserve the Welsh language. One was the Reformation: received in Wales with no great wave of enthusiasm, it nevertheless, with its emphasis on making the Scriptures available to every man in his own tongue, saved Welsh from declining into a mere patois. Queen Elizabeth's reign saw the translation of the complete Bible and the Common Prayer into Welsh, while the revised Welsh Bible of 1620 is still in use. Like their English equivalents, the Welsh Bible and Prayer Book were classics and monuments; in the case of Welsh, a language under threat of extinction was confirmed and enriched. Banned from so many other important areas of life, it took refuge, not for the last time, in religion.

The Renaissance was the other great movement that, while encouraging the study of Greek and Latin, gave a new impetus to the national tongues. In Italy, France, Germany, and England scholars and writers show a new awareness of the possibilities, the particular strengths of their own languages and literature. From the Italy of Petrarch and Boccaccio it spread to France with Ronsard, Rabelais, Du Bellay, and to England with Spenser, Sidney, and Shakespeare. In Wales, a little more backward, the Welsh grammar and the Welsh dictionary of 1621 and 1632 were part of the same movement, helping to establish Welsh as a genuine national language.

From the Reformation to the Industrial Revolution Welsh remained the language of the countryside; in the towns and near the borders English was also spoken. While the Anglican church became increasingly associated with English patronage, English bishops, and abuses such as pluralism and absenteeism, the Methodist revival of the eighteenth century was strongly Welsh. The hymns of William Williams Pantycelyn, the sermons of men like Daniel Rowland, were powerful blood-transfusions for the language. The 'circulating schools' of Griffith Jones Llanddowror in the eighteenth century, and the Sunday schools later, gave the Welsh farmworker, for the purposes of Bible-reading, it is true, a standard of literacy in his own tongue.

Since the Industrial Revolution the pressures for and against the Welsh language have been both powerful and complex. With the rise of industry came a revolution in transport and communications: the railways in particular opened up the farthest corners of Wales to the traveller and the entrepreneur. In the south-east, where the iron and coal industries were concentrated, a flood of non-Welsh immigration after 1850 – workers from the Midlands, the West Country, Ireland – diluted the native speakers to a degree that even the steady arrival of Welsh country girls and boys could not remedy. By 1901, in a typical valley town such as Ebbw Vale, only one in five spoke Welsh. (By 1961 it was one in twenty-seven.) Most of the ironmasters were English; English was the language of opportunity, of industry, and of commerce beyond the local grocery store.

In 1870 the Education Act made English the medium for compulsory primary education in Wales, and in the 1890s this was extended to the secondary system. The Welshman, with his respect for education, and his natural desire to see his children get on, had to pay a hard price. 'I lost my native language / For the one the Saxon spake / By going to school by order / For education's sake', wrote Idris Davies, a valleys' poet. Gradually English and education came to seem synonymous. Small children caught speaking Welsh in school were made to wear a placard, the 'Welsh Not', around their necks, and were punished at the end of the day. The ordinary Welshman came to feel that his language, suitable enough for private matters such as family life and chapel, was somehow intrinsically inferior. Thus in the end he connived at his own linguistic oppression. Nor is this difficult to understand, in a wider context. Victorian England was at the height of her powers; and if large areas of Africa, Asia, and India were learning to despise their 'lingo' and to read and write in that superior language, English, it is hardly surprising if Wales, nearer and smaller, did the same.

The nineteenth century, with its steamboats and its railways and the astonishing growth of literacy, saw the beginnings of that shrinkage of the world into the global village of today where a few major languages dominate international finance, industry, science, and diplomacy. It also saw the rise of nationalism in Europe, the emergence of the scientific study of languages, and a new interest in national and regional folklore, all of which were to help Welsh to survive. As early as 1789 a group of London Welshmen began to revive the *eisteddfod*, the medieval Welsh contest in music and poetry, which had fallen into decline. In 1791 the eccentric and scholarly patriot Iolo Morgannwg (Edward Williams of Glamorgan) re-invented the ceremony of the *Gorsedd*, an assembly of bards, with rites he claimed went back to the ancient Druids. Welsh literary societies with influential patrons were established at towns like Brecon (1823) and Abergavenny (1833). The movement for a Welsh university began in the 1860s, and with its founding some years later (though its teaching was entirely in English) came a Welsh literary revival, new editions of Welsh texts, new Welsh grammar books, and a new interest in

Celtic studies generally. In 1885 the Welsh Language Society started to campaign for the use of Welsh, alongside English, in schools. Wales even had its own colonial episode: in 1865 a radical Nonconformist minister, Michael Jones, set up in Patagonia a Welsh-speaking, self-supporting, cooperative, and democratic society, whose descendants still speak Welsh today. And in Wales itself writers unknown outside her frontiers but famous within them, such as O. M. Edwards, an Inspector of Schools, made Welsh history and culture available in a popular, readable, but in no way vulgarized form.

In the present century the pressures against the language have not abated. Emigration of the Welsh-speaking young from rural west Wales, immigration of English-speakers into the industrial south-east, and more recently into the countryside as weekend cottagers, the expansion of secondary and higher education, the prestige of the film, the entrenchment of radio, television, and newspapers, all these have steadily eroded the numbers of native speakers. The percentage of the latter in the population shows a gradual decline, from 35 per cent in 1911 to 27·2 per cent in 1951 and only 19·6 per cent in 1971, the latest count. Indeed the 1971 Census gives only 542,425 declared Welsh-speakers out of a total population (also decreasing) of roughly two and a half million. Monolingual Welsh-speakers – 32,725 – tend to be concentrated in two main age groups: the very old, and the very young who have not yet started school. Geographically, of course, one must discriminate. In Dyfed, predominantly rural, the proportion of Welsh-speakers remains relatively high: seven out of ten in Cardiganshire, and a good two thirds also in Carmarthenshire. In Glamorgan it drops to one in eight, and in Gwent to one in forty-seven. Radnorshire has only 655 Welsh speakers out of its sparse 17,510 inhabitants. Pembrokeshire ('Little England beyond Wales') and Breconshire both have about one in five.

There are signs, however, of a stemming of the tide. On the one hand, there has been forceful, occasionally violent, campaigning by a new breed of Welsh activist, young, articulate, well-educated, and passionate for commitment. At the same time there has been a change of attitude among certain sections of the middle class: it has become acceptable, fashionable even, to send one's children to the new Welsh-language schools. And while the old inferiority complex about Welsh has tended to persist in the countryside (where it is used most), what the urban middle class does today, the farmer may well do tomorrow.

One might add, what America does today, Britain does tomorrow. The present movement in American linguistics is towards the acceptance and indeed the encouragement of minority languages, even including the American English spoken in the black ghettoes: long written off as ignorant and incorrect, this is now recognized as a 'dialect', a branch of English with rules and patterns, and a vitality and validity of its own. In Britain the last decades have seen an increasing acceptance of the regional accent, and one need only listen to old BBC news bulletins to appreciate this change. Thus if Englishmen can now be proud of their Geordie or West Country speech, how much more so can a Welshman be of his language, which has not only a long history but centuries of written and spoken literature.

From the outside the activities of the Welsh-language campaigners often seem petty and trivial: refusing English tax forms, daubing paint on English road-signs, blowing up the occasional television transmitter. Even within Wales scorn and annoyance are frequent reactions. And certainly – since sentences are usually light, and Welsh magistrates often sympathetic – all this seems a far cry from the bloody struggles of other minority groups. One must understand, however, that these apparently unproductive acts of vandalism have a meaning more symbolic than real; the tax form, the road-sign, stands for the imposition of English in law and government, the TV transmitter for the flood of English unleashed daily into the Welsh home. The logical retort is that since the majority, indeed almost four fifths, of the population speak no Welsh, why should education, the media, local government, the legal system not use English? Unfortunately, and also fortunately, the campaign for Welsh is not a logical matter; minorities have usually been coerced into respecting the rights of majorities for too long to be tolerant.

This is not to say that the English-speaking majority in Wales are either bullies or villains, though successive governments at Westminster have indeed done their best to delay and obstruct progress within Wales. What is needed, here and elsewhere, once the rights of the minority have been recognized, is freedom of choice, not, that is, an illusory freedom based on the power to pay, but genuine alternatives: Welsh schools alongside English ones, Welsh radio and television as well as the English channels, Welsh used freely in local government, politics, the law. The Welsh Language Act of 1967 gave the right to use Welsh in all legal proceedings, and stated that in future Acts of Parliament the word 'England' should no longer automatically include Wales. (Very few trials have so far been conducted entirely in Welsh, and in bilingual cases, owing to lack of practice, standards of interpreting have not been high.) In 1972 a Committee recommended that all traffic signs be bilingual within ten years; certain areas, with few Welsh speakers, have been reluctant to comply. The reorganization of local government boundaries in recent years took, it is claimed, little account of the language factor.

Two areas are particularly sensitive. Education and the media affect the quality of life and language more profoundly than any other source. After considerable agitation from groups such as the militant Welsh Language Society the Government has finally agreed to provide a fourth, Welsh-language, television channel. This will satisfy those who, like the writer Saunders Lewis, see television in its present form as the 'chief killer of the Welsh language', and who have pointed out that BBC radio broadcasts more Polish, Portuguese, and Serbo-Croat than Welsh. It will also remove an irritation for those English-speaking viewers in Wales who resent finding a slab of Welsh replacing a more congenial programme. However, at present, funds are short, and none of the British regions is able to have the sort of network it deserves.

If there are not enough Welsh books, periodicals, and newspapers one can argue that the Welsh themselves are to blame: who else do they expect to produce them? But Welsh readership obviously depends on a fully literate Welsh-speaking population, and this in its turn depends very largely on the provision of education in Welsh. In the schools of Wales English has had the upper hand since the Tudors, and only in the last fifty years or so have serious efforts been made to redress the balance. Primary education was, as often, the pioneer. In 1939 an independent Welsh-language school was set up at Aberystwyth, sponsored by the Welsh-language youth movement; a great success, it was later taken over by the local authority. Others followed, especially in the industrial south, and nursery schools sprang up to prepare children in Anglicized areas. Secondary education lagged. Not until 1956 was the first school to teach all subjects, except science, through the medium of Welsh established, at Rhyl in North Wales. In the South bilingual and Welsh-only schools have been set up since 1962. In colleges and university more teaching is now done through Welsh, in specially designated institutions such as Bangor and Aberystwyth. Paradoxically, it is the Anglicized counties such as Radnorshire (Powys) and Gwent that are now the most anxious to learn and use Welsh; in west Wales teaching in schools still tends to be through the medium of English.

The Welsh language is a burning political issue in Wales today, yet it is perfectly possible to travel the country without feeling the heat of the flames. Whole cities, counties even, appear to be using nothing but English, while in the west Welsh can be heard in common use, uttered unselfconsciously, and courteously changed to English when the occasion requires. From the traveller sympathy and respect are all that are needed; it may be human to laugh at sounds one cannot understand, consonants that seem unpronounceable, but it is hardly polite. Indeed, it only confirms the Welsh in their private belief that the English are the true barbarians, who can only use one language (and that often badly) where they can use two.

At present the very acts of speaking and, especially, of writing Welsh are a political statement, an affirmation of an identity that feels itself under threat of engulfment. It is perhaps naïve to hope for a time when people can stop talking about which language they are using and start worrying about what they are using it for. The problem of the writer in Wales is a real one. The choice between Welsh and English is a choice between an audience of less than half a million and one that embraces, if one is lucky, the whole of the Anglo-Saxon world. The challenge of bilingualism and its related problems of identity is not of course confined to Wales: Switzerland, Belgium, Canada, and India are confronted with a similar kind of dilemma.

For a country whose population never reached three million, Wales has an extraordinary literary tradition. Its poetry, in Welsh, dates back to the ninth century and possibly even earlier, to a time when most of Britain was a Celtic land. The earliest medieval poets in Welsh continue the functions of the ancient bards; their heroic poetry – praise for the prince or hero, lament for his fall – is intended for recital rather than reading, and partakes of the semi-magical nature of the prophecy and the spell. The great age of medieval Welsh poetry comes later, however, in the twelfth century, perhaps after the introduction of Irish poets and musicians to a North Wales royal court. These 'family bards', attached to princely houses in Wales and Ireland, evolved strict poetic forms, elaborate and disciplined metres ornamented with intricate patterns of imagery and sound. (Compare the Celtic crosses with their combination of exuberance and control.) Not all poetry was 'official', of course: there is love poetry, and nature poetry, sharply observed. Medieval Welsh poetry reaches its climax in the work of Dafydd ap Gwilym (fl. 1340–70). Working in the European as well as the native tradition, Dafydd is amazingly various, a superb craftsman, nostalgic, witty, anti-clerical, moving, erotic, open to bird- and wind-song as well as to the profane love of married women.

The poetry of medieval Wales can be found in anthologies such as the *Penguin Book of Welsh Verse* or the *Celtic Miscellany*. But some of its special qualities evade translation, and more accessible to the modern reader, perhaps, is the collection of medieval prose tales, epic and romance, known as the *Mabinogion* (Everyman). These are stories of kings and giants, hags and monsters, the magic Head, the mythical boar, the woman changed into a mouse, the lovers Culhwch and Olwen, dreams and visions, journeys, hunts, feasts, and battles. Written down from the late eleventh century, they reflect a much older society, its myths and folk-traditions: the magic Cauldron perhaps an echo of Iron Age religious rites, the wading of the giant to Ireland an ancient memory of a far-off epoch before the raising of the sea-level around Britain, which took place in prehistoric times. At the same time, here is no Celtic twilight: the stories are as sharp and colourful as a medieval illuminated manuscript, their magic and monsters oddly down-to-earth, accepted by the teller as normal and necessary parts of life.

After 1536 Welsh poetry declined. English was now the official language of the country, of her gentry, and her professional classes, those who formerly provided patronage for poets. Many of her brightest children left for London or had their Welshness educated out of them at Jesus College Oxford. The monasteries, too, were gone, monasteries that had sheltered and encouraged the native culture. There were few towns, and no capital city, to form an artistic centre. Verse-making continued but the heart had gone out of it.

In the eighteenth century the Methodist movement both damaged and nourished the native literary tradition. What was considered 'pagan' - dancing, harping, and certain kinds of poetry – was violently condemned. At the same time, however, the hymns of William Williams Pantycelyn are among the greatest poetry written in Welsh, and Williams himself has been claimed as Europe's first great Romantic poet. Meanwhile, under different influences, scholarly interest in Welsh literature revived. The *eisteddfod* was disinterred, with its prizes for the traditional themes and metres.

Given this sort of history – the disappearance, that is, of the patronage system – it is not surprising that Welsh writing has remained a more classless activity than writing in England. Competitors for the Bardic Chair have been teachers and ministers, farmers and railwaymen. Though the audience for Welsh poetry has been by its nature a small one, the appetite for the Welsh sermon, that astonishing flower of rhetorical prose, in the true tradition of ancient oral literature, has until recent times been enormous.

Writing in English by Welsh men and women also has a long tradition, but its early stars are either exceedingly minor (John Dyer, Sir Lewis Morris, for example) or, like George Herbert, have only limited connexions with Wales. The term 'Anglo-Welsh literature' only really becomes relevant in the early twentieth century, when large areas of Wales became English in speech without losing their underlying consciousness of Welshness: 'Despite our speech we are not English', as R. S. Thomas's poem puts it. The label itself only dates from the 1920s, and has gradually gained acceptance. Discussions about labels are rarely as fruitful as tasting the bottle's contents. As Dylan Thomas pointed out, 'It's the poetry, written in the language which is most natural to the poet, that counts, not his continent, country, island, race, class, or political persuasion'.

A lot of good writing, poetry and prose, connected or not with Welsh life and problems, has come out of a small country in the last seventy years or so. Neither W. H. Davies nor Richard Hughes write much that is directly concerned with Wales, nor do the three great War Poets, Edward Thomas, Wilfred Owen, and Alun Lewis. Dylan Thomas absorbed and transcended Welshness and Anglo-Welshness; R. S. Thomas, vicar of an upland parish in mid Wales, writes in anger, disgust, and compassion of the life of the Welsh countryside. From the industrial valleys of the south there has tended to come an excitable brand of prose, a wordy revelry from the pit-head, the pub, and the chapel. Best known in England, perhaps, are the popular novels of Richard Llewellyn; good work by Gwyn Thomas, Gwyn Jones, Rhys Davies, Alun Richards, and others can be found in collections of Welsh short stories.

Gwlad beirdd a chantorion, 'land of bards and singers', runs one line of the Welsh National Anthem, composed in 1856 by two weavers of Pontypridd, and no one who has heard a Cardiff Arms Park crowd on International day will dispute the claim. Music and poetry are certainly the primary arts of Wales, and those most able to survive its poverty. Painting, sculpture, architecture, the theatre, once it moves beyond the folk-drama, are all costly arts, which require expensive materials, wealthy patrons, the audience of a courtly or highly urban society. In Wales good voices have been cheap and plentiful, early instruments were simply made, and the performers are often their own best audiences. One could add, too, if it is not too slick a theory, that music and poetry are the most directly emotional of the arts, and that this may have some connexion with the Celtic character.

For the half million or so Welsh-speaking inhabitants, the annual festival of music and poetry, with some arts and crafts, is the National *Eisteddfod*. A late-eighteenth-century revival of a genuine medieval tradition, the *Eisteddfod* is now very much alive. Held alternately in North and South Wales, it lasts for the whole of the first week in August; there is as much jockeying for the privilege of holding it as formerly for the Olympic Games. The only national institution to conduct its proceedings entirely in Welsh, its passions, rows, rivalries, and successes are largely closed to the outsider. (As a legacy of the Puritan nineteenth century, it is teetotal 'on the field', but the peripheral pubs do an excellent trade.) Competitions are held in solo and choral singing in a large variety of categories, in verse recitation, and in the playing of musical instruments. One of the most testing of the musical forms is the ancient art of *penillion*, whose complex rules involve, basically, playing one tune, fully harmonized, on the harp, while singing a quite different tune, as a sort of counterpoint. A Bardic Chair and a Crown are awarded for Welsh poetry. The *eisteddfod* ceremonial – white-robed bards, harpists, bands of dancing children – has survived a lot of affectionate ridicule; some of it, the great cry, 'Is there peace?' and the presentation of visiting expatriates from all over the globe, has more serious significance.

Eisteddfodau (the plural) are not confined to 'the National'. The Llangollen International Eisteddfod, another annual event, is a colourful festival of folk-music and dancing, much more rewarding as a spectacle for the non-Welsh visitor. Meanwhile, all over Wales, smaller local *eisteddfodau* take place regularly, in which amateur singers, musicians, and choirs compete for honours and small monetary prizes. And on 1 March, St David's Day, celebrated in Wales with an enthusiasm equal to the apathy accorded to St George in England, schools all over the country contribute their own concerts and *eisteddfodau*, with their rash of bogus Welsh costume and their very real odour of bruised ego and leek.

Folk-dance in Wales has, alas, none of the splendid vigour of the Scots reel or the trance-like abandonment of the Irish jig, and one can only conclude that in this area the religious revivalists did their job well. Folk-song, on the contrary, is jealously preserved, and there are many fine examples, most of them poignant and melancholy, and in minor modes. Today, outside the *eisteddfod* and the school, they are sung mostly by young people, with guitars rather than harps, who are keeping Welsh folk-song alive with new, topical additions to the repertoire. Earlier, there was, as in Ireland, a tradition of the solo (male) ballad-singer: Phil Tanner of Gower, for example, who died in about 1950 and was singing until well into his eighties, and another (or the same?) old man who could be heard occasionally on the radio about twenty years ago, singing in a strong, high-pitched, musical scream. Folk-song has suffered, in Wales as in England, from the attentions of prettifiers, who add twiddly piano accompaniments and the refinements of 'trained voices'. It comes as a shock, too, to discover that some of our best-loved 'folk-songs' are in fact last century's compositions, or earlier melodies transformed out of all recognition into Victorian front-parlour sentimental songs. Not so surprising, however, when one remembers how firmly the nineteenth century left its mark on modern Wales.

Since the arrival of Nonconformity, at least, music and religion have been close partners in Wales, and in a puritanical form of worship without ritual or vestments, music and the sermon are the natural outlets for emotion and the artistic sense. Englishmen are constantly surprised at the way in which Welshmen burst into hymn-singing, in pubs, coaches, or the rugby stand. (Welshmen, if they get that far, are often shocked at the skinny, bloodless singing in an English church.) The singers may well not be chapel-goers (for chapels are closing now in Wales), and they may well follow the hymn with an equally traditional 'rugby song' of entirely opposite moral assumptions. The hymn, then, has become in this context less of an address to the Creator than an affirmation of solidarity, a cry of pleasure at being one of a great mass of Welshmen.

Choral singing still survives in the chapels, of course, with the *Cymanfa Ganu*, a festival of hymn-singing that at the height of its popularity sometimes lasted for days. The male-voice choir, too, essentially an urban, industrial phenomenon, continues, though anyone who has seen one recently will have noticed that the average age of the choir is well over thirty. The choirs are eclectic in membership and in choice of programme; indeed, their taste in music does not always match the genuine beauty of the sound, as adjudicators in foreign festivals have sometimes pointed out. The choirs are at their best, in fact, not in the over-arranged folk-songs or the selections from *Oklahoma!* but in the simple, full harmonies of the Negro spiritual or the traditional Welsh hymn. As in the industrial North of England, too, which has its own great choirs and brass bands, there is the *Messiah* or an oratorio at Christmas, bursting the small chapels with sounds that could fill a cathedral.

Classical music in Wales has suffered from the same disabilities as the more expensive art-forms mentioned earlier. Opera-singers have until recently left for England, and anyone who knows opera in Britain can reel off a long list of Welsh-born international stars. The Welsh National Opera Company has, with enthusiasm and subsidies, built itself into a fine company, and, rightly, welcomes singers from outside Wales. Apart from the BBC Welsh, there is no national professional orchestra, though there is a flourishing Youth Orchestra, and important music festivals at Swansea and Llandaff. There are numbers of young Welsh composers, and some well-established ones – Daniel Jones, Alun Hoddinott, William Mathias, Grace Williams – but their work is (like that of most modern English composers) little known outside their own frontiers.

The musical life of Wales, with its two and a half million people thinly spread, can hardly compete with that of London with its seven millions, its concert-halls and opera-houses. Yet there is some truth in the cherished old national chestnut that Wales is a musical nation. In England certain kinds of music-making are thought of as middle-class activities, and this can lead to a sort of stultifying pride in Philistinism; in Wales, where the middle class, when it existed, has done less to lead or to stifle, this constraint is much less apparent.

The Welshman, it has been said, is a born actor. His language, unlike English, does not tolerate being pronounced sloppily; his taste for oratory and rhetoric is an ancient one; his whole character, indeed, seems to impel him to inflate into comedy and tragedy the ordinary incidents of his life. His favourite occupations have been teaching, politics, and the Ministry, all professions that require a 'performance'. As for organized theatre, on the other hand, this has long been weak in Wales; lack of money, of towns, 200 years of Nonconformity, the usual culprits. In recent times new theatre companies working in Welsh and English have received much more encouragement, and drama is fostered at the university colleges. Purpose-built theatres, like concert-halls, are uncommon in Wales, but the new smaller experimental troupes can be accommodated in a variety of other buildings. A Welsh ballet company has recently been formed, but has not yet had time to establish a reputation.

Sport, too, is a kind of art, a performance, an expression, and a group ritual. (I am talking here of sports that are part of the national culture, and not of the wider variety open to visitors.) As in rural England, the Wales of earlier centuries had its violent village football, played with two distant church porches as goals, its wrestling, its cock-fighting, its fabulous long-distance runners, its early forms of hockey and other sports. Today sport in Wales is very similar to sport in England, but with some persistent under-lying differences.

Welshmen have not used the natural facilities of their own countryside as much as have Englishmen, and this again is probably a question of money and leisure. While Welshmen have always made good sea-captains, sailing as a sport has only fairly recently become a popular leisure activity. Fishing, for trout or salmon, has been less of a sport than a second occupation. The Welsh breed good horses, but they are not very interested in racing. Fox-hunting, however, has long been popular, in a more functional, less class-based way than in England. Farmers are obviously the most usual participants, but in the Valleys there is a hunt made up largely of miners. The Welsh fox-hound, too, is slightly different from his English counterpart: probably descended from French hunting-dogs introduced into the Vale of Glamorgan by the Normans, he has a wiry coat, a lightish colour, a good nose, and a loud voice.

Organized team sports are by and large an urban phenomenon, confined to the South, to the industrial valleys and the coast. Village cricket is played, though less than in England, and a Welsh team, Gowerton, carried off the village championship at Lords in 1975. But Glamorgan is still the only Welsh county to run a full cricket team. Founded in 1885, Glamorgan remained a second-class county until 1921. Its perform-ance has been erratic: it has won the county championship only twice, in 1948 and 1969, and its team has recently benefited from the arrival of non-British immigrants. It is rare for Welsh cricketers to make the top, and Tony Lewis is the only Glamorgan player to captain (briefly) England.

Rugby football is just over a hundred years old in Wales, but in that time, in the South at least, it has attained the status of a national mania. Wales was, in fact, the last of the home countries to take up the game; she has, however, made it peculiarly her own. Rugby was introduced into Wales by public schoolboys and Oxbridge under-graduates, but its violent physical excitement quickly gained for it a broad popular following. On the industrial south coast the six major clubs – from east to west, Newport, Cardiff, Aberavon, Neath, Swansea, Llanelli – were in business by 1876. In 1881 the

Welsh Union was founded at Neath, in response, it is thought, to a national defeat in which England trounced Wales by the equivalent of sixty-nine points to nil. From 1900 to 1914 there followed a Golden Age of Welsh rugby, then a slump, until the late 1930s when the game revived. Since the Second War it has gone from strength to strength. In recent years the Welsh R.U. has pioneered coaching techniques and squad training, with great success.

Rugby is still confined to the industrial south-east of Wales, the coastal towns, and the valleys. Within these geographical limits, however, it has an almost boundless following: in the streets of a South Wales town, on an International Saturday afternoon, not a man is to be seen. In Cardiff the crowds are excitable but rarely threatening; at Twickenham their singing is swelled by the nostalgia of all those London Welsh exiles whose comfortable life in England requires the occasional shot of *hiraeth* (a passionate longing for home). On the field the game is, more than in England, democratic. At its best, the Welsh game is witty, resourceful, courageous, swift, and full of panache; at its worst, it is underhand and ugly, the product of violent partisan feeling over-riding the sense of fair play. At least, like the French, whom they somewhat resemble, the Welsh team is never dull.

If sport in Wales has been the art-form of the ordinary man, cooking should perhaps be that of the woman, however much such old-fashioned distinctions are to be deplored. The old Welsh kitchen (to be seen at St Fagan's Folk Museum, for instance) with its iron range, its sturdy hooks for cured hams and strings of onions, its Welsh oak dresser, with blue-and-white china and copper-lustre jugs, cries out for the smell of warm bread, cooking chickens, leek pie, and toasted cheese. Yet if a rugby match can be easily located in South Wales on a winter's Saturday, good Welsh cooking, on the contrary, is hard to find. Cheap and medium-priced restaurants everywhere serve the ubiquitous steak, plaice, scampi, chips, peas; smarter ones go in for what might be called international French, and with varying success. Many hotels and restaurants are run by English people, for the Welsh though naturally hospitable do not seem to be a nation of hoteliers. The best coffee-bars and ice-cream parlours are Italian. There are a few exceptions – a Welsh restaurant (owned by an Italian) opened recently in Cardiff, for example – but it would be pointless to name them. This is not France, where one can expect a good restaurant to be still in business fifty or a hundred years later.

Good English cooking is country-house cooking, the product of the prosperous upper and middle classes. Good Welsh cooking is, traditionally, home cooking, and farmhouse cooking to be more precise. It is essentially unpretentious, using the simple ingredients available in a country where the soil is often thin and the sunshine none too reliable. The rich have always lived well, of course: Vicar Pritchard's moral verses, in the early seventeenth century, castigate those who demand six-course meals and wine twice a day. His peasants survived (more healthily perhaps) on cottage vegetables: garlic, onion, parsnip, marrow. Arthur Young the economist, travelling in South Wales in the 1770s, before the improvement of agricultural methods had taken hold there, noted in Pembrokeshire the frugal diet of the poor. The cottagers around Narberth lived on 'bread and cheese, and milk, or water; no beer, nor meat, except on a Sunday'; near St Clears it was 'barley-bread, cheese, and butter; not one in ten have either cows or pigs. . . . Their little gardens they plant with cabbages, carrots, leeks, and potatoes'. In the uplands one can only assume that conditions were equally as bad.

Like most peasant cooking, in Europe, the basic Welsh dish is a stew or soup, generally made in this instance with mutton or ham, and with vegetables added according to season. *Cawl* (pronounced 'cowl') is the Welsh equivalent of Irish stew, Lancashire hotpot, French *pot-au-feu*: boiled or simmered for as long as necessary, depending on the age of the meat, it has no fixed ingredients, though leeks and potatoes give it its characteristic Welsh flavour. For special occasions a roast chicken, or, best of all, a leg of best Welsh lamb – for if the valley sheep are fatter, the mountain sheep are certainly sweeter – are usual fare.

Beefsteak is not a national dish – the Welsh preferred to sell their cattle to England – but dairy produce is excellent. Carmarthenshire butter and real Caerphilly cheese are extraordinary delicacies. Toasted cheese (*Caws pobi*, 'Welsh rarebit') has been a Welsh favourite for centuries, and there is an old joke that in order to make some room in heaven, St Peter stood outside the pearly gates and shouted 'Caws pobi!' thereby emptying Paradise of all its Welshmen. 'Glamorgan sausages' is another good, filling snack, a mixture of cheese, breadcrumbs, egg, and onions, formed into sausage shapes and fried; it was enjoyed by George Borrow in the 1860s.

Fish and seafood are especially good in Wales. Inland, fresh Teifi or Towy salmon, trout, and sewin (sea-trout) are well worth paying for. Shellfish of all varieties from oysters to mussels are plentiful, though not made enough of. Cockles, traditionally dug at Penclawdd in Gower, are eaten alone with beer and vinegar, fried in batter, baked in pies. Oddest of all to the foreigner is laverbread, a special kind of seaweed gathered on the south coast and sold ready washed and boiled, a dark shiny greenish-black purée, in Swansea Market. Laverbread is traditionally fried in oatmeal and eaten with bacon; it also makes a good sauce for Welsh lamb. (Seaweeds are also eaten in Ireland and in the East, and they are highly nutritious.)

Like other regions of Britain, Wales has its own wide variety of bread, buns, and cakes, of the kind that provide wholesome filling rather than a dainty bite of choux pastry and cream. *Bara brith* is a cross between bread and cake, rather like the *barm brack* of Ireland: it is made with flour, yeast, spices, sugar, and dried fruit, and can be mixed with milk, milk and water, or cold tea. *Teisen lap* is more of a fruit cake, and is served spread with butter. These two are baked in the oven. Several other Welsh dishes – pancakes, oatcakes, 'Welsh cakes' – are cooked on a griddle or bake-stone. 'Welsh cakes' can be bought in tea-shops: small, round, flat, slightly browned, they have a pleasant dryish taste enlivened by currants and spice. *Crempog las* are a variety of savoury pancake, a thick batter that includes parsley and chopped spring onions ('shibbons' as they are known in South Wales); these can be cooked in a frying-pan and are eaten hot with butter.

That South Wales has still a distinctive personality of its own will probably not be disputed by any traveller west of Cardiff. But the clichés of its culture – as seen through foreign eyes, that is – should not always be accepted at face value. Take, for example, the Welsh Sunday, that traditional Slough of Despond. It is true that there are still places in Wales (but not many in the South) where you cannot drink in a pub on a Sunday, though members of clubs and residents of hotels can be served. Strict Sabbatarianism has firm roots in Wales, though they are not really very long ones, and date only from the Nonconformist fervours of the last century. In a study of Tregaron, a small market-town in the south-west, written in the 1940s, Emrys Jones describes how it was felt irreligious even to buy a Sunday paper. Yet until quite recently chapel-going was in fact no penance but a source of some very real pleasures, and not only of a religious kind. The full-blooded Welsh sermon was a high art in itself, combining poetry, rhetoric, theatre, and philosophy with a firm grip on the realities of belief. Hymn-singing was a religious and social ritual, a source of physical enjoyment, and an affirmation of the one-ness of the group. In the countryside chapel was an occasion, like market-day, to meet neighbours separated by miles of lanes; in the towns it was an opportunity to wear one's best finery. No self-respecting woman would be seen on Whit or Easter without a new coat and hat, a modern version of an old homage to the gods of spring. Perhaps the decline of the chapels in the present generation has less to do with the falling-off of religious belief than with the satisfaction by other means of these basic social necessities: radio and television now provide the drama, rural neighbours can be easily contacted by car and telephone, entertainment and social life with their 'dressing-up' are more diversified, and women are now accepted in pubs.

Outside the industrial south-east, South Wales is made up of small towns and scattered farmsteads. This pattern of life has encouraged a capacity for self-reliance, something found in all such societies, and, since many farming tasks have to be done in common, places a high value on family and neighbours. The importance of the family in South Wales has survived industrialization, the rapid growth of towns, and most other vicissitudes. Everyone still seems to be related to everyone else, and the ramifications of kinship still affect local elections and (unfortunately) local government and the appointment to certain kinds of jobs. There is at the same time a great respect for individual achievement, and if a child is promising the family does not stand in its way. Welsh names, source of merriment to foreigners, reflect this dual emphasis on family and individual. Those famous surnames – Jones, Williams, Evans, Thomas – which make a Welsh telephone directory a surrealist experience, are clearly personal names; they are an adaptation to English custom (after the Acts of Union) of the Welshmen's prized genealogy. Thus Sion (John) ap Ifan ap Tomos (etc.) became plain John Evans, for administrative purposes. The 'p' of *ap* ('son of') gave the numerous surnames in P and B: Parry, Bevan, Pritchard, Penry can easily be deciphered as *ap* Harri, *ap* Ifan, *ap* Richard, *ap* Henry. Christian names, too, had a traditional, family quality: the first boy would often be named after the father, the second after the maternal grandfather, and so on. And if a child died in infancy another would be given its name, a practice that can be verified in churchyards.

Given the confusion that such reduplication could generate, two methods of distinguishing the individual were widely used. One is the unusual Christian name, which gives flavour to the inevitable Jones or Thomas. Some are Welsh (Gwynfor, Eurfron, Eiddwen, Gwenllian, and so on), others Biblical (Daniel, Ebenezer, Theophilus, Christmas even), some, occasionally, musical (Handel, Haydn, Verdi). The other method is the nickname, a habit that out of basic necessity has persisted in Wales long after the Curthoses and Crookbacks have disappeared, as a living tradition, in England. Those were fortunate whose nicknames focused on trade or place of residence – Jones the Milk, Williams Pant-du, for example – for satire can be merciless: Lord Cut-glass and Evans Alleluia are among the milder versions.

If family and individual form one paradox of Welsh culture, home and exile are another. Like Ireland and Scotland, and for similar reasons, Wales has seen a steady seeping-out of her population, her most enterprising and ambitious young people driven out by the Depression, or, even in better times, attracted elsewhere by money, a wider arena, a less closed-in society. Teachers are a traditional Welsh export, while the old occupations of the countryside (farming itself, and cloth-weaving), translated into London terms, give the Welsh drapers and the small Welsh dairies, which can still be seen around Bloomsbury and elsewhere. The arrival of the young Welshman in London has, with Dylan Thomas, Rhys Davies, Dannie Abse, become almost a literary theme. There are no Welsh ghettoes, for the emigrant tends to be a professional or a small businessman, but there are thriving Welsh clubs and chapels. Many London Welsh, like Irishmen in America, dream of eventually retiring to the homeland; the gravestones of small country churchyards like Pontrhydfendigaid, with their Maida Vale and Putney addresses, show that this is sometimes achieved, if too late. The position of the exile, whether his state be self-imposed or not, is always ambiguous: he comes to feel at home in no place, and when he goes back on a visit he starts to remember why he has left.

Not all of this may be apparent to the visitor, even if he manages to discard the blurring lens of national stereotypes, which make the world a comic-strip inhabited by beréted Frenchmen and kilted Scots. Indeed he may well (and legitimately) lack curiosity, preferring to enjoy mountains, sea, or forest on their own terms, as if they had no nationality – though sooner or later a Welsh drizzle will force him into the town. The gazetteer that follows concentrates, however, not on the beauties of scenery, which need no explanation, but on history and architecture, and the marks of man on the landscape.

Short-stay Guide

This page is intended for the person whose time in South Wales is limited to a few days. What, out of all that is described in this book, is most worth visiting? The question is an invidious one, but below are some unashamedly subjective thoughts on the matter. The items are *not* listed in order of preference.

Not all of the items in the list are the subject of a separate gazetteer entry: it is suggested that the index will provide the most convenient way of tracing descriptions.

Castles
Caerphilly
Cardiff
Carew
Cilgerran
Castell Coch
Kidwelly
Pembroke
Raglan
Chepstow
Manorbier

Churches and Ruined Abbeys
St David's Cathedral and Bishop's Palace
St Govan's Chapel
Llandaff Cathedral
Ewenny Priory
Tintern Abbey
Patrishow church

Land- and Sea-scape
National Parks: Brecon Beacons;
    Pembrokeshire Coast
Areas of Outstanding Natural Beauty:
    Gower Peninsula; Wye Valley
Radnor Forest (Llandegley)
Vale of Glamorgan
Upper Neath and Tawe valleys
Teifi Valley around Cenarth
Devil's Bridge and the Rheidol Valley
Cwm Einion ('Artists' Valley')
Preseli Mountains
Elan Valley reservoirs (Rhayader)
Llyn-y-fan fach Lake (Myddfai)
South Gower coast and Rhosili Bay
The estuary at Laugharne

Pembrokeshire coast: Bosherston;
    Broad Haven; St David's Peninsula;
    Strumble Head, Fishguard; etc.
Cardigan Bay coast: Llangranog
Dovey Estuary

Monuments
Offa's Dyke (near Presteigne, Knighton,
    Montgomery)
Pentre Ifan cromlech (Newport, Dyfed)
Caerleon Roman amphitheatre
Nevern High Cross
St Fagan's Folk Museum (Cardiff)

Seaside Towns and Villages
Aberaeron
Aberystwyth
Lower Fishguard
Laugharne
Llangranog
New Quay
Port Einon
Tenby

Inland Towns and Villages
Brecon
Cardiff
Carmarthen
Grosmont
Haverfordwest
Llantwit Major
Monmouth
Montgomery
Presteigne
Skenfrith
Swansea

Gazetteer

Abbreviations

NT for National Trust

Entries in the Gazetteer

The first figure of the map reference supplied to each entry refers to a page number in the map section at the back of the book. The subsequent letter and figure give the grid reference.

Population figures are based on the 1971 Census.

TOP: *Abbey Cwmhir: the abbey ruins*   BOTTOM: *Abbey Cwmhir church (1866)*

Abbey Cwmhir Powys 7F1
10km. from Rhayader (Rhaeadr Gwy)
It was a principle of the monks of the Cistercian Order that their Houses should be built in places remote from all human habitation, and at Abbey Cwmhir they seem to have fulfilled this obligation most successfully. Today, there is virtually no public transport, and the walk from Rhayader is a hilly one. Nor does very much survive of the abbey: a few grey stones remain to mark the outer walls, the bases of piers, and parts of the transepts. But the setting is beautiful; the small Clywedog River forms a pool here, perhaps the remnant of the monastic fishpond. The mountains retain their wildness, beneath a growing coat of forestry.

The abbey was founded as a daughter-house of Whitland, in 1143, by a Welsh prince. It continued, naturally enough, to have patriotic sympathies. In 1231, for example, during Henry III's skirmishes with the Welsh, one of the Cwmhir monks directed the English to a 'ford', where their horses were mired and they were trapped at the mercy of the Welsh leader Llewellyn. Henry retaliated by burning down a grange of the abbey and fining the abbot. Privileges granted to Cwmhir that same year include the condition that the monks 'do not abuse their liberty by assisting the king's enemies in Wales'. It seems likely that the corpse of Llewellyn the Last, headless, was brought here for burial, after his rather mysterious death at Cilmeri near Builth, in 1282. During the Glyndwr rebellion (c. 1400) – it is not known which side the monks supported – the abbey suffered severely, and was never fully restored. The Dissolution completed its destruction: an arcade was removed, it is said, to Llanidloes church, while the rest was, as usual, treated as a quarry. (One Thomas Wilson Esq. is described as having built a 'small but elegant house' in the Elizabethan style, using materials from the abbey.)

Even in its heyday, Abbey Cwmhir, 240m. above sealevel, and in mountainous land, was never a rich house by English monastic standards. Yet its nave, 72½m. long, was exceptionally ambitious, and it had the usual extensive pasture lands for its sheep and cattle. Its stud farm was such that in the early thirteenth century it was obliged to supply the Welsh prince Llywellyn ab Iorwerth with two colts annually 'of their superior breed'. At that time, too, the mountains would have been covered with their indigenous oak forests, source of fuel and of timber for building. (By 1848 these were almost denuded; they are now being replaced, but not by oak.)

Abbey Cwmhir village is clustered around the Happy Union pub, a Victorian Gothic mansion, and an eccentric neo-Byzantine church of the same vintage (1866). The latter two were built by the Philips family, on the proceeds of Manchester cotton; hall and church have been described as a 'lively and muscular couple'. The church contains a stone coffin lid, decorated and inscribed, from the grave of Abbot Mabli.

Aberaeron Dyfed 6A2 (*pop.* 1,324)
A unique example of Regency town-planning in Wales, Aberaeron is the creation of the Revd Alban Thomas Jones Gwynne, who in 1807 obtained an Act of Parliament to build two piers at the mouth of the Aeron, 'with convenient wharfs, cranes, and storehouses, at an expense of about £6,000'. Further harbour development in the years following gave the little port prosperity. In 1848 it was importing coal, timber, and groceries, and exporting Welsh butter and oats; thirty boats with a seven-man crew each were engaged in a lucrative herring fishery.

Aberaeron is not flamboyant; its Georgian houses and harbourside buildings are well proportioned but modest.

C9 Celtic cross-shaft, Llanddewi Aberarth church

More recently a planned campaign of colourwash has emphasized its charm. The Town Hall in Market Street is an impressive neo-classical building. The town's English street-names run from Waterloo and Wellington to Albert and Victoria: their Welsh 'equivalents', which are springing up all over the town, usually revert to topographical description. Alban Square, named after the Revd Alban Gwynne, has attractive Georgian houses. The town's other centre of interest is the harbour itself, which reaches right into the town. Here a row of small houses and the harbourmaster's taller house (now a hotel) look out onto the pleasure yachts, which have replaced the old fishing fleet. At the entrance to the car

C10 hog-backed stone, Llanddewi Aberarth church

park south of the harbour, a curious tiny building was used as a weigh-house for lime.

The railway reached Aberystwyth in 1864, and the Cardigan Bay ports declined thereafter. Aberaeron now survives very largely on tourism, which it caters for conscientiously. There is sailing in plenty, and good fishing, for salmon, trout, and sewin (sea-trout). The beach is shingly but safe for bathing. In summer months a regatta, a carnival, an art exhibition, and sheep-dog trials are held.

In the church porch at LLANDDEWI ABERARTH (on the hillside, 2½km. east) are a ninth-century Celtic cross, and a tenth-century hog-backed decorated stone, rare in Wales.

Aberdare (Aberdâr)   Mid Glam.   11E2
(*pop.* 37,760)
Aberdare, near the head of the Cynon Valley, is an industrial town created on iron and coal. Already early last century a traveller noted the delightful vale of Cynon, 'remarkable for picturesque and romantic scenery', but complained that the working of coal and iron ore, while it added to the wealth and number of the inhabitants, had materially defaced the beauty of the neighbourhood. The number of inhabitants had certainly increased, but their wealth was a relative matter; most were 'rich' only in comparison with those who had stayed behind on the hill-farms of the west. And conditions of life in the new mining towns were hard indeed. Aberdare had its share of the unrest caused by those conditions, by the fluctuations of wages and the insecurity of employment. In 1857 four or five thousand miners in the Aberdare Valley stayed out on strike for seven weeks, in protest against a wage reduction of 15 per cent. Although this battle was lost (the miners had to return to work with a 20 per cent reduction), others succeeded. The Trade Union Act, which recognized the legality of unionism, was passed in 1871; the Liberal Home Secretary who guided it through Parliament was a Welsh coal-owner and ironmaster who later took the title of Lord Aberdare. A statue of him stands in Aberdare Park. And at Cwmbach, near Aberdare, the first cooperative store in Wales was opened, in 1860. This was a step towards breaking the stranglehold of the 'company shop', in which men were forced to spend their wages.

Aberdare has a strong musical tradition. In Victoria Square 'Caradog' stands in bronze, conducting the Great Choir of five hundred that won the chief choral prize at the Crystal Palace in 1872 and 1873. Here too, the son of a schoolmaster, was born Alun Lewis (1915–44), one of the finest of the Second World War poets.

St John the Baptist's church in Aberdare is an ancient building whose registers date back to the early eighteenth century. The church of St Mary in Maesydref was built in 1865, in French Gothic style. The architect, Sir A. W. Blomfield, had at that time a young assistant; his name was Thomas Hardy.

The Iron Trambridge at Robertstown in Aberdare, a nineteenth-century tramroad bridge, has been recommended for scheduling as an industrial monument. Industrial archaeology is also one of the attractions of the Dare Valley Country Park, which has four nature trails and several walks, providing a good introduction to the flora and fauna of the coalfield.

Aberedw Powys 7F3
'Oh, Aberedw, Aberedw. Would God I might dwell and die by thee. Memory enters in and brings back the old time in a clear vision and waking dream, and again I descend from the high moor's half encircling sweep and listen to the distant murmur of the river. . . . Once more I stand by the riverside and look up at the cliff castle towers and mark the wild roses swinging from the crag and watch the green woods waving and shimmering with a twinkling dazzle as they rustle in the breeze and shining of the summer afternoon, while here and there a grey crag peeps from among the tufted trees'. The Revd Francis Kilvert's eminently readable diary breaks out, on 13 April 1875, into a more than usually intense celebration of the beauty of this landscape. Justly so, for Aberedw stands at one of the finest stretches of the consistently beautiful Wye. Aberedw Rocks, south of the village, form a magnificent 1½km.-long terrace of lime-

St David's church, Cregrina, Edw Valley, showing C15 screen

stone rising above the brown river. In the village itself, a fine Early English church has a fifteenth-century rood-screen, a wooden roof of some antiquity, and an ornamented porch.

On the hill high above the river are the ruins of a castle that was once a stronghold of the Welsh prince Llewellyn the Last. Its destruction was helped along by the Cambrian Railway, which drove through the site and has now itself shunted on into history. In the Aberedw Rocks, a cavern about 1½m. square goes by the traditional name of Llewellyn's Cave. Here he is thought to have hidden, shortly before his death, near Builth, in 1282.

The Edw Valley has a number of attractive, if isolated, churches. Llanbadarn-y-garreg, beside the river; Rhulen, a fourteenth-century building, on the side of the mountain; Cregrina, restored in 1958, with a Norman font and fifteenth-century screen. GLASCWM (Glasgwm), today, is one of the most remote. Yet this was one of the 'mother-churches' of Wales, a semi-monastic foundation of the Celtic Church, which pre-dated the Normans and their new organization into bishoprics. Its unusual size reflects this ancient status. Kilvert describes a visit to the Vicarage there, on 22 May 1871. The Vicar entertained him with bread and butter

and Herefordshire cider, and took him to see the 'Cathedral': 'The Cathedral lay a little distance down a pretty lane overarched and avenued with sycamores and limes. It was one of the very large Welsh Churchyards, 2 acres in extent and thinly peopled. The church long, low and whitewashed, an unbroken line of roof without a tower or bell-turret of any kind. An immense chancel and an equally large belfry and a small nave. The belfry is the village school. . . . There used to be three good bells in Glascwm Church brought by the enchanted bisons from Llandewi Brefi. Just before the present Vicar came there was a tremendous wedding of a farmer's daughter. . . . One bell did not ring loud enough to satisfy the people so they took an axe up to the bell and beat the bell with the axe till they beat it all to pieces'.

The stone circle known as the Fedw, near Glascwm, is one of the largest of its kind in Wales.

Abergavenny (Y Fenni)   Gwent   7G6
(*pop.* 9,388)
Abergavenny is an ancient and attractive market town set at the point where the Usk flows out into the lower-lying lands of Gwent. The Romans built a fort some-where here, named Gobannium; tiles of the Second Augustan Legion, based at Caerleon, have been found.

C14 St David's church, Rhulen, Edw Valley

This fort may have occupied the same site as the Norman castle, which was founded before 1090 by Hamelin de Balun to control this section of the Usk Valley. The medieval lordship of Abergavenny extended from Pontypool to the Monnow River. One of its most notorious incumbents was William de Breos. In 1176, shortly after succeeding to the lordship, de Breos invited Sitsyllt ap Dyfnwal and a number of other local chieftains to a banquet at the castle. Once at table, the guests were set upon and murdered by the Norman's armed retainers. De Breos was guilty not only of treachery but also of violating one of the most sacred traditions of Celtic culture, the duty of hospitality. He ended badly, though not for another thirty years or so (*see* Painscastle).

From de Breos's time there remain only some fragments of the curtain wall. Most of the ruins are later – from the thirteenth and fourteenth centuries – and the gatehouse may date from the Glyndwr rising (*c.* 1400), when the whole town was sacked and burned. Today, in the castle grounds, stands the District Museum, which has collections relating to local history, costume, and folk-life, including a Welsh border kitchen.

St Mary's church in Monk Street formed part of the Benedictine Priory, founded by de Balun shortly after the Conquest as a daughter-house of the Abbey of St Vincent at Le Mans. The tower is a fourteenth-century structure but much of the fabric has been restored. Inside, the church is rich in detail. Twenty-four elaborately-carved choirstalls from the late fourteenth century have survived intact, and there are numerous splendid tombs with wooden and alabaster effigies. Note in particular a huge figure of Jesse carved in wood, with a branch growing out from the body; this is probably the base of a Jesse tree, which would have culminated in a figure of Christ.

Picturesquely situated among its mountains, Abergavenny became a tourist centre early last century. In 1811 the Breconshire and Monmouthshire Canal was completed; this now provides an additional leisure attraction. Earlier visitors fished the Usk, cycled, were driven out to Llanthony, Raglan, or Crickhowell. The nineteenth century also saw a brief but passionate revival of Welsh culture in the town. Sir Benjamin Hall and his wife, later Lord and Lady Llanover, encouraged the founding of a literary society and annual *eisteddfod*. This was part of a wider awakening of national consciousness in Wales at this time. For this particular seed, however, Abergavenny, in the Anglicized border-lands, was stony ground. The Welsh revival did not long survive the death of its patrons.

Abergavenny makes an excellent centre for exploration both of the Brecon Beacons National Park and the Gwent–Hereford border country. Its immediate circle of mountains includes the triangular Sugar Loaf (NT) and the Great Skirrid, a Holy Mountain whose huge western ravine was thought to have been rent at the Crucifixion. On its summit an Iron Age fort can still be traced, and a much ruined chapel where, during the

Figure of Jesse, Abergavenny

persecutions of the seventeenth century, Roman Catholics are said to have gathered for Mass. Blorenge, on the opposite side of the town, is an outcrop of the coal-field, and marks off Abergavenny from the industrial valleys to the west.

The Three Castles – Skenfrith, Grosmont, and White Castle – are within easy reach. Seven km. north-east, at Llanfihangel Crucorney (Llanfihangel Crucornau), Llanfihangel Court is a fine Elizabethan mansion, open to visitors on summer Sundays.

Abergwesyn Powys 6D3

The village of Abergwesyn, in the Irfon Valley, is separated from any town of size by km. upon km. of desolate, heathery moorland, populated only by the particularly hardy brands of Welsh sheep. This was not, however, always a lonely or isolated place. The recently-surfaced road west to Tregaron was one of the main 'Drovers' Roads', along which great herds of black cattle journeyed to London and the South. Cattle-rearing was the traditional occupation of the Welsh tribesmen from the earliest times, a natural and necessary choice in a country composed mainly of uplands. Records of Welsh cattle being driven to London for slaughter go back to the Middle Ages; and as London and its needs grew, so did the drovers' trade. In Elizabeth's reign drovers had to be licensed annually at the Quarter Sessions; this was partly to ensure they did not get confused with vagabonds, of whom 'the most that walke about be Welchemen'. The eighteenth and nineteenth centuries were, however, the most prosperous period for the cattle trade. The herds (cattle, mostly, but also sheep and ponies) were assembled at various points and shod *en masse* at centres such as Tregaron, Pumsaint, and Painscastle. As far as possible they were kept off the main thoroughfares, in order to avoid the payment of tolls. Pubs and inns in England and Wales still mark the old journeys with the name 'Drovers' Arms'. Once in England the cattle were either fattened in the Home Counties, or sold at once for slaughter at markets such as Barnet and Smithfield.

The drover held a key position in the Welsh agricultural economy. He was responsible for seeing that the cattle fetched a good price, and the risks he took were thus considerable. On top of this, he was entrusted with commissions in London or other large towns, paying rents and taxes, delivering letters. Eventually he became a sort of banker, and indeed drovers set up country banks at Llandovery, Aberystwyth, and Carmarthen, issuing their banknotes stamped with the heads of sheep or oxen. He brought, too, a vital breath of freedom, a link between the remote hill farmers and the outside world.

About 4km. further up the valley, LLANDDEWI church has traces of earlier buildings and a primitive carved Celtic cross. An early vicar there was Thomas Howell, whose son James (*c.* 1594–1666) became Charles II's Historiographer Royal, and a well-known poet and propagandist. His *Familiar Letters* were read and praised by writers from Defoe to Thackeray, and can still be perused with pleasure.

Abergwili Dyfed *see* **Carmarthen**

Aberllynfi Powys *see* **Glasbury**

Abermule (Abermiwl) Powys 3H5

On a hill commanding the Severn Valley the fragmentary ruins of Dolforwyn Castle await excavation. It was built by Llewellyn ap Gruffydd (Llewellyn the Last) in 1273, one of a number of sophisticated fortresses intended to stand firm against the English king. Recognized Prince of Wales by Henry III at the 1267 Treaty of Montgomery, Llewellyn lost most of his power and possessions in his ten-year conflict with that king's successor, Edward I. His death near Builth in 1282 put an end to his attempts to achieve unity and independence for Wales. The castle passed to the Mortimer family.

The name Dolforwyn means 'Virgin's meadow', and this may be a survival of an old legend, noted by the fanciful medieval historian Geoffrey of Monmouth. According to this tale, the British king Locrine had a daughter Sabrina, by Estrildis, who was not his wife. The queen, Gwendolen, in a fit of jealousy, had the girl drowned, here, in the river. In another version Locrinus divorces Gwenddolan for Essyllt, whereupon Gwenddolan drowns both Essyllt and her daughter Havren. This maiden is the 'Sabrina fair', symbol of chastity, in Milton's masque *Comus*. The legend may well be a poetic attempt to explain the origin of the river's name (Severn-Sabrina-Hafren, in Welsh): many folk-tales arise in such a way.

The once praised and now neglected epic 'The Fleece', by the eighteenth-century poet John Dyer, describes rather charmingly a pastoral feast on the banks of the Severn somewhere near Abermule:

> From Wreakin's brow to rocky Dolvoryn,
> Sabrina's early haunt, ere yet she fled
> The search of Gwendolen, her stepdame proud,
> With envious hate enrag'd. The jolly cheer
> Spread on a mossy bank, untouch'd abides
> Till cease the rites; and now the mossy bank
> Is gaily circled, and the jolly cheer
> Dispers'd in copious measure; early fruits,
> And those of frugal store, in husk or rind;
> Steep'd grain, and curdled milk with dulcet cream
> Soft temper'd.

('Steep'd grain and curdled milk' would appear to be that traditional Welsh dish known as 'flummery'.)

Aberporth Dyfed 9E1

The presence of the nearby Government Experimental Rocket Station does not deter the boaters and bathers at this popular sandy cove on Cardigan Bay. The beach is safe, and the village provides the usual facilities. Tresaith, a few km. away, is another small, sandy beach, with a waterfall and rocky cliffs. From accessible headlands (some are Government property) can be seen on a clear day Snowdon, Cadair Idris, and the Irish coast; look out for seals and porpoises off shore.

On the main coast road, a little inland, Blaenannerch village and its Calvinistic Methodist chapel were the starting-point for the great Welsh religious revival of 1904.

Abertillery (Abertyleri) Gwent 11G1 (*pop.* 21,140)

From Brynmawr down to Aberbeeg the terraces run in relays almost the whole length of the Ebbw Fach, or Western Valley, a striking landscape to those unfamiliar with it, though reafforestation and new building are softening its harsh impact. Abertillery is an industrial town that grew with the coal-mines in the late nineteenth century and is now struggling to adjust to their decline. A small museum in the town reflects its industrial past. NANTYGLO and BRYNMAWR, further up the valley, grew earlier. In 1810 the Yorkshire brothers Joseph and Crawshay Bailey took over the furnaces there; workers flooded in, from agriculturally-depressed west Wales, from England and Ireland. Nantyglo Iron Works in the following decade built up a world-wide reputation for the manufacture of iron rails. Crawshay Bailey's Tramroad, from Nantyglo to the Brecon–Newport Canal at Govilon, was opened in 1822; now abandoned, it once carried the famous 'Crawshay Bailey's Engine', immortalized in Welsh popular song. Another of Bailey's constructions can, however, still be seen at Nantyglo. This is a fortified tower built as a refuge from rioting workmen. No idle paranoia, either, for unrest born of inhuman working conditions and the fluctuation of pay and employment could indeed take violent forms. In the 1830s, for example, a rudimentary form of Unionism was enforced by the 'Scotch Cattle', a secret society of men disguised and blackened, who held midnight meetings on the hillsides, and intimidated blacklegs, agents, and truck shop keepers in the pay of the ironmasters. Chartism, in the '40s, more sophisticated in political terms, could also lead on occasion to bloody clashes. Men from Brynmawr, led by a shoemaker known as King Crispin, marched to Newport and were met with musket-fire. A strong political tradition has survived in the valleys, fed and tempered by the chapels, which are everywhere in evidence.

Brynmawr is on the southern fringe of the Brecon Beacons National Park and only minutes away from the magnificent scenery of the Clydach Gorge, where the native beech woods are now protected by a Nature Reserve.

Aberystwyth Dyfed 2D6 (*pop.* 10,680)

Aberystwyth combines the respectability of the Welsh seaside landlady with the vitality of the college student.

Still very much a small town, its triple function – summer resort, administrative centre, university town – gives it an atmosphere unique in Wales. The visitor expecting a 'Welsh Brighton' (as the old guide-books styled it) may perhaps be disappointed; but anyone who has lived or studied at 'Aber' comes away with a lasting affection for the place.

From the pier (second version, which dates from 1872) the promenade curves north with a row of high, gabled, and bay-fronted villas to the foot of Constitution Hill, which can be climbed by cliff-path or funicular railway. At the opposite end of town Pen Dinas headland has the remains of a fine Iron Age hill-fort, and an uncompleted nineteenth-century column set up to commemorate the Battle of Waterloo and originally intended to carry an equestrian statue of the Duke of Wellington. Both headlands give magnificent views over town and coast.

Aberystwyth's history as a town dates back to the Middle Ages. An early castle stood inland, on a hill above the Ystwyth River. Then, during the revolt of the Welsh under Llewellyn the Last, in the late thirteenth century, Edward I undertook a massive programme of castle-building in North Wales. Flint, Conwy, Harlech, Caernarvon were all raised at this time. At Aberystwyth the new castle was built in 1277–9, near the mouth of the Rheidol; its scanty remains stand among pleasure gardens on a promontory in the angle of the New Promenade. The castle was captured by Glyndwr during his rebellion in the early fifteenth century. Shortly before the Civil War Thomas Bushell minted coins there, from silver extracted from the local mines: some of these can be seen in the Ceredigion Museum. Like Caernarvon and Conwy, Aberystwyth was a walled town. Great Darkgate Street was one of the medieval thoroughfares; there was a second gate near the bridge, and Eastgate was a third.

Until the late eighteenth century Aberystwyth's main *raison d'être* was as a port serving the mines of the Cardiganshire uplands. 'This town is enrich'd by the coals and lead which is found in its neighbourhood, and is a populous, but a very dirty, black, smoaky place, and we fancy'd the people look'd as if they liv'd continually in the coal or lead mines', wrote Daniel Defoe in 1724, with a description that seems more appropriate to a South Wales valley town in the early years of this century. The harbour was improved in 1780, and it was about the same time that the town began to develop as a fashionable watering-place.

Before the coming of the railway, in 1864, Aberystwyth had, it seems, a strong Regency flavour; visitors (to what was in those days a rather inaccessible spot) were aristocratic. After 1864 the town became a popular resort for the ordinary family. The Marine Baths were built by 1810, followed by the Assembly Rooms in 1820 (later to be used as a students' Union). High Street was laid out in the eighteenth century, and there are still some Georgian houses in Laura Place and the Pier Street area. Further from the centre, in North Parade, for example, Victorian buildings predominate. Look out for chapels of varying styles.

For some, the most interesting building in the town is the old 'College by the sea', the original university on the sea-front. Thomas Savin, an enterprising businessman who had helped push the railway to the Cardigan coast, had this built by J. P. Seddon in the 1860s, a fantastic hotel intended to take the new railway tourists. Savin went bankrupt in about 1865, whereupon a group of Welshmen subscribed £10,000 to buy the premises for a new, non-denominational, Welsh university. Seddon was in the process of adapting the building when in 1885 most of it burned to the ground. The south wing is all that remains today of this extraordinary monument of the Victorian imagination.

The University College is presently housed in modern, mainly post-war, buildings on Penglais Hill. The first constituent college of the University of Wales, it opened its doors to twenty-five students in October 1872. For the following ten years, government assistance having been refused, the College relied entirely on voluntary subscriptions. Some were large ones (David Davies of Llandinam, the coal and railway millionaire, made substantial contributions) but mostly it was the 'pennies of the poor' that kept the place going. Finally, in 1884, after two new colleges had been opened at Cardiff and Bangor, the college at Aberystwyth received its first government grant. Its charter came four years later. In 1907 a charter was also granted to the National Library of Wales, whose imposing white buildings (1911–55) stand on the same hill. Glamorgan and Monmouthshire miners agreed to a levy of a shilling a head on their wages as a contribution towards a building fund. The National Library is a deposit library (that is, it automatically receives a copy of every book published in the UK), and has an unrivalled collection of Welsh books, manuscripts, prints, and drawings. There is an exhibition gallery at the Library, and an Arts Centre at the Great Hall of the University College.

For the holiday visitor Aberystwyth offers bathing (safer north of the pier), boating, and fishing; there are films and concerts, and a summer season of plays and children's entertainment put on by the University theatre. The Ceredigion Museum (of Cardiganshire life and history) is in Vulcan Street and there are summer exhibitions dealing with the town's history in St Paul's, Upper Darkgate Street. CLARACH (over Constitution Hill) has another good beach. LLANBADARN FAWR, now a suburb of Aberystwyth, was the birthplace of Dafydd ap Gwilym, the fourteenth-century Welsh poet of European stature. The church of Llanbadarn stands on the site of a Celtic monastery founded by Padarn (Paternus), a Breton missionary saint, in the sixth century. The present building dates from the thirteenth century, with a carved fifteenth-century south door. The interior is austere, but has some fine memorial tablets in the chancel. There are two impressive Celtic crosses, one a tenth-century granite pillar cross elaborately carved, and the other, shorter, of local sandstone, and of roughly similar date.

No summer visitor to Aberystwyth should miss the journey to Devil's Bridge (qv) on the VALE OF RHEIDOL RAILWAY. Opened in 1902, this narrow-gauge line was originally intended to serve both tourism and the owners of the lead-mines, who could use it to transport ore to Aberystwyth harbour. Evening trains in the early days even took the devout to revivalist meetings in valley chapels. Two wars and the closure of the mines hampered the line's prosperity. In 1954 it decided to become unashamedly a tourist attraction, and has continued in well-deserved popularity ever since. It runs from the

The sea-front at Aberystwyth

Nanteos (1739), SE of Aberystwyth

main-line station at Aberystwyth, and from Easter to mid October. For philatelists there are railway letter stamps and first-day covers.

Passenger coaches dating from 1923 and 1937 are pulled by steam locomotives, built or rebuilt in 1923, up the 19km. and 204m. to Devil's Bridge. (This is the last steam railway operated by British Rail.) From Aberffrwd the gradient is one in fifty, a climb of 144m. in 6½km. On its journey the train passes Llanbadarn, Capel Bangor, the Cwm Rheidol Reservoir, and the Rheidol Falls; towards the end the line runs high along the mountainside, emerging from a narrow ravine into the tiny Devil's Bridge station. The trip takes an hour each way.

NANTEOS means 'stream of the nightingale', though, as the poet Edward Thomas said, the nightingales of Wales 'have no wings'. One of the rare country houses in the Principality, Nanteos lies in a wooded valley about 4km. south-east of Aberystwyth. It has a charming Victorian Italianate lodge, and a fine stable-block and entrance-screen in early-nineteenth-century Greek Revival style, designed by one of the Cockerells. The house itself is Georgian, built in 1739, in dark stone, with a creeper-grown façade. Inside, visitors (summer afternoons) can see an early kitchen, a Victorian morning-room, and an impressive music-room that has an Italian marble fireplace and excellent plasterwork. Wagner is said, though the story is unlikely, to have composed part of his music-drama *Parsifal* at Nanteos, drawn presum-ably by the ancient wooden cup long kept at the house and thought to be the legendary Holy Grail itself. The vessel, much eaten away by sufferers seeking a miraculous cure, was said to have been brought by Joseph of Arimathea to Glastonbury, from where it passed to the monks of Strata Florida, and, at the Dissolution, to the Nanteos family for safe keeping.

Ambleston (Treamlod) Dyfed 8C3

Ambleston with its Norman church tower lies between two streams of the Western Cleddau, which runs down through Haverfordwest. Nearby, 'Castle Flemish' is a Roman site, one of very few known in this corner of west Wales. The irregular rectangular enclosure with rampart and ditch is thought to have been a fortified farm settlement, occupied in the late first or second century AD. The local name commemorates more peaceful 'invaders' from Flanders, who, in the eleventh century, were settled in the Haverfordwest area by Henry I as part of the subjugation of the south-west of Wales. At Ford, a few km. west, another Roman site has not yet been fully identified as fort, farmstead, or villa. There is not much to see today.

Scollock West Farm, just south of Ambleston, has in one of its fields a striking modern piece of statuary. The marble couple of John and Mary Llewellyn are dressed for chapel (?), and an inscription praises their thrift and industry.

Sealyham Hall, near Ambleston, is famous for its dogs. Here, Captain Jack Edwards, a Master of Foxhounds in the middle of last century, produced a new breed. The Sealyham is a cross between the local (Pembrokeshire) corgi and a rough-haired terrier, with a soupçon of Dandy Dinmont.

Ammanford (Rhydaman) Dyfed 10C1
(*pop.* 5,795)

Like so many of South Wales' industrial towns, Ammanford with its coal tips and the scars of opencast mining lies only minutes away from the wildest and most beautiful mountain scenery. The Amman River rises in the Black Mountain, and runs down through Brynamman and Glanamman to Ammanford; it joins the Loughor near the boundary with Glamorgan. The town of Ammanford expanded with the anthracite-coal industry late in the nineteenth century. The name College Street commemorates the school opened in 1880 by Watkin Hezekiah Williams ('Watcyn Wyn', 1844–1905), who taught his scholars a delight in literature and especially poetry. The literary sessions held here between poets and learners were a modern continuation of the medieval bardic system of disciple and master. After Watcyn's death, 'Gwili' (the Revd John Jenkins), a famous Archdruid of Wales, took over the work.

At the Farmers Arms in Brynamman (then called Gwter Fawr), George Borrow spent a night; he had crossed the Black Mountain on foot from Llandovery, meeting gypsies and Methodists on the way. Here, in a depressing Welsh drizzle, he breakfasted on Glamorgan sausages, tea, and toast, then, with characteristic intellectual curiosity, visited the local iron foundry.

The mountain road over the summit of Mynydd Betws to Pontardawe passes at its highest point the ruins of Penlle'r Castell. From the tower of this motte-and-bailey fortress can be seen the distant Black Mountain of Carmarthenshire and the watchtower of Carreg Cennen Castle, 8km. due north, on its huge limestone crag.

Amroth Dyfed 8D5

At exceptionally low tide there appears on Amroth beach the remains of a petrified primeval forest. An arrowhead found in the skeleton of a small pig caught in the roots of a tree was estimated to be about 10,000 years old. Other traces of the life of the earliest hunters in this region include flint flakes, stags' horns, and fossilized hazel nuts.

Amroth Castle, in medieval times, was according to some accounts the scene of a sumptuous banquet given by Cadwgan ap Bleddyn for the neighbouring lords, among them Gerald de Windsor, Lord of Carew, and his beautiful wife, Nest. It was soon after this that Cadwgan's son carried off Nest by force from Carew Castle. The present 'castle' is a nineteenth-century building, described in 1848 as an 'elegant marine castellated villa', and residence of the Revd Thomas

Shrapnel Biddulph. It is now a holiday centre, with flats, cottages, and caravans.

Nineteenth-century Amroth was noted for its excellent coal, which, smokeless and odourless, was much in demand for the drying of malt and hops. Amroth today is an attractive village and resort. It is notably the eastern starting-point of the Pembrokeshire Coastal Footpath, which follows the coast through magnificent scenery almost without interruption to Cardigan.

In the neighbourhood, Colby Lodge, to the north of the village, is a Nash house. Ludchurch, 3km. inland, has an attractive old church with a ruined plague cross. The beach at Wiseman's Bridge, further south along the coast, and named after a fourteenth-century lord of the manor, was used in 1943 for a dress-rehearsal of the Normandy landings, in the presence of Sir Winston Churchill.

Angle Dyfed 8B5

Angle, formerly called Nangle, is set in a corner (Latin *in angulo*) of Milford Haven. The single main street with its colourful cottages and Georgian Globe Hotel joins the two small harbours. West Angle Bay is a popular sandy beach, from which a boat leaves for Thorn Island where a nineteenth-century fort has been converted into a hotel and restaurant. On the eastern rim of Angle Bay, and opposite Angle, there are jetties for oil tankers. Popton Fort (1863) now serves as offices for the BP tanker terminal.

Angle and its surroundings have been inhabited from very early times. On Broomhill Burrows stands the Devil's Quoit, a Neolithic burial chamber, on the ancient ridgeway that crossed south Pembrokeshire from end to end. At Castle Bay and West Pickard can be seen traces of Iron Age promontory forts. From the late Middle Ages there survive some unusually long, narrow fields near the village, which are said to be the remnants of the system of strip farming introduced by the Normans. Angle 'Old Rectory' is a single square tower, now deserted, with a rounded projection housing a corner stair. As in many medieval houses of this sort, the main entry and living-room were at first-floor level. Above were two small, heated chambers, and a corbelled wall-walk; not the most comfortable of dwellings, but secure. Angle dove-cote, a listed building, is a reminder of the difficulty medieval people had in providing meat through the winter months.

In the nineteenth century Angle limestone was used for purposes as diverse as mantelpieces and manure, and there was a flourishing oyster fishery. Angle church is restored; the 'Fisherman's Chapel' in the churchyard dates from 1447.

Baglan W. Glam. *see* Port Talbot

Barry (Y Barri) S. Glam. 11F4 (*pop.* 41,578)
Barry was one of a number of small ports on the

Glamorganshire coast that sent shipping to and fro across the Bristol Channel from Elizabethan times and even before. In 1848 its population was 104, and it remained at about that figure until, in the 1880s, David Davies and the newly-formed Barry Railway Company proceeded to build a dock here, with the express intention of bypassing Cardiff and its crippling port-taxes. By 1891, thanks to the ever-increasing demand for high-quality Welsh coal, Barry's population had jumped to 13,000; by 1921 it was almost 39,000. Since then coal exports have declined to nothing, and Barry Docks now deal mainly in bananas.

The docks lie immediately north of a horse-shoe-shaped peninsula known as Barry Island. It is said that the seventh-century St Baruch was buried here and a chapel raised to his memory; this gave the town its name. At Nells Point in the nineteenth century stood a holy well renowned for the cure of eye diseases. On Holy Thursday women flocked to wash their eyes in the waters, each one dropping a pin into the well as she left. A large Butlins Holiday Camp now stands near the spot. Whitmore Bay and Jackson's Bay on the 'Island' both have sandy beaches.

To the west and beyond Knap Point, The Knap, or Cold Knap, is a rather bleak and respectable beach backed by a high bank of pebbles. It has a large open-air swimming-pool and boating-lake. Behind and above The Knap is Porthkerry Country Park, crossed by an old viaduct. There are very slight remains of a castle on Old Village Road. For holidaymakers Barry also offers tennis, sailing, bowls, and golf, plus a small private zoo opened in 1962. CADOXTON, once a village and now part of Barry, has an ancient church with a rood-loft staircase behind the pulpit, a Saxon (?) font, and medieval wall-paintings.

FONTYGARY (Ffontygari), 6½km. west, is a small seaside resort with a beach of sand and pebbles below high cliffs, and a large caravan park. At RHOOSE (Y Rhws), 5km. west of Barry, is the Cardiff Airport, and a large cement works.

PENMARK (Penmarc), 6½km. north-west, has the remains of a Norman castle: two round towers and part of a curtain wall standing on the edge of a ravine above the Waycock brook. The castle's outer ward originally adjoined the church of St Mary. On the latter's outside south wall notice the 'scratch dial', an early method of indicating the times of services.

Beguildy (Bugeildy) Powys 3H6

Beguildy ('Shepherd's House') lies in the Teme Valley, which forms the English border here (Offa's Dyke lies out to the west, a few km. distant). All around is emptiness, wild uplands browsed by sheep and only half tamed by reafforestation. There is a 'Black Mountain' to the north, in England, and another, to the south-west, in Wales. Beguildy church has a fine thirteenth-century rood-screen, and a Jacobean pulpit and altar-table.

Berriew (Aberriw) Powys 3H4

Berriew is an attractive old village with half-timbered houses, standing, as the Welsh name tells us, at the confluence of the Rhiw River with the Severn. It was once an important point on the Shropshire Union Canal, which was constructed in the eighteenth century to transport wool from the Severn Valley sheep farms to the mills of Manchester and the Midlands.

It was at Berriew that the sixth-century Celtic saint Beuno began his religious life. According to his early biographer, he left the place as soon as he heard the hated English tongue on the other side of the Severn. His missionary churches are mostly in North Wales, but Betws Cedewain, a village in the uplands between Berriew and Newtown, has a Beuno dedication.

Bishopston W. Glam. see Gower Peninsula

Blaenafon Gwent see Pontypool

Borth Dyfed 2D5

Borth is a long, straggly seaside resort that has 5km. of good sands. It lies on the edge of a great expanse of marshy bog, the Cors Fochno, part of which is now a Nature Reserve. Cors Fochno is a rare example of a raised peat-bog; it is a habitat for abundant mosses and rare plants and over seventy varieties of moth and butterfly. Birds and animals of many kinds have retreated there to breed.

About halfway along the coast between Borth and Aberystwyth, Sarn Cynfelyn (Cynfelyn is a Welsh form of Cymbeline) is marked on maps. This is one of a number of sarnau, or causeways, stretching out for several km. into Cardigan Bay. According to legend these are all that remain of the lost land of Cantre'r Gwaelod (the 'Lowland Hundred'). Once, long ago, where Cardigan Bay is now, there was a fertile plain, with sixteen noble cities in it. The low-lying land was protected against the sea by a system of dykes and sluices. In the reign of King Gwyddno the keeper of the embankment was Seithennin, and he was an arrant drunkard, one of the 'Three Arrant Drunkards of Britain', according to one version. One night, after a great feast, Seithennin forgot to close the sluices; Cantre'r Gwaelod and its king and people were drowned for ever. Since then, on clear days, boatmen have seen the walls of palaces shimmering under the waves, while others have heard the watery chimes of the 'bells of Aberdovey'.

This attractive story, related more amusingly by Thomas Love Peacock in his comic novel *The Misfortunes of Elphin*, is, of course, pure fabrication. Most of the details were invented by nineteenth-century *littérateurs* on the basis of a few obscure references in medieval Welsh poems. The *sarnau*, according to scientists, are natural ridges or shoals, formed by the accumulation of pebbles and boulders derived from glacial deposits.

The legend should not therefore be dismissed as mere eyewash. Geological investigations show that Cardigan Bay was indeed once a fertile plain, and that the sea gradually encroached upon it. Stumps of an ancient forest can be seen at Borth at low tide. The Dovey Estuary, like the Severn, is a flooded river valley, and it may well have been possible at one time to wade from 'Wales' to 'Ireland', as does a character in the medieval Welsh *Mabinogion*. But this invasion by the sea took place not in the Dark Ages, as the legend has it, but in the Bronze Age, that is, perhaps as long ago as 2000 BC. The memory of this flooding must have been handed down from prehistoric hunters, who were forced to leave their territory as the sea-level rose.

Bosherston Dyfed 8C6

Past St Michael's church with its fourteenth-century churchyard cross and stone effigies, Bosherston Lakes, or Lily Ponds, are a series of fresh-water pools formed either

St Michael's church and C14 cross, Bosherston

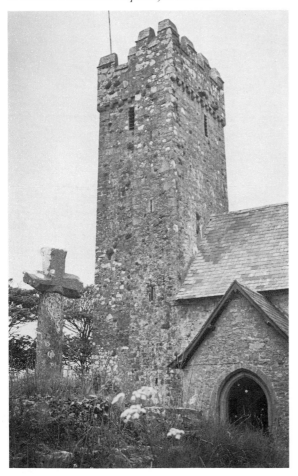

by natural sand bars, or, as some say, as the result of a man-made dam that dates back to the time when Napoleon was a possible invader. (There is good pike-fishing, by permit.) On one arm of the pools, until fairly recently, stood Stackpole Court, eighteenth-century seat of the Earls of Cawdor. Its gardens can still be visited. The church at Cheriton, a few km. north, has fourteenth-century effigies of Richard de Stackpole and his wife, plus a seventeenth-century canopied monument to Roger Lort, his wife, and their twelve children.

Thanks to the Army's tank-firing range at Castle-martin the wild and spectacular coast near Bosherston is restricted in access. Well out of range, however, to the north, Barafundle Bay is cut off from the road by whitish cliffs and a warren of sand dunes. Broad Haven is another good sandy beach (not to be confused with Broad Haven on St Bride's Bay). Nearer the fire of artillery, St Govan's Chapel can be reached by following the road through Bosherston village. This tiny, primitive building, in a fissure of limestone cliffs, stands on the site of a much earlier hermitage. The cell, stone altar, and piscina, or holy-water stoup, are still in place. Mystery and superstition surround the spot. Even the identity of the holy hermit is unknown. For some, he is one of King Arthur's knights, Sir Gawaine, who spent his latter days in pious and solitary meditation. This ties up with another legend, according to which Bosherston Pools are the lake of the mysterious and magical sword Excalibur. For others, he is Gobham, Irish abbot of Dairinis and contemporary of St David. Or the saint may have been a woman, Cofen, the wife of a Celtic chieftain of the sixth century.

The flight of steps leading down through the chapel to the holy well are, according to another tradition, impossible to count; you will, it maintains, never get the same total going up as coming down. The well itself, now dried up, was reputed to have miraculous healing properties, especially for eye diseases. In a rock close by, a silver bell, the original bell that once hung in the chapel bellcote, is reputedly immured. Stolen by pirates, the bell was rescued by sea-nymphs who placed it in the rock, which will ring out if struck.

The limestone cliff scenery between St Govan's and Linney Head is unequalled in beauty and full of surprises. West of the chapel you come first to Huntsman's Leap, a natural ravine between the cliffs where a horseman who had just jumped the chasm is said to have dropped dead with fright at the very thought. Further on, two huge detached pinnacles of rock standing out to sea are covered with sea-birds. These are Elegug Stacks, where breed thousands of guillemots (Welsh *elegug*), kittiwakes, razorbills, fulmar petrels – to mention a few – on the sheer jagged walls and the green tops thick with tree-mallow. A little further west, the Green

OPPOSITE: *St Govan's Chapel, nr Bosherston*

The Elegug Stacks, W of Bosherston

Bridge of Wales is a great natural arch of limestone, and to the east of the Stacks, the Cauldron, or Devil's Punch Bowl, makes an extraordinary spectacle as the sea rushes in.

From Stackpole (Greenala Point) to Linney Head a series of Iron Age forts have been discovered. At Bosherston itself, Fishponds Camp is one of the largest; it was inhabited during the Early Iron Age (*c.* 4000–*c.* 2000 BC) and may have been chosen as a good landing-place. There are remains of a promontory fort on the cliff-top overlooking Bullslaughter Bay, and other traces of pre-historic inhabitants at Flimston Bay and Linney Head. The Flimston area, now in the tank range, is unique in South Wales for its deposits of pipe clay; the old workings are abandoned and overgrown.

Boverton S. Glam. *see* **Llantwit Major**

Brecon (Aberhonddu) Powys 7F5 (*pop.* 6,283)
Brecon is a town almost encircled by mountains. To the north, Mynydd Epynt, made even more desolate by the Army firing zones; to the east, Mynydd Llangorse and the Black Mountains of the border country; to the south, the barren splendour of the Beacons, only partly tamed as a National Park; to the west, the upper Usk Valley, and that of the Gwydderig, which provides a narrow pass into the Vale of Towy. Yet in spite of this protective

bunkering of uplands, Brecon itself has not remained Welsh, if indeed it was ever so. Towns, especially in hill country, are not a Welsh phenomenon. Brecon, like others, was essentially a Norman creation, while the Usk Valley, its main communication link with the outside world, is, like the Wye, a finger of England pointing into Wales.

Settlement here goes back well before the Normans. In the Iron Age the summit of Pen-y-crug was fortified (the climb gives marvellous views). Three Roman roads crossed at this point, the confluence of Honddu and Usk. One ran from Isca (Caerleon) to the gold-mines at Dolaucothi, a second from Cardiff to Castell Collen near Llandrindod, and a third from Neath north-east to Kenchester. There are remains of a fort and of a villa in the vicinity. Of the Celtic Dark Ages, little survives except place-names. Brecon itself is thought to be a version of Brycheiniog, the name of the Welsh kingdom reputedly carved out in the fifth century by a Welsh or part-Irish prince, Brychan. It seems likely, too, that there was a Celtic church at Brecon before the Normans came.

Bernard of Newmarch, or Neufmarché, half-brother of the Conqueror, marched into Brycheiniog from Herefordshire in 1091. Styling himself Lord of Brecon, he used the rising ground between the two rivers to build a castle that would serve as military and political centre for the lordship. The present ruins are dispersed between

Cathedral church of St John from the NW

the grounds of the Castle Hotel, where two towers and part of the great hall stand on the river bank, and those of the residence of the Bishop of Brecon. Here, Ely Tower, a polygonal tower on a motte, is said to have been the prison of the Bishop of Ely, who with his jailer, the second Duke of Buckingham, plotted against Richard III two years before the Battle of Bosworth. Buckingham paid with his head, but the Bishop escaped to Flanders. The dilapidated state of the castle is partly due to the good sense of the seventeenth-century townspeople who hoped, by destroying it, to prevent its use by either faction in the Civil War.

Bernard atoned – or gave thanks – for his bloody victory at Brecon by founding a monastery. He granted his confessor, a monk from Battle Abbey, the church of 'St John the Evangelist without the walls'. A new church was built, and a religious community established, an offshoot of the Benedictines of Battle in Sussex. (A village near Brecon may be named Battle because of this association, or, according to another tradition, as a memory of the encounter between Bernard and Rhys ap Tewdwr in 1093.)

Unlike Cistercians, Benedictines allowed their abbey churches to be used for parish worship. Hence at the Dissolution of the Monasteries, St John's survived, although it lost valuable treasure, including the great

BRECON

golden cross, or rood, which with its screen had been one of the glories of the pre-Reformation church. Of the medieval Dominican friary, which stood in the quarter known as Llanfaes (on the opposite bank of the Usk), the church also survived, while the friary itself was turned in 1541 into a new grammar school. This later became Christ College, one of the very few boys' public schools in Wales; the medieval chapel is still in use, but the main buildings are Victorian and twentieth-century.

St John's remained a parish church until 1923 when it was chosen as cathedral of the new diocese of Swansea and Brecon. It is a sober and pleasing building of pinkish-grey stone, dating largely from the thirteenth and fourteenth centuries. Though it has a number of fine and interesting features, its relatively humble origins mean that it cannot fairly be compared with the great medieval cathedrals of Britain.

The nave of St John's is fourteenth-century Decorated, with octagonal piers and a finely-traced west window (there is no early glass). Near the door, a strangely primitive font with Latin inscriptions is a survival from an earlier building. Above it hangs an ornate eighteenth-century chandelier. The thirteenth-century choir is Early English; but its vaulting was done by Sir Gilbert Scott during restoration in 1874–5. The tower, transepts, and chancel also date from the thirteenth century. In the sanctuary, on the south side, can be seen triple sedilia, and, more unusual, a triple piscina.

Brecon's historic connexions with trade and with the military find visual expression in this parish church. The north and south aisles were formerly separated from the nave and used as craft-guild chapels: Weavers and Tuckers to the south, Corvizors and Tailors to the north. Of these, only the Corvizors' (Cordwainers or Shoemakers) Chapel survives. It is thought that this chapel was originally dedicated to St Crispian and St Crispinian, patron saints of shoemakers. Among the memorial slabs in the floor of the church are some bearing trade emblems. The north transept was known as Battle Chapel, because of its use by the parishioners of Battle. The south had the traditional name of 'Capel-y-cochiaid' ('chapel of the red-headed men'), which may refer to the fair-haired Normans of the early garrison. The fourteenth-century Havard Chapel, with its squint and Aubrey tomb, was restored in 1922 and given as regimental chapel to the South Wales Borderers, who until recently had their headquarters in the town.

A few other features repay inspection. One is the cresset stone, a medieval lamp – and an unusually large one – with holes for thirty oil lights. In the south aisle are Jacobean effigies of a royal justice and his wife, and an earlier wooden figure, graceful though mutilated, in

OPPOSITE: *Looking S along the Honddu Valley; Brecon is at the confluence of the Honddu and the Usk*

sixteenth-century ruff, head-dress, and stiffly pleated robe. This is a lady of the Gam, or Games, family, one of whose members, Sir Davy, saved the life of Henry V at Agincourt (a battle fought on St Crispian's Day, as readers of Shakespeare will know). Also buried in the church is Dr Hugh Price, treasurer of St David's, who in 1571 obtained from Queen Elizabeth a charter to set up a college at Oxford. This was Jesus College, the first Protestant foundation of the University; its Welsh connexions have continued unbroken ever since.

In spite of its medieval churches and ruined castle, Brecon's atmosphere is, rather, under the influence of the eighteenth and nineteenth centuries. Its narrow streets, elegant town-houses, and small, old-fashioned shops are more reminiscent of Jane Austen or Mrs Gaskell than of Chaucer. The eighteenth century saw the growth of Brecon as a corn-market and agricultural centre generally. By 1848 a traveller could describe it as a desirable place of residence, where the society was 'remarkably select'. Places of interest that date from this period include the inn in High Street where Sarah Siddons, née Kemble, was born in 1755; her parents were on a theatrical tour (see Swansea for further Welsh connexions of the Kemble family). Captain's Walk, between the river and the Shire Hall, is reputedly so named from the fact that French officers, captured in the Napoleonic Wars, were allowed to take exercise there. The classical Shire Hall was erected in 1842, and the Brecon Barracks, now the headquarters of the Army in Wales, also dates from the nineteenth century. In Llanfaes eighteenth-century almshouses erected to house 'twelve decayed female housekeepers' are still in use.

In Captain's Walk the Brecknock Museum has permanent exhibits covering local geology, natural history, archaeology, and folk-life, including Roman remains from Y Gaer, several Ogham stones, and an early dug-out canoe from Llangorse Lake. The museum of the South Wales Borderers and Monmouthshire Regiment is in the Watton.

Relics of a much earlier army should be visited at Y Gaer, or Brecon Gaer, the Roman auxiliary fort near Aberyscir (Aberysgir) about 5km. west, and first excavated by Sir Mortimer Wheeler in 1924–5. (Access is restricted between May and July when the hay crop is standing.) The fort was built about 75 at roughly the time that the Second Legion moved to Caerleon, that is, at the very beginning of the Roman conquest of Wales. Strategically placed at the junction of five Roman roads, the early fort was made of earth and timber. At the turn of the first century it housed a Spanish cavalry regiment possibly 500 strong. In mid second century stone defences were added and the main internal buildings also reconstructed in stone. At the end of that century the fort suffered some damage; the gates had to be rebuilt and a new well and bath-house were constructed within the fort. In about 290 the garrison abandoned the

fort, returning some time in the fourth century when they carried out further repairs. By the early fifth century the Roman occupation of Britain (never much of a success in Wales) was over.

Today, after excavation, three gateways, remains of angle turrets, and part of the north-east wall are visible. The west gate has two unusual projecting rectangular guard-chambers. None of the buildings within the fort – headquarters, granary, baths – can now be seen. The presence of the bath-house within the walls has suggested to archaeologists that the garrison may have been much reduced in numbers by the late second century, for these large buildings were usually placed outside. The earlier bath-house may lie under the medieval farm-house to the north-west of the barn. A Roman tomb-stone carved with the figures of a couple, found near the site, is now in the National Museum at Cardiff.

On the edge of the National Park, Brecon is an excellent base for excursions by foot or car into the surrounding mountains. The National Park's major information centre is at Libanus, about 6km. south-west. Pen-y-fan (872m.) can be reached in good weather and by good walkers; the view embraces the Bristol Channel and the Malvern Hills. Here in the Beacons nature dwarfs man, reducing fort and church alike to insignificance. On the perimeter of the great expanse of bare uplands, however, a few ancient villages have pleasant old cottages and medieval, though usually restored, churches. LLANDDEW, 2½km. north, has a small medieval church and fourteenth-century holy well. In the vicarage gardens there still remain traces of the much older building where Gerald the Welshman (Giraldus Cambrensis), the twelfth-century cleric and writer, lived during his twenty-five years as Archdeacon of Brecon. LLANFRYNACH, a few km. south-east, is a charming village with an Elizabethan manor-house. The Roman villa, first discovered in 1783, is no longer visible.

Bridgend (Pen-y-bont ar Ogwr)   Mid Glam.
11E3   (pop. 14,531)
Bridgend has escaped the heavy industries that have disfigured Port Talbot, Neath, and Swansea. On the edge of the Vale of Glamorgan, it has retained something of the atmosphere of a country town. It owes its origins to the Normans, who protected the crossing of the Ogmore River with a castle. The town is divided traditionally into Oldcastle, on the east bank of the Ogmore, and Newcastle, on its west bank. There is no trace of the 'old' castle. The 'new' one, a mid-twelfth-century structure, stands in ruins on the spur of a hill above the river. Part of the curtain wall, a rectangular keep-tower, and an excellent Norman gateway are all that now remain. St Illtud's church, adjoining the ruins, was largely rebuilt in the mid nineteenth century.

Most of Bridgend was built in the nineteenth and twentieth centuries. One of its most striking buildings is the Town Hall, in early-nineteenth-century Greek Revival style, with massive columned portico; it has recently been under threat of demolition. There is a pleasant riverside park.

PENCOED, an old colliery village 6½km. north-east, was (like Llangynwyd, near Maesteg) one of the last places in South Wales to keep alive the old tradition of the *Mari Lwyd*. The name means 'grey mare' (as in nightmare) or 'grey Mary'. A horse's skull, its lower jaw fixed with a spring, causing a loud snap, was stuck on the end of a long pole that was draped with a white sheet and decorated with ribbons, glass, and bits of cloth. Underneath was a man, accompanied by a varied party: the 'leader', the 'sergeant', 'Merryman', and 'Punch and Judy'. On Twelfth Night, and for some days afterwards, this procession went the rounds of the households exchanging verses and demanding money and drinks; a lot of horseplay and mock fighting took place. Pubs in the Welsh valleys used on occasion to engage a special 'poet' to match wits with the revellers, for if they once gained entry free drinks were the rule.

LLANGAN, 6km. east, is named after St Canna. Its churchyard holds two ancient crosses. One, possibly a ninth-century work, is a Celtic wheel cross with a crude carving of the Crucifixion. The other, more elaborate, dates from the fifteenth century, and is carved with saints and another Crucifixion scene.

Broad Haven Dyfed 8B4

On St Bride's Bay, Broad Haven and Little Haven are two popular resort beaches separated by a steep cliff. Above Little Haven an Iron Age hill-fort has been excavated. On the spectacular cliffs, whose folds show in places the coal measures that Pembrokeshire once exploited, large boulders are strewn, carried here from St David's by the invading ice. There is a Countryside Unit at Broad Haven car park, providing information, and arranging tours, walks, and lectures for visitors to this area. (N.B. Do not confuse with the Broad Haven near Bosherston.)

Bronllys Powys 7F4

The Norman Bernard of Newmarch on his first advance into Wales from Hay and the Wye Valley built a series of castles along his route. Bronllys, Hay, and Talgarth were thus all fortified in 1088, probably with motte-and-bailey constructions, to be later rebuilt in stone. The fine round tower that now stands at Bronllys is a keep built in the thirteenth century, though the mound beneath it is earlier. Round keeps were a feature of thirteenth-century castle building, replacing square or rectangular ones, which were much more vulnerable to collapse if mined. There are not all that many round keeps to be seen (though there are several in this area and on the Welsh Borders), for soon afterwards medieval military architects turned their attention to strengthening the outer defences rather than the inner ones. The former

could after all be used more effectively to provide a counter-attack, whereas the keep was a largely passive and defensive structure.

Bronllys church was rebuilt in 1887, but its curious detached tower dates from the fourteenth century. This may have served as a place of refuge when the castle fell into ruin, with the added security of being on hallowed ground.

Brynmawr Gwent *see* **Abertillery**

Builth Wells (Llanfair-ym-Muallt) Powys 7E3 (*pop.* 1,481)

'Romantically situated' on the River Wye, as one nineteenth-century traveller put it, Builth is a meeting-point for a number of roads that cross the wild uplands of central Wales. It is a fine centre for fishing, walking, or pony-trekking, though a large section of Mynydd Epynt, to the south-west, is a military firing-zone, and is best left to the war games. For wet days the town library should have copies of the novels of Hilda Vaughan (Mrs Charles Morgan), which are mostly set in this locality. In early summer Builth, normally quiet, prepares itself for its great annual event, the Royal Welsh Agricultural Show, an explosion of activity and spectacle that takes place during one week of July. Here the native Welsh breeds of cattle, sheep, pigs, and ponies can be seen alongside the newer crossbreeds and the Border Country animals.

Nothing but a mound now remains to show that in the thirteenth century Edward I chose to raise a castle in the town, part of a network of new fortresses built to contain the Welsh. The latter, under Llewellyn the Last, were refusing to be quietly conquered. Had Builth Castle survived it might have been as impressive a structure as its contemporaries in North Wales – Conwy, Harlech, or Caernarvon. It is to these years, too, that there belongs an old Welsh tradition about the people of Builth. Llewellyn had been promised protection here; in 1282 he came to the castle, but the 'Traitors of Builth' refused to harbour him. In some obscure way this seems to have led to his death; somewhere nearby, in the countryside, perhaps at Cefn-y-bedd, he was cut down, unrecognized, by an English trooper. A modern monument to this event now stands at Cilmeri, 2–3km. west on the road out of Builth. Llewellyn's Cave, part of the same tradition (or legend), is at Aberedw (qv).

In 1691 Builth town burned to the ground in a great fire, and was raised again from its ashes by moneys sent from all over Britain. The town plan is therefore essentially one of the eighteenth century. The handsome bridge over the Wye dates from 1770. It was around that time that Builth began to enjoy a new prosperity. Mineral waters became fashionable, and the little cluster of spa-towns in mid Wales became miniature rivals of Bath (which itself owed its fortunes largely to a Welshman, Beau Nash). The Pump Room and Old

The amphitheatre at Caerleon, c. AD 80

Crown Hotel are vestiges of this former glory. Builth's reputation as a health resort was heightened by the visit in 1808 of Lady Hester Stanhope, the adventurous and amorous aristocrat, who spent the last years of her life in retirement at nearby Glan Irfon.

Builth has its prehistoric remains and its legends. On a mountain not far away, Cefn Carn Cafall, a cairn is surmounted by a stone that is said to bear the impress of a dog's paw. This was allegedly the print of Arthur's hound, Cafall, who passed here once while hunting. Arthur, it is said, built the cairn and placed the stone on top; if removed, the latter is supposed always to return to its original position.

A more credible piece of folklore, perhaps, is connected with Nant-yr-arian, a small brook running about 1½km. west of the town. The name, which means 'Moneybrook' or 'Brook of the silver', is said to come from the fact that in times of plague the brook was used as a kind of market-place. Provisions would be placed there by the country dwellers, and, to avoid the spread of infection, the payment thrown into the brook.

Builth Road railway station, some distance from the town, is a rather curious and grandiose piece of nineteenth-century railway architecture, now converted into flats. It has the grassgrown, strangely desolate atmosphere of all abandoned railways – except that the railway is, miraculously, still in use (1975).

Burry Port Dyfed   *see* **Pembrey**

Caerleon (Caerllion) Gwent 11H2 (*pop.* 6,235)
Present-day Caerleon is somewhat unprepossessing, but is well worth visiting for the Roman remains, which are certainly the most impressive in Wales. This was Isca, one of the two main garrisons for Roman Wales, and, with York, one of the three permanent legionary bases in Britain. Isca, home of the Second Augustan Legion, was erected by Frontinus in 74–5; it had an earth rampart and timber buildings. A stone facing was added in the early second century, and further extensive reconstruction took place about a hundred years later. By the end of the third century it seems that the garrison had left, and part of the legion had transferred to Richborough in Kent.

The fort originally covered 20ha. Sixty-four barrack blocks were laid out symmetrically, each housing a *centuria* (eighty men). The total population of the fort could have been as high as 6,000. Among the other buildings were a granary (outside the walls), a hospital, cookhouses, and baths. Excavations in recent years have also revealed a massive quay beside the Usk, built of timber and stone, with ballast of Preseli Grey slate. Here ships of 1½m. draught could have docked, at high tide.

The west corner of the fortress, at Prysg Field, is still

visible, with the remains of cookhouses and a latrine with stone sewer. One barrack-block can be clearly seen, plus some modern reconstructions. Besides this, Caerleon possesses the only completely excavated amphitheatre in Britain. Constructed in about 80 (and a contemporary of the Colosseum in Rome), the amphitheatre is oval, with an earth bank, originally over 8m. high, that held tiers of wooden seats. A stone wall 3½m. high surrounded the arena; its surface was covered with a smooth mortar to ensure that no beast or man gained foothold. In places where this mortar coating has perished inscriptions have been found marking the work of the various military units engaged in the construction.

Two main entrances, one at each end, lead into the arena; two others lead up to what were private boxes, and a small half-domed recess in front of one of these may have held a statue of Nemesis (Fate). Other entrances lead to the tiers of seats, which are estimated to have held an audience of several thousand. What exactly the Romans watched here must remain a matter for conjecture, but it was probably military parades and exercises as well as more gory gladiatorial combat.

It has recently been made possible to excavate the Roman Baths, which date from 85 and are thus the earliest stone buildings so far identified within the fort. The Baths lie under the ground between the Bull Inn car park and Backhall Street and are already known to include a Cold Bath (*frigidarium*) and a Plunge Bath (*natatio*). They should be revealed to view within the next few years. Meanwhile, the excellent museum, on the main road, has good displays of, among other things, weapons, sculpture, and inscriptions.

In the Middle Ages the remains of the fort were apparently much more extensive, and legends grew up connecting these signs of a vanished and sophisticated civilization with the court of King Arthur. 'Caer Llion on Usk' is one of Arthur's royal seats in the collection of Welsh tales known as the *Mabinogion*. The thirteenth-century *Dingestow Chronicle* describes a great feast held by King Arthur at Caerleon, which was the 'fairest place in the isle of Britain'; at its quays were ships from all the corners of the world, its houses were resplendent with gold, it had two churches and an archbishop, and some 200 schools with teachers of numerous arts. It was this association with Arthur that brought Alfred Lord Tennyson to Caerleon in 1867; he wrote part of the *Idylls of the King* at the Hanbury Arms.

Caerleon church stands on the site of the Roman basilica. It is much restored but has a Norman arch in the south wall of the west end. The hotel called the Priory, near the museum, is now thought unlikely to have stood on the site of a medieval abbey. 'Caerleon Abbey' was, in fact, the same as LLANTARNAM ABBEY, a few km. distant. At the Dissolution Llantarnam, a Cistercian house, and daughter of Strata Florida, was purchased by William Morgan, a wealthy local squire, and its remains incorporated into a new manor-house.

(A common fate, cf. Margam – *see* Port Talbot – and Ewenny.) In 1836 the premises were practically rebuilt.

Caerphilly (Caerffili)　Mid Glam.　11F3
(*pop.* 40,689)
The road from Cardiff runs over Caerphilly Mountain, and the railway, from a long tunnel beneath it, emerges into Caerphilly, an ordinary-looking but lively small town, whose nineteenth-century terraces and twentieth-century supermarkets are dominated by the huge carcase of one of the largest castles in Europe. Among the most magnificent of medieval castles, Caerphilly's setting is disappointing but instructive; life is not a museum, and from the wall-walks and towers can be seen the pit-head gear at Bedwas Colliery and the town sprawling into the mouths of the valleys.

The interest and the extraordinary impact of Caerphilly Castle derive from its enormous size (in Britain only Windsor is larger) and from the complexity of its defences. It was built by Gilbert de Clare, the Anglo-Norman Lord of Glamorgan, as a protection against the Welsh, whose leader, Llewellyn, had in 1268 been acknowledged prince of all Wales. Gilbert's first castle on this site, which he had taken by force from the local Welsh ruler, was destroyed by the enemy soon afterwards; in 1271 he began the present castle. Other South Wales castles – Kidwelly and White Castle, for example – were being heavily refortified at this time, while in the North Edward I was very shortly to embark on the massive programme of castle-building that was to bring the Welsh finally under control. The scale and number of castles in Wales, both North and South, shows not only the strength of the English but, even more, the great fear they had of the Welsh. Thus two centuries after the Norman conquest of Wales these alien lords were still not able to command the support of their feudal subjects.

Thanks to Llewellyn's retreat from South Wales, and his death near Builth in 1282, the new castle at Caerphilly was not put to the test until 1316, when a local leader, Llywellyn Bren, besieged it without success. In the winter of 1326–7 it was again under siege when Queen Isabella and her party chased the hapless Edward II through to Neath. At the close of the Middle Ages the castle fell gradually into decay. Like many another medieval stronghold, it was revived, briefly, during the Civil War. Recognizing its potential, Cromwell's army took the trouble to knock it about a bit, draining its lakes and blowing up the towers. One of the towers still leans very precariously today, showing either the strength of the medieval construction or the inferior quality of Cromwellian gunpowder. The castle was carefully and extensively restored by the third and fourth Marquesses of Bute and, later, by the State (without any of the fanciful medievalism exhibited by the third Marquess at Cardiff Castle and Castell Coch).

Caerphilly is a fine example of a fully-developed concentric fortress. The Crusaders had brought back from the East new techniques of fortification that had been developed to withstand corresponding advances in methods of attack. Walls alone could no longer provide adequate defence. The aim was rather to divide the castle into separate portions, each one of which would have to be gained before the castle fell. At the same time, the defenders were given better facilities for counter-attack inside the castle: thus, at Caerphilly, the projecting drum-towers of the inner ward could be used for firing both down into the outer ward and over and beyond it to the south platform.

The outermost circle of defences was composed of a series of moats and lakes. At the eastern side a curtain wall of nearly 300m., with towers and buttresses, and a strongly fortified gatehouse with barbican and double drawbridge, protected the main entrance. On the west a hornwork, surrounded by water, had its own gates and drawbridges. Behind the curtain wall and south platform another, inner, moat cut off the main body of the castle. Further gatehouses protected the entry to the outer ward, and to the inner ward, which was the central core of the castle. This latter contained the essential living quarters, including four solars (private apartments), a chapel, and a well. The Kitchen Tower projects into the outer ward, and has recesses for cooking. The Great Hall, dating from the fourteenth century in its present form, was probably built by Hugh le Despenser, favourite of Edward II. It has mostly been restored,

though some of the moulding around windows and doorways is original; it is used for banquets and concerts.

The Rhymney Valley Arts Festival takes place annually; some of its events are held at Caerphilly. The town is still famous for its white, crumbly cheese, though this is only very rarely made here now.

Caersŵs Powys 3G5
Black-and-white half-timbered houses proclaim the wealth of the fertile Severn Valley and provide a visual link with Shropshire and the Border Country. They contrast strongly with the small slate-roofed stone cottages of upland Wales, which surrounds the valley to north, south, and west.

Caersŵs may have been the ancient Mediolanum, the name given by Ptolemy to one of the chief 'towns' of the Ordovices, who occupied the area north of the Severn in early times. What is certain, however, is that the Romans established a military camp here. Tiles of the Twentieth Legion, based from 86 at Chester, have been found in the town. The station was served by a Roman road from Viriconium (Wroxeter); others may have run to Brecon and to Chester. There were silver and lead mines to the west. There is not much left to see of the Roman fort; indeed the main road runs through it on its way west out of the village.

Today Caersŵs is a centre for farmhouse holidays and for pony-trekking. The church at LLANWNNOG, about

Caerphilly Castle: the E side: see also *colour plate facing p. 86*

Llanwnnog church, 3km. NW of Caersŵs: late-C15

3km. north-west, has a very fine rood-screen and loft. 'Ceiriog', one of Wales' best-known nineteenth-century poets, is buried there.

Caerwent Gwent 12A3

For anyone interested in Britain under the Romans, Caerleon and Caerwent are most conveniently placed. Less than 25km. apart, they illustrate very nicely the two poles of Roman activity in Britain. Caerleon is strictly a military site; Caerwent is the remains of Venta Silurum, the 'market-town of the Silures', a unique example of a civilian settlement in Wales, and perhaps one of the most impressive sites in the whole of Roman Britain.

Venta Silurum was founded about 75, not long after the Romans first conquered the country. It remained in occupation well into the fourth century. Here were all the usual buildings of a tribal capital: forum, basilica (assembly-hall), temples, baths, houses, and shops, laid out in characteristic grid pattern each side of the main Roman road. The forum was placed at the intersection of the town's two main thoroughfares; it had shops, including possibly a fishmonger's or oyster bar, on its south and east sides. The basilica, which adjoined the forum, was partly heated, and had painted walls and mosaic floors. The public baths were also heated, by underfloor hypocausts. Some of the houses were spacious and well decorated; examples of the wall-painting found here can be seen in the museum at Newport.

Not all of Caerwent has been fully excavated, and some lies under the village. What remains visible today is none the less impressive. A considerable stretch of the city wall can be seen, 5m. high in places; this was built in the late second or early third century. In the fourth century polygonal bastions or towers were added to provide extra cover, and a well-preserved single-arched passageway in the south gate seems also to have been blocked up at this time, a time, perhaps, of increasing unrest. (Cardiff was fortified at the same period.)

The war memorial stands at the centre of the Roman town, and the road through the village is the old Roman road from London to Caerleon. On the south side of Pound Lane are the remains of two Roman houses. To the east of these houses lie the traces of a small temple of Romano-Celtic type, with a central shrine and surrounding ambulatory.

Finds from Caerwent have mostly been placed in the museums at Newport and Caerleon. However, two inscribed stones of great interest can be seen in the church porch at St Stephen's, Caerwent. One is a dedication to the war-god Mars Ocelus. The other is a record of a dedication to a man named Paulinus, commander of the Second Augustan Legion and later governor of two Roman provinces in Gaul. The inscription includes the phrase '*Ex decreto ordinis res. publ. civit. Silurum*' ('by decree of the local senate the community of the Silures [set this up]') – evidence of the machinery of self-government accorded to the tribal system in Britain by the Romans.

About 2km. north-west of Caerwent, Llanmelin Wood Camp provides a fascinating contrast. This Iron Age hill-fort, set on the tip of a spur of Wentwood, consisted of a small inner enclosure defended by a series of multiple ramparts and ditches. Finds here point to an agricultural settlement, dating back to the third century BC and occupied during the Roman period. This culture must be that of the Silures, the tribe whose territory in south-east Wales the Romans overran by force; it was this kind of site that those who accepted 'Romanization' left for the 'new city' of Caerwent.

Caldicot Gwent 12A3 (*pop. c.* 8,000)

Caldicot, beside the M4, has grown in little over a decade from a village into a sizeable town with new shops and industrial estates. The Romans had potteries here in the third century AD when Caldicot stood on the Via Julia, which ran to Caerwent. Caldicot Castle is a Norman foundation, with some later additions. The keep, built in the late twelfth or early thirteenth century, stands on a motte; it is an impressive example of a round tower, and one of a number of circular keeps built in Wales around this time. (Skenfrith, Bronllys, and, of course, Pembroke are others.) The early gateway is at the west end of the castle; the rectangular gatehouse, on the south side, with flanking towers, dates from the fourteenth century, and was built by Thomas Woodstock, a son of Edward III. By the early seventeenth century the castle had long been in disrepair, and it remained so until the nineteenth century, when a traveller could describe it as a 'graceful and picturesque ruin'. It has been carefully restored, and is now used for 'medieval' banquets with traditional musical entertainment. No borough grew up around this castle. SHIRE NEWTON (the Welsh version is Drenewydd Gellifarch), an attractive village on a hill about 5km. north, was (despite its name) the centre of the 'Welshry' of Caldicot lordship.

Caldy Island (Ynys Pŷr) Dyfed 8D5/D6

Frequent motorboat services in summer months take the visitor from Tenby Harbour to Caldy Island, rich in history and natural life. Men lived there from earliest times, and the bones of great animals – mammoth, rhinoceros, Irish elk – found in Nanna's Cave have shown that prehistoric Caldy was no island but a low hill rising out of the Forest of Coedrath. In the so-called Dark Ages, the 'Age of Saints' of the Celtic Churches, the Welsh named the island Ynys Pŷr ('Pyr's Island', as Manorbier was 'Pyr's Manor'), and founded a monastic

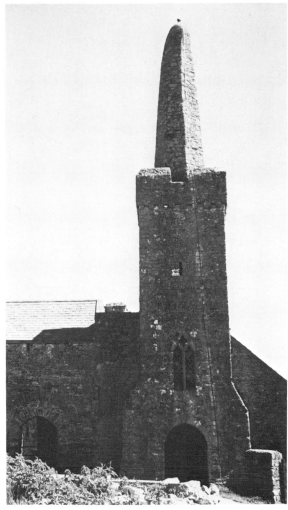

ABOVE: *St Illtud's church, Caldy Island. C13 and C14*

OPPOSITE: *Ogham stone with added Latin inscription, St Illtud's church*

community. Perhaps Pyr was the first abbot. St Illtud is thought to have held a school here, where he may have taught St David and St Samson (patron saints of Wales and Brittany). From this period dates an Ogham stone in St Illtud's church on the island (Ogham is a form of script representing Roman letters by means of long and short strokes cut on each side of an edge or line, here the side of the stone). Another monument, of the ninth century, reads 'And by the sign of the Cross [which] I have fashioned upon that [stone] I ask all who walk here that they pray for the soul of Cadwgan'.

In the ninth or tenth century the invading Norsemen arrived from the sea, renaming the place Cald-ey (Cold Island) and laying waste the Celtic monastery. The monastic tradition continued, however, with the granting of the island in the early twelfth century to the Benedictine monks of St Dogmaels, near Cardigan. At the Reformation the community was disbanded, and the abbey fell into ruin. The church was used over the years as a laundry and even as a brewery. In 1897 the Revd Donne Bushell, of Harrow, bought the island and began to repair the buildings. By 1906 a community of Anglican Benedictines was able to settle; they converted to the Roman Catholic order in 1913, rededicating the church to St Samson and importing relics from his cathedral at Dol in Brittany. This changeover lost the monks valuable financial support, and in 1929 they transferred to Prinknash Abbey, Father Aelred, the abbot, leaving for America. The present monks are Cistercians (Trappists) from Chimay in Belgium. They farm the island successfully, and sell their produce. They also sell perfume in Tenby gift-shops, which is odd when one considers that their attitude to women does not allow the latter to visit the monastery.

St Illtud's church, in the monastery farmyard, dates from the thirteenth and fourteenth centuries, but retains a strangely primitive air. The unusual stone spire is well out of true. The sanctuary, the oldest part of the church, is paved with large black pebbles from the beach.

Paul Jones the pirate is said to haunt Caldy's cliffs, and a bay is named after him. One is, however, much more likely to see seals and sea-birds, on rocks too precipitous for wise fishermen to land.

St Margaret's Island, to the west, is a small nature reserve managed by the West Wales Naturalists' Trust. Landing is by permit only.

Capel-y-ffin   Gwent   *see* **Llanthony**

Cardiff (Caerdydd)   S. Glam.   11F4
(*pop.* 278,221)

Cardiff is a rags to riches story, with the second Marquess of Bute as Prince Charming. In 1801 Cardiff's population was 1,870; in 1905 it became a city, and by 1913 it was the foremost coal-exporting centre of the world. In 1957 it was chosen as the capital city of Wales. Cardiff does not engage the emotional loyalties of all Welshmen, nor does it, obviously, have the long traditions of Dublin or Edinburgh. Indeed, for a North Walian – a man from Bangor, say, or Caernarvon – it is as remote as London, and much less easy to get to. Economically, too, it is no longer on such sure ground. To the visitor, none the less, it makes a fine impression. Its huge Norman-cum-Victorian castle, and its magnificent Edwardian civic centre set among flowering trees, lawns, and daffodils, give it an individual character; it has museums, theatres, a university, a cathedral, and sports facilities of international repute.

The Normans under Robert FitzHamon arrived in Cardiff in the eleventh century and built a castle on the site of a derelict Roman fort. A borough was established by 1100; as usual, non-Welsh settlers were especially encouraged. The walled town and castle suffered from a

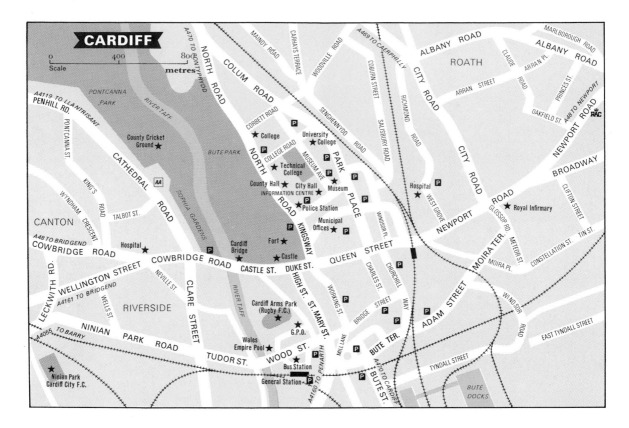

number of attacks from the Welsh of the surrounding areas. In 1158, for example, Ifor ap Meurig, the Lord of Senghenydd (Caerphilly), kidnapped the Norman Lord of Glamorgan and his countess, releasing them only after promise of redress of wrongs. Medieval Cardiff had houses of Black Friars (Dominicans) and Grey Friars (Franciscans), both established in the thirteenth century; churches (St Mary's and St John's, plus the cathedral at Llandaff) were built and embellished.

The town continued quietly enough, as a market-centre and port. It traded by sea with the Bristol Channel ports and even with La Rochelle. Fishing in the Taff and Rhymney rivers was an important minor industry; the old Welsh craft known as a coracle (*see* Cenarth) was said to have been in use up to the late nineteenth century. Until the beginning of that century, indeed, Cardiff's atmosphere was that of a small country town, with pigs and cows strolling in the streets. Town life was dominated by the castle and its occupants, who owned much of the land.

Cardiff's industrial development at first lagged behind that of Swansea, Neath, and Merthyr Tydfil. Improvements in communications in the late eighteenth century, however, prepared the way for the boom to come. The first real impetus was the construction of the Glamorganshire Canal from Abercynon to Cardiff, which the iron-

masters Crawshay, Homfray, and Guest promoted in 1792–4. This canal, and the demand created by the French Wars, gave enormous stimulus to the export of iron, Cardiff's first major commodity. In 1830 the second Marquess of Bute, who owned the Cardiff estates, invested £350,000, most of his capital, in the building of the town's first dock. The Bute West, opened in 1839 on the marshy east bank of the Taff Estuary, made possible the growth of Cardiff's coal export trade, though transport from the coalfields was still inadequate. In 1836 a private Act of Parliament was obtained for a new railway to run from the Merthyr and Dowlais ironworks to the new docks. The Taff Vale Railway, opened in 1841, was the first in South Wales; constructed by Isambard Kingdom Brunel, it was a remarkable feat of engineering. The changeover of shipping from sail to steam, the technical developments that enabled the deeper pits of the Rhondda and Aberdare valleys to be exploited, all these contributed to the phenomenal rise of Cardiff after 1850. Further docks were opened in 1857, 1874, 1887, and 1907. The South Wales Railway, from Chepstow through Cardiff to Swansea, also by Brunel, opened in 1850. Many of these developments involved the Bute estates; the second Marquess died in 1848, but his son reaped a fabulous fortune from the town's prosperity.

Cardiff Castle

Of pre-nineteenth-century Cardiff, the castle is the most striking survival. (Llandaff (Llandaf) – *see later* – was not part of the city until this century.) Even here, however, the Victorian energies of the Butes have left an astonishing imprint. The site of the castle was Roman, a 3¼ha. walled enclosure, constructed after 300 and probably similar in concept to the Forts of the Saxon Shore in south-east England. Surviving Roman masonry is outlined by a band of reddish stones running along the present walls; see especially the south section, facing Duke Street. The north gate has been well reconstructed. The Romans had civil as well as military settlements in this area. At Ely, about 6km. west, and now in the suburbs, a Roman villa and traces of ironworkings have been discovered.

In the remains of these Roman fortifications the Norman invaders built their own motte-and-bailey castle. Originally a timber construction on a high mound, and surrounded by a moat, it was rebuilt in stone in the late thirteenth century. A fine circular shell keep, and part of the medieval curtain wall, survive in a corner of the present castle enclosure.

All this tends to pale, however, in comparison with the quite extraordinary re-creation of the castle undertaken from 1865 by the architect William Burges for the third Marquess of Bute. Out of the proceeds of the vast family

estates in England, Scotland, and Wales, and in particular from the Cardiff Docks, the third Marquess was able to indulge his passion for archaeology, medievalism, architecture, and religion. At Cardiff Castle imagination and money ran riot. Burges, who had similar enthusiasms, created not only a fantastic and fairytale skyline for the city but a series of lavishly decorated rooms that sum up the mock-serious, anti-quarian, luxurious tastes of his patron. Medieval-ism and symbolism are everywhere, especially in the Chaucer Room (paintings and stained glass inspired by Chaucer's works) and the Summer Smoking Room, which, with its emblems of the universe, the elements, metals, and so on, looks out over the city and the docks from the topmost storey of the zodiac-bedecked Clock Tower. The Chapel, or Oratory, where the second Marquess collapsed and died in 1848, reflects his son's Catholic piety. The Arab Room, in gold, marble, and cedarwood, is an overwhelming piece of magnificence. The Library reminds us that Lord Bute was a serious scholar; his languages included Greek, Hebrew, Assyrian, and Egyptian (statues representing the world of Antiquity sit in Gothic niches over the fireplace, together with his own). Bute's castle may not appeal to every modern taste; it lacks all restraint, screams out wealth, appears to have lost all touch with reality. As a

Cardiff Castle: statues in the library representing the world of Antiquity and its languages

period-piece, however, it is of absorbing interest. The castle was given to the city in 1948.

The church of St John's is the only other building of medieval origin, and this, too, has been considerably restored. The main body of the church is Perpendicular in style; the interior is well proportioned, with a clerestory in the chancel, a rood-loft staircase, and thirteenth-century arcading in the south choir. The altar-piece is by Sir William Goscombe John. The north chapel, which has Renaissance screenwork, contains an Elizabethan monument to two members of the Herbert family, unusual in that both effigies are of the same sex. The finest feature of the church is perhaps the tower, which was built in the fifteenth century; it is of West Country type, with elaborate parapet and crocketed

pinnacles. The architect may have been John Hart, who erected Wrexham steeple and that of St Stephen's in Bristol. There are some scanty remains of the Black Friars' priory, excavated by Lord Bute in 1887–8, in Bute Park, adjoining the castle.

Much of Cardiff is the creation of the nineteenth century and of the Bute family enterprises. In 1849–53, for example, the Taff River was diverted to remove the danger of flooding and to make sites available for the new railway bridge and station. (Its former course ran through what is now Cardiff Arms Park.) New housing developments – Butetown, near the Docks, Temperance Town (in the area of the present bus station) – catered for the expanding population. After the Church Building Act of 1818 a spate of new churches and chapels also appeared. The chapels were mostly Gothic in style. Some of the churches are fine examples of Victorian work, in particular, St German's, Roath, and St Margaret's, Roath, with the enormous marble Bute mausoleum. The Market Hall, which has an upper, balcony, floor, was rebuilt in 1890–1, and the main shopping-streets are joined by attractive old-fashioned arcades. Sophia Gardens and Roath Park, both formerly part of the Bute estates, were granted to the city in 1858 and 1887 respectively.

In 1898 the city fathers acquired from the Marquess of Bute the 24ha. of Cathays Park. With impressive Edwardian confidence they proceeded to lay out a spacious and dignified civic centre. The buildings – the City Hall (1901–6), the Law Courts and University Registry (1904), the Glamorgan County Hall (1912), and the Temple of Peace and Health (1938) – are mostly neo-classical, of white Portland stone, separated by wide avenues and green spaces. Across the park are the University College of South Wales and Monmouthshire (1909, originally opened in 1883) and the National Museum of Wales. The latter received its charter in 1907; its first stone was laid in 1912, but it was not completed until 1927. Sir Mortimer Wheeler, who was its Keeper of Archaeology and later Director, gives an account of its early difficulties in his *Still Digging*. Both museum and university college have expanded dramatically in recent years. The National Museum has fine collections relating to Welsh history, natural history, archaeology, industry, and so on; its art galleries include an important group of French Impressionists. Folk-life exhibits are centred at St Fagan's (*see later*), and a new Industrial and Maritime Museum, like St Fagan's partly open-air, is now under construction on the site of one of the early Bute docks.

About 3km. west of the city centre, LLANDAFF CATHEDRAL stands quietly in a hollow; the Green nearby, with preaching-cross and ruined Norman belfry, and the simple, old-fashioned houses and cottages of the village, give an air of spaciousness and tranquillity. As a cathedral, Llandaff is neither fully medieval nor fully modern, neither Lincoln nor Coventry; instead, its history and architecture reflect every important change in religious life and in building since the twelfth century and before.

The site of the present church had been used for burials as early as Roman, pre-Christian times, and it was here in the sixth century that the Celtic missionary-saint Teilo is traditionally believed to have founded a *llan* or Celtic monastery. A small church only 8½m. by 5m. stood on or near the site until some years after the Norman Conquest. The tenth-century Celtic cross found in 1870 in 'Teilo's Well' (in the Bishop's Palace garden) is the only relic of this first period.

For the Normans, the rebuilding and reorganization of the Celtic churches was an essential part of their conquest; it seems probable that they both sincerely

The National Museum of Wales, Cardiff

believed in it as a spiritual necessity and recognized its potential as a method of psychological domination. Urban, the first Norman bishop of Llandaff, began the present cathedral in 1120. As was usual, building continued for well over a century. After dedication in 1266 changes continued to be made to the finished structure up to the end of the fifteenth century. Some excellent Norman and later work has survived from the medieval cathedral: the fine, roundheaded, carved, and moulded arch dividing the high altar from the Lady Chapel; the Transitional north and south doorways, which are also richly carved; the west front (*c.* 1220); the late-thirteenth-century Lady Chapel with Perpendicular windows; the north-west 'Jasper' Tower, named after its builder, Jasper Tudor, uncle of Henry VII. The medieval stone reredos is now in the Dyfrig Chapel.

The Reformation was a disaster for Llandaff. Its treasures were hidden or sold; the fabric deteriorated badly through a combination of neglect and poverty. In the Civil War Cromwell's troops notoriously turned the place into a beer-house, stabling animals there and burning its books. They even took pot-shots at a few daring Easter communicants. Two great storms, in 1703 and 1723, brought down the roof of the nave and the south-west tower. The 'poor desolate church of Llandaff' had declined into a ruin.

The eighteenth century set out to remedy this in its own style. John Wood, the architect of fashionable Bath, began to reconstruct the building; he chose to create an Italianate temple, with classical plaster-work, domed tower, and entrance portico. Perhaps fortunately, funds

OPPOSITE: *Llandaff Cathedral from the SE*   ABOVE: *Rossetti's 'Seed of David' triptych, Llandaff Cathedral*

failed; two of Wood's classical urns, which once stood on the temple roof, can be seen outside the old Prebendal House, on the north-west side of the cathedral.

The resultant hybrid, unfinished, a 'ball-room with Venetian windows', as one eighteenth-century observer described it, remained in place until 1835, when the nineteenth-century restorers began their work. Medieval Gothic was now the main inspiration for most church-building. The architect at Llandaff was John Prichard, later joined by J. P. Seddon. Prichard's remarkable restoration included the new south-west tower with spire, modelled on the Gothic churches of Normandy, and a large number of important details (the portrait heads of English monarchs from Richard III onwards, on the outside walls of the nave, are one of his unusual features). Seddon was responsible for commissioning from D. G. Rossetti the 'Seed of David' triptych (for the high altar, and now in the Illtud Chapel). Rossetti's models included William Morris (David) and his wife

(the Virgin Mary), Swinburne, and Burne-Jones, all important members of the Pre-Raphaelite fraternity. (The Bishop of Llandaff is said to have called on Rossetti in London to see the pictures in progress. To his enquiries, a maidservant who opened the door replied, 'Oh, lor', Sir, Mr Rossetti is married and he don't paint now'.) Six porcelain panels in the Dyfrig Chapel are also Pre-Raphaelite work, designed by Burne-Jones, with Elizabeth Eleanor Siddal, inspiration of Rossetti and Swinburne, as model; these, however, came to the cathedral much later. Of the surviving Victorian furnishings, the neo-Gothic Bishop's throne is little short of a masterpiece.

A fine Victorian restoration was thus blown to bits when in January 1941 a German land-mine exploded on the south side of the cathedral. Of all the British cathedrals only Coventry suffered more than Llandaff. Reconstruction began once more; medieval and nine-teenth-century features were carefully restored where possible. The new church refused, however, to live entirely in its past. At the point where the medieval builder placed his rood-screen – between nave and sanctuary – the twentieth-century architect has thrown an immense parabolic arch of reinforced concrete. On the cylindrical organ-case that surmounts the arch Jacob Epstein's aluminium 'Christ in Majesty' forces the gaze upwards, reminds the visitor that this is not a museum of architecture or craftsmanship but a living and uncompromising place of faith. The other major new work is the Welch Regiment Memorial Chapel (1956), built of river-washed stones from old Llandaff cottages in course of demolition. Among recent work, notice the bronze panels in the Lady Chapel, each representing a wild flower whose Welsh name connects it with the Virgin Mary. There is a John Piper window over the high altar.

No visitor to Cardiff nor indeed to South Wales should miss the Welsh Folk Museum at ST FAGAN'S (Sain Ffagan), 6½km. west. From the remains of a Norman castle, Dr John Gibbon in the mid sixteenth century built a large gabled mansion; this, with extensive grounds, was given by the Earl of Plymouth to the National Museum of Wales in 1948. The castle itself has been carefully restored and furnished. In the 40ha. of woodlands old buildings from every part of Wales have been reconstructed in accurate detail. Cottages, farms, early chapels, a working woollen-mill, a tannery, and many other buildings that would otherwise have been demolished or left to decay have been brought stone by stone to give an authentic and unique picture of the social life and architecture of rural Wales. Craftsmen demonstrate the old techniques of – to take three examples – weaving, basketry, and wood-turning.

St Fagan's itself is a charming, hilly village, with a thirteenth-century church. Near here, on 8 May 1648, Cromwell's army won a particularly bloody battle, the most significant encounter fought during the Civil War in Wales.

Cardigan (Aberteifi) Dyfed 8D2 (*pop.* 3,800)
Once a flourishing sea-port, and enriched by the Cardiganshire lead mines, Cardigan lost its harbour with the silting up of the Teifi Estuary. In 1840 (*pop.* 2,925) it was still exporting grain, butter, oak, bark, and slate, and importing timber, coal, limestone, and manufactured goods. The railway reached Cardigan in 1888, but this too has now departed. Cardigan remains, in its beautiful riverside setting, an attractive, old-fashioned little town.

The scene of fierce battles between Welsh and conquerors (in 1136, for example, Gruffydd ap Rhys ap Tewdwr and his men took on and routed a combined force of English, Normans, and Flemings), Cardigan retains from that period its medieval stone bridge with its cutwaters and recesses. The castle was a fortress of the Lord Rhys. It was here at Christmas 1176 that he held

the first recorded *eisteddfod*, after a year of proclamation in 'Wales and England and Scotland and Ireland and the other islands'. There were two kinds of contest: one in poetry, for the bards, and one in music, for the harpists, pipers, and others. Two chairs were set for the victors, and ample gifts rewarded them. Welsh culture, which flourished even among the bloody rivalries of the native princes, was ousted from the castle by the Norman invader. Cardigan was captured by Gilbert Marshall, Earl of Pembroke, in 1240, and later that century, after the uprising under Llewellyn the Last, Edward I placed his own hated English officials in this and other strongholds. Little now remains of the castle, and it is not open to the public.

Cardigan also had its monastic foundation, a Benedictine priory – a Norman legacy – fragments of which are incorporated in the parish church of St Mary. The chancel is of the fourteenth century and there is some original medieval Flemish glass (rare in Wales) in the upper part of the east window. The octagonal font is a fifteenth-century feature. The adjacent building, now a hospital, has the original Gothic windows in the west front, but the remainder was rebuilt in 1802, perhaps by Nash. A free grammar school, founded in 1653, had in 1840 twenty-eight scholars; of these, six were 'on the foundation', that is, learning free of charge Greek and Latin, history and geography, but paying one guinea annually for instruction in writing and arithmetic.

In the High Street note the Georgian Shire Hall, since converted into a furniture showroom, and Tabernacle, a fine chapel. Bethania Chapel (1847) in William Street has the original pews and gallery. There is a covered market at the Guildhall (1859).

Cardigan is within easy reach of good bathing at Poppit Sands, Gwbert-on-sea, and MWNT, with its small, ancient, white-washed church almost on the beach. CARDIGAN ISLAND is a nature reserve, and not accessible to the public.

Carew (Caeriw) Dyfed 8C5
Most of the village of Carew and its antiquities – castle, high cross, and tidal mill – lie on the A4075 just after it turns off north from the main Pembroke–St Clears road (A477). There are old cottages, inns, and a round stone chimney of the kind locally called 'Flemish'. The parish church and rectory are at Carew Cheriton, down a lane to the south of the crossroads with the A477.

The castle, a rather elegant ivy-grown ruin, stands on an arm of the Cleddau River, where flocks of seagulls wheel and settle. A demesne of the Princes of South Wales, it passed in Henry I's reign into the hands of Gerald de Windsor, the Norman castellan of Pembroke, who had married the daughter of Rhys ap Tewdwr. The daughter was the notorious Princess Nest, famous for her beauty and her adventures, great grandmother of a bishop and of Gerald the Welshman, the twelfth-century cleric and writer. Nest's son William took the

Caerphilly Castle

Epstein's 'Christ in Majesty', Llandaff Cathedral

Carew Castle from the Cleddau River, showing a mixture of C13 and Elizabethan features

name of Carew, and it was probably one of these early Carews who built the castle's west front with its huge defensive round towers typical of the late thirteenth century.

In the late fifteenth century the Welsh retrieved the castle. An improvident Carew mortgaged it to Sir Rhys ap Thomas, one of the most ardent supporters of Henry Tudor, the future Henry VII. When that prince landed near Milford Haven in 1485 he is said to have spent a night at Carew Castle before marching on to Bosworth, where Rhys was knighted. In Sir Rhys's time the house became famous for its lavish hospitality and the patronage of bards. One of his banquets, for St George's Day, is said to have lasted a week.

In the following century an equally individual owner again transformed the castle. Sir John Perrott (1527?–92) was the living image of red-haired King Henry VIII, and conclusions were drawn accordingly. One of four gentlemen chosen to carry the canopy of state at the coronation of Queen Elizabeth, he was soon afterwards appointed Vice-admiral of the seas about South Wales and Keeper of the gaol at Haverfordwest. His rashness and his appetite for a brawl were unlimited. As governor of Munster during the Fitzmaurice rebellion, he was said to have killed or hanged over 800 Irishmen. He returned exhausted. Retiring to Wales, he was next appointed Commissioner for piracy in Pembrokeshire, even though (or because?) not long before he had been accused of trafficking with pirates himself. In 1584 he was sent back to Ireland as Lord Deputy. Eventually his hot tongue was his undoing, and his presumption of blood relationship with the Queen was not enough to

save him. He was accused of speaking contemptuously of Her Majesty, and other treasonable acts, and died in the Tower of London in 1592. At Carew his extensive alterations were, not surprisingly, never completed.

Carew Castle illustrates clearly (and with great charm) certain important developments. The early, thirteenth-century, parts of the castle are mainly defensive: stout walls and massive towers with great buttresses. The riverine site, too, was chosen for security as much as for convenience. Feudal land-owners lived thus in a constant state of embattlement, defended against their own tenants as well as against the encroachments of other great men. The portions added by Sir Rhys ap Thomas show a new concern for elegance. However, this more elaborate style is confined to the inner, courtyard, face of the building; the exterior could still be needed to withstand attack. The north side, on the contrary, shows how by Elizabeth's time castles were giving place to manor-houses. Windows are now much larger and far more decorative; defence has given way to comfort. The house no longer looks inward onto its enclosed courtyard, but outwards to the community. The new monarchy of the Tudors had brought comparative stability, even to such far corners of the Kingdom. This security was not to last for ever; Carew was twice besieged during the Civil Wars of the following century and suffered accordingly.

On the Cleddau, just below the castle, a corn-mill has been in existence since before 1560. The present 'French mill', a three-storey rectangular structure, dates from the late eighteenth century. It is open to visitors as a working museum. The mill is a tidal one, that is, water

enters at high tide and is dammed up by a barrage; it can then be let out gradually, at a controlled flow, to turn the mill machinery.

Carew Cross, near the entrance to the castle, is one of the most spectacular Celtic crosses in Britain. While Irish crosses of this type often have carvings of men or animals, the Welsh ones are almost without exception geometrical. Carew Cross, probably an eleventh-century work, is a wheel-headed cross resting on a huge shaft that is inscribed with a variety of traditional patterns. The inscription commemorates Margiteut, who is thought to be Maredudd ap Edwin, King of Deheubarth (south-west Wales) and great grandson of Hywel the Good, who died in battle in 1035. Note the swastika pattern on the top panel; this represents a Sanskrit word meaning 'well-being', and the Celts considered it lucky. The other patterns may also carry a symbolic meaning. Carew Cross is a remarkable technical achievement, showing extraordinary sureness of eye and hand on the part of the Celtic sculptor.

At Carew Cheriton, St Mary's is a fine plain church with a slim square tower (c. 1500) that is topped by a pointed turret. The chancel and transepts are of early-fourteenth-century date; the tiles in the sanctuary may have come from the castle (the raven they bear was one of Sir Rhys ap Thomas's heraldic devices). The nave is earlier, and its architectural detail – small capitals, wave-moulding, and four-leaved flowers – points to the influence of Bishop Gower, who was responsible for the very fine Bishop's Palace at St David's. In the chancel are three effigies: a priest in vestments; a crusader (perhaps Sir Nicholas Carew); and a small female figure holding a heart. This last may be a child's effigy, or it may be a 'heart burial', the body lying elsewhere. The ancient building in the churchyard has been variously described as a charnel-house and a chantry chapel. In 1848 Samuel Lewis notes it as a parochial school, with a master appointed by the Vicar.

Carmarthen (Caerfyrddin) Dyfed 9F4
(*pop.* 13,072)
Visitors have always been pleased with Carmarthen. Taylor said of it in 1652 that it was 'one of the plentifulest towns that I ever set foot in . . . there is nothing scarce, dear, or hard to come by, but tobacco pipes'. Defoe in the next century described it as 'an antient but not a decay'd town, pleasantly situated on the River Towy, or Tovy. . . . The town indeed is well built, and populous, and the country around it is the most fruitful, of any part of all Wales'. Defoe's assessment, if a little colourless, seems to capture the sober liveliness that

LEFT: *Carew Cross (C11): one of the most spectacular Celtic crosses in Britain*

OPPOSITE: *Tower (c. 1500) of St Mary's church, Carew Cheriton*

characterizes Carmarthen still. This atmosphere is compounded of a long history, a pleasing but unflamboyant architecture, a rich tradition of religious energy and controversy, plus the vitality and excitement of the regular markets, which draw in the population of the surrounding countryside. Carmarthen is also a college town and is the administrative centre of the new county of Dyfed.

Carmarthen has long been identified with the Roman station of Moridunum, and recent excavations have revealed the extent of this settlement. On the site of an earlier hill-fort, a walled town of about 6ha. was laid out in the second century AD with buildings of timber or stone, some of which had tessellated floors and hypocausts. The town seems to have continued in use at least until the end of the fourth century. Moridunum, which may have been the tribal capital of the Demetae, was the most westerly of all the known Roman settlements in South Wales; from there the Roman road turned sharply north towards Bremia (Llanio). Today the only visible feature is part of the amphitheatre mound (off Priory Street, past Merlin's Oak). Finds from the excavations can be seen in the County Museum; one object, a Roman domestic altar, has been placed in the porch of St Peter's church.

The next builders to leave their mark were the Normans, who fortified the hill above the river. Their early motte-and-bailey structure was replaced by a stone castle in the reign of Henry I. During the Middle Ages the castle was frequently captured and frequently enlarged. The main body, however, failed to survive the Civil War. John Nash built the county gaol on the site in 1789; the gaol was replaced earlier this century by the present County Hall. The remnant of the Norman castle, a fourteenth-century gateway with sturdy towers and machicolations, can be seen in Nott Square, engulfed by the modern town.

Under the Normans the castle provided the nucleus for a 'new town', which grew up outside its walls. Separate from this was the Welsh community or 'old town', which came under the jurisdiction of the Augustinian Priory that the Normans themselves had founded. Squabbles between the two towns persisted until well after 1546 when Henry VIII granted the 'new town' a charter that incorporated both.

The Priory of St John the Evangelist played an important part in the life of medieval Carmarthen, holding St Peter's and other churches, and providing courts of justice, fairs, and markets. At this priory was written the oldest surviving Welsh manuscript, a collection of poems known as the 'Black Book of Carmarthen' (now in the National Library at Aberystwyth). Both the priory and the Franciscan friary were dissolved at the Reformation; their buildings have disappeared, though street names indicate their sites. In 1450 Carmarthen was the scene of a famous *Eisteddfod*, held under the patronage of Gruffydd, Lord of Dinefwr. Here were laid down new rules for the Welsh poetic metres, many of which are still in use today.

The Reformation caused comparatively little up-heaval in Wales. Carmarthen, however, was the setting for one of the three executions that took place in Wales under 'Bloody Mary'. Bishop Robert Ferrar of St David's had already in the previous reign come into conflict with his chapter, which had managed to secure his imprisonment. On the accession of Mary, Ferrar, still in a London gaol, refused to accept the return to Roman Catholicism. He was tried, condemned, and sent back to Carmarthen to be burned in the market-place in March 1555. A plaque in Nott Square commemorates his martyrdom.

Ferrar's fate catches the imagination, but in fact it had few repercussions in Carmarthen. Much more significant for the town was the religious and educational revival of the eighteenth century. Peter Williams, one of the leaders of Welsh Methodism, was the first minister of Heol Dwr (Water Street) Chapel; Penuel Baptist Chapel dates back to 1785 (it was rebuilt in 1910); Heol Awst (Lammas Street) Chapel, Independent Methodist, was set up in 1726, and was later associated with the Presbyterian College for Ministers, which was active in the town in the late eighteenth and nineteenth centuries. Isaac Carter moved his printing press here from New-castle Emlyn in 1725, and in the course of the century the town became well known in South Wales as a centre of printing and of Nonconformity.

Many of the town's most distinguished buildings date from the eighteenth century, when its vitality was per-haps at its height. The neo-classical Guildhall was erected in 1767; the Public Library retains the façade of a Georgian town house built for the local ironmasters. There are a number of elegant terraces (Quay Street is one example), though some are in need of repair. John Nash spent the years 1784–96 in the town and some of the houses may perhaps be his work.

The nineteenth century saw further church and chapel building in an interesting variety of styles. In 1848 Trinity College was founded as an Anglican teacher-training college for men. (It is now coeduca-tional and forms part of the Faculty of Education of the University of Wales.) In 1852 the railway reached Car-marthen, and, together with the silting up of the Towy, contributed to the town's decline as a port. Other events that century left little trace for the visitor, but are per-haps worth remembering. Paxton's election campaign in 1802, for example: the candidate spent £15,690 4s. 2d., which included the bills for over 11,000 breakfasts, nearly 37,000 dinners, 25,000 gallons of ale, 11,000 bottles of spirits, and £786 worth of ribbons. Un-fortunately he lost by forty-five votes. Forty years later Carmarthen had its share of the agricultural unrest known to historians as the 'Rebecca Riots'. In June 1842 three or four hundred men on horseback entered the town in broad daylight (most of 'Rebecca's' activities took place at night). Carrying placards reading 'Justice', they ransacked the workhouse before being scattered by a troop of dragoons. This incident did much to bring the farmers' genuine grievances to the attention of the nation at large.

Present-day Carmarthen has a number of sights to interest the visitor. Merlin's Oak, in Priory Street, should not be omitted, though its withered stump en-cased in railings is perhaps not much of a spectacle. It was the fanciful medieval historian Geoffrey of Mon-mouth who first connected Carmarthen with the en-chanter Merlin, probably by means of a false etymology (Caer-Fyrddin = Merlin's town). The old rhyme runs: 'When Merlin's Tree shall tumble down, / Then shall fall Carmarthen Town'. A local tradesman once tried to kill it, out of sheer irritation at the crowds it drew; its pitiful remains are now under Council protection.

St Peter's church, nearer the centre of town, is well worth a visit. Most of the fabric dates from the thirteenth century, though there was a place of worship here earlier. There are a number of interesting monuments and memorials, including the much restored tomb of Sir Rhys ap Thomas, who struck the blow that felled Richard III at Bosworth (and put Henry Tudor on the throne of England). A brass tablet on the south wall commemorates Sir Richard Steele (1671–1729), the essayist of the *Spectator*, who is buried here in the vault of his wife's family, the Scurlocks. Steele died in what is now the Ivy Bush Inn in King Street. Also buried some-where here, in 1576, was Sir Walter Devereux, first Earl of Essex, and father of Queen Elizabeth's favourite. His body was brought back from Dublin to his native Car-marthen. Notice, too, the old Faculty Pew, and the Victorian roof, which replaced Nash's plaster ceiling in 1861. For Nash's cornice, put up in 1785, the workmen are said to have robbed the alabaster tomb of Hywel y Pedolau, son of Edward II's wet-nurse, and reputedly so strong that he could break a horse-shoe with his bare hands.

From St Peter's one can return to the town centre via King Street and Nott Square, the latter named after General Nott of Afghanistan – his father kept the Ivy Bush – whose statue, cast from Indian guns, stands on the square. Through Lammas Street, with its modern shops, one should make for Friars Park and 'The Bulwarks', a ditch-and-rampart defence constructed by the townspeople during the Civil War.

Market-day at Carmarthen (Wednesday and Satur-day) should not be missed. In and around the market hall with its old clock, local produce such as the famous Carmarthenshire butter is on sale. Auctions in the cattle-mart are well worth attending (proceedings are in English) and since everyone knows his neighbours there is no chance of the visitor accidentally acquiring a prize pig by an ill-timed sneeze.

The County Museum is an interesting collection, its exhibits spanning the centuries from a dinosaur's foot-

ABOVE: *Carmarthen cattle-mart* BELOW: *Carmarthen: aerial view from the S*

print to a nineteenth-century butter churn. There are two ancient stones inscribed in Latin and Ogham: the Voteporix stone, in memory of a sixth-century King of Dyfed, and the Paulinus stone, named after the saint who is reputed to have taught St David. Finds from the Roman gold-mines at Dolaucothi are on display, as are medieval sculpture and relics of rural life and work. In 1975 the museum was still in Quay Street, but the house had become unsafe, and it is planned to move to the Bishop's Palace at Abergwili, where more of the collections can be shown.

ABERGWILI is a village just outside Carmarthen on the A40. It was chosen in Henry VIII's reign as the site of the new Bishop's Palace for the diocese of St David's. Bishop Barlow (1536–48) was responsible for this move; it involved, so tradition has it, his stripping the lead from the roof of the glorious palace at St David's, which he considered a 'barbarous and desolate corner'. Here at Abergwili Salesbury and Bishop Richard Davies worked on their translation of the Bible and Common Prayer into Welsh. The Prayer Book and New Testament were published in 1567, at the expense of a Carmarthen merchant, Humphrey Toy; they are monuments in the history of the Welsh language. The Bishop's Palace was rebuilt in the early nineteenth century.

On the opposite bank of the Towy, LLANGUNNOR (Llangynnwr) was for some years the home of Sir Richard Steele (*see above*), who had married a Carmarthenshire woman, Mary Scurlock ('Dear Prue'). Tŷ Gwyn, the Scurlock farm, has been rebuilt. The church at Llangunnor has a memorial to Steele and the tombs of Sir Lewis Morris, the Victorian poet, and David Charles, a famous Welsh hymn-writer. There are splendid views over the Towy Valley.

Another Welsh hymn-writer is celebrated at CONWIL ELVET (Cynwyl Elfed), about 8km. north of Carmarthen on the A484. An old farmhouse, 'Y Gangell', has been converted into a museum to honour the name of 'Elfed'. H. Elfed Lewis (1860–1953) was the eldest of eleven children. In his long life he became well known and well loved as poet and preacher. Like many Welsh bards, he took his poet's name from his birthplace.

Carreg Cennen Dyfed 6C6, 9G4
1½km. E of Trapp
Dramatically sited on its great limestone crag, the mass of Carreg Cennen Castle is brutish and powerful. The castle is remarkably isolated: Trapp, a tiny village, is more than a km. away, and the bus route even further. It is also quite uncluttered by later settlement. There is

Carreg Cennen Castle

a stiff climb up from the farmyard beneath its walls; once at the castle there are magnificent views south over the Black Mountain.

The first fortress here was built by the Welsh as a stronghold of the Lords of Deheubarth, whose main seat was at Dinefwr (near Llandeilo). The Lord Rhys (*c.* 1135–97) and his sons had succeeded in forcing the Normans to recognize their rule. But disunity was the downfall of the medieval Welsh, and the Normans used this to their advantage. After the death of the Lord Rhys, squabbles broke up his inheritance. Rhys Fychan, his son, had to fight his uncle, and even his own mother, the Norman Matilda de Breos, who out of spite had given Carreg Cennen into English hands. The uncle, Maredudd ap Rhys Gryg, of Dryslwyn Castle, joined forces with another Welsh prince, Llewellyn, and evicted Rhys from his domain. Twenty years later, in 1277, the castle fell to Edward I of England; it remained in English hands for most of the rest of its active life.

The present buildings date mostly from the time of John Gifford, to whom Edward I gave the castle in 1283, or of his son, John Gifford the younger. The latter was executed for rebellion in Edward II's reign, and the castle was then granted to that king's favourite, Hugh Despenser, Lord of Glamorgan. Despenser was hanged four years later when Edward's sad reign was brought to a violent end.

Subsequent owners included John of Gaunt and Henry of Bolingbroke; when the latter became King the castle became Crown property. It suffered in the revolt of Owain Glyndwr and had to be substantially repaired. In the Wars of the Roses it stood out for the Lancastrians, but was surrendered to the King's Chief Justice in 1462. Later that year it was decided to demolish it for fear that local brigands might use it as a lair. Five hundred men with picks and crow-bars were paid £28 5s. 6d. to reduce it to ruin.

Carreg Cennen illustrates very clearly the late-medieval theory of fortifications that had evolved to meet more sophisticated techniques of attack. The inner ward was constructed first, protected on one side by a sheer precipice and on the others by towers and ditches. After this came the great barbican, the most remarkable feature of the castle. A stepped ramp, originally flanked by walls, approaches the main gateway, taking a sharp right-angled turn (which would slow down the attacker) and passing over a series of five pits crossed by drawbridges. The gatehouse itself was protected by its own towers, while from the north-east tower of the castle the defenders could adequately cover the approach with their fire. Somewhat later the outer curtain wall was added; it too had towers at its corners, and a well-fortified gate. This arrangement of defences within defences, typical of the Edwardian period of castle-building, should by rights be called concentric; but at Carreg Cennen the lines of construction are square rather than round, which contributes to its fearsomely

primitive appearance. It has also been pointed out that the outer square is accurately aligned on the four points of the compass.

One especially evocative feature of this castle is the 'secret passage'. This is a roughly-hewn corridor with a vaulted roof, lit by openings cut in the outer wall, that leads along the southern cliff face down to a natural cavern in the rock. The purpose of this cave remains uncertain: there are signs of its having served as a dovecote,

The 'secret passage' at Carreg Cennen

and water may have been collected there. Water supply could well have been a serious problem at Carreg Cennen. Rainwater seems to have been collected in cisterns behind the gatehouse and in the clay-lined ditch that formed part of the inner ward's defences; but, though upland Wales is proverbially rainy, this might still not have provided sufficient to withstand a long siege.

This is a strangely desolate castle. Guarding no strategic road or waterway, lacking in any signs of comfort, and above all clearly failing to provide the nucleus of a thriving town (as at Pembroke, Kidwelly, Haverfordwest, and other Norman sites), Carreg Cennen seems to stand as a monument to brute force exerted to no good purpose.

Cascob Powys *see* **Presteigne**

Castell Coch S. Glam. 11F3 Tongwynlais
Just off the main Cardiff-to-Merthyr road, at Tongwynlais, Castell Coch is a fascinating example of Victorian medievalism. The 'Red Castle' was a small fortress built in the early thirteenth century by Gilbert Earl of Gloucester (who was probably also responsible for the castle at Caerphilly). In 1870 it was in ruins. The third Marquess of Bute, who had inherited a fortune of £300,000 a year from his father, had not long left Oxford, where he had been converted to Roman Catholicism. There, too, he had met William Burges, a budding architect, whose passion to recreate the spirit of medieval art matched Bute's own. In 1865 Burges was engaged to report on the possibility of restoring Cardiff Castle. Work on Cardiff was already in progress – the well-known clock tower was rising above the ruined battlements – when Bute, in 1871, commissioned a new report, this time on Castell Coch.

Castell Coch was a remarkable architectural achievement. Re-creation rather than restoration, it was 'a medievalist's fantasy in wood and stone, set in woodlands garlanded with wild garlic and surrounded by the Marquess's own vineyards'. For the external structure Burges used French sources, with details from Carlisle Castle and the Tower of London. The effect of the cylindrical towers is massively Norman; their pointed conical roofs, on the other hand, are archaeologically unsound, a charming proclamation of almost Bavarian fantasy.

The framework was finished in 1879, but when Burges died in 1881 the interior was hardly begun. His plans were executed as closely as possible by William Frame, who had worked with him on Cardiff Castle. Inside, the octagonal drawing-room with its fantastic rib-vaulted ceiling, blue and gold, and spangled with birds and butterflies, and the extraordinary bedroom designed for Lady Bute, with its murals and Gothic wash-stand, are minor masterpieces of the Victorian imagination.

Bute should not be dismissed as an eccentric and extravagant aristocrat (his charities to hospitals, schools, universities, and religious causes, to name a few beneficiaries, were considerable). He was an enlightened and strongly individual patron of architecture, a learned and deeply religious man with a passion for archaeology. He was in some ways the epitome of a certain kind of Victorian.

Castell Coch was never much used by the family; indeed, it was intended as a sort of superior summer-house. The Marquess's vineyard, however, planted in 1875, yielded a commercially viable crop for some forty-five years. Visitors to the castle would be served with the wine (some of which was reserved for the altar) and asked their opinion. Sir Herbert Maxwell is said to have replied, 'Well now, Lord Bute, it is what I should call an interesting wine'. 'I wonder what he exactly meant', remarked His Lordship thoughtfully, some time later.

In the Second World War the castle was fortified as a machine-gun post. It is now in the care of the Department of the Environment.

Castlemartin (Castellmartin) Dyfed 8B5
The 'castle' here seems never to have been more than an earthwork or at most an enclosure with a wooden stockade. Castlemartin village, once flourishing, now forms a rather melancholy part of an extensive tank and artillery range. (Firing times must be consulted before you venture into this area.)

The church of St Michael is Norman, and its organ (1842) once belonged to Mendelssohn. Castlemartin gave its name to a distinct breed of Black Cattle, now merged into the Welsh Blacks. The local militia, the Castlemartin Yeomanry, turned out in 1797 to deal with the French 'invasion' near Fishguard. For this they were awarded the only battle honour given to a regiment for an engagement on British soil.

Cenarth Dyfed 9E2
The old bridge and tumbling falls make Cenarth a favourite beauty spot, and indeed it is very pretty. On this stretch of the Teifi, between Cenarth and Cilgerran, one may occasionally still see coracle fishing, an ancient technique once common in Britain, but now confined to this and one other river, the Towy at Carmarthen. The Romans remarked on the coracle of the 'ancient Britons' when they arrived in the first century AD, and the craft was probably already old then. The basic frame of the boat is made of interwoven ribs of ash, willow, or hazel, and is covered with tarred canvas or calico (which has replaced hide). The Teifi coracle is rounded, and waisted amidships; it lies deeper in the water than the Towy coracle, which is more oval in shape. The traditional construction is handed down in families. Coracles work in pairs: fish are caught in nets drawn between the two and a club or 'priest' (*pren pysgod*) with a leather thong is used to kill the catch. To avoid over-fishing, the number of pairs on the Towy is now limited to twelve.

Chepstow Castle, showing the Great Tower

The coracle weighs about 13kg.; a characteristic sight in this area is the black turtle shape of a fisherman walking down to the river with his coracle strapped to his back. The only similar boat still in use elsewhere in Great Britain is the Irish curragh, a larger and more pointed craft, used for sea-fishing off the west coast of Ireland and around the Aran Islands.

Chepstow (Cas-gwent) Gwent 12A2 (*pop.* 8,037) For visitors who enter the Principality by the impressive Severn Bridge (1966), Chepstow is the first town 'over the border'. A fine starting-point for explorations of the Wye Valley, the Forest of Dean, or the South Wales coast, Chepstow is also worth looking at in its own right, as a town full of character and with living remains of its past.

Chepstow Castle, conspicuous on a cliff above the Wye, has the distinction of being the earliest stone castle built by the Normans in Wales. It was founded by William FitzOsbern, who, as recently created Lord of Hereford, pushed down into Gwent in the five years immediately following the Battle of Hastings. At Chepstow the cellar and the two lower storeys of the Great Tower date from this earliest foundation. In 1115 the

King granted the Marcher lordship of Chepstow (then known as Striguil) to the powerful de Clare family, and the castle became the military and administrative centre of their territory. Later generations added to and strengthened the castle. William Marshall, for example, who built the immense round keep at Pembroke, was responsible for the curtain wall with towers and gateway that divides the lower and middle baileys. In *c.* 1190 this use of rounded or semicircular towers to strengthen a wall's defences reflected the most advanced notions of fortification science. The residential quarters in the lower bailey date from the thirteenth century, as does Marten's Tower, with its chapel.

The castle withstood and survived the revolt of the Welsh under Owain Glyndwr, but saw active service during the Civil War. The Earl of Worcester, who owned both this and Raglan Castle, was one of the most ardent Royalist supporters. Raglan endured a lengthy siege; Chepstow was twice besieged, and on the second occasion Cromwell himself took part in the action. In 1645, during the Second Civil War, he left a strong Roundhead force outside the walls; the castle was reduced by hunger but refused to surrender. As a result, and in contrast to what happened at Raglan in similar circumstances, the commander was killed, with some forty of the garrison. A plaque commemorating Sir Nicholas Kemeys, who led this Royalist defence, can be seen in the Lower Court. During Parliament's ascendancy Jeremy Taylor, the Royalist divine and writer, was kept prisoner here, briefly, before his retirement to Golden Grove in Carmarthenshire. After the Restoration the castle was again used as a prison, this time for Henry Marten, who had signed the King's death warrant. Marten had escaped execution on condition of perpetual imprisonment. His rooms, in the tower that bears his name, seem to have been reasonably comfortable. In any event, he remained there twenty years, until his sudden death, in 1680, at the age of seventy-eight.

Like other Norman towns in Wales, Chepstow's fortifications included not only a castle but a town wall. Substantial remains of this are still visible, curving around from the castle to join the Wye, whose loop here protected the northern and eastern flanks. This late-thirteenth-century wall has traditionally been known as the Port Wall, a name that reflects the town's former importance as a haven. Until the Act of Union in 1536 abolished the Marcher Lordships, Chepstow had enjoyed exemption of toll on all goods destined for foreign trade. Indeed, its wharfs and warehouses remained in use well into the nineteenth century, when Newport and Cardiff, nearer the coalfield, outstripped it.

The town gate, in Bridge Street, once a major obstacle to traffic in and out of South Wales, dates originally from the thirteenth century, and was part of the wall. It was rebuilt in 1524 by the Earl of Worcester, who placed his coat of arms on the façade. The windows and battlements are of later date. From the fourteenth century all cattle and goods brought through this gate for sale in the town had to pay duty to the Marcher Lord of Chepstow. A small local museum is now housed in the upper room.

St Mary's church was formerly part of a Benedictine priory founded by FitzOsbern at the same time as the castle. It has been much restored, leaving the nave and the five-arched west door as the only original Norman work. There are some interesting later memorials, including the grave and epitaph of Henry Marten, removed to the nave from their earlier place in the chancel by a bigoted vicar named Chest, who objected to a regicide lying so close to the altar. The verse on Marten's stone is said to be his own composition.

Of later centuries, there remain some fine old houses, including the Montague Almshouses (1613), and the Powys Almshouses, about a hundred years more recent. The iron road bridge over the Wye dates from 1816, and is one of the earliest in Britain. Brunel's railway bridge, built in 1852, lasted in its original form until 1962, when it was reshaped.

About 2km. south of Chepstow the Bulwarks, a fine hill-fort with multiple ramparts, probably dates from just before the Roman conquest. It is now in danger of engulfment by suburban development. At MATHERN (Matharn), 4km. south-west, an interesting old church is dedicated to the sixth-century saint Tewdric, a Celtic king who ended his days as a hermit. His supposed coffin was reburied in the chancel in 1610. Nearby, the Bishop's Palace, now a private house, was a residence of the Bishops of Llandaff, who used it from the time of the Glyndwr rebellion (*c.* 1400) up to 1705. It has some medieval and some Tudor features, and a glorious garden. Moynes Court, another old house, near the village, bears the coat of arms of Bishop Godwin, the prelate who was responsible for reburying St Tewdric in Mathern church. It is essentially a seventeenth-century building, though its gatehouse is considerably older.

On the same side of Chepstow, off a minor road that joins Shire Newton and Crick, RUNSTON CHAPEL is a small ruined chapel of the early twelfth century. This is all that remains of a once sizeable medieval village, deserted for some unknown reason, probably economic; traces of it were still visible in the late eighteenth century. To the north are two curious museums: the Imperial Russian Museum and Gallery (open afternoons only) at St Arvan's, and at Wolves Newton (10km. north-west), the Model Farm Folk Collection.

Cilgerran Dyfed 8D2

Early tourists approached Cilgerran Castle not through the long main street of the quiet old-fashioned village, but by river, from Cardigan. Out of the Teifi Gorge the ruins rise dramatically on a high bluff; from this angle painters such as Turner and Richard Wilson captured its extraordinary visual excitement.

The original castle must have been raised in the early

years of the Norman conquest of Wales and would have been a simple motte-and-bailey construction. The present inner ward probably corresponds to the old motte and the outer to the bailey. What remains today dates mostly from the thirteenth century: two great round towers built by the son of William Marshall (another William), Earl of Pembroke, and parts of the curtain wall and a rectangular tower of slightly later date. There are remains of a lime-kiln, but no well, so that there must have been easy access to the river. The local slate, grey with traces of rust-colour, cut in small slices, gives the castle its particular character. There are some fine round-headed Norman doorways and windows.

Despite its apparently strong position above the river, the castle was batted back and forth between Welsh and Normans. The Lord Rhys took it, with Cardigan Castle, from the Normans in 1164; William Marshall of Pembroke, Strongbow's son-in-law, retrieved it for them in 1204. Llewellyn the Great used Cilgerran in 1215 as a base from which to reconquer most of Pembrokeshire, summoning, as a result of this victory, a Council of all Wales, at Aberystwyth. The second William Marshall took the castle again for the Normans in 1223, and built the present towers and parts of the wall. By 1326 Cilgerran, like Conwy and other Welsh castles, had been allowed to fall into ruin. Later that century, fearing a French invasion and possibly also a Welsh rising, Edward III ordered Cilgerran, Pembroke, and Tenby refortified. The French did not come to Wales, but Glyndwr's revolt did, and the castle was once more briefly in Welsh hands (1405).

Cilgerran was occupied from the Tudor period by the Vaughan family, who had received it from Henry VII for services rendered. Fortified residences were now giving way to comfortable manor-houses; like many another Elizabethan and Jacobean family with wealth and position, the Vaughans deserted their castle, early in the seventeenth century, for a new residence in the neighbourhood. Unlike Pembroke, Cilgerran seems to have played no part in the Civil War.

Cilgerran churchyard has a sixth-century Latin and Ogham inscribed stone to the memory of Trenegussus, son of Macutrenus. There are coracle races on the Teifi in mid August (for coracles, *see* Cenarth).

Clyro (Cleirwy)　Powys　7G3
An extensive Roman military station at Clyro served as a base for the legions' expeditions into Wales, where they hoped to find valuable minerals. (A recent archaeological handbook warns that visitors to the site are not very welcome.) Not very much remains of the Norman castle built by William de Breos. Apart from its own quiet beauty, Clyro's chief interest is for literary pilgrims or anyone who has read the diaries of Francis Kilvert, curate here from 1865 to 1872. Kilvert's delight in nature, his sense of humour, his eminently Victorian

sensibility (he loved not only his job, which he did well, but good food, young ladies and little girls, railway travel and sight-seeing, croquet and ice-skating), and, not least, his vivid and personal style, all these make his *Diary* one of the minor classics of his time:

> Sunday, 14 April. The beauty of the view, the first view of the village, coming down by the Brooms this evening was indescribable. The brilliant golden poplar spires shone in the evening light like flames against the dark hill side of the Old Forest and the blossoming fruit trees, the torch trees of Paradise blazed with a transparent green and white lustre up the dingle in the setting sunlight. The village is in a blaze of fruit blossom. Clyro is at its loveliest. What more can be said?

Kilvert is of more than just literary interest. He records, for example, that the last Welsh-speaking parishioner died in the early 1870s; he describes the custom of dressing graves with flowers on Easter Eve, and on May Eve that of putting birch and 'wittan' over the door to keep out witches.

LLOWES, a village about 3km. south of Clyro, was a favourite haunt of Kilvert's. In the churchyard, the Great Cross of St Meilig is formed of two crosses, one dating from the seventh century, and one from the eleventh.

Coity (Coety)　Mid Glam.　11E3
Coity Castle was one of a rash of castles built to defend the fertile Vale of Glamorgan from the envy of neighbours and the wrath of its earlier rulers. The land was acquired by Payn (Payen, i.e. 'pagan') de Turberville, one of the followers of Robert FitzHamon, the Norman conqueror of Glamorgan. According to Welsh tradition, Morgan, the aged Lord of Coity, came out to meet the invader, his daughter in one hand and a sword in the other. Payn chose the heiress and a quiet life, took the land, and built a castle. The oldest surviving buildings – the square keep and polygonal curtain wall, on the edge of the earlier moat – date from the late twelfth century. Later were added east and west gatehouses, residential quarters, and a three-storeyed round tower that jutted out over the moat and provided cross-fire along the curtain. The outer ward was built in the fourteenth century. Further additions were made in Tudor times, the keep enlarged and the high chimneys erected. In Elizabeth's reign the Coity heiress, Barbara Gamage, married, against royal wishes, Robert Sidney, brother of the poet Philip Sidney; their happy marriage and life together at Penshurst Place in Kent were celebrated by Ben Jonson.

To the east of the castle, Coity church is a fine early-fourteenth-century building in Decorated style; the central tower, with its gargoyles, is somewhat later. Each transept has a squint and a piscina with trefoiled head. In the chancel an ancient oak chest with carvings of the Passion is thought to be an example of a portable

Coity Castle: the round tower and the hall

Easter Sepulchre; if so, this is very rare. On the north side of the church are two miniature stone effigies of fourteenth-century Turberville ladies.

Conwil Elvet Dyfed *see* **Carmarthen**

Cowbridge (Y Bont-faen) S. Glam. 11 E4
(*pop.* 1,221)
This is a distinctive small country town, the number of inns and ale-houses along its one, long, main street testifying to its age and importance as a market-centre. Settlement here may date back to the Romans; however, like most ancient Welsh boroughs, Cowbridge was essentially a Norman creation. Part of the fourteenth-century town walls and one gateway still survive, on the south-west side of the town. There is, however, no castle in the town itself. A grammar school for boys was founded in about 1609 by the Stradlings of St Donat's; later that century its administration was transferred to the Principal and Fellows of Jesus College, Oxford (well known for its Welsh connexions). The present school buildings were put up in 1847.

Before the Industrial Revolution, Cowbridge was one of the more important inland towns of South Wales, serving as it did an unusually rich and fertile countryside. At 70 Eastgate it had the first printing press in Glamorgan, set up in 1770 by Rhys Thomas. It also had the county gaol or 'Bridewell', which was converted into the present Town Hall in about 1830.

A plaque in the main street commemorates one of the county's most colourful eccentrics, Edward Williams (1746–1826), who kept a bookshop here. Williams took the bardic name of Iolo Morgannwg, 'Iolo of Glamorgan'. Patriot, radical, and poet, he collected old Welsh manuscripts and legends, enthusiastically inventing what he was unable to discover. His work is thus both genuinely valuable and horribly confusing for later scholars. Iolo's main claim to fame is as one of the moving spirits behind the revival of Welsh national consciousness that took place around the time of the French Revolution; in particular, he was responsible for much of the present ritual of the National *Eisteddfod*. He is buried at Flemingston, his birthplace, about 5km. south-east.

Between Cowbridge and the coast lies the VALE OF GLAMORGAN, not a valley but a coastal plateau, a quiet green landscape whose village names – Boverton, Flemingston, Llanbethery, Llantwit – reflect a mixture of Norman and Welsh influence. LLANBLETHIAN (Llanfleiddan, or Llanbleiddian), 1½km. south-west, is the parish in which Cowbridge lies. Thomas Carlyle, a frequent visitor, described the village as a 'little sleeping cataract of white houses with trees overshadowing and fringing it'. On the hill overlooking the hamlet, the church of St John the Baptist has a high Perpendicular tower. A sepulchral slab of the early fourteenth century has an inscription in Norman–French, to the wife of 'Walter Torig'. The castle, popularly but wrongly known as St Quintin's (for the St Quintin family had left the region by this time), stands at a loop in the Thaw River. It was built (and never finished) by Gilbert de Clare, who was killed at Bannockburn in 1314. Parts of the walls and a fine three-storey gatehouse remain. An earlier castle is thought to have stood on the opposite side of the valley, on Llanblethian Hill, which has traces of an Iron Age hill-fort.

LLANDOUGH (Llandŵ), about 3km. south of Cowbridge, should not be confused with the Llandough near Cardiff. Here the ancient, restored church of St Docco, or Dochau, contains an early memorial brass (rare in Glamorgan); on the south wall of the nave a curious tablet commemorates the Bassett family, three children of which all died within a month in 1713. The couplet reads: 'William died first, and lies outward of all, / John in the middle, and Friswith next the wall'. The church lies in the grounds of the great house, Llandough Castle, a modern mansion in pseudo-medieval style.

PEN-LLIN CASTLE, 3km. north-west, can be seen on the right of the A48 as you go west towards Bridgend. The original castle was destroyed by Owain Glyndwr in the early-fifteenth-century rebellion; fragments of it now form part of the stable-block. Pen-llin church, standing dutifully at the castle-gate, is 'modern'. The old parish church is at LLANFRYNACH, nearly 3km. south. On the old main road, and near the entrance to the lane that leads to this ancient and simple church, may be seen a coffin-stile; this one and another at the lower end of the field (where field meets churchyard) are thought to be the only examples in Glamorgan. A block of stone set between two stiles held the coffin while the bearers clambered over into the field.

ST HILARY, 3km. south-west of Cowbridge, is a charming hamlet of thatched cottages looking out over the Vale towards the coast. The church is Norman, its corbelled and embattled tower enlivened by small gargoyles. There are effigies, monuments, and memorial tablets within, some belonging to the Basset family of BEAUPRE CASTLE. The ruins of the latter, also known as Old Beaupre (pron. 'Bewper'), lie about 1½km. from St Hilary and can be reached by climbing a stile near the bridge at Howe Mill on the St Athan–Cowbridge road, then crossing the fields by way of a track along the banks of the Thaw. The castle is a rare example of Renaissance architecture in South Wales. A medieval manor-house was remodelled in the sixteenth century by its owner, Richard Basset. The gatehouse, dated 1586, is a delightful fusion of Tudor Gothic and early Italian Renaissance. In the courtyard Basset added, in 1600, an elaborate three-storey porch, which uses the three Orders (Doric, Ionic, and Corinthian) to set off the family escutcheon.

Coychurch (Llangrallo) Mid Glam. 11E3
Once a separate village, and now joined to the outskirts of Bridgend by a sizeable industrial estate, Coychurch has one of the finest churches in this part of the country. A late-thirteenth-century building, and cruciform in plan, it is dedicated to St Crallo. Only the tower, which fell in 1877, and the south transept, damaged in its fall, have been rebuilt. The west front is simple and pleasing; the interior is spacious, with a fine fifteenth-century wagon-roof bearing carvings. Masons' marks are visible on the fine arcading of the nave. The chancel has a piscina and handsome sedilia. There are late-medieval effigies, including one of a Coychurch parson who died in 1591. The font, a plain octagonal bowl, dates from the thirteenth century. In the churchyard is buried Thomas Richards, a curate of Coychurch and compiler of an important Welsh–English dictionary (1753). Two ancient crosses, worn and damaged, are thought to

commemorate 'Ebisar', whose name also occurs on an eighteenth-century stone at Llantwit Major.

Craig-y-ciliau Powys see **Crickhowell**

Craig-y-nos Powys 6D6
Just out of reach of the industrial towns and villages that straggle up the valleys, Craig-y-nos Castle is a Victorian romance. First built in 1842, it was bought in 1878 by Adelina Patti, the world-famous and fabulously wealthy soprano. Madame Patti had recently married the Italian tenor Nicolini, her second husband. In search of happiness in a romantic setting, she lavished money and enthusiasm on her 'castle', adding a winter garden, an aviary, and a miniature theatre modelled on Drury Lane. After every concert tour she returned to Craig-y-nos, travelling by special train and alighting at Penwyllt station, where her private waiting-room was lavishly furnished. Nicolini died in 1899, and Patti married a Swedish baron, at Brecon. When she died, in 1919 at the castle (she was buried in Paris), Baron Cederström sold the property. It later became a sanatorium. Its future is at present uncertain; the grounds may be opened to the public as a Country Park. The Winter Gardens were dismantled and re-erected in Swansea's Victoria Park as the Patti Pavilion. The theatre, which seats 200, was reopened in 1963, and has a summer season of opera provided by a local semi-amateur group.

A little further up the valley a spectacular tourist attraction was unknown to earlier travellers. The DAN-YR-OGOF caves honeycomb the limestone rock, which lies in a narrow band between the coalfield on one side and the Old Red Sandstone of the Beacons on the other. These are among the finest and largest caverns in Britain. They were not seriously explored until the late 1930s and not opened to the public until the '60s. There are huge, chilling underground lakes, natural bridges, impressive stalagmites and stalactites, all now lit by electricity. The caves are still being explored by experienced clubs, and new finds may yet be expected.

Turning southwards from Craig-y-nos, a minor road at Pen-y-cae leads to COELBREN and the magnificent Henryd Waterfall. The Nant Llech plunges 27m. into the Tawe, over a cliff whose strata show a thin seam of coal. This is NT property, and a convenient car park has been provided. Between Coelbren and Banwen (near Onllwyn) there stood a Roman camp (Y Gaer); the Roman road north-east towards Brecon Gaer (another Roman station) can still be traced. It is as straight as the Romans could make it on such a terrain.

Crickhowell (Crucywel) Powys 7G6
Crickhowell, on the banks of the Usk, is a small market-town that has remained largely content with its size and situation. The Usk Valley provides its main lines of communication. The Norman Bernard of Newmarch

passed through the valley on his conquest of the King-dom of Brycheiniog; he gave this site to a de Turberville, who built a castle. Fragmentary remains of this – it was destroyed by Owain Glyndwr in the early fifteenth century – can be seen near the Post Office, and there are good views from its 'tump'. There is another, perhaps earlier, castle mound visible at Maescelyn (1½km. north-west).

The church of St Edmund King and Martyr was founded early in the fourteenth century. It was exten-sively repaired in the eighteenth when the two side aisles were taken down. In 1830 a new south aisle provided an extra 150 sittings. Porth Mawr ('Great Gate'), on the west side of the town, is a fifteenth-century castellated gateway, all that remains of a long-vanished Tudor mansion that belonged to the Herbert family. Herbert memorials may be seen in the church.

The Usk at Crickhowell has long attracted the angler. Salmon and brown trout are plentiful, though here as elsewhere permits are required. One of the town's most attractive features is the thirteen-arched medieval stone bridge (restored in 1818), with its cutwaters, its pre-carious greenery, and the shallow weir below.

In earlier times Crickhowell was a flannel-manufacturing town: Smollett in *Humphrey Clinker* makes reference to Crickhowell flannel. But this had already died out by the 1830s. Shoe-making was also once a local industry. At present handtools and furniture are made, and the town is growing as a dormitory. Its population in 1831 was just over a thousand, and it has taken over a century to double that.

Outside the town, on the A40 going north-west, Gwernvale Manor (*c.* 1800) was the birthplace of Sir George Everest, the Surveyor General of India who gave his name to the mountain. It is now a hotel. One and a half km. in the opposite direction, Cwrt-y-gollen has the barracks of the Welsh Brigade, whose museum is open to the public several days a week. The famous regimental goat, Taffy, is on show.

The mountains around Crickhowell provide excellent walking and riding. Table Mountain, its characteristic shape clearly visible from the town, has on its sliced-off summit the traces of an Iron Age fort. Pen-cerrig-calch (690m.) is an isolated outlier, the only one north of the Usk, of the carboniferous limestone that forms the narrow ridge of cliffs and crags to the south. Its Welsh name records this: *pen* (head or peak), *cerrig* (stones, rock), *calch* (chalk, limestone).

Numerous small villages nearby repay exploration. South of the town and almost adjoining it, LLANGATTOCK (Llangatwg) climbs up the hillside, with its cottages built to house quarrymen and weavers. Sixteenth-century St Cadoc's church has been restored; inside may be seen the old village stocks and whipping-post. The old tramroad, built in 1816 to transport limestone from the quarries to Brynmawr and the Nantyglo iron works, now makes a good straight track for walking the Llan-gattock Mountain. The Newport–Brecon canal, con-structed between 1797 and 1812, also for the iron works, and recently cleaned and restored, runs through Llangattock; there are fine walks along the towpath.

Some of the cliffs and old quarries of Llangattock Mountain have been set aside as a National Nature Reserve, CRAIG-Y-CILIAU. Here the steepness of the terrain protects even from Welsh sheep a rich limestone vegetation, and in particular several rare species of whitebeam that grow nowhere else outside the Brecon Beacons Park. The narrow limestone belt (here only a few km. wide), which terminates in the Llangattock cliffs, is particularly rich in caverns and in sink- or swallow-holes. One of these caves is known as Eglwys Faen ('stone church'), and may have served as a refuge for those fleeing from religious persecution. Another, Agen Allwedd, an exceptionally long cave, has over 14km. of passageways.

LLANGYNIDR, a little further west, also has its moun-tain, and a splendid stone bridge (*c.* 1600) over the Usk, which here rejoins the canal. A minor road from the village climbs up and over Llangynidr Mountain to meet the Heads of the Valleys road near Ebbw Vale. In the Rhiangoll Valley, on the Talgarth road, CWM-DU has a large parish church with a fourteenth-century tower. During some long-past rebuilding a sixth-century burial stone, inscribed with Latin, was reset into one of the buttresses of the south wall. On the hills above are traces of a Celtic camp, and a Roman one at Pen-y-gaer. LLANBEDR, at the foot of Pen-cerrig-calch, at the mouth of the narrow and unspoiled Grwyne Fach Valley, is another attractive village with old cottages and a restored fourteenth-century church.

Dale   Dyfed   *see* **Milford Haven**

Dan-yr-Ogof   Powys   *see* **Craig-y-nos**

Defynnog and **Sennybridge** (Pontsenni)
Powys   7E5
Defynnog was a market centre until Sennybridge, better served by road and railway, outpaced it. The church has a font with a Runic inscription (unique in Wales) and a fifth- or sixth-century Latin- and Ogham-inscribed stone built into the base of the tower.

Sennybridge now has the markets and a military camp, which practises its skills on the Mynydd Epynt firing range. In the late Middle Ages Sennybridge had a fortress, Castell Ddu ('Black Castle'), where offenders against the hunting laws were imprisoned by the Constable of Fforest Fawr. Fforest Fawr was the Great Forest of Brecknock, an immense expanse of wild upland to the south of the town. Never fully wooded, the title 'Forest' denoted, here as elsewhere, a royal hunting-ground. Richard III reduced to some extent the severity of the game laws. After the Middle Ages the Crown farmed out the land, but its 16,000ha. remained un-

The Mynach River nr Devil's Bridge

Devil's Bridge (Pontarfynach) Dyfed 6C1
The Mynach River cascades down a wooded gorge in a series of magnificent falls; this, plus the curiosity of the three bridges, has made the spot one of the most visited in Wales. The summer crowds and the turnstile into which you put your fee to see the falls make it difficult nowadays to react like Wordsworth, who felt, here, that the world had only just been created. Perhaps the best plan is to accept that this is a tourist sight, and that one is, after all, a tourist. Ideally, the trip to Devil's Bridge should be made from Aberystwyth on the Vale of Rheidol narrow-gauge steam railway, another unashamedly enjoyable tourist activity.

Precipitous steps and paths lead down one side of the oak-, fir-, and beech-wooded ravine and up the other. (Halfway down a notice warns the elderly and infirm that they might prefer to give up at this point.) From a number of places the spectacular waterfall, the Cauldron, and the three bridges appear; seasons and rainfall vary the treecover, the foliage, and the force of the cascade. The bridges are built each directly above one another. The lowest, a simple pointed arch of stone, is medieval, probably the work of the monks of Strata Florida. Legend has it that the Devil, hearing a bridge was needed, offered to provide one, in return for the first living thing to cross the finished structure. As usual in such tales, he is outwitted: the first creature sent across is a small dog. Above this old bridge, a second, with a flatter arch, was constructed in 1753, at a time when lead-mining still flourished in this part of Cardiganshire. The present road bridge dates from 1901.

A leaflet on such topics as the natural history and geology of the gorge can be obtained from a roadside kiosk or from the Hafod Arms Hotel, which owns the falls and maintains the footpaths. This hotel, a large Swiss chalet, was built in the 1830s by the fourth Duke of Newcastle, who bought the Hafod Estate (*see* Pontrhydygroes) and spent a considerable amount of money and effort on agricultural improvement.

Disserth Powys *see* **Newbridge-on-Wye**

Ebbw Vale (Glynebwy) Gwent 11F1
(*pop.* 26,049)
Ebbw Vale was still a village in the last decade of the eighteenth century, when its first iron-works was opened. The town grew up like its valley neighbours, unplanned, around the iron-works and coal-mines, which attracted large numbers of Welsh and foreign migrants. Its enormous expansion, in the mid nineteenth century, came with the growing need for iron on the new railway networks of Europe and North America. Coal was also easily available. By the turn of the century the giant Ebbw Vale Steel, Iron and Coal Company was not only making steel, but manufacturing its own plant, supplying its own limestone, making coke from its own coal, and importing iron ore from Spain and

enclosed until 1815. Today Fforest Fawr is a paradise for walkers, naturalists, and geologists. Motorists can gain some idea of its attractions by taking the minor road via Heol Senni, which comes out into the magnificent upper Neath Valley.

On the Brecon road, Pen-pont is a seventeeth-century house with a classical façade added in 1813. The Usk Valley estate was carefully landscaped by the Williams family in the eighteenth century; the fine larch plantations are among the oldest in the country. This family was also responsible for the restoration of Pen-pont church, undertaken by Gilbert Scott in 1865. It has a round tower, and an organ that was brought from Brighton Pavilion.

Norway, where it controlled supplies. The importation of iron ore was in fact to be the key to its decline. Local ore contained too much phosphorus, nor could it sustain the immensely increased demand. The steel industry of South Wales was moving inexorably to the coastal belt, where imported iron ore could be worked without need for further transport. By the time of the Depression the Ebbw Vale steelworks was derelict. In 1935 it was revived, as a deliberate act of social policy, by the British government. Today the town's fortunes still depend very largely on the steel industry's precarious future.

Population has declined since the 'twenties throughout the Ebbw Valley. Coal mines have closed, and some new and more diversified factory development has taken place. The landscape, despoiled and deforested by industry, is gradually taking on a more cared-for look; it is perhaps churlish to complain that conifers, more 'economical', have replaced the native oak.

Elan Valley Powys *see* **Rhayader**

Ewenny Mid Glam. 11E4

The priory church of Ewenny is one of the finest relics of the Normans in Wales and one of the best examples of a fortified monastery in Britain. It stands, indeed, as a visual symbol of the dual domination of the invader, temporal and spiritual, castle and church. Its battlements are also a reminder that the Benedictines (unlike the Cistercians, who succeeded in integrating with the Welsh) remained alien to the native population; English or French, they were foreigners, and could expect hostility.

The abbey church survived the Dissolution to serve the parish; there remain also considerable stretches (partly restored) of the precinct walls and defences. The conventual buildings, however, were sold by Henry VIII to Sir Edward Carne, who was the last British ambassador to the Holy See before Henry broke off relations with the Papacy. Carne built an imposing mansion within the abbey walls, which remained in his family until, in 1700, it passed to the Turbervilles.

The style of the church is very early Norman, and it may have been founded by William de Londres, the first Norman lord of Ogmore, who was dead by 1126. His son Maurice gave the priory to the Abbey of St Peter in Gloucester in 1141. A sepulchral slab, probably of the late thirteenth century, commemorates Maurice in Norman–French: '*Ici gist Morice de Lundres le fundur Deu li rende son labur Am.*' ('Here lies Maurice de Londres the founder; God reward him for his services, Amen'). The original church was cruciform in plan; its single-aisled nave has the rounded arches and massive circular piers of the early-Norman period. The nave, used by the villagers, was originally separated from the eastern end, where the monks worshipped, by a $2\frac{1}{2}$m.-high stone wall. Beyond this, the crossing, the vaulted chancel, and the

south transept (the north transept was demolished in the early nineteenth century) are more elaborate and slightly later in date. There are a hagioscope (squint) and a fine double piscina, and a fourteenth-century wooden screen. The north porch is Tudor. The church contains, besides the grave-slab of Maurice de Londres, a number of interesting effigies and memorial tablets. The outside wall of the south transept bears a 'Mass Dial', four radiating lines that probably represent the four main daily offices: *prime*, or first hour, *terce*, or third hour, *sext*, which was midday, and *none*, the ninth hour.

The fortifications include the church tower itself, with its stepped battlements, and a precinct wall with two gateways and stout towers. These date from the late twelfth or early thirteenth century. A wall-walk can be reached from the tower. It is not clear whether these features were seriously intended for defence or merely as a sort of warning, since according to one authority the eastern and most vulnerable side remained unfortified throughout the Middle Ages.

Ewenny Potteries were opened in the seventeenth century, and the descendants of the original potters can still be seen at work. Ewenny ware was widely known in the seventeenth, eighteenth, and nineteenth centuries, when the village lay on the old coaching road into Bridgend.

Fishguard (Abergwaun) Dyfed 8B2/C2
(*pop.* – with Goodwick – 4,933)

Sheltered by the two massive headlands of Pen Caer and Dinas 'Island', Fishguard is in reality three settlements. At Goodwick (the name means 'good harbour') the London railway meets the sea. Here Fishguard Harbour with its 600m.-long breakwater was completed in 1906 as a port of call for the great Atlantic liners. At present it serves mainly the Irish ferries to Rosslare; Atlantic liners are too big for it, and in any case are a dying breed. Behind Goodwick, and up a fierce hill, an ugly modern housing estate on the headland is known as Harbour Village. There are magnificent views from the top.

Opposite the railway terminal, up another steep hill, Fishguard itself is an attractive small town with narrow streets and ancient inns. In one of these, the Royal Oak, was signed the treaty between the British and the French that ended the pathetic skirmish known grandly as the 'last foreign invasion of Britain'. At Carreg Wastad, an unsuitable spot on the western headland (but they had been unable to make Bristol), and at an unsuitable time of year (22 February 1797), an Irish–American named Tate landed a force of 1,200 French composed mostly of convicts. The French had been led to believe that the disaffected Welsh would join them to march on London. Instead, Lord Cawdor rushed to the rescue with the Fishguard Fencibles and the Castlemartin Yeomanry. The French, apparently half-starved, were well on the way to being defeated by the fat pigs and poultry from the farms they looted. They were further abashed by the sight of 'troops' to the number of several thousand: a few hundred local militia, in fact, plus, as tradition has it, a large crowd of Welsh women in red shawls and tall black hats. Jemima Nicholas, a formidable character who is reputed to have used a pitchfork to round up several Frenchmen single-handed, is buried in St Mary's churchyard.

If one continues through the main street another steep hill winds down to the delightful harbour village of Lower Fishguard. At this point the Gwaun River enters the sea out of its mysterious valley. Lower Fishguard has so far remained remarkably unspoiled. Once a flourishing herring and pilchard fishery, it now caters mainly for yachtsmen and tourists. On the cliff to the east a short climb along the beginnings of the Pembrokeshire Coastal Path brings you to the remains of a Napoleonic fort, complete with cannon.

Lower Fishguard has literary and historical connexions through the Fenton family. Samuel Fenton built the pier that served the pilchard fishery. His niece Mary was lamed by a broadside fired by Paul Jones who arrived in the harbour at the time of the American War of Independence and demanded a ransom of 500 guineas. Mary's brother, Richard (born 1747), was the author of *A Historical Tour through Pembrokeshire* (1811), *Memoirs of an old Whig* (1815), and other books; he was a friend of Goldsmith, Garrick, Burke, and Dr Johnson. Fenton's attractive eighteenth-century house, Glyn-y-mel, is now a guest-house and is being restored to its original elegant state. In the grounds can be seen a number of Latin-verse epitaphs to a series of favourite dogs.

Fenton and his French wife were involved in contemporary politics as well as in literary and antiquarian pursuits. In the early nineteenth century rural Wales was torn by struggles against the enclosure of common land by landlords who were often English and absentees. Fenton had been sued by the Crown for encroaching on a Crown manor. When the Crown sold the land to a private buyer the case was dropped; however, a mob of five or six hundred gathered to destroy the new landlord's newly built houses. On 27 August 1824

A painting in Carmarthen Museum showing the surrender of the French 'invasion' force nr Fishguard in 1797

Mrs Fenton, now a widow, was given the privilege of removing the first stone from the new cottages.

Fishguard's magnificent coast will please the historian as much as the naturalist. To the east, Strumble Head is a huge cliff of volcanic lava 1,080m. thick. At LLANWNDA numerous prehistoric remains cannot always easily be distinguished from the immense grey boulders left by glaciation. There are, however, three or more burial chambers, and two standing stones, while Garn Fawr is a great hill-fort with traces of hut-dwellings. Llanwnda church has early cross-inscribed stones incorporated into its walls. TREFASSER (Trefaser) is reputed to have been the birthplace of Bishop Asser, one of King Alfred's closest counsellors and author of an important chronicle of his reign.

West of Fishguard, the GWAUN VALLEY exercises a special fascination. It is one of the few places in Wales where Old New Year's Eve (*Hen Galan*) is still celebrated on 12 January, with singing and home-made beer. Llanychaer has an old bridge and mill-wheel; Pontfaen church has ancient inscribed stones. At Llanllawer the 'Field of the Dead' (*Parc y Meirw*) is the largest megalithic alignment in Wales, 42m. long, with four out of eight pillars still standing. The Gwaun Valley has a wealth of wild flowers and birds: buzzards, owls, kestrels, warblers, dippers, and kingfishers. Behind the valley rise the rounded heights of the Preseli Mountains.

Flat Holm   S. Glam.   *see* **Penarth**

Furnace   Dyfed   2D5
Furnace has not only a spectacular waterfall but also, as the name implies, a unique industrial monument, which is in the process of being restored. The site, on the River Einion and close to the navigable Dovey Estuary, had already been occupied in the seventeenth century by furnaces smelting silver. In 1755 Jonathan Kendall, a forge-owner from Staffordshire (whose family were later involved in the development of the iron industry in Breconshire and Monmouthshire), set up a blast furnace for iron ore. The fuel was local timber, and water-power came from the river via a water-wheel. The iron ore was imported from Cumberland, and presumably landed at a nearby point on the Dovey.

Kendall's enterprise is a fine example of an eighteenth-century charcoal-fired blast furnace set in its original rural environment. The square chimney stack has disappeared, but traces of the cast house (into which the molten iron flowed) can be seen in the west wall. The furnace building itself was on two levels; the Gothic archway on the upper floor was the charging-hole for the iron ore and the charcoal. Furnaces were commonly built into a sloping bank, in order to make charging easier. The lower level would have housed the bellows that provided the blast.

When Kendall began his operations at Dovey, iron was already being produced more efficiently in South Wales using coke instead of charcoal. The Dovey furnace thus went out of use about 1813, and the building and its water-wheel were adapted for sawing pit-props and later for grinding bone-meal for fertilizer. It is now hoped to open the buildings to the public when preservation work has been completed. The land is owned by the Royal Society for the Protection of Birds.

From Furnace a minor road turns off east into CWM EINION (Cwm Einon), 'Artists' Valley', with magnificent hill and forest scenery, picnic sites, nature trail, and, further on, Anglers' Retreat, a remote fishing lodge set near lakes and falls. Care should be taken when walking in this boggy country.

Gelligaer   Mid Glam.   11F2   (*pop.* 33,670)
Gelligaer is a colliery town between Quakers' Yard (named after an early Friends' burial ground) and Blackwood. The Roman road that ran from Cardiff to Brecon Gaer passed this spot, and here the Romans built a fort capable of housing a cohort of 500 foot. Roughly 120m. square, the fort would have enclosed within its walls a headquarters, commandant's house, construction shop, and granaries, as well as accommodation for the infantrymen. Gelligaer is in fact a classic example of a Trajanic fort of this dimension. Unfortunately, the stone walls have entirely disappeared, and only the mound of the ramparts can still be traced (north of the B4254 and just west of the church). Further north, on Gelligaer Common, five Roman practice camps are known, two of which can still be traced with the help of a large-scale map. Practice camps were small fortifications 30 or 60m. square, made, literally, to give the soldiers practice in fort-building. Walls, which are easily made, are therefore short, and attention is focused on corners and defensive gateways.

Gelligaer Common also has a number of ancient tumuli and stone cairns. At Carn Bugail, near Bedlinog, Dark Age house-sites have been discovered.

Glasbury   (Y Clas-ar-Wy)   Powys   7F4
Glasbury is a pleasant, small place in the Wye Valley and a good centre for walking, pony-trekking, and fishing. Its Roman camp was discovered in recent years, on a spur of high ground near the old railway line. Clyro Camp, clearly part of the same strategic advance, is visible from the site.

The name Glasbury is an Anglicization of the Welsh *Clas-ar-Wy*, which indicates that a Celtic monastery (*clas*) or religious community once stood here. Later, the settlement was a Norman village; its castle and church stood on the Radnorshire bank of the river. In the sixteenth century the Wye's course shifted, so that the old church was then in Brecknockshire. The present church replaced it in 1838. Glasbury today has more the air of an English village than of a Welsh one. Maes-yr-onen chapel (1696) is an early Nonconformist meeting-house with a largely unspoiled interior.

A little further up the river, at ABERLLYNFI, or Three Cocks (as the old inn is called), is Gwernyfed Old Hall, a fine early-seventeenth-century house with a twelfth-century doorway and a celebrated avenue of walnuts. A school now occupies the grounds. LLYSWEN, beyond this, and at a great loop in the Wye, was the site of a Welsh princely palace and later a Norman castle. The present great house, Llangoed Castle, is an early-seventeenth-century building and stands in park-land about 3km. outside the village.

Glascwm Powys *see* **Aberedw**

Gower Peninsula (Gŵyr) W. Glam. 10A2/B3
Geographically, Gower is a peninsula; in less literal terms, it is more like an island. Like Pembrokeshire, which it resembles in more ways than one, many of its medieval settlers were English, possibly Flemings, but certainly West Country men, whose dialect, especially in south Gower, survived until recent times. Cut off from the rest of South Wales by the wide marshy Loughor Estuary and the scarp of Pennant sandstone that begins at Swansea, Gower has escaped railways, towns, and all industry except cockle-fishing. The south, crowded in summer, has a magnificent coastline of limestone cliffs, sandy, sloping beaches, and caves where prehistoric men and animals have left traces. Inland is farmland, and small, ancient villages; their primitive, uncompromising churches have low, embattled towers, a reminder of the days of sea-raiders. On the northern side of Cefn Bryn, the narrow ridge that forms a sort of backbone, heathery moorland slopes down to marshes and 'burrows' at the edge of the estuary. Swansea has spread into the south-east corner round to Caswell Bay, and inland to Killay and Dunvant, but most of Gower, scheduled as an Area of Outstanding Natural Beauty, is protected by the NT and by the Gower Society (Royal Institution, Swansea), which publishes a comprehensive guide. To anyone who thinks of South Wales east of Llanelli and south of the Beacons as one huge industrial disaster area, Gower will come as an enormous and rewarding surprise.

From Mumbles (*see* Swansea) cliff-paths follow the coast all the way round to Worms Head. Not all the beaches are accessible by car. Directly behind the Mumbles, Bracelet Bay and Limeslade Bay are two small, popular, sandy coves. Langland Bay, a wider stretch of sand, has an imposing hotel built by the iron-masters of Merthyr as a seaside villa on a large scale. Caswell is another sophisticated beach, with hotels and restaurants; its pine-trees, sloping limestone cliffs, and firm sands preserve its character. From Caswell a short cliff-walk leads west to Brandy Cove (the name is self-explanatory) and to Pwll-du. There, beneath Pwll-du Head, a stream emerges from the sands; it runs underground near the village of BISHOPSTON, forming a beautifully wooded 'dry valley'. (This, like most of the

coastline, is NT property.) Bishopston itself has a small, grey church with some Norman features, including a font. 'Old Castle', marked on large-scale maps to the north of the village, is the earthwork remains of a prehistoric camp; there is another behind Pwll-du Head.

Between Pwll-du and Oxwich Bay the sloping limestone cliffs contain two important caves, which can be reached by some cautious scrambling. Bacon Hole and the larger Minchin Hole have both yielded bones of long-extinct animals – mammoth and woolly rhinoceros among them – and the pottery and bone tools of prehistoric man.

Three Cliffs Bay is the rocky corner of Oxwich Bay where Pennard Pill enters the sea. On both banks of this stream sand has encroached since early times, sometimes overwhelming, sometimes shifting to reveal the evidence of former settlements. On the east side of the Pill is PENNARD BURROWS, where the old church has been excavated from the sand. The 'new', medieval church was built about $1\frac{1}{2}$km. east and on much higher ground; it contains an eighteenth-century barrel-organ. Pennard Castle, in ruins, and less than a km. from the shore, also shows the sands at work. There are remains of curtain wall, gateway, round towers, and domestic buildings, dating from the late thirteenth or early fourteenth century; on the windward side the dunes confront the castle at ever closer quarters. (Pennard Castle can also be reached from Parkmill.)

On the Pill's opposite bank is another stretch of dunes, PENMAEN BURROWS, under which lies the vanished medieval village bearing the unusual and puzzling name of Stedwarlango. A small, primitive church excavated here had fragments of holy vessels still on its altar, suggesting a hasty retreat from the sand. Under the dunes may yet be found other, perhaps earlier, remains. At the point where Penmaen Burrows meets Three Cliffs Bay is a fine prehistoric promontory fort with trenches and dykes and the traces of stone hut foundations. About $1\frac{1}{2}$km. west of the buried church a Neolithic chambered tomb has been revealed in the sand.

Inland from Three Cliffs, PARKMILL has some recent development and some quiet corners. The watermill may still be working. A small road leads off from here to PARC-LE-BREOS (Park le Bruce), 800m. north-west. The name refers to the 200-ha. deer park enclosed in the thirteenth century by the Norman William de Breos; the main attraction now, however, is the fine Neolithic chambered tomb, one of the best preserved in the country. A cairn of about 20m. length originally covered a central passage and four side-chambers where the remains of at least twenty bodies were found. Like Tinkinswood and St Lythan's, in the Vale of Glamorgan, Parc-le-Breos is an example of the Cotswold–Severn type of cairn, one of the features of which is the rounded 'horns' flanking the forecourt.

Not far from here, at Trinity Well in Ilston Cwm, a

Three Cliffs Bay, Gower

modern memorial commemorates the first Baptist congregation in Wales, founded in 1649 by John Myles, who in 1660 led his fellow worshippers to New England where they founded a new Swansea in Massachusetts. (Brown University, Providence, R.I., has the church records, which show that members came from as far afield as Llandeilo and Margam.) ILSTON (Llanilltud Gŵyr) itself, on the edge of Fairwood Common, has a small, heavily-defensive church with typical saddle-back roof. It is dedicated to St Illtud, whence the village name, a characteristic fusion of Welsh and English elements. In the thirteenth century Ilston church was given by William de Breos to the Knights of St John of Jerusalem.

Beyond Three Cliffs is the wide, sandy curve of OXWICH BAY. In summer a Countryside Centre for information on Gower and on its Nature Reserves (of which Oxwich is one) is set up in the capacious car park. At this western end of the bay, Oxwich church stands on a rocky ledge near the sea. Its small chancel contains sculptured Delamere tombs. Oxwich 'Castle', on a hill above the village, was a Tudor mansion built by Sir Rice Mansel of Penrice, in 1541. Partly a farmhouse, Oxwich Castle has been restored. The gateway bears the Mansel crest; there is a large, round, stone pigeon-house (or 'culver-house', in Gower dialect – Latin *columbarium*).

The Mansels came to Oxwich from PENRICE (Pen-rhys), about 2km. north. The medieval castle they abandoned there can be seen from Oxwich Bay; it stands in ruins on a steep outcrop of rock. Old Penrice Castle was built in the late twelfth century and early thirteenth; there are remains of a gatehouse, of curtain wall with semicircular bastions, and of a round keep-tower, which was three storeys high but had no staircase (ladders and trapdoors were used instead). The Old Castle looks down onto the 'new' Penrice Towers, a late-eighteenth-century house with a Victorian wing. Penrice Park, a highly successful piece of Georgian landscape design, was created at the same time as the new mansion. The Penrice Woods, the meres, the road (which provided a more direct route from castle to church), these have contributed to the present enchant-ment of Oxwich. Penrice church is ancient but restored. According to an old tradition it was connected by secret passage to Sanctuary Farm, nearby, which may be on the site of a medieval nunnery.

PORT EINON, the next bay west, has a quite different atmosphere. The village is an old port and fishing-hamlet, which once traded across the Bristol Channel in limestone and pigment. Tales of piracy and wrecking abound, while a churchyard statue commemorates a lifeboat hero. The bay is wind-blown, in spite of its cliffs, almost treeless, with huge breakers rushing at the white cottages. On the Point, at the base of a reef known as the Skysea, is the ruin of the Salthouse, whose great vaults once held contraband wine.

There is a spectacular cliff-top walk from Port Einon Point along the limestone headlands to Mewslade and Rhosili. A number of fascinating caves can be visited, with due care for the tide and the unreliable rocky paths. Culver Hole, very near Port Einon, is not always easy of access. It is a large natural cavern whose entrance has been almost blocked up, at some unspecified date, by masonry. Inside, it has the appearance of a three-storey stronghold. According to one theory this was merely a medieval pigeon-house (as the name suggests) that be-longed to a now vanished castle at Port Einon. Further along, and about 5km. west of Port Einon, are Paviland Caves, below Golden Top, a hill named for its yellow lichen. Here in 1823, in the Goat's Hole, a headless, red-stained human skeleton came to light. Familiarly dubbed the 'Red Lady of Paviland', it proved, a century later, to be the remains of a youth ritually buried with red ochre about 18,000 years ago, in the Early Stone Age. Stone tools of a variety of Neolithic periods were also found in the cave. Nowadays the Hole is not an easy place to reach; in Stone Age times it looked out not onto the sea (for the Bristol Channel did not yet exist) but over a thickly-wooded plain.

Mewslade, the last of the south-facing beaches, can only be reached by footpath; it is considered by many to be the most attractive of all the bays. There are the remains of Iron Age settlements on Thurba Head and by Lewes Castle.

RHOSILI, 5km. of sands and breakers, must be one of the finest beaches of Europe. Open to sky, winds, and the Atlantic, it is immense and yet enclosed; the Worms Head sits stonily and in shadow at its southern end, Burry Holms, a small bird-island, at its north, and, behind the beach, the dunes and rising moorland of Rhosili Down. The road stops at the village, well above the beach. An old, primitive-looking church, with saddle-back tower, has a late-Norman south doorway, and a 'scratch dial' for the times of Mass. Captain Edgar Evans, a local man who died on Scott's last South Polar expedition, is commemorated inside the church. Be-tween here and the Worms Head are the remains of a medieval open-field or strip-farming system. Worms Head itself is a nature and geological reserve; it can be reached by causeway at low tide.

On the desolate but bracing Rhosili Down, walkers can find the 'Swine-Houses', or Sweyne's Houses, which are two Neolithic chambered tombs of c. 2500 BC. More traces of ancient history – prehistoric defences, frag-ments of medieval or early-Celtic monastic buildings, and a tiny ruined church – can be explored on Burry Holms, the tidal island now given over to seabirds.

From Rhosili beach it is a good walk to LLANGENNITH (Llangynydd), a small village in a hollow beneath Llanmadog Hill. The church is the largest in the Gower, and is dedicated to St Cennydd, whose Celtic monastery here later became a Norman priory. Motorists at Rhosili can only turn back inland and rejoin the winding lanes that cross the peninsula from north to south.

REYNOLDSTON, a village with a green, is almost the central point of Gower. It stands on the slope of Cefn Bryn (186m.), a long hilly ridge of Old Red Sandstone with an outcrop of older, Silurian rock. Over the summit of Cefn Bryn and about 1½km. north-east of Reynoldston is Arthur's Stone, a prominent landmark and focus for legend. Four stones, no longer upright, support a huge capstone of millstone grit, which rises 3m. above the ground. The capstone is split, traditionally by Arthur, or by St David, who recognized that this ancient burial site (it is of course a Neolithic chambered tomb) would attract superstition. Like other standing stones or crom-lechs, it is said to go down to the sea and drink (or bathe) on Midsummer Eve (or All Hallows).

North Gower villages stand back from the sea, for here as elsewhere in South Wales sand has changed the coastline. The limestone cliffs that face the sea directly on the peninsula's south coast here rise well inland; they look out over marsh and burrows to the silted flats of the estuary. Less populated by holiday-makers than the south coast, this is excellent bird country. Whiteford Burrows is a scheduled Nature Reserve.

The villages of North Gower have an air of some isolation but they do not lack charm. LLANMADOG and CHERITON, under Llanmadog Hill, almost run into one another. Llanmadog church is restored Early English with the usual fortified tower. Cheriton church, very prettily situated, contains wood carvings by a local

ABOVE: *Weobley Castle, Gower* BELOW: *Standing stones on Llanrhidian village green*

historian and former Rector of the dual parish, the
Revd J. D. Davies. Davies discovered a huge smugglers'
cellar underneath his own Rectory at Llanmadog.

Between Cheriton and Llanrhidian, in a fine exposed
setting, are the ruins of WEOBLEY CASTLE, less a fortress
than a heavily defensive medieval manor-house. The
hall and kitchen wing date from the late thirteenth
century, the work of Henry Beaumont Earl of Warwick
and one of the Norman rulers of Gower. The solar,
gatehouse, and chapel appear to have been added in the
following century. There is a fascinating variety of
windows and towers.

At LLANRHIDIAN, on the edge of a marsh, St Rhidian's
church is a nineteenth-century rebuilding of an ancient
edifice. A curiously carved stone in the porch bears the
letters A and C and a cross; its purpose is still unknown.
On the village green are two standing-stones and the
old village stocks. Above the church and to the east, Cil
Ifor Top is crowned by an extensive Iron Age fort with
clearly defined terraces.

This final north-east corner of Gower coast is famous
for one thing: cockles. PENCLAWDD, a sprawling settlement from which can be clearly seen the chimneys of
Llanelli across the estuary, is the centre of this industry.
Until quite recently the cockle-women, in bonnets and
flannel dresses, were a familiar sight on the sands,
leading their donkey-carts out at low tide and bending
down to dig below the surface for the cockle-beds.
Cockle-harvesting continues, but in modern dress. Penclawdd cockles can be bought in Swansea Market.

Grassholm Dyfed *see* **Skokholm Island**

Grosmont Gwent 7H5
With its neighbours, Skenfrith and the White Castle,
Grosmont formed the Trilateral, a defensive triangle of
fortresses designed to protect a vulnerable section of the
borderland. Grosmont – the name is Norman–French,
and means 'large hill' – still stands on the border, which
curves around beneath its walls in the shape of the
Monnow River.

Grosmont Castle consists of a single ward protected by
a deep ditch or moat. The remains of the Great Hall, a
two-storey building with ground-floor kitchen and the
hall itself on the first floor, date from about 1210. Much
of the castle was built by Hubert de Burgh, Royal
Justiciar, who held the Three Castles from 1201 to 1243,
and who was reputed to have spent vast sums on their
reconstruction. De Burgh built the curtain wall and
gatehouse; its semicircular towers are typical of
thirteenth-century castle construction. The three-storey
building outside the north curtain wall was added in
about 1330, when the castle was held by the Earl of
Lancaster.

As a royal fortress, Grosmont's history is marked by
two major events. In 1233 Henry III was in residence.
He had come, with his queen and his army, to suppress

the rising in the Marches in which Llewellyn the Great
and the Welsh had joined with his own discontented
barons. The army, encamped outside the walls, had here
no outer ward to protect them (as at White Castle). A
surprise attack led by Richard de Clare, under cover of
darkness, routed the royal force and drove the King and
Queen into ignominious flight. Of more long-term
significance than this episode was the defeat of the Welsh
at Grosmont in 1405. Owain Glyndwr's army besieged
the castle, and Harry of Monmouth (later Henry V)
marched from Hereford to relieve the garrison. Over
800 Welshmen were said to have been slain at this encounter, from which Glyndwr's cause never recovered.

Grosmont today is a charming relic of what was once
an important medieval borough. St Nicholas's church
with its octagonal tower and elegant spire is said to owe
its spacious plan to a French architect engaged by
Queen Eleanor, wife of Henry III. The Town Hall was
rebuilt in 1832, when Grosmont was still a Borough (its
two officers were Mayor and Ale-taster). Inside stands a
fourteenth-century stone. On market-day the first
woman to place her basket on this stone escaped toll.
Two upright stones (of which one remains) outside the
Hall were also 'toll stones', in that any goods laid down
on the road between them were subject to duty.

Gumfreston Dyfed *see* **Tenby**

Gwaun Valley Dyfed *see* **Fishguard**

Halfway Powys 6D4
At this small hamlet on the A40 between Llandovery and
Trecastle a curious roadside memorial is worth looking
out for. It commemorates a stage-coach accident that
occurred here in 1835 after the driver had imbibed more
than he could take of drink. The victims (not seriously
hurt) are recorded on the pillar, with due regard for the
social hierarchy.

Haverfordwest (Hwlffordd) Dyfed 8C4
(*pop.* 9,101)
Haverfordwest is an excellent example of how medieval
towns grew up around a castle when the site of the latter
was well chosen. The east-facing Norman fortress here
was built on a hill, at a point on the Cleddau where the
river could be both forded and used for waterborne
trade. Town life was never part of the indigenous
culture of medieval Wales; at Haverford Henry I settled
Flemings, a people, according to Gerald the Welshman,
'brave and robust, ever most hostile to the Welsh . . .
well versed in commerce and manufactories'. This unpleasant act also helped the little town to flourish.

The three basic elements of medieval life under the
Normans (and which find expression in architecture)
can still be seen at Haverfordwest. Best preserved is the
castle, begun by Gilbert de Clare, Lord of Pembroke, in
the early twelfth century, and completed by William de

Valence in the thirteenth. But not all the townspeople could live within the castle precinct. Haverford's medieval town walls can here and there be traced in a garden or backyard, while the pattern of its streets can be seen from the heights of the castle. At Haverfordwest, sometime around 1200, Robert Fitztancred, one of the town's Norman governors, founded a house of Black (or Augustinian) Canons. The ruins of the Priory of St Mary and St Thomas now stand neglected in a riverside meadow.

Haverford received a series of royal charters, from the twelfth century on, that gave it considerable liberties and privileges. Thanks to a strong local government and to its natural advantages as a port, it became the most important trading centre in Pembrokeshire. In 1545 Henry VIII made the town itself into a separate 'county'; it had already, in 1536, ousted Pembroke as county town. At the same time, its history was not without violence. It suffered in the various revolts of the Welsh, and was burned by both Llewellyn the Great and Owain Glyndwr. During the Civil War the town surrendered to Parliament, but after the Pembroke revolt Cromwell none the less gave orders for the castle to be 'slighted'. This cost the townsfolk £20 4s. 10d. The age of castles was over; Haverford's fortress became successively a gaol, a police station, and a museum.

Three churches and a priory testify to the vitality of Haverford's religious life. The priory was stripped and emptied at the Dissolution. During the same century William Nichol of the town was one of the few martyrs in Wales to go to the stake in the Marian persecutions. A recent memorial at the corner of High Street and Dark Street marks the place where Nichol paid with his life for refusing to return to the Roman Church. Much later, on the site of the present County Hall, George Gambold and John Sparks founded the only Moravian chapel in Wales. Gambold's brother John, who became its minister in 1768, was the author of a Welsh Moravian hymnary.

The town continued to flourish as a trading centre for the surrounding area and its seaborne trade. The mayor of the town still bears the title of Admiral of the Port; the fine warehouses and original Custom House on the Old Quay are worth inspection. Haverford had a flourishing paper-making industry, and an important iron foundry; the latter came to a violent end when its boilers burst, raining bricks on the town. The port has gradually declined since the arrival of the South Wales Railway (1853) and the modern growth of Milford Haven.

In Haverford the castle can be visited both as Norman fortress and as the home of the county museum. There are remains of the thirteenth-century rectangular keep and a round north tower, curtain wall, and a well originally 36m. deep. Under the courtyard lies a secret underground passage. The museum collections include sections relating to archaeology, folk-life, local industry, and art. Of the three medieval churches, St Martin's is the oldest, but has been heavily restored. St Thomas's, dedicated to the martyr of Canterbury, has a thirteenth-century tower and, inside, the graveslab of a palmer, with a palm branch and floriated cross. St Mary's is one of the finest churches in Wales. It dates mostly from thirteenth century, with a fifteenth-century north aisle and clerestories. The lancet windows are Early English. Notice the oak roof, the carvings on the capitals of the arcades (which include a pig playing a *crwth*), and the effigy of a pilgrim whose scallop-carved purse shows he had made the long journey to Santiago de Compostella (he may have been on his way to St David's when he died). Albany Chapel, Tabernacle Congregational Chapel, and the Wesleyan Methodist chapel are all very old foundations. (Quakers from Haverfordwest founded Haverford County, in Pennsylvania, USA.) Haverford also has some good Regency and early-Victorian houses; see, for instance, the ornate iron balconies in Barn Street, a touch of New Orleans in Pembrokeshire.

Haverfordwest makes a good centre for exploring the surrounding countryside. In the immediate neighbourhood, near Merlin's Bridge, Haroldston, now in ruins, was a home of the Perrott family (*see* Carew). Here Addison (of the *Spectator*) was entertained with a masque in the classical mode; Sir Herbert Perrott may, it is said, have been an inspiration for the character of Sir Roger de Coverley. Now at the British Museum, the 'Haroldston Calendar' is a fine fourteenth-century manuscript with illuminations showing the medieval peasants of Pembrokeshire at their seasonal tasks.

Picton Castle (Castell Pictwn), a few km. east of Haverford, is a Norman foundation much restored and long occupied by the Philipps family. The magnificent gardens are sometimes open to the public, and it is planned to open a gallery of the work of Graham Sutherland. The Philipps family produced some notable characters. Sir John Philipps (1666–1737) was a friend of the Wesleys and a founder member of the SPCK. Dr Johnson approved of Picton, which served as a centre of culture and hospitality for the neighbourhood. In Queen Elizabeth's reign Morgan Philipps of Picton married a local 'widow' and heiress, whose seafaring husband later turned up after many years of slavery on the Barbary coast. After a lawsuit, the widow was returned.

Wiston Castle (Cas-wis), on a minor road, also to the east of Haverford, but north of the A40, has the remains of a stone shell-keep on a motte; its bailey survives as an earthwork. Wizo the Fleming is said to have built this castle in the twelfth century; Llewellyn the Great destroyed it in 1220.

Hay-on-Wye (Y Gelli)   Powys   7G4   (*pop* 1,230)
Hay was a frontier town in the time of the Normans, who gave it its name (Norman–French *la haie*, 'the wood', Welsh *Y Gelli*) and built a castle here. The first version

Looking S over Caban Coch Reservoir, Rhayader. The 'expression' of such reservoirs, according to R. S. Thomas, is 'a pose/For strangers'

'Dylan Thomas' by Augustus John (the National Museum of Wales)

Haverfordwest : old town and Norman castle

was a motte-and-bailey construction, raised, together with the original parish church, in Henry I's reign. The second, a stone castle, was given by King John to the notorious de Breos family. Castle and town walls were sacked by Glyndwr in about 1400; the castle was repaired extensively under Henry IV. Fragments of it were later incorporated into a Jacobean mansion with Dutch gables and towering chimneys. Hay church was rebuilt in 1833 and extended again later. The clock tower, in the town centre, dates from 1884.

For centuries Hay has been a busy agricultural centre (its stock market is known as the 'Smithfield'). Times were not, however, always untroubled. In 1795, for example, there occurred what one historian has called the 'revolt of the housewives'. On 23 August some women of the town stopped a wagon loaded with bags of flour, and took the flour into the market-house to be divided the next morning. This curious incident was one of a number of sporadic and relatively non-violent Corn Riots, which took place in Wales between 1793 and about 1801; scarcity of corn and the resulting high prices goaded the community into taking the law into its own hands.

Modern Hay – town and castle – is gradually being transformed into one huge bookshop, where second-hand books in thousands are bought and sold in person

and by post. Booth's Bookshop is fast becoming one of the seven wonders of modern Wales.

Booth's or no, Hay is a fine centre for exploring the Marches, that ambivalent and beautiful border country where Welsh place-names have infiltrated England (as Llanveynoe) and English ones have slipped into Wales (as Newchurch or Painscastle). Hay itself has long been English-speaking. The Baptists, when they had just opened a church in the town in 1653, rejected a minister sent from Monmouthshire because he could not preach in English. (However, a few km. south, at the same period, Llanigon Independent church held services mainly in Welsh.)

Hirwaun   Mid Glam.   11E1

Hirwaun is a bleak town in bleak and imposing country at the junction of a number of mountain roads. On the northern rim of the South Wales coalfield, the town was the site of ironworks from the mid eighteenth century. South of the town, on Hirwaun Common, stand the ruins of Crawshay's Tower, an industrial folly put up by Francis Crawshay, son of William Crawshay the Iron King, in about 1858. Ten m. high, it housed two brass cannon and could be inhabited during summer months. It was abandoned after the closing of the Hirwaun ironworks.

'Came to Irvan, an enormous mining-place, with a spectral-looking chapel, doubtless a Methodist one'. George Borrow's remark of 1854 is a reminder not only of his own stolid intolerance but also of the rapidity with which Nonconformist chapels sprang up to minister to the needs of the new population of the industrial valleys. The Anglican Church lagged sadly behind, and its services were conducted mostly in English.

The road from Hirwaun through Treherbert to the Rhondda passes near Llyn Fawr Reservoir, which lies, with another, smaller lake, beneath the crags of Craig-y-llyn. There, in 1911, when the natural lake was drained, a significant hoard of Bronze and Iron Age artefacts (*c.* 600 BC) was discovered. These included bronze axes of local make; two great bronze cauldrons, possibly from Ireland; bronze ornaments for men and horses; and the iron sword of a chieftain from south-west Germany or eastern France. Archaeologists believe these objects may have been cast into the lake as offerings to the spirits of the waters. It is well known that the early Celts had numerous gods of river, well, and stream, while magic cauldrons play a part in the *Mabinogion*, the collection of old Welsh epic and romance, which was written down much later but that seems to reflect earlier beliefs and customs. The Llyn Fawr hoard can be seen in the National Museum at Cardiff.

Ilston   W. Glam.   *see* **Gower Peninsula**

Kenfig (Cynffig)   Mid Glam.   10D3
Before the steel works came to Margam a wild belt of sand-dunes, or 'burrows', stretched along this coast from Porthcawl almost to the Afan River. Of this strange landscape, a paradise for naturalists, Kenfig remains, with rolling dunes and a mysterious freshwater pool only 900m. from the sea. It is increasingly encroached upon, by industry, road-building, and caravans; it retains, however, much of its desolate charm.

Stone walls, which can be clearly seen emerging from the sands and the pool, have given rise to legends of a drowned and buried city, a 'Pompeii of sand' overcome for its sins by the avenging elements. The reality is more complex. Dunes formed extensively along the South Wales coast in prehistoric times: Kenfig itself has yielded evidence of occupation in the Iron and Bronze Ages. By the mid twelfth century there was a castle here, and a church dedicated to St James; a port at the river-mouth held twenty-four ships. In the following century the sands became menacing. A new church had to be built, on higher ground and farther from the sea. It was dedicated to St Mary Magdalen, and gave the village its present name, Maudlam (pronounced locally Mow-glum). The pool seems to have come into existence by 1365, formed most probably by the blocking up by sand of the Kenfig Estuary. Gradually, a marsh was created, and finally the sand cut off its outlet to the sea, leaving the freshwater lake or pool. Then, in the early sixteenth

century, a tremendous sandstorm overwhelmed what remained of the castle and village. The borough survived as an independent corporation until 1886; its 'guildhall', with charters and civic records, is the upper floor of the village inn.

Maudlam church, squat and grey, has a restored Norman chancel arch and a fine Early Norman font with cable-moulded rim and fish-scale decoration. Between here and the sea lie the hills and valleys of sand-dunes, interspersed with moorland rich in birds and plant-life. The pool, often chilly, can be used for bathing, with reasonable care.

Kidwelly (Cydweli)   Dyfed   9F5   (*pop.* 3,076)
This ancient borough grew up around its Norman castle, one of the finest in South Wales. It was founded in Henry I's reign by Roger, Bishop of Salisbury, a spiritual lord with an evident eye for temporal power; the earthwork defences date from this period. Late in the thirteenth century, and with the threat of Welsh rebellion ever present, Payn de Chaworth constructed the inner ward. The chapel, which juts out over a cliff, was added around 1300. In the early fourteenth century the outer curtain and gateway completed the defences; the towers of the inner ward were raised by a storey to provide a clear view for the garrison.

The castle fell in and out of Welsh hands during the medieval period. Maurice de Londres, Lord of Kidwelly, was faced in 1136 by an army of Welsh led by Gwenllian, the wife of Prince Gruffydd ap Rhys. In a field in the Gwendraeth Valley, still known as Gwenllian's Field (*Maes Gwenllian*), the Normans won a bloody victory, capturing and beheading Gwenllian and her son, Morgan. Kidwelly was badly damaged in the Glyndwr rebellion of the early fifteenth century. Under Henry IV it passed to the Crown, but by this time it had lost its strategic importance.

Kidwelly is a striking and well-preserved example of the concentric castle, which was the fine flower of late-medieval military architecture. This type of castle had two complete sets of defences, one within the other. The inner ward would have a high, strong wall with drum towers and gate defences. The outer would have similar wall, towers, and gate, but lower in height. Sometimes, as at Kidwelly, a fortified town adjoined the castle, its walls meeting those of the fortress in one unbroken enclosure. Kidwelly's town wall appears to have been interrupted on the north side. On the south side, the early-fourteenth-century town gate is still in existence. Outside the walls, ditches and moats often provided extra security.

The concentric design at Kidwelly is modified by the demands of the site, a naturally strong one overlooking a ford on the main road to west Wales. The steep bank of the Gwendraeth Fach River on the eastern side forms a straight line, which the inner and outer wards curve around to meet, in a half-moon shape. The most im-

Kidwelly Castle: the S gatehouse

pressive features of the castle today are the massive south gatehouse, three-storeyed, with semicircular towers, and the chapel, whose high buttresses rise from the river bank. The hall that stands in the outer ward is much later than the rest of the structure; it was probably added by Sir Rhys ap Tewdwr, who had received the castle in return for his support of Henry VII.

On the opposite bank of the Gwendraeth, and across a fourteenth-century bridge, the priory church is a survival from the Benedictine house founded in 1130 as a daughter cell of Sherborne in Dorset. The building is a fine example of Decorated style. Its spire was a later addition to a thirteenth-century tower. A fourteenth-century alabaster statue of the Virgin and Child has been replaced in the church having long been buried in the churchyard to prevent superstitious veneration.

Kidwelly was once a flourishing seaport. FERRYSIDE, the next station on the railway line west, has a sandy beach on the estuary, with a fine view of Llansteffan Castle on its hill across the water.

Knighton (Trefyclo) Powys 7G1 (*pop.* 2,010)
Knighton is a delightful small market town on a rise between hills in the gentle Teme Valley. It stands on the

border, and has done at least since Offa's Dyke was built; the Dyke can be clearly seen to the west of the town. Knighton is the half-way point for those walking the Offa's Dyke Path and is the headquarters of the Offa's Dyke Association. The town charter dates back to the thirteenth century. Knighton's church, restored, is partly Norman and there are some charming old houses and inns.

At BLEDDFA, several km. west on the A488, which crosses Radnor Forest, the church is set on a prehistoric mound. The building is mostly of thirteenth-century date, with a fourteenth-century roof.

KNUCKLAS CASTLE (Cnwclas), 5km. north-west of Knighton, is a ruin high on a hill. Legend connects it with King Arthur. This was, the legend asserts, the home of the giant Cogfran, where Arthur married the giant's daughter, Guinevere. More prosaically perhaps, Knucklas was the birthplace of Vavasor Powell (1617–70), who has been called the most remarkable Welshman of his day. One of the early Welsh Nonconformists, and a fanatical Puritan, Powell frequently travelled a hundred miles in a week, preaching in two or three places daily. When Cromwell declared himself Lord Protector in 1653, Powell and others turned against him. They had come to believe in the Fifth Monarchy, the imminent reign of the saints on earth, which was to follow the four great empires of Assyria, Persia, Greece, and Rome. To this utopian vision Cromwell was a serious obstacle. Powell attacked him in a violent sermon, and fled to Wales, some thought to provoke a rising. But in 1660, instead of the Second Coming, the Stuart monarchy was restored. Royalist Wales greeted it with rejoicing. The Puritans were out of favour; Powell spent almost the whole of the rest of his life in prison. His best-known work, *The Bird in the Cage, Chirping*, was written in gaol.

Lampeter (Llanbedr Pont Steffan)   Dyfed
6B3   (pop. 2,189)

Lampeter is a small but busy market centre at a point in the upper Teifi Valley where a number of main roads converge. In term-time it bulges with students from St David's College. Now coeducational and a constituent part of the University of Wales, St David's was founded in 1822 by the Bishop of St David's, an Englishman named Thomas Burgess. Concerned at the state of the Anglican clergy in Wales, Burgess carried through a number of reform projects, setting up schools, establishing libraries, encouraging the SPCK. He took the then unusual step of requiring proof of Welsh-language proficiency from incumbents sent to Welsh-speaking parishes. Burgess's great ambition was to create a theological college in his own diocese. He put aside a tenth of his own income for this purpose and encouraged his clergy to do the same. By 1820 the fund had reached £11,000, and in 1822, with grants from the King and the Universities, the foundation stone was laid at Lampeter. The quadrangular block was designed by

C. R. Cockerell, and praised by Sir Gilbert Scott as 'a most charming example of the early Gothic revival'. In 1852 the college was given the right to grant the degree of Bachelor of Divinity. The building was enlarged in 1880, and further expansion has taken place in recent years.

St Peter's church (1870) is also neo-Gothic. St David's College School was founded by Vicar Ebenezer Williams in 1805. Under a later vicar-headmaster, John Williams, the fame of this grammar school reached Sir Walter Scott, who sent his son here (*see also* Ystrad Meurig). The school can be seen from Station Terrace, a name that also reflects history, for Lampeter has lost its railway.

The mound of a medieval castle is visible in the grounds of the college (which was built on 'Castle Field'), and earlier fortifications have left traces on the surrounding hills, at Goitre and Allt Goch. Running from north-east to south-west, on the opposite bank of the Teifi is a stretch of Sarn Helen, the Roman road named after the legendary (?) Helen, Welsh wife of Magnus Maximus, or Macsen Wledig, who married her after seeing her in a dream, and who made an abortive bid for the imperial crown in AD 383. Another Helen was the British mother of Constantine, the first Christian Emperor, who was born at York. Just to confuse matters, Sarn Helen may also derive from the Welsh for angle (*elin*) (this road is unRoman in its jagged course) or for Legion (*y lleng*).

Further up the valley, and in one of Sarn Helen's angles, LLANFAIR CLYDOGAU has a church with a primitive carved font. There are Bronze Age cairns and a burial chamber in the parish. On the west bank of the river, Derry Ormond House, designed by Cockerell, has been demolished, but Derry Ormond Tower, built to commemorate the Battle of Waterloo, is a local landmark.

Midway between Lampeter and Aberaeron, FELIN-FACH has a new arts centre, which runs summer schools in Theatre Art and Design and puts on plays and concerts in both English and Welsh during the year.

Lamphey (Llandyfai)   Dyfed   8C5

Lamphey was one of the seven medieval manors of the Bishopric of St David's. Here, in a more comfortable climate than that of the western peninsula where the cathedral stands, the bishops had a splendid country seat built, with fishponds, gardens, and orchards. Some of the buildings are earlier than the corresponding palace at St David's itself: an early-thirteenth-century hall and service rooms, and a private apartment possibly built for Bishop Richard Carew later that century. However, Lamphey bears the unmistakeable imprint of Bishop Henry Gower (1327–47), who had a hand in Swansea Castle and was largely responsible for the magnificent Palace at St David's. Gower's characteristic arcaded parapets are clearly visible at Lamphey,

Lamphey Palace, showing the arcaded parapets

though they are simpler here, perhaps the result of using less-experienced masons. Later work included a very fine Perpendicular east window in the chapel. In Henry VIII's reign Bishop Barlow exchanged the Palace for the rich living of Carew; the King sold Lamphey to the Devereux family. Elizabeth's favourite, Robert Devereux Earl of Essex, thus spent much of his boyhood here. As at Carew Castle, modifications were made to bring the medieval building into line with the new Renaissance standards of taste and comfort.

Lamphey Court, near the Palace, is a small but elegant Georgian house (*c.* 1820) with a great colonnade of pillars forming the façade. HODGESTON, between Lamphey and Manorbier, has a fourteenth-century (Decorated) church well worth visiting for its chancel, sedilia, and piscina.

Laugharne (Lacharn) Dyfed 9E4

Laugharne (the *ugha* is silent) is a small town the size of a fishing-village. Norman, Welsh, medieval, eighteenth-century, it has, somehow, and in spite of its obvious attractions for tourists, persistently retained an air at once distinctive and abstracted. This is partly due to its position at the end of the country lane that is the A4066

from St Clears; though the road continues, at a tangent, to Pendine, it is easy to be aware that there is nothing beyond Laugharne but the marshes and dunes of the Burrows, and the widening estuary.

Like Gower and south Pembrokeshire, Laugharne also acquired a certain peculiarity from its medieval settlers, English brought in as a sort of security by the Norman lords who created the borough. In 1804 Laugharne was still divided into an English and a Welsh part, though by the mid nineteenth century the former had shrunk to a small area within the town, and the majority of field-names in the parish were once more Welsh. The charter granted in 1307 by Sir Guy de Brian, or de Brienne, however, still governs the town. The Corporation Court Leet and Court Baron meet on alternate Mondays in the delightful eighteenth-century Town Hall; the Portreeve, as chief officer, presides over business.

Llansteffan on the next estuary and Laugharne were both fortified by the Normans to protect the sea approaches. Laugharne Castle stands almost at the water's edge: two twelfth-century towers, from the time of Rhys ap Gruffydd (who entertained Henry II there), and the remains of a reconstruction done in Elizabeth's

reign by the braggardly and adventurous Sir John Perrott, a natural son of Henry VIII, who also reshaped the castle at Carew. (Laugharne Castle is undergoing restoration.)

St Martin's church also dates from the Norman era. A thirteenth-century foundation, it was rebuilt in the mid fourteenth century by a later member of the de Brian family. Its square central tower has strongly defensive features. Inside, a largely fifteenth-century interior has been restored to its earlier simplicity. There are a small tenth-century Celtic cross, fourteenth-century piscina and sedilia, and a number of interesting memorial tablets. A box in the church contains the remains of a Beaker Folk burial.

Of the yewtrees, planted in 1720, the one nearest the porch was known as the 'fox-tree'; the heads of foxes, polecats, and other predatory animals were hung on it for three successive Sundays, after which the catcher received the usual rate for the job. On 17 November 1802 Samuel Taylor Coleridge visited Laugharne and was moved by its tombstones; he pitied the living even more: 'Cottages favourable only to vegetable life – Hotbed of wild weeds on their roofs and ivy on their walls – but the shrivelled shrimps of cold and hunger – swarthied tenants'. The grave of Dylan Thomas is in the new part of the churchyard, a simple white wooden cross.

It is difficult, indeed, to see Laugharne through eyes other than those of Dylan Thomas, who lived here from 1938 to 1940 and again from May 1949. According to those who knew him, Dylan spent some of his happiest and calmest days in Laugharne, 'this timeless, mild, beguiling island of a town, with its seven public-houses, one chapel in action, one church, one factory, two billiard tables, one St Bernard (without brandy), one policeman, three rivers, a visiting sea, one Rolls-Royce selling fish and chips, one cannon (cast-iron), one chancellor (flesh and blood), one port-reeve . . . and a multitude of mixed birds'. Dylan's first house in Laugharne was a fisherman's cottage in Gosport Street, found for him by the novelist Richard Hughes, who lived in the Georgian house adjoining the castle. Later he moved to 'Sea View', a tall white-washed house at the 'posh end' of the town. In 1949 the Thomases moved back again to Laugharne: Dylan, his wife, and children to the Boat House, a 'house on stilts' halfway up a cliff on the edge of the tide, and his parents to 'The Pelican', a cottage near Brown's Hotel. (Brown's and the Cross House Inn were Dylan's drinking-places in Laugharne.) The Boat House has been neatly tidied into a museum, with records, photographs, some furniture, photostats of manuscripts of which the originals are in America. More evocative is the small wooden lock-up shed or garage, further up the cliff path, where Dylan retreated to work; looking out over the estuary, he wrote and re-

OPPOSITE: *Dylan Thomas in the graveyard at Laugharne*

BELOW: *In this shed on the cliff near the Boat House Dylan Thomas wrote* Under Milk Wood *and some of his finest poems*

TOP: *Late-C15 or early-C16 rood-screen, Llananno*   BOTTOM: *Early-C18 musicians' gallery in St Cynllo's church, Llanbister*

wrote *Under Milk Wood* (based partly on Laugharne and partly on New Quay, but set mostly in the Wales of his own imagination) and his last poems. 'Poem on his birthday' and 'Over Sir Johns Hill' (the latter is just south of the town) grew out of this seascape.

Llananno and **Llanbister** Powys 7F1
In the Ithon Valley, between Llandrindod and Newtown, two churches are well worth taking the trouble to find. Near the junction of the A483 and B4356, Llanbister church stands on a hilly site. This is a restored thirteenth-century building with a musicians' gallery, or singing loft, that dates from 1716. Readers of Thomas Hardy's *Under the Greenwood Tree* will be able to imagine the music of the band. Further on towards Newtown, Llananno church lies below the road and on the riverbank. It possesses a magnificently carved rood-screen, one of the finest in Wales. Intertwining leaves, flowers, bunches of grapes, an exuberance of natural forms disciplined into a pattern both intricate and controlled. Twenty-five tabernacled niches on the western side hold figures of saints, but these are not the originals; it would have been a miracle indeed if they had survived the image-breaking fervour of the Reformation.

Llanarth Dyfed 6A3
The village lies partly on the main Aberystwyth road and partly on a hillside around the old church. The latter has an eleventh-century font, an Ogham stone inscribed '*Gurhir.t.*', and a display of early Welsh and English Bibles. At Wern, now a farmhouse, Henry Tudor is said to have stayed the night on his way from Milford Haven to Bosworth Field. From Llanarth, lanes wind down past unobtrusive holiday sites to a small, sandy beach, Cei Bach.

Llanbadarn Fawr Dyfed *see* **Aberystwyth**

Llanbadarn Fawr Powys *see* **Llandrinod Wells**

Llanbedr Powys *see* **Crickhowell**

Llanblethian S. Glam. *see* **Cowbridge**

Llancarfan S. Glam. 11F4
Now a growing village, Llancarfan was one of the holy sites of Celtic Wales. According to his medieval biographers, the sixth-century saint Cadoc, son of a South Wales king, spent fifteen years studying in Wales and Ireland. Hiding one day in a wood from a murderous swineherd, he saw near a fountain an enormous wild boar. The animal made three huge bounds, staring, after each one, at the stranger who had disturbed him. Cadoc marked the site with three branches; these spots were to become the church, dormitory, and refectory of Llancarfan Abbey. (In fact, Celtic 'monasteries' were not built on the same plan as the later, Latin ones,

introduced by the Normans.) The name meant 'Church of the Stags', for one day two deer came out of the forest and replaced with their labour two idle, disobedient monks who had refused to carry timber for the monastery buildings. Cadoc's history is in reality more obscure. However, the number of churches dedicated to him in South Wales – the Llangadogs, Llangattocks, Cadoxtons – shows the result of his enormous missionary effort. The thirteenth-century church at Llancarfan was rebuilt early last century. The five-lighted window in the north chancel wall is an early-sixteenth-century feature. The size of the church probably reflects the awareness, in medieval times, of a strong, local, religious tradition. The Carfan Valley also had several holy wells.

Llandaff S. Glam. *see* **Cardiff**

Llanddew Powys *see* **Brecon**

Llanddewi Powys *see* **Abergwesyn**

Llanddewi Aberarth Dyfed *see* **Aberaeron**

Llanddewi Brefi Dyfed 6C3
A quiet village beautifully set in the hills above the Teifi Valley. George Borrow in *Wild Wales* describes how 'an ancient church stands on a little rising ground just below the hills, multitudes of rooks inhabit its steeple and fill . . . the air with their cawing'. This thirteenth-century church, St David's – much restored – is traditionally connected with an episode in the life of the patron saint of Wales. Here in the fifth century was held the Synod called by the Welsh Church to discuss the doctrines of Pelagius, notably the denial of original sin. (Pelagius is thought by some to have been a Welshman or an Irishman.) David, summoned from Pembrokeshire, produced a swift refutation of the new ideas. The story goes that, as he addressed the crowd, the ground miraculously rose beneath him, forming a natural platform; a white dove fluttered down to settle on his shoulder.

At Llanio Issa farm nearby, a Roman camp (Loventium?) still lies buried. It stood on a route north from Carmarthen, and is not very far from the Roman goldmines at Pumsaint.

Llanddowror Dyfed *see* **St Clears**

Llandegley Powys 7F2
Llandegley's Norman church has a fine font and openwork screen. It is dedicated to St Tecla, a sixth-century saint for whose disease, a 'falling sickness', the neighbourhood's mineral waters were reputed to provide a cure. The saline, sulphur, and chalybeate waters brought the place considerable fame as a spa in the eighteenth and early nineteenth centuries. Its proximity to Llandrindod Wells, and its lack of any other economic function, however, prevented it developing further than a village.

A small stone thatched building, 'The Pales' (1745), is the oldest surviving Quaker meeting-house in the country. It has a rarity value, too, for Quakerism has never been very strong in Wales. George Fox came on a missionary tour in 1657, but, preaching in English, he was confined in his success to the Anglicized parts of Radnorshire, Montgomeryshire, and 'little England beyond Wales' (south Pembrokeshire). Severe persecution of Quakers under Charles II led to mass emigration from the Welsh meeting-houses. Welsh Quakers bought 16,000ha. (40,000 acres) in Pennsylvania, settling there in large numbers from 1682. The American community flourished, while the Friends at home, bled of their most vigorous members, declined. Other Nonconformist sects seem to have appealed more strongly to the Welsh character.

From Llandegley Rocks (520m.) there are magnificent views north-east over the wild expanse of Radnor Forest.

Llandeilo Dyfed 6C5 (*pop*. 1,794)

Llandeilo is a small market-town of character, built on one of the humpy hills that are scattered along this stretch of the Towy Valley. The road from Carmarthen crosses the river over a fine stone bridge (1848) then rises steeply up past slate-roofed cottages and a sixteenth-century coaching inn, bisects the parish churchyard, and becomes the main street of the town itself. The latter's buildings are sober, mostly early-Victorian, a mixture of elegance and dilapidation. There are some fine chapels. The church, which retains a thirteenth-century tower, was restored by Sir Gilbert Scott in 1850; it is surrounded by an attractive lopsided 'square'.

If it were not for the lorries, which bump and grind relentlessly day and night through the patently too narrow main thoroughfare, Llandeilo would indeed appear to be untouched by modern times. There is no coffee-bar, and Welsh is the language most often heard in the teashop. On Saturdays a market is held 'above the town'. Fresh Towy salmon is worth paying for; it is often described, on local menus, somewhat ambiguously, as 'poached'.

At the top of the town is the entrance to the Dinefwr (Dynevor) Estate. In magnificent parkland stand a nineteenth-century mansion and the ruins of old Dinefwr Castle. This latter was from 877 the principal residence of the princes of South Wales. The remains include parts of the keep, towers, stairways, and curtain wall. Dinefwr commanded a breathtaking and strategic view over the Towy Valley. Within the park, the church of Llandyfeisant is said to have been built on the site of a Roman temple; a hoard of silver Roman coins was dug up nearby some years ago.

Eight km. to the west, Dryslwyn rises, another ruined castle on a mound. From this fortress began the revolt of Rhys ap Meredudd (1287-8), who was disappointed at what he had got out of his cooperation with Edward I. During a three-week siege in August 1287 the attackers

mined one of the towers, which fell down, crushing a number of them to death with its fall. The dead included William de Monte Casino, who had earlier tried to end the conflict by challenging Rhys to single combat. The present remains are largely those of the chapel; again, there are splendid views out over the valley. From here can be seen a more modern monument, Paxton's Tower, a triangular crenellated folly erected by the extravagant Mayor of Carmarthen, Sir William Paxton, in honour of Lord Nelson. The architect was Samuel Pepys Cockerell, who also designed Middleton Hall (near Llanarthney), of which only the late-eighteenth-century stable block now remains. Paxton's Tower is owned by the NT. It has on each of its three doors an inscription to Nelson, in Welsh, Latin, and English respectively.

A few km. up the valley from Dryslwyn, and on the opposite bank of the Towy, stands the nineteenth-century Gothic pile of what is now the Gelliaur Farm Institute. This was Golden Grove, one of the Welsh seats of the Earls of Cawdor. In a previous house on this site, Jeremy Taylor (1613-67) took refuge. Taylor had been a chaplain with the Royalist army; taken prisoner at Cardigan, he came here on his release to join a friend who kept a school in the neighbourhood. At Golden Grove he spent ten years of his life, composing among other things his *Holy Living, Holy Dying* and *The Golden Grove* (1655). His wife, Joanna, was the heiress of Mandinam House near Llangadog.

Llandough S. Glam. *see* Cowbridge

Llandovery (Llanymddyfri) Dyfed 6D4 (*pop*. 1,999)

'A small but beautiful town situated amongst fertile meadows', according to George Borrow in *Wild Wales*, and 'about the pleasantest little town in which I have halted in the course of my wanderings'. Small, sober, peaceful, full of character, Llandovery is an old-established Welsh market-town; its Welsh name, 'church among the waters', refers to the meeting of the Bran, Gwydderig, and Towy rivers. There is an attractive old square with Town Hall, and the remains of a Norman castle – two round towers on a bramble-grown tump – near the cattle-market.

The town has not grown much since the eighteenth century, when it was noted for its stocking-fairs. It was also an important centre of Welsh printing, especially in the nineteenth century; the Rees-family press printed scholarly editions, including Lady Charlotte Guest's translation of the medieval Welsh tales known as the *Mabinogion*. In 1848 St David's College was founded, one of the very few public schools in Wales. The school chapel has a Graham Sutherland Crucifixion.

Llandovery has more than one literary association, and, as is often the case in Wales, literature is closely allied to religion. Rhys Pritchard (1579-1644), Vicar

Dolauhirion Bridge, 3km. from Llandovery: by William Edwards

of Llandingat (near the town), was the author of religious verses known as the *Welshman's Candle*. Immensely popular in his day, these verses provide a valuable picture of social life in seventeenth-century rural Wales. Vicar Pritchard bemoans, for example, the passing of the simple life: while the peasantry live on soup and vegetables (garlic, onion, parsnip, and marrow), the aristocracy demand six-course meals, with fine sauces, and wine twice a day. A more recognizable name for the non-Welsh visitor is perhaps that of William Williams Pantycelyn. Pantycelyn, a fine eighteenth-century farmhouse, stands near the hamlet of Pentre Tŷgwyn, about 1½km. east of Llandovery, on the Brecon road. William Williams was one of the great writers of the eighteenth-century Methodist movement. He is best known for his hymns, among them 'Guide me, O thou great Jehovah'. Williams is buried in the churchyard at Llanfair-ar-y-bryn (on the outskirts of Llandovery); his descendants still live at Pantycelyn.

Three km. outside Llandovery, on the Lampeter road, Dolauhirion bridge is a graceful stone structure, the work of the self-taught builder William Edwards, who built the famous single-arch bridge at Pontypridd. To the north, and beyond Cilycwm, an NT village with a medieval church and early Wesleyan Methodist chapel, the road leads up into the mountains and to the new reservoir, Llyn Brianne, opened in 1972. A lake of 88ha., formed by the Towy and the Camddwr, is held back by a dam 88m. high. In contrast to the Elan Valley, no occupied dwellings were drowned here; under the water lie coniferous forest and moorland sheep-runs. Llyn Brianne supplies the Swansea area.

Llandrindod Wells Powys 7F2 (*pop.* 3,379)
The waters at Llandrindod were known to the Romans, who named them Balnae Silurum, 'the Baths of the Silures', and to the seventeenth century, but the town was not developed as a spa until the eighteenth century,

Llanfihangel Helygen church, nr Llandrindod Wells

when the fame of Bath had made such places desirable. Llandrindod became, very briefly, the rival of the West Country resort. Poems such as the following: 'Let England boast Bath's crowded springs, / Llandrindod happier Cambria sings' contributed to a flourish of popularity, which led in its turn to the arrival of disreputable persons and gamblers, and to the eclipse of the place as a fashionable spa. Then in 1817 a Dr Williams of Aberystwyth published a pamphlet on the medicinal virtues of the waters. Llandrindod returned to fashion; new hotels were built, and the railway (in 1865) helped to consolidate the town's popularity. Sufferers from gout, rheumatism, bronchial complaints, dyspepsia, anaemia, insomnia, and gravel all flocked to its thirty various mineral springs.

The town still has the solid, prosperous – some might say stuffy – appearance of a mainly Victorian spa. It is, however, very pleasantly full of space and greenery. Its large red-brick hotels, un-Welsh-looking, are now much used for conferences. In summer it offers bowling festivals, including the Welsh National Championships in August. In the centre of town there is boating on an agreeable lake, and there is good coarse fishing here and on the Ithon at Llanyre (Llanllŷr). The eighteen-hole golf course, at 330m. one of the highest in Britain, has magnificent views of the surrounding hills. Llandrindod's Museum holds folk-life collections, dolls, and finds from the Roman sites in the area. At the Automobile Palace, Tom Norton's Veteran Cycle Collection, a private museum, is open all year round. The town itself has become a centre for national and international motoring and motor-cycle events.

Just outside Llandrindod, near Llanyre, and over-looking a large bend in the Ithon River, Castell Collen ('fort of the hazel') is the impressive visible remains of a Roman fort. In about 75–8, during the campaign of Julius Frontinus against the Silures, a large square fort was erected here; built of turf and timber, it was capable of holding an infantry garrison a thousand strong. In about 140 the defences were faced in stone. The following century the Romans reduced its area by building a cross wall, and isolating a bank and ditch to the west (near the farmhouse). They continued to occupy the fort, though not continuously, into the fourth century. The banks and ditches of the whole enclave can still be traced. In the centre there are dilapidated remains of some stone buildings. Archaeologists have identified these as a headquarters, in the centre, a granary, to the north, and a commandant's house, to the south.

Castell Collen stood on the Roman road running north from Brecon Gaer, while another may have con-tinued north to Caersŵs. Not far away from the fort, and just south of Llandrindod, the Romans made practice camps, small mock fortifications built as training for troops. There is little to see there now, for the earth-works are rarely more than a $\frac{1}{2}$m. high. None the less, this is the largest known group of such camps in the whole of the Roman Empire; there are eighteen here, each 30 or 60m. square.

A number of interesting churches may be visited from Llandrindod. On the A483 going north, and just before Cross Gates, is LLANBADARN FAWR, not to be confused with the parish of the same name near Aberystwyth. This one has a church with a carved tympanum of Norman style – a rare feature in Wales. Its two mytho-logical animals are set one each side of a lily-plant, which is probably a symbol of the Incarnation. Also in the porch, a Roman centurial stone inscribed '*Valflavini*' is built into the fabric. Such stones were used to mark buildings used as garrisons by detachments of a hundred. At LLANFIHANGEL HELYGEN, which stands on a minor road about 4km. north-east, the small church has an ancient font, stone-slab floor, oak pews, and a pen for children. LLANFIHANGEL RHYDIEITHON, further along the A488 towards Bleddfa, is also worth a visit.

Llandybïe Dyfed 6C6

On the railway line that still runs from Shrewsbury down to Llanelli, Llandybïe has suffered from recent 'development'. There is, however, an interesting medieval church, which has an impressive seventeenth-century monument to Sir Henry Vaughan of Derwydd. The lime-kilns at the Llandybïe quarries are an excellent example of Victorian Gothic, here applied to the Vic-torians' second religion, industrial progress. Designed by R. K. Penson, better known for his churches, the kilns have arches reminiscent of Piranesi.

Glynhir Mansion, about 2km. east, has a fine octagonal dovecote, and the fall of the Loughor River, within its grounds, but these cannot normally be visited. Derwydd, north of Llandybïe, was a residence of Sir Rhys ap Thomas, the local magnate who was one of Henry Tudor's most ardent supporters. The house contains his bedstead and a number of other historic relics.

Somewhere near Llandybïe, and not far from Glyn-hir, a limestone cavern in the hills is said by tradition to be the resting-place of Owain Llawgoch ('Owen of the Red Hand'), who with his band of men was blocked up by enemies and left to starve. In 1813, according to the nineteenth-century travellers Mr and Mrs S. C. Hall, this cave yielded ten human skeletons, 'with skulls and bones of larger size than those of the present race'. This legend clearly connects with that other story according to which the same Owain and his men remain sleeping, in a cave on the banks of the Cennen. They will wake when Wales has most need of them.

Llandysul Dyfed 9F2

A small old-fashioned market-town, Llandysul's nine-teenth-century terraces are built in the local grey and rust-coloured slate. In the main street, a fine chapel is now the Labour Exchange. The church, with its square Norman tower, stands above a bend in the shallow Teifi River. There is a stone in the church with a sixth-century inscription: '*Velvor filia Broho*'.

The local woollen mills, once a staple of the Cardigan-shire economy, are now being revived to serve the new industry, tourism. Maesllyn Mill, towards Rhydlewis, is a working mill and museum.

The area around Rhydlewis is associated for Welsh people with the bitter and brilliant stories of Caradog Evans. It was partly as an antidote to the portrayal of Welsh rural life as nasty and brutish that D. Parry-Jones wrote his affectionate and nostalgic memoirs, *Welsh Country Upbringing*, *Welsh Country Characters*, and so on. Parry-Jones was also brought up near Llandysul, at Llangeler.

Llanelli Dyfed 10B2 (*pop.* 26,320)

Llanelli was little more than a village in the mid eighteenth century (when the ill-fated poet Richard Savage fell in love with Mrs Bridget Jones, a young and beautiful widow of the place). A century later, thanks to the coal, tinplate, and anthracite industries, it was 'thriving but ungainly', enveloped in smoke that could be seen 'three miles away'. Some of these industries have passed on from Llanelli, and the port has closed; the town's industrial present and short-term future depends largely on the steel and tinplate works at Trostre.

Few buildings are older than Early Victorian. Stepney House, near the church, has a Georgian façade. Stradey Castle (at Stradey Park) is an eighteenth-century building with a west wing of 1874. This sort of antiquarianism seems irrelevant, however, in a town like this. The visitor would do better to visit the covered market (famous in west Wales), spend a winter Saturday afternoon at a rugby match in Stradey Park (equally famous), and Sunday morning at one of the Nonconformist chapels (which have given poets and radicals to the town). As for museums, Parc Howard offers local collections, South Wales pottery, relics of industrial history, and paintings by Welsh artists.

Llanfair Clydogau Dyfed *see* **Lampeter**

Llanfrynach Powys *see* **Brecon**

Llanfrynach S. Glam. *see* **Cowbridge**

Llangadog Dyfed 6C5
Llangadog is a small town or large village with old cottages, a fifteenth-century coaching inn, and a large Cooperative Society creamery, which, with the sheep and cattle-sales, keeps the town alive.

Llangadog's name means 'church of Cadog', or 'Cattwg'. Cadoc was the son of a king of South Wales. After many years of study in Ireland, Cadoc returned to Wales and founded a monastery at Llancarfan in the Vale of Glamorgan. The Saxon invasions of the sixth century forced him to flee to Brittany, but he came back, drawn to 'console the Christians of Britain'. In Northamptonshire he met the inevitable martyrdom at the hands of a Saxon chief. Cadoc's medieval biographers ascribe to him a series of wise sayings. Of these, the most appropriate locally might be: 'The best patriot is he who tills the soil'.

Between Llangadog and Llandeilo is Bethlehem, a village, like many in Wales, named after its chapel, and a popular posting-place at Christmas. On the high ridge south of the village, Carn Goch is a huge Iron Age encampment, perhaps the largest in Wales. Its two forts extended over 800m.; the larger one had a great stone rampart 6m. high, some of which remains in place today. The climb up gives magnificent views over the Vale of Towy and the hills of what was until 1974 Carmarthenshire.

Llangammarch Wells Powys 7E3
The tiniest of the Welsh spas, Llangammarch Wells is a village and a railway station; the main roads pass it by. Here the Pump House Hotel dispensed its bariumchloride waters, of special efficacy for heart complaints. The hotel had its own golf course, tennis courts, and shooting facilities; less active visitors could sit peacefully in the gardens around the triangular lake, or walk the paths carefully 'graduated to provide resistance exercises'. Much of this remains, but the hotel has changed its name to 'The Lake', showing that taking the waters has given place to taking the trout. Walking, ponytrekking, fell- and rock-climbing now attract younger and healthier visitors.

Llangammarch church has the graves of Vicar Theophilus Evans, who discovered the wells at Llanwrtyd, and his grandson, Theophilus Jones, author of a classic history of Breconshire. The parish's most famous son, however, was the Puritan John Penry, born here in 1563. Shortly after leaving Oxford, Penry published a treatise attacking the clergy in Wales, who could not preach in the people's native language, and calling for a translation of the complete Bible into Welsh. This brought him a month in prison. Later, under the influence of Scots Presbyterians, he came to deny the doctrine of the supremacy of the state in religious matters, and joined a group of 'separatists' who wanted a totally independent church. This was politically and theologically dangerous; Penry was quickly arrested, on suspicion of complicity in the writing of the 'Marprelate Tracts', a series of pamphlets attacking the Anglican bishops. In 1593, aged barely thirty, Penry was hanged.

Llangan Mid Glam. *see* **Bridgend**

Llangasty Tal-y-llyn Powys *see* **Llangorse Lake**

Llangathen Dyfed 6B5
A by-road off the main A40 from Llandeilo to Carmarthen brings the traveller to Llangathen, a small cluster of houses around an old church. The latter is worth looking into; it has a thirteenth-century tower and an impressive Jacobean monument to Bishop Rudd. The hamlet is chiefly of interest, however, to the literary pilgrim, for here at Aberglasney House lived John Dyer (*c.* 1701–57), poet and painter, whose poems 'Grongar Hill' and 'A Country Walk' impressed Wordsworth and helped to make popular a new conception of the Picturesque. Grongar Hill itself, close by, is one of a number of humpy hills scattered in this part of the Towy Valley. It is crowned with the remains of an ancient hill-fort (on private farm-land). Dyer celebrates this patch of country, 'that soft track / Of Cambria deep embay'd, Dimetian land, / By green hills fenc'd, by ocean's murmur lull'd / Nurse of the rustic bard', in verse that combines eighteenth-century order and artificial elegance with a new appreciation of the beauties of landscape. In 'A Country Walk', less well known than 'Grongar Hill', the scene is still very near to home:

> Up Grongar Hill I labour now,
> And catch at last his bushy brow . . .
> See below, the pleasant dome,
> The poet's pride, the poet's home . . .
> See her woods, where Echo talks,
> Her gardens trim, her terrace walks,
> Her wildernesses, fragrant brakes,
> Her gloomy bow'rs and shining lakes.
> Keep, ye Gods! this humble seat
> For ever pleasant, private, neat.

The gods have failed Dyer; though his reputation has endured, if only as a literary curiosity, his house, Aberglasney, is in ruins.

Llangattock Powys *see* **Crickhowell**

Llangeitho Dyfed 6B2
Llangeitho, in the Aeron Valley, is an attractive village
grouped around a square. It is chiefly remembered in
Wales as the parish of Daniel Rowland (1713–90), one
of the giants of the Welsh Methodist movement.
Rowland was curate here until 1763, when the ecclesiastical authorities suspended him for unorthodoxy. He
continued preaching in a meeting-house, on the site of
the Calvinistic Methodist chapel, where his statue now
stands. Crowds flocked from all over Wales to hear his
fiery sermons. Some idea of the ardent, Biblical rhetoric
of Rowland's preaching may perhaps be gained from
the elegy on his death written by William Williams
Pantycelyn, who wrote many of the most famous and
well-loved Welsh hymns. Even in translation it retains
its extraordinary vitality:

> When dark night covered Britain without a sign of
> dawn Daniel sounded the clear trumpet of Sinai, shaking
> solid rocks with its powerful echo. His name was
> Boanerges, son of the loud, fiery, thunder which shook
> terrifyingly, the pillars of heaven and earth. In Llan-
> geitho, he began to shout the destruction of the ungodly
> world, thousands fled thither from South and North,
> terror, amazement, fear caught the people, great and
> small, every face lost its colour, knees trembled with the
> thunder as if death itself had taken possession of every
> one in the crowd, and the cry 'What shall we do to save
> our souls' arose from every side. That is how Daniel
> began. The sound came over Dewi's hills like a flame
> consuming flax till it echoed in the rocks of Towy and
> the old chapel of Ystradffin, where counties congregated
> in a host of common people without number, at the
> strong echo of the clear trumpet of high heaven's
> message. They were like the days of Sinai, the sound of
> a trumpet and the voice of words, mist, tempest, smoke
> and fire, and a great mountain intensely quaking and
> shaking from the depths of the earth, revealing the
> divine wrath against all manner of sin.

Daniel Rowland is buried in the parish church of St
Ceitho, which was restored and enlarged early this
century.

Llangorse Lake (Llyn Syfaddan) Powys 7F5
Reedy Llangorse Lake is the largest natural lake in South
Wales. Its wind-rippled waters have collected a store of
legends over the years. Giraldus in medieval times speaks
of blood flowing in the lake (this could be caused, it is
suggested, by the River Llyfni flowing in over deposits of
a red sandy clay) and of voices crying (Giraldus himself
suggests this could be due to the crackling and moving
of winter ice). Less susceptible of natural explanation is
his claim that the flock of wild waterfowl rise crying from
the lake only when they recognize the true royal blood
of Wales; the Norman lords of the Marches, passing on
horseback, apparently could not win such acknowledgement.

Llangorse Lake has, too, its sunken city. Once,
according to the legend, there was dry land here, and a
great heiress living in a royal court. A young man
aspired to her hand; too poor to win her, he remedied his
fortunes by murdering a rich carrier and taking the
wealth that was on him. The lady refused to marry him
until the ghost had been appeased. The young man
visited the grave; whereupon a voice cried out, 'Is there
no vengeance for innocent blood?' Another answered,
'Not until the ninth generation'. The lady, hearing this,
was for enjoying themselves while they might, for by the
ninth generation they would all be rotting in their
graves. Many years passed. Then, when the royal couple
were very old, they invited all their offspring to a huge
and magnificent banquet. When the merriment was at
its height, a terrible earthquake swallowed king, queen,
guests, and palace; the land where they stood was
drowned under a lake.

There is, of course, no scrap of evidence that any
princely court ever lay under Llangorse Lake. The lake
was formed soon after the disappearance of the glaciers
that covered most of South Wales during the Ice Age.
The only dwellings possible would have been the mud
huts of primitive hunters. In 1925 a 'dug-out' canoe was
dredged up from the mud of the lake; its date was uncertain, but archaeologists connected it with the island
in the lake, which is a 'crannog' or stockaded island,
partly built up artificially with stones and piles, of the
sort made by prehistoric lake-dwellers (such as those at
Glastonbury). Thus the legend could be an elaboration
of an ancient folk-memory relating to the real inundation
of some very early form of settlement. (*See* Professor F. J.
North's fascinating book *Sunken Cities*, which applies
archaeology and other sciences to the numerous Welsh
legends of drowned lands.)

Waterfowl and sunken palaces today share the lake
with campers, caravanners, sailers, and anglers. There
is an Adventure Centre for young people, which provides holiday courses in sailing and canoeing.

LLANGASTY TAL-Y-LLYN, on the south side of the lake,
is a village revived in the mid nineteenth century by a
reforming Victorian, Robert Raikes, and his family.
Raikes, a Yorkshireman, had been strongly influenced
by the Tractarian, or Oxford, Movement, which re-
vitalized the Anglican Church. The school and church
at Llangasty were built first (on principle); designed by
J. L. Pearson in about 1848, they are small, unpretentious, and charming. The church interior, with its
stained glass, glazed tiles, and brass candelabra, is in
typical Tractarian style. Raikes's house, Treberfydd –
also by Pearson – with its many gables and chimneys, is

OVER PAGE: *The church of Llangasty Tal-y-llyn (S side of
Llangorse Lake), with the lower slopes of the Black Mts in the
background. In the centre is the snow-covered summit of Mynydd
Troed*

St Idloes' church, Llanidloes, showing the N arcade and hammer-beam roof thought to have been salvaged from Abbey Cwmhir

one of the most attractive of Victorian country houses. It is still lived in by the Raikes family.

Llangranog Dyfed 9E1

A curiously-shaped outcrop of rock like an old lizard's head gives the sandy beach at Llangranog its special character. The village, mostly slate-roofed nineteenth-century houses and cottages, lies constricted in its narrow ravine between the coastal hills. In summer the beach can be very crowded, especially when the Welsh League of Youth (*Urdd Gobaith Cymru*) are at camp here. There are excellent NT cliff-top walks, with magnificent views of the Cardigan Bay coast-line. Motorists should explore the minor roads that lead from here to New Quay, Penbryn, and so on.

Llangunnor Dyfed *see* **Carmarthen**

Llangurig Powys 3F6

Llangurig is a pretty village with an old, restored church. It is the highest settlement in the Wye Valley. Salmon and brown trout may be fished here, by permit.

The Aberystwyth road (A44) climbs up over Plynlimon (Pumlumon), where determined walkers may search for the sources of both Wye and Severn. The 'summit' of Plynlimon-fawr (not easily recognizable) is Pen Plynlimon-fawr (741m.). It is signposted from the main road at Dyffryn Castell, near Ponterwyd. An extraordinary sense of the oldness and emptiness of upland Wales emanates from these great unremitting expanses of grey and brown moorland. Forests and reservoirs made by man have encroached only a little on the wilderness.

Llangynfelyn Dyfed *see* **Talybont**

Llangynidr Powys *see* **Crickhowell**

Llangynwyd Mid Glam. 10D3
The old village stands on a hillside around its church, while the new estates spread down towards the main road to Maesteg, an industrial town of the nineteenth century, with a market well known locally. In the old village, St Cynwyd's church, restored in 1893, has a heavily defensive tower, and over the porch, a figure of the patron saint holding the church in his hands. This parish is the setting for the popular romantic legend of the Maid of Cefn Ydfa. In the early eighteenth century Ann Thomas, heiress of the estate, fell in love with a poor thatcher, Wil Hopcyn, author of a famous Welsh air. Her parents refused to hear of the match, locked up their daughter, and married her against her will to a wealthy young lawyer from Bridgend. Wil left the village. Called back by an insistent dream some two years later, he found Ann dying. Both lovers are buried at St Cynwyd's, Wil under a yew tree and Ann in the chancel. His name is also marked on the column of famous local men, which stands outside the churchyard.

About 2km. west of Llangynwyd, on Margam Mountain, are the remains of a large Celtic, probably Early Iron Age, camp. Near the earthworks and concentric enclosures, known as Y Bwlwarcau (The Bulwarks), have been found traces of several primitive farmsteads, those of the hill-dwelling herdsmen who inhabited Wales before the Romans came.

Llanidloes Powys 3F5 (*pop.* 2,333)
Once one of the busiest industrial towns in Wales, Llanidloes now lives quietly on its past, its black-and-white half-timbered market-hall turned into a museum. These upland regions of Wales were never, of course, rich. The farming families supplemented their income by spinning their wool and weaving it into a coarse and hardwearing cloth, used by the Army in the eighteenth century and on the slave plantations of the West Indies and America. A related cottage industry was knitting. Men, women, and children in the Welsh hill country could be seen on the roads knitting as they walked; knitting evenings were held by parties of friends in one farmhouse or another. By the mid eighteenth century woollen manufacture at Llanidloes had reached the factory stage, though the mid-Wales textile industry was on too small a scale to produce an 'industrial revolution'. The Severn Valley woollen towns declined in the nineteenth century; they were too far from a coalfield, and the railways were late in coming to mid Wales. When they did come, the market was flooded with Welsh flannel made in Rochdale, which sold at a price the local mills had no hope of matching.

Another once flourishing industry has left its marks near Llanidloes. At the foot of the present Clywedog dam, the Bryn Tail lead mines began production in the late eighteenth century, and were at their most productive between 1845 and 1867. This industry, too, suffered from its isolation and the lack of transport facilities. At Bryn Tail parts of old walls, a gable-end of the main building, and a ruined water-wheel pit and engine-house are among the extensive remains. These have now been scheduled as an Industrial Monument.

Llanidloes has plenty to offer the visitor. Besides the fascinating local museum in the old Market Hall, St Idloes' church, a partly thirteenth-century building, has a north arcade and fine hammer-beam roof that are thought to have been salvaged from the Cistercian Abbey Cwmhir at the Dissolution. The town is surrounded by the wildest of Welsh mountain scenery, and for those who like waterworks, the Clywedog dam and reservoir are indeed impressive. Llyn Clywedog, 246ha. and 50 thousand million litres of water, regulates the level of the Severn and provides security of water supply for Birmingham, Wolverhampton, Bristol, and several English counties. It is stocked annually with brown and rainbow trout; it also offers sailing and a 4km.-long nature trail. There is good fishing, too, in the Severn and Clywedog rivers.

Llanina Dyfed *see* **New Quay**

Llanrhian Dyfed 8B3
In Llanrhian church, which has an uncharacteristic tower for this area, the octagonal font bears the arms of Sir Rhys ap Thomas (*see* Carew). On the coast, Porthgain and Abereiddi once had flourishing stone quarries and a large brickworks. The ruins impart a melancholy atmosphere to the magnificent coastline. At Abereiddi, fossil-hunters can search for *Didymograptus bifidus* in the black rocks; at Porthgain, the greedy or discerning eater can sample fresh crab, lobster, and other sea-food in season.

Llanrhidian W. Glam. *see* **Gower Peninsula**

Llanrhystyd Dyfed 6B2
A small, old-fashioned village on the coast road between Aberaeron and Aberystwyth. The River Wyre flows through to the sea about 1km. away; there is a sandy beach fairly near. Llanrhystyd Castle, of which only the mound remains, was built by Cadwaladr, a twelfth-century prince of North Wales. The church was rebuilt last century, when the original tower was buttressed and topped with a broach spire, unusual in this part of the country.

Llansantffraid (Llansanffraid) and **Llanon** Dyfed 6B2
These two small villages meet along the main coast road to Aberystwyth. St Bride's church (which gives the first village its name) has a thirteenth-century tower and an unspoilt late-eighteenth-century interior, with gallery, box-pews, clear window-glass, and brass chandeliers.

Llanon, on the landward side, may be named after St
Non, the mother of St David. There are the ruins of a
medieval chapel behind the post-office. The beach,
½km. away, is pebbly.

Llansantffraed (Llansanffraid)   Powys   7F5
Literary tourists will want to visit the tomb of Henry
Vaughan the Silurist, in the graveyard of the church of
St Bride (rebuilt in 1885). Henry and his twin, Thomas,
were born in 1621 or 1622 at Newton, near Scethrog, a
little further up the valley; this was a younger branch of
the Vaughan family who held Tretower Court. Both
brothers were Royalists and both were interested in
alchemy and hermetic philosophy. Thomas was Vicar at
Llansantffraed for a few years, but was ejected in 1650.
Henry had studied law, and served in the King's army,
but returned to Brecknockshire to practise medicine. He
married twice, his second wife being his first wife's
sister, and had four children by each marriage. At the
age of about thirty, a serious illness, coupled with a
reading of the work of George Herbert (another poet
with Welsh connexions), caused his mind to turn in-
wards, to matters spiritual. His poetry, previously con-
ventional love pieces, became deeply religious and
mystical. For Vaughan, the external world is the expression of spiritual harmony; to apprehend this, he attempts to regain the purity of vision associated with
childhood. His own allegorical journey begins and ends
here in the Vale of Usk, or Isca, as Vaughan addresses it:

   When I am laid to rest hard by thy streams
   And my sun sets where first it sprung its beams.
Vaughan died in 1695; a memorial service is held
annually.

Llansteffan   Dyfed   9E4
The Normans with their genius for strategic sites fortified
Llansteffan on their first advance into Wales early in the
twelfth century. Extensive ditches remain, some of them
from this period. The present stone ruins date from the
rebuilding of the castle in 1284, possibly by Geoffrey de
Chamville. There is a fine gatehouse-cum-keep, which
was used as the main living quarters. High on its hill,
the castle looks out over the mouth of the Towy River
and into the wide estuary where Towy meets Taf and
Gwendraeth. On the sands below, cockle-pickers with
their donkeys were once a familiar sight.

   Like Laugharne, on the next estuary west, Llansteffan has Dylan Thomas connexions. In the short
story *A Visit to Grandpa's* it is after an afternoon at
Llansteffan that the old man sets out for Llangadog, in his
best waistcoat, 'to be buried'. '"There's no sense in lying
dead in Llansteffan", he said. "The ground is comfy in
Llangadock; you can twitch your legs without putting
them in the sea"'. On the road to Carmarthen, at
Llangain, is the farmhouse 'Fern Hill', where Dylan's
aunt Ann Jones lived. Here Dylan spent in childhood
those paradise-like holidays described in the memor-

able imagery of his poem 'Fern Hill' and in his affectionate and humorous prose. For this aunt, too, he wrote
'After the Funeral', a poem in which the 'stuffed fox' and
'stale fern', symbols of Welsh Nonconformist respectability, vie with the 'ferned and foxy woods', nature,
love, and fertility.

Llantarnam   Gwent   *see* **Caerleon**

Llanthony (Llanddewi Nant Hodni)   Gwent   7G5
The magnificent remains of Llanthony Priory owe their
origin to the sudden conversion of a Norman knight.
William de Lacy, hunting here in his brother's lordship,
the Vale of Ewyas, stumbled on a ruined chapel dedicated to St David (hence the Welsh name, Llanddewi).
Something in the beauty of this isolated place made him
form the resolve to become a hermit. He was joined by
the Queen's chaplain, Ernisius, in 1103, and by others
attracted to the contemplative life. Gradually, a religious community grew up; land was given (by de
Lacy's brother), a church built and consecrated. The
informal gathering became, in about 1118, a regular
priory of Augustinian canons.

   One of the very few houses of Augustinian or Black
Canons in Wales, Llanthony, the first such foundation,
prospered. In the disastrous reign of Stephen, however,
conditions everywhere were so bad that the chroniclers
claimed 'Christ and his angels slept'. In Wales, in
particular, an oppressed population took the opportunity
to rise against their conquerors. The Llanthony canons,
as an alien foundation, took refuge at Hereford. After
1137 they were given land near Gloucester. Here they
founded a new Llanthony (Llanthony Secunda), and
gradually removed their possessions to the new house.

   The de Lacy family, which had fallen into disgrace,
recovered its estate in Ewyas in the 1150s. Gifts of land
and churches in Ireland made by the fifth Baron to the
Black Canons probably led to the rebuilding of the
priory. This took place, with a few breaks, between 1175
and 1220; some canons returned, and the two Llan-
thonys parted company for the time being.

   The remainder of the priory's life was by no means a
quiet one. Their wealth from Ireland and from local
estates appears to have corrupted the monks, while the
revolt of the Welsh under Owain Glyndwr at the turn of
the fifteenth century, together with the incursions of the
English kings, laid waste the house and its property. In
1448 the priors were granted exemption from tax-
collecting as their lands could no longer support the
charges. In 1481 the priory was once more placed in the
care of the sister-house at Gloucester, only the Prior and
four canons remaining in Wales.

   The priory stumbled along until the Dissolution of the
Monasteries, when a royal servant named Arnolde
bought it for £160. An eighteenth-century owner converted the south tower into a shooting-box, and built a
house for his steward (this is now the hotel). In about

The small chapel-of-ease at Capel-y-Ffin

1807 the poet Walter Savage Landor bought the abbey, repairing roads and planting Spanish chestnuts as part of a scheme of improvements. His plan for a model estate foundered on bitter disputes with tenants and neighbours. In 1814, disenchanted, he moved abroad, addressing Llanthony, from a safe distance, with the following ironical couplet: 'I loved thee by thy streams of yore, / By distant streams I love thee more'.

The south-western tower of the church and most of the west range of the monastic buildings – the outer parlour, and the vaulted basements, probably used for storage of food and wine, with the canons' dormitory above them – are now occupied by a hotel. The non-resident visitor can, however, be content with the extensive remains of the church and lesser fragments of the claustral buildings. The church dates from *c*. 1180–1220; its solid yet graceful remains show very clearly the transition between the Norman or Romanesque style (round-headed arches) and the later Gothic (pointed arches). Both the main windows, east and west, have disappeared, the latter within the last 200 years. The west front retains, none the less, a mutilated grandeur.

The cloister, to the south of the church, is now a grassy square; its own south wall is much rebuilt. On its eastern side, the 'slype', or covered passage-way, still has a fine vaulted ceiling of thirteenth-century date. Immediately beside this, the chapter-house (one of the priory's

administrative centres) was an ornamental and spacious structure. Of the outbuildings, the priory gatehouse has been incorporated into a farm to the south-west of the ruins. St David's church, also of the thirteenth century, appears to have been transformed out of the infirmary hall and chapel.

CAPEL-Y-FFIN ('Chapel on the boundary') can be reached from Llanthony, or over the Gospel Pass from Hay-on-Wye. Remote in its valley, it has a Youth Hostel and a curious variety of ecclesiastical buildings. There are an early Baptist chapel, and a small Anglican chapel-of-ease with square windows and a cottage-like porch – 'squatting like a stout grey owl among its seven great black yews', as the Revd Francis Kilvert described it. Kilvert also provides a vivid account of the personalities involved with the third and most ambitious of these buildings, the Anglican Benedictine monastery founded by 'Father Ignatius' (the Revd J. L. Lyne) in 1870. He visited the site in that year, when the monks were still working on it – 'They looked very much like old women at work in the garden' – and again later in the year with Father Ignatius's parents (Mrs Lyne, it being Friday, 'had wisely taken the precaution of bringing with her an honest leg of mutton and two bottles of wine'). Kilvert describes Lyne's extraordinary gentle innocence (which led to his being cheated right and left) and the hostile reactions to the new community from local people.

White Castle, 3km. N of Llantilio Crossenny: the finest of the Three Castles

Capel-y-ffin Monastery fell into disrepair after the death of Father Ignatius in 1908. In the 1920s part of it was reoccupied for a few years by the sculptor Eric Gill; the London–Welsh poet and painter David Jones spent some time with him there. It later became a girls' school. Abergavenny Museum has some items connected with Father Ignatius and his venture.

Llantilio Crossenny (Llandeilo Gresynni)   Gwent 7H6

Llantilio church stands on a mound, within an entrenchment, a good example of Christian re-use of an earlier, perhaps pagan, site. In the village, where the road turns towards White Castle, a rectangular enclosure surrounded by a wet moat is all that remains of Hen Gwrt ('Old Court'), a medieval moated dwelling.

From Llantilio, the WHITE CASTLE lies about 3km. north, in the direction of Llanvetherine (Llanwytherin). Walkers can take the slightly longer route of the Offa's Dyke Footpath, which runs between Llantilio and Llanvetherine, avoiding the roads. White Castle formed, with the castles at Grosmont and Skenfrith, a strategic triangle against the unruly Welsh. It stands isolated on a hill, remote from any civil settlement and intent purely

on defence. White plaster still visible here and there on the masonry is thought to have given the castle its name (though another tradition has it that it was called after a Welsh chieftain, Gwyn).

The earliest reference to a castle at Llantilio is in 1161–2, though it may well have been there for some time by that date. By the end of the twelfth century the castle consisted of a small rectangular stone tower surrounded by a plain curtain wall, now the inner ward. In the following century, when the Welsh rose twice, under the two Llewellyns, the castle was extended and heavily refortified. In 1244 a new hall, buttery, and pantry were built. In the 1260s or 1270s the inner wall was strengthened with semicircular towers, a powerful gatehouse was added, and the outer ward enclosed by its own curtain wall with flanking towers. The old square keep was demolished, and residential buildings were put up within the inner ward.

The strategic value of the Three Castles can be gauged from the fact that they remained almost continuously in the hands of the Crown, rather than in those of powerful families who might use their position against the King. Hubert de Burgh, Royal Justiciar, held them from 1201 to 1232, with an interval of fourteen years in the reign of

King John. De Burgh spent considerable sums on the three castles, though it seems likely that Skenfrith and Grosmont received a greater share. After 1234 another royal officer, Waleran the German, took charge of the castles, and in 1254 they were granted to the Lord Edward, later Edward I. In 1267 they passed to his younger brother, the Earl of Lancaster.

White Castle does not seem to have been called on to prove its strength. Llewellyn the Last and his army came almost as far as Abergavenny, 11km. away, but this frontier was never crossed, and after 1277 the Welsh retreated. The castle continued in use as an administrative centre for the collection of rents and levies. By the sixteenth century, with the breakdown of the old feudal system, it had already fallen into disrepair.

The castle's plan is satisfyingly easy to grasp. Its core is the inner ward, where domestic buildings – hall, solar, kitchen – stood in a pear-shaped courtyard within a strong curtain wall. Four semicircular towers project from the curtain, one of them housing a chapel. On the north-west, a powerful gatehouse controlled a drawbridge and portcullis. Around the inner ward are a steep ditch and moat; to the south, a hornwork, or separate defensive outwork, was also surrounded by water. On the opposite side, and facing the gatehouse, an extensive outer ward large enough to camp an army had its own curtain wall with towers, its own gatehouse, and its own moat (which was probably dry).

Small-scale but powerful, White Castle was very much a military matter. From the outside, its cylindrical towers make no concessions. Inside, a well, a chapel, and the remains of fireplaces and latrines show that there was at least a rudimentary standard of comfort.

Llantrisant Mid Glam. 11F3
The church, ruined castle, and sober, slate-roofed cottages of Llantrisant stand on a hill looking out south over the Vale of Glamorgan. In 1967 the new Royal Mint was established on a site below the hill, and extensive new housing development has followed.

The 'three saints' of the village's name are Illtud, Wonno, and Tyfodwg. The church, originally Norman, was rebuilt in the sixteenth century and again in 1873; the sturdy-looking west tower is probably Tudor. Six eighteenth-century bells (1718) were cast on the spot, in a foundry that was discovered under the belfry at the last restoration. Inside, there are an octagonal thirteenth-century font, and some interesting memorials, including an upright stone effigy built into the north wall and thought to represent Cadwgan Fawr of Miscin, a local knight of the mid thirteenth century. A Pre-Raphaelite window (1873) portrays an unbearded Christ.

Llantrisant Castle was built about 1250, by the Norman Richard de Clare, to protect the Vale of Glamorgan from attacks from the hill country to the north. It was in ruins by the end of the Middle Ages; today, only the fragment of a round tower remains. It was

somewhere near Llantrisant, in 1326, that the unfortunate Edward II was captured with followers such as Hugh le Despenser, Lord of Glamorgan. He was led from here to Berkeley Castle, where he spent ten months in captivity and was finally most horribly murdered.

Llantrisant is famous in South Wales as the home of Dr William Price, an eccentric medical man and self-styled Archdruid of Wales. In 1884 he caused a scandal by attempting publicly to cremate the body of his young son, Iesu Grist (Jesus Christ). Tried at Cardiff Assizes, Price's case was dismissed with a farthing's costs; cremation was pronounced in no way contrary to the law of the land. Price himself, a familiar figure in scarlet vest, green trousers and coat, and foxskin cap of the kind now known as a 'Davy Crockett', died in 1893, aged as old as the century. His own public cremation drew a crowd of thousands.

The Caerau ('camps'), a few km. east on a hill, are the earthworks of a circular prehistoric hill-fort with impressive triple bank and ditch defences.

Llantwit Major (Llanilltud Fawr) S. Glam. 11E4
Llantwit Major is an attractive and ancient town of considerable character, somewhat tempered in more recent years by its proximity to the RAF station at St Athan. South of the town, a lane runs down alongside the Col-hugh River to a largely unspoiled beach about 2km. away. Along the coast, and a little to the west, Tresilian Bay with its caves and cliffs was once noted for smugglers' passages and secret marriage-ceremonies.

Much of Llantwit's history is visible in its old buildings, but much, too, has remained buried. It is a great pity that the Roman villa at Caermead field, north-west of the town, is no longer worth a visit. One of the few known Roman villas in Wales, it occupied about 3ha. in all. Excavations in 1888 uncovered painted walls and a colourful mosaic pavement; the skeletons of forty-three humans and three horses, and the evidence of burned masonry, suggested that the villa was attacked by Irish raiders, early in the fourth century, and its inhabitants massacred. A copy of the pavement may be seen in the National Museum at Cardiff.

In the centre of the town, a prominent old two-storey building is the Town Hall or Church Loft, whose origins date back to the late thirteenth century. Sacked by Owain Glyndwr during his rebellion (c. 1400), the structure was rebuilt in the fifteenth century, and this is the building we see today. The bell in the turret is pre-Reformation and is inscribed, in Latin, 'St Illtud, pray for us'. All kinds of community events were held at the hall, from fairs and markets to courts of justice. John Wesley preached outside it, in the eighteenth century. The Old Swan Inn, nearby, is thought to have served in medieval times as a monastic or a manorial mint.

Llantwit's major historical significance is, however, as a religious centre. Traditionally, it was here that Illtud, one of the Celtic missionary saints, and a native of

Brittany, set up, in the fifth century, a school or monastic community. As a centre of learning and of piety, Llantwit became famous throughout the Celtic Church. The list of Illtud's pupils at what has sometimes been called the first British university include SS David, Samson of Dol, Paulinus of Leon (Paulus Aurelianus), Taliesin the bard, and Gildas the historian. The community lasted until the Normans came; the buildings may have occupied the site of the present church. Early references to Illtud's arrival from the sea may well have some foundation in fact. Colhugh Point was used as a port in Norman times, and perhaps earlier, while an old oak breakwater on the beach has yielded a carbon-dating of *c.* 1305–*c.* 1495.

The present parish church of St Illtud is ancient and unusual, with a number of interesting features. It is in reality two churches, joined by a central tower. The West, or Old, church, originally a late-twelfth-century building of simple cruciform plan, was reconstructed in the fifteenth century, which makes it newer than the East, or New, church, which itself remains a largely thirteenth-century building. Notice in the East church a Jesse tree in a finely carved niche; a fourteenth-century stone reredos, possibly a rood-screen originally; some remnants of wall-paintings; and a memorial to 129-year-old Matthew Voss, who died in 1534. The Western church retains its Norman south door and porch; its roof is of Irish bog-oak and is splendidly carved with heraldic devices. This part of the church is now used as a museum of early stones and monuments.

The two earliest stones, probably from the eighth century, are decorated but have no inscriptions. The 'Cross of Samson' commemorates a king (?) who is otherwise unknown; it also bears the names Iltu [tus], Samuel, and Ebisar. The cross of Howel ap Rees, a slab cross with carved wheel head, was set up by King Hywel of Glywysing, a ninth-century ruler mentioned in the medieval *Book of Llandaff*. 'Abbot Samson's pillar' is a quadrangular cross shaft with decorated panels (*c.* 800), raised by the Abbot for the repose of his soul and for that of King Iuthahel (Ithel), Artmal (Arthmael), and Tecan (the 'deacon'?). There are some fine effigies from later periods: in particular, that of a lady in full elaborate late-sixteenth-century costume, with a bust of her child at her shoulder.

BOVERTON, a village 1½km. east of Llantwit, is on the edge of the RAF station and has developed accordingly. A large ruin in the village is all that remains of Boverton Place, a fortified manor-house with stabling for more than sixty horses. LLANMAES, 1½km. north-east, on a minor road, has an Early English church with Norman font and some faded wall-paintings. The parish registers record the death of Ivan Yorath, allegedly aged 180, in 1621 (he had fought at Bosworth in 1485, and lived 'muche by fishing') and that of another parishioner who, we are told, lived to be 177.

About 4km. north of Llantwit, towards Cowbridge,

ABOVE: *The cross of Howel ap Rees in St Illtud's church, Llantwit Major. The Latin inscription reads:* [I]N INOMINE DI PATRIS ET / [S]PERETUS SANTDI ANC / [CR]UCEM HOVELT PROPE / [RA]BIT PRO ANIMA RES PA / [TR]ES EVS *(In the name of God the Father, and of the Holy Spirit, Hovelt prepared this cross for the soul of Res, his father)*

OPPOSITE: *Double-beaded plaitwork in a late-C9–C10 Celtic cross-shaft: St Illtud's church, Llantwit Major*

and down a small lane from the village of Sigingston, LLANMIHANGEL PLACE is an attractive old Tudor mansion, all angels and gables. The spectre of a fifteenth-century heiress, Eleanor Dee, is said to haunt the neighbourhood. Believed to have magic powers, she was branded as a witch, and tethered, in her moments of frenzy, by an iron ring attached to her wrist. She met her death by drowning in the pool that lies near the church, and has been seen rising in the white mists that gather there at twilight.

The coast-road east from Llantwit leads to St Athan and to ABERTHAW (Aberddawan), a flourishing port in pre-industrial times and now utterly destroyed by cement-works and a power-station. A few old cottages still remain.

Llanwenog Dyfed 6B3
A small village on the edge of the mountains that separate the Teifi Valley from the sea, Llanwenog has an attractive inn and an interesting old church. The tower is a fifteenth-century one, with carvings, waterspouts, and heraldic devices. Inside, an early and primitive font bears grotesque carved faces. The bench-ends, carved by a Belgian refugee early this century, give a pictorial history of the locality. There are an eighteenth-century barrel-roof, local stained glass, and, on the north wall, the Creed and Ten Commandments in Welsh.

In the old days, Llanwenog was the scene of an annual inter-village football match, played on 'Old New Year's Day' (the calendar was changed in 1752). As much folk ritual as sport, the game was played as follows. The 'ball' was placed on a ridge halfway between Llanwenog and Llandysul, which are about 10km. apart. The 'teams' were the entire male population of each village, some on foot and some on horseback; the 'goals' were the church porch of each respective parish. Unlike modern football, the winner was expected to get the ball into his own, not his opponent's, goal. The game was often violent and lasted most of the day. In 1833, after an accidental death had occurred, the Vicar of Llandysul succeeded in replacing the game with a Sunday School Festival that included a recital of catechisms and singing of anthems.

Llanwnda Dyfed　*see* **Fishguard**

Llanwnnog Powys　*see* **Caersŵs**

Llanwrtyd Wells Powys 6D3
The waters at Llanwrtyd are said to have been known to the Romans; they were certainly found in 1732 by the Revd Theophilus Evans of Llangammarch. Evans suffered from a chronic condition of scurvy, in a form almost as bad as leprosy. After two months of internal and external treatments with the sulphurous waters, he was completely cured. Llanwrtyd had in fact a variety of mineral springs, but it was the sulphur that was most

in demand; it was the strongest in Wales and more palatable than the famous and equally strong Old Sulphur Well water at Harrogate.

The spa had long been a favourite place of resort for South Wales. The coming of the railway helped to draw in the English visitor as well. To the Pump Room and to the large and comfortable hotels, the Victorian sufferer (or over-indulgent diner) brought his ulcers, gout, sciatica, liver and kidney complaints. Llanwrtyd could not offer the sophisticated amusements of Baden-Baden, but it did have the quiet pleasures of the countryside. For the active, there were rambles, golf, even some shooting; in the season, the day would close with a concert in the spa grounds.

Llanwrtyd has been called the most beautiful of the Welsh spas, and certainly its sheltering mountains and the charming Irfon Valley have enabled it to retain some hold on the traveller now that the waters are no longer in fashion. Fishing, boating, pony-trekking have replaced sulphur and chalybeate as the key to health and relaxation; golf and country walks are still well provided for. There are fine views from old Llanwrtyd village, a little further up the valley, where the famous Welsh hymn-writer William Williams Pantycelyn was curate for a few years in the 1740s.

Once a stopping-point on the drovers' road from Abergwesyn, Llanwrtyd still retains (1975) the luxury of a railway station.

Llanybydder Dyfed 6B4
A small market-town in the Teifi Valley, Llanybydder stands at the crossing of numerous roads. Normally quiet, it is internationally famous for its horse-fairs, held on the last Thursday of each month. The surrounding area once had a thriving woollen industry. Many of the old riverside mills have now fallen into disuse; but some have recently reawakened, to cater for the new interest in local crafts. Traditional Welsh tapestries, blankets, skirts, and ties make hardwearing and colourful souvenirs.

Llawhaden (Llanhuadain) Dyfed 8C4
The castle at Llawhaden, which looks out from its hill over the Eastern Cleddau and the Preseli Mountains, was a fortified residence of the medieval bishops of St David's. Originally a circular enclosure with a rampart of earth dug from the surrounding ditch, some form of castle was already in existence here when Giraldus Cambrensis, Gerald the Welshman, visited the spot during his tour of Wales in 1195. The present ruins, however, date from the early fourteenth century. The best-preserved portion is the south-east face: a drum-towered gatehouse and a stretch of curtain wall with lancet windows and projecting pentagonal towers. The strongly defensive nature of the building indicates how insecure were the medieval lords spiritual, especially when they were almost all foreigners to their flock. The

castle would probably have been staffed by mercenary soldiers. The chapel, which is reached by a fine Perpendicular stair tower, was added in the early sixteenth century, during the episcopate of Bishop Vaughan. One of his successors, the black sheep Bishop Barlow (1530–48), is said to have taken the lead from the roof to pay off his debts (certainly during his time, the residency moved to Abergwili near Carmarthen), and the castle deteriorated thereafter.

Nearby, there are remains of a medieval wayfarers' hospice, built by Bishop Bek in 1287. Llawhaden church, across an ancient bridge, was rebuilt in the late fourteenth century, and is curious for its two towers.

Llowes Powys see **Clyro**

Llyswen Powys see **Glasbury**

Llywel Powys see **Trecastle**

Loughor (Llwchwr) W. Glam. 10B2 (pop. 26,845)
Road and railway cross the Loughor River here, at a point just above the broadening out of the estuary. Near the river, and south of the main road, the remains of a small castle stand on a Norman mound, itself very near to the probable site of the Roman fort of Leucarum. A single rectangular tower and part of a curtain wall date from the late thirteenth or early fourteenth century. Loughor now forms part of the almost continuous industrial ribbon running from Swansea to Llanelli. Within a few km., however, lies the perfect unspoiled countryside of the Gower Peninsula.

Lydstep Dyfed 8D5
The first Viscount St David's was largely responsible for erecting this coastal village. The ruined 'Palace of Arms' in the centre is claimed as a hunting-seat of Bishop Gower of St David's, though it may have been merely an armoury. Lydstep Haven is a caravan site; Lydstep Head, to the west, is NT property, and there is a nature trail organized by the West Wales Naturalists' Trust. The caverns, beyond Lydstep Head, are worth a visit, but with the exception of the Smugglers' Cave can be inspected only at low tide. The beach is sandy, and there are magnificent views out towards Caldy Island.

Machynlleth Powys 3E4 (pop. 1,766)
Machynlleth is an attractive and historic small town on the south bank of the Dovey River, a river that is often considered as the border between North and South Wales. Trees and hills seem to come down almost into the streets, where ancient houses and eighteenth-century inns mix with the prim bow-windowed fronts of more recent villas. The Victorian clock tower with its pinnacles, which bestrides the main thoroughfare, was put up in 1873, in honour of the Marquess of Londonderry,

who had acquired the local *Plas* by marriage; it replaced the earlier Market Cross. Plas Machynlleth, built in 1691 and extended in the nineteenth century, was given to the town by the Londonderry family before the Second War. It is now used for council offices, and its grounds provide a fine public park.

Maen Gwyn Street is named after the town's oldest surviving relic of the past, a prehistoric direction-stone that marked the Dovey Valley trackway before the Romans came. The stone, broken in later times, perhaps as a rejection of pagan superstition, stands against the wall of a house in this street. Traces of an Iron Age encampment have been found on the hills above Machynlleth, and there are more prehistoric signposts at Penegoes and Abergwydol.

The pride of the town, however, is the old stone Parliament House of Owain Glyndwr, which stands in Maen Gwyn Street opposite the gates of the Plas. The original building now forms the library, and the whole, extended structure has been rechristened the Owain Glyndwr Institute. Last century it served as a storehouse and carding-room for the wool trade; it now provides municipal offices and a place of 'rest and culture' for the town.

Glyndwr is known to the English largely as the Glendower of Shakespeare's *Henry IV*, a poetical, somewhat boastful magus, plotting against the English King. The Welsh, naturally enough, see him in the light of their own national history. Starting with a territorial quarrel with the Earl of Ruthin in 1400, Glyndwr's rebellion spread quickly through the whole of Wales. By 1403 the English in Wales were cowering in their walled

The Parliament House of Owain Glyndwr, Machynlleth

towns and castles; administration had largely broken down and royal expeditions into Wales had as yet little lasting effect. Glyndwr determined to exploit the weakness of the English Crown. With the great families of Mortimer and Percy, who had their own reasons for discontent, he conspired against the usurper Henry IV. Under an agreement signed with Mortimer and Henry Percy (Hotspur) in 1405, the Kingdom once conquered was to be divided between them; Glyndwr was to receive the whole of Wales and the Border Country. He negotiated alliances with the Irish and Scots, and, in particular, with the French King Charles VI, who was only too pleased to find an opportunity to weaken his traditional enemy. In 1405 a French force landed in Milford Haven; it marched almost to Worcester, where it met the English army and retreated. This was the beginning of the end for Glyndwr. The English pushed relentlessly back into Wales, capturing castles, and reasserting their power in the more Anglicized, lowland regions. By 1413 northern Cardiganshire alone still held out for Glyndwr.

The latter was not, however, merely an unsuccessful freedom fighter. He saw his rôle in Wales as that of statesman as well as of general. The Parliament he set up at Machynlleth (others were held at Dolgellau and Harlech) was to be representative of Wales, with four members chosen from each commot. At Machynlleth, in 1404, tradition has it that he was crowned prince of all Wales, with envoys from France and Scotland in attendance. That same year, the people of the Shropshire border decided to ask for a peace treaty with the 'land of Wales'. Glyndwr's negotiations were not confined to military matters. With the French monarch he discussed freeing the Welsh Church from its dependence on Canterbury (this would have meant recognizing the Avignon Pope), and making St David's an archbishopric. He proposed, too, when the war was won, to set up universities in Wales, one each for the north and south of the country.

The short-term consequences of the failure of Glyndwr's revolt were bitter ones for Wales. Destruction of towns, castles, and manors was wholesale. Many monasteries were injured almost beyond repair. The Welsh were forced to pay out vast sums in compensation, partly for arrears of rent, and partly also in fines for failing to hold the courts of justice. The country further suffered from the hatreds and rivalries of a divided people, and from the banditry that was the result of the refusal of the outlawed to make their surrender. Glyndwr himself, after the fall of Harlech (1409) and the loss of his wife and family possessions, vanished into the hills. The time and place of his death are unknown, and this mystery has added much legendary force to his memory. He is one of several Welsh princes whom legend has it sleep somewhere in a lonely cave, an armed band at their side, ready to awake when danger threatens Wales. What is certain is that the passions aroused by

his ten years of Welsh independence awoke again to greet Henry Tudor on his march to Bosworth in 1485.

Machynlleth refuses, wisely enough, to live on its past. For the visitor, its seasonal fairs, sheep-dog trials, and fox-hunt (with a foot-pack of hounds of French descent, suitable for this special terrain) are attractions additional to the magnificent scenery of the Dovey Estuary and the hills. There is splendid walking, into Plynlimon, in the Llyfnant and Dulas valleys, to Forge or Glaspwll, or to Pengoes (1½km. east), birthplace of the eighteenth-century landscape painter and watercolourist Richard Wilson.

Manorbier (Maenorbŷr) Dyfed 8C5
This must be one of the most delightful castles in Wales, with its solid military lines tempered by a flowery courtyard, its round, 'Flemish' chimneys, and its unspoiled setting next to the sea. It was built by the de Barri family, Norman barons who consolidated their victories with marriages as strategic as their castles. William de

Manorbier Castle

Barri, who is probably responsible for much of the present castle, married Angharad, herself the offspring of a dynastic union between Norman and Welsh (Gerald de Windsor, Steward of Pembroke, and Nest, the much-seduced heiress of Rhys ap Tewdwr, Prince of South Wales). Most of the castle – a rectangular inner ward, with sturdy gate-house and curtain wall protecting the usual domestic buildings – was completed by 1300. There is a well shaft with smugglers' passage. The castle is inhabited, but is open to the public in summer.

Inside the castle, a waxwork figure represents Giraldus Cambrensis, 'Gerald the Welshman', one of William de Barri's sons, who was born at the castle in 1146. The sons of the medieval nobility had only two careers open to them: Army or Church. William's other sons took a prominent part in the Norman conquest of Ireland. Gerald chose the Church, and achieved a lasting fame through his writings, which remain very readable today. He accompanied Archbishop Baldwin of Canterbury on the latter's tour of Wales, undertaken to

preach the Third Crusade; one result of this was the *Itinerary*, Gerald's illuminating account of their travels. Half-Norman and half-Welsh, Gerald's overriding ambition was to be appointed Bishop of St David's and to free that see from its dependence on Canterbury. This was never granted, and Gerald remained merely Archdeacon of Brecon.

Gerald's description of Manorbier, 'Maenor Pyrr' or manor of Pyrrus, as he calls it, cannot be omitted. The castle is 'excellently well defended by turrets and bulwarks, and is situated on the summit of a hill extending on the western side towards the seaport, having on the northern and southern sides a fine fish-pond under its walls, as conspicuous for its grand appearance, as for the depth of its waters, and a beautiful orchard on the same side, enclosed on one part by a vineyard, and on the other by a wood, remarkable for the projection of its rocks, and the height of its hazel trees. On the right hand of the promontory, between the castle and the church, near the site of a very large lake and mill, a rivulet of never-failing water flows through a valley, rendered sandy by the violence of the winds. Towards the west, the Severn sea, bending its course to Ireland, enters a hollow bay at some distance from the castle; and the southern rocks, if extended a little further north, would render it a most excellent harbour for shipping. . . . This country is well supplied with corn, sea-fish, and imported wines; and what is preferable to every other advantage, from its vicinity to Ireland, it is tempered by a salubrious air'. Gerald concludes, therefore, that Manorbier is 'the pleasantest spot in Wales; and the author may be pardoned for having thus extolled his native soil, his genial territory, with a profusion of praise and admiration'.

Medieval castles were thus not only materially strong but also well supplied, almost self-sufficient, in food. With their mills, fish-ponds, orchards, hazel-groves, and vineyards, the Barris evidently could live in some comfort. Nor was Manorbier in the twelfth century a charming backwater or haven of peace from the world. Gerald's remarks about shipping remind us that this western corner of Wales was the springboard for the invasion of Ireland.

Across the stream, which once powered the castle corn mills, Manorbier church with its tall square tower stands halfway up the hillside. The original building was probably contemporary with the castle; the nave is of twelfth-century date, and other sections were added or rebuilt later. There are traces of wall-painting, and, in the chancel, the effigy of a crusader. The rood-loft is a fourteenth-century feature.

Below the castle are a sandy beach with tidal pools and rocks of Old Red Sandstone. On the eastern headland, the King's Quoit is a collapsed cromlech marking a prehistoric burial chamber.

Marcross   S. Glam.   *see* **St Donat's**

Margam W. Glam. *see* **Port Talbot**

Marloes Dyfed 8A5
Marloes has a number of prehistoric remains: a large Early Iron Age promontory fort, on the headland known as the Deer Park, and, on Gateholm Island, which can be reached on foot at low tide, extensive traces of a Romano-British settlement. These rectangular huts were occupied, it is thought, in the third century, possibly by a monastic community.

In later times, Marloes men practised wrecking and leech-gathering (the latter for the supply of Harley Street). Here, too, until the nineteenth century, the ceremony of 'Hunting the Wren' survived. This pagan rite took place on Twelfth Night. A wren, symbol of the evils of winter, was captured and placed in a carved and beribboned 'wren-house'. Four men carried it around the town, singing traditional verses, and collecting moneys and drink at every house. The Marloes wren-house may be seen at the Welsh Folk Museum at St Fagan's (*see* Cardiff).

From Marloes, boats leave for the island nature reserves of Skomer and Skokholm. Marloes' cliffs are a habitat of the rare prostrate broom (*Sarothamnus scoparius* ssp. *maritimus*), which differs from common broom in its manner of spreading closely pressed to ground or cliff face.

Mathry (Mathri) Dyfed 8B3
Mathry church, in its pre-Christian (?) circular enclosure, is dedicated to the 'Seven Saints'. These legendary septuplets, unwanted, were saved from drowning by a monk, St Teilo, who reared them on fish miraculously provided daily by the Cleddau River. Mathry fair has a charter that dates back to Edward III; it is still an annual event. Abercastle (Abercastell), about 2km. north-east, along the coast, is a delightful small harbour.

Between Abercastle and Trevine (Trefin), at Longhouse, Samson's Stone (Carreg Samson) is a fine example of a Neolithic passage-grave. A polygonal burial chamber was incorporated in a round mound, with access provided by a passage-way through the mound itself. At Longhouse the mound has not survived, but there remains the enormous capstone resting on a number of uprights, not all of which support its weight.

Merthyr Mawr Mid Glam. 10D4
A delightful village of old, thatched cottages (which are not all that common in Wales), Merthyr Mawr is one of the prettiest spots in the Vale of Glamorgan. Narrow lanes lead down to the hamlet, one of them crossing a medieval four-arched bridge with holes for sheep-dipping. St Teilo's church is neo-Gothic, with an octagonal font that may be original. In and around the church are a number of ancient stones and effigies, including a Celtic cross.

Beyond the village, farmland almost immediately gives way to a great waste of sand-dunes, the 'Warren'. The ruins of Candleston Castle, a fifteenth-century fortified manor-house, stand on the edge of this expanse, protected by a limestone cliff. Once a fertile medieval manor, Candleston was gradually overtaken by the blowing sands. The house, however, was occupied well into the nineteenth century.

Today the dunes are of special value to athletes, who train here, and to archaeologists, who have made significant discoveries during the last hundred years or so. One of the numerous tumuli proved to contain a Beaker Folk burial, with six skeletons (some in the crouching position) and some characteristic pottery. The shift of sands has also uncovered Iron Age, Bronze Age, and Romano-British tools and ornaments.

Merthyr Tydfil (Merthyr Tudful) Mid Glam. 11F1 (*pop.* 55,215)
Merthyr Tydfil is a town of little beauty but of great interest to anyone concerned with social history. It has been called the archetypical town of industrial South Wales; it has experienced every phase of industrial development since about 1760. It has spent most of this century throwing off the legacy of the last.

Merthyr grew as fast as any American boom town. A village in 1750, by 1801 it was the most populous place in Wales; it remained the largest town in the Principality for sixty years. Its phenomenal growth was due to iron, and, later, coal. Four great iron works – Cyfarthfa, Dowlais, Penydarren, Plymouth, controlled by dynasties of ironmasters, Crawshays, Guests, Homfrays – drew in a huge new population from rural Wales and from England.

Richard Crawshay had made a million by 1810. His rival, Samuel Homfray, in 1803, bet him 1,000 guineas that a load of ten tons of bar iron could be conveyed by steam power along the new tramroad from his works to the canal at Navigation (Abercynon) – a distance of nearly 16km. Richard Trevithick, the Cornish engineer, was engaged to build a steam locomotive. In February 1804 the historic journey took place. The first steam locomotive in the world drew its five wagons, carrying ten tons of freight and seventy men, at an average speed of 8km. per hour. During the journey, the engine's brick chimney stack hit a bridge and both were damaged. Trevithick repaired the stack and continued the run. The 'railway' came into general use ten years later, although Trevithick's first engine collapsed after three trips. Part of the Penydarren Tram Road line has recently been scheduled as an industrial monument, while other relics of the original journey can be seen in the National Museum at Cardiff.

In nineteenth-century Merthyr wages were (comparatively) high, but the quality of life was not. In one of Anthony Trollope's novels a young curate faints on hearing he is to be sent there. Carlyle visited the town in 1850. 'It is like a vision of Hell', he exclaimed, 'and will never leave me, that of these poor creatures toiling all in sweat and dust, amid these furnaces, pits and rolling mills. The town might be one of the prettiest places in the world. It *is* one of the sootiest, squalidest and ugliest; all cinders and dustmounds and soot'. Poor housing and food, bad drainage, pollution, long hours of work, brought high rates of disease and mortality. The average life-expectancy in 1845 was thirty-two for tradesmen, for working-men, seventeen. Workers lived huddled in long rows of cottages with primitive washing and lavatory facilities. William Crawshay, meanwhile, in 1825, spent £25,000 on his mock-medieval Cyfarthfa Castle.

Given these conditions, industrial unrest was inevitable. In 1816, for example, Josiah John Guest and other ironmasters had to barricade themselves in Dowlais House; from there, they fired into a violent mob, killing at least one person. The Merthyr Riots of 1831 produced at the Castle Inn a massacre more bloody than Peterloo; a 23-year-old miner, Dic Penderyn, almost certainly innocent, was hanged for his part in the death of a soldier and was buried at Abcravon (a Welshman in Pennsylvania later confessed to the crime). (*See* Alexander Cordell's novel *The Fire People*, for a colourful account of this period of Merthyr history.) The 1831 Riot at least ensured the town a seat in Parliament under the new franchise laws. From then on, the town has had a consistently radical political tradition. Its Members have included Henry Richard, the pacifist from Tregaron, and Keir Hardie.

Changes in the use of fuel and in the technology of steel production robbed Merthyr of its economic advantages. By the 1930s it was a Distressed Area. Political and Economic Planning suggested in all seriousness that the town be abandoned, and its people rehoused on the coast and in the Wye Valley. The Second World War provided a temporary respite from the desperate unemployment of the Depression years. Since the War, government policy has created new jobs, in engineering and consumer-goods manufacture, but Merthyr still does not wear much of an air of affluence.

Rebuilding in Merthyr and Dowlais has changed the face of the old, nineteenth-century town centre. Some of the early industrial terraced housing still remains, however; long low rows of cottages in grey Pennant sandstone, with slate roofs and (sometimes) cobbled yards and outhouse walls. In these older parts of town, inns, chapels, and shops were often classical in form. (In 1851 Merthyr had eighty-four churches and chapels, of which sixty-five were Nonconformist.) The 'Triangle', a well-known early development at Pentre-bach, represents an attempt to provide simple housing with some privacy and access to open space. Later terraces have characteristic red and yellow brickwork around doors and windows. The modern houses, healthier, of course, and more comfortable, are unfortunately not always more pleasing to the eye than these older buildings, whose local materials fitted better into the landscape.

Cyfarthfa Castle (1825), in mock-Gothic style, overlooks the site of the old Cyfarthfa Iron Works (Crawshay evidently believed in living near his job). It now houses an art gallery and museum. VAYNOR (Y Faenor), 4km. north, is on the edge of the Brecon Beacons National Park. Its Gothic church was built by Robert T. Crawshay, who was buried here in 1879; his grave bears the words 'God forgive me'. On a much-quarried ridge across the valley stand the remains of Morlais Castle, a late-thirteenth-century fortress that may never have been completed. The ruins include parts of the curtain-wall, and two drum towers, one of which was probably the keep and has a gracefully vaulted polygonal chamber in its lower storey. There are also remains of a well-shaft and of domestic ovens.

Milford Haven (Aberdaugleddyf)   Dyfed   8B5
(*pop.* 13,745)
Milford (the 'ford' is probably 'fiord', reflecting the Viking connexion) is a *ria* or drowned valley, and a natural harbour well known to early seafarers. It may well have been the shipping-place for the Preseli bluestones at the start of their long journey to Stonehenge. There are Neolithic remains (including the Long Stone at Sandy Haven) all along this coast. Here, too, in the old Welsh romance *Culhwch and Olwen*, King Arthur searches for the whelps of Rhymhi the she-wolf. St Brynach landed here on his way to Nevern, guided by an angel. Shakespeare's Imogen in *Cymbeline* starts her wanderings here; nearby, at Mill Bay, Henry Tudor had landed, in 1485, and collected local support on his way to the Battle of Bosworth and the English crown.

There was some medieval settlement at Milford; the remains of Priory Pill, a late-eleventh-century Benedictine house founded by Adam de la Roche (of Roch Castle), stand north of the docks. However, the present town-centre dates largely from the turn of the eighteenth century. In 1790 Sir William Hamilton, who owned the estate, obtained an Act of Parliament to build quays and docks. His nephew and heir, Charles Greville, was entrusted with the implementation of the scheme. On a carefully chosen site, Greville laid out, with the aid of a French architect, a pattern of parallel streets, the lowest fronting the water. Observers noted that the style of building was superior to the usual local models. By 1815 there were some 160 houses, many of elegant design, and a chapel endowed by Greville. A colony of North American Quakers from Nantucket Island were brought over, to be nearer to London, their main market for lamp oil. This plan was not entirely successful, however. Milford became more a fishing port than a base for South Sea whalers (or a Naval dockyard, which had been Greville's other ambition).

At present, after a number of vicissitudes, Milford's future seems assured by the overwhelming presence of the four huge oil refineries and the oil terminal. Care has been taken to protect a naturally beautiful landscape

MONMOUTH

from the impact of these developments; this includes even the choice of paints for the tanks and other structures.

Surrounding villages have remained relatively unspoiled. At St Ishmael there is an attractive church dedicated to a sixth-century associate of the great Celtic missionary-saint Teilo. The bay near the church is called Monk Haven, reflecting perhaps the enterprises of the Milford Benedictines. Dale is a rather charming seaside village. It lies on the edge of a saltmarsh rich in shore plants. Among them are thrift, purple sea lavender, and white-flowered scurvy-grass (a source of Vitamin C, whose Welsh name, *morlwyau meddygol*, means medicinal sea-spoons). Dale has Iron Age promontory forts at Great Castle Head and Dale Point, and a modern castle probably built on an earlier site. Robert de Vale, the thirteenth-century lord of this manor, was an ancestor of both Owain Glyndwr and Henry Tudor. Dale Fort Field Centre, on Dale Point, is a nineteenth-century fort used as a base for field study and courses. There are good beaches (though West Dale rollers can be ferocious), and facilities for yachting.

Monknash S. Glam. *see* **St Donat's**

Monmouth Gwent 12A1 (*pop.* 6,545)
This ancient border town is full of character, with curious associations and some fine old buildings. Of its earliest days as the Roman station of Blestium, nothing has survived. Its visible history begins with the Normans, or rather, in this case, Bretons, who built the first castle, founded a priory, and fortified the river-crossing.

The Monnow gateway is the only fortified bridge gateway in Britain and one of the few in Europe. Built in 1262, it has the combination of solidity and rounded grace that characterizes the best of Norman or Romanesque architecture. Monmouth Castle has not worn so well. Founded by William FitzOsbern in the early years after the Conquest, it suffered badly in the Civil Wars, and was slighted in 1646. The present remains consist largely of a rectangular two-storey tower of the twelfth century (with later additions), which contains the great hall of the castle. Somewhere within its walls was born Harry of Monmouth, later to become Henry V, the victor of Agincourt, and, thanks to Shakespeare, one of the 'favourite' English kings. The strength of Harry's place in the popular patriotic myth can be seen exemplified in Great Castle House adjoining the castle. This mansion was built in 1673 by the first Duke of Beaufort for the sole reason that he wanted his first grandson born near the spot where 'our great hero' Henry V was born. (The Duke preferred myth to archaeology – he used the stones from the castle to build

OPPOSITE: *The Monnow Bridge, Monmouth*

RIGHT: *The font in the S aisle of St Thomas's church, Monmouth*

his new house.) For about the last 100 years Great Castle House has been the headquarters of the volunteer Royal Monmouthshire Engineer Militia (now part of the Territorial Army). It has some fine woodwork and an excellent decorated plaster ceiling (not normally on view).

Monmouth Priory was a Benedictine house founded by FitzOsbern in the eleventh century and affiliated to the French abbey of S. Florent at Saumur. St Mary's church was built on the site of this priory, and of this only the tower is unrestored. (The church of St Thomas the Martyr has retained more of its Norman character.) The priory was connected with Monmouth's other powerful myth-maker, Geoffrey of Monmouth, the twelfth-century cleric and author of the influential and imaginative *History of the Kings of Britain*, which includes stories of King Arthur, Cymbeline, and Lear.

Medieval Monmouth was also famous for a more prosaic artefact, the round knitted cap, an example of which can be seen in the local museum. The 'Monmouth Cap' was famous by Shakespeare's day (though it is unlikely that it was worn at the Battle of Agincourt, as he suggests in *Henry V*). At one time a whole area of the town was given over to its manufacture; indeed, Monmouth seems to have been a pioneer of the art of knitting, which arrived there from the Continent.

In the early eighteenth century Daniel Defoe wrote that Monmouth was 'rather a decay'd than a flourishing town'. Yet it was about the same time (1724) that the imposing neo-classical Shire Hall was completed, in Agincourt Square. Here, from his pedestal high up on the façade, Henry V harangues the back of the Hon. Charles Stewart Rolls, who appears more interested in his model biplane. The statue of Rolls, by Sir William Goscombe John, commemorates the pioneer of motoring and aviation, co-founder of Rolls-Royce (1904), associate of the Wright brothers, and the first man to fly the Channel non-stop in both directions (1910). C. S. Rolls was born at Hendre House near Rochfield, a neighbouring village; he died in a flying accident at Bournemouth in 1910.

Rolls's mother, Lady Llangattock, gave the town its collection of Nelsoniana, now housed in Priory Street with the local history museum. Nelson's connexions with Monmouth are tenuous; he visited it in 1802 and was made a freeman of the borough. Of particular interest to him would have been the Naval Temple on the Kymin Hill, a tower and summerhouse built that same year to honour the heroes of the French Wars. This is now NT property.

The villages around Monmouth are small and peaceful, with a mixture of Welsh and English names. At Mitchell Troy, St Michael's contains the treble stocks of

OPPOSITE: *St Thomas's church, Monmouth, showing the Norman chancel arch*

Montgomery

the village. St Peter's at Dixton is a primitive-looking building founded in the seventh century by the Celts and rebuilt in the early-Norman period.

Montgomery (Trefaldwyn) Powys 3H4
(*pop.* 968)

This small market-town, facing out over the Camlad Valley towards England, was from Tudor times until April 1974 the county town of Montgomeryshire. It has, however, none of the air of an administrative centre. Its wide main street, almost a market-square, with Georgian red-brick houses and bow-fronted shops, has, equally, escaped the rash of antique shops that often afflicts towns of this age and grace. At the end of Broad Street, the Town Hall is a well-proportioned late-Georgian building. The ground floor, whose arches were originally open, dates from 1748; the upper storey was reconstructed in 1828. Arthur Street has some charming early-nineteenth-century cottages, some of which, half-timbered, may be the renovated remains of Tudor buildings. Cobbled paving adds to the charm. All in all,

Montgomery gives a good impression of what a small country market-town must have felt like in, say, 1830: its dimensions, spaces, buildings, and its nearness to the fields. An English market-town, that is, for Montgomery has none of the characteristic Welsh flavour of Tregaron, Llanidloes, or Carmarthen.

Traces of the district's earliest inhabitants – a hill-fort, or Neolithic settlement, heavily fortified sometime later, during the Iron Age – can be found on the hill beyond Old Castle Farm, about 1km. north-west of the town. This site, which has extensive earthworks, and a view that on a clear day can stretch to Cadair Idris, is more impressive than the remains of the Roman fort excavated in recent years. The fort, Lavobrinta, was an important military outpost, occupied intermittently from 75 until the late fourth century; only the outline (near Forden) has survived.

As a town, Montgomery is really a Norman creation. Roger de Montgomery, its founder, was one of the Conqueror's most trusted knights. Among his extensive grants of land in newly conquered England was a tract

Montgomery Castle (early-C13), birthplace of the poet George Herbert

in the Hundred of Chirbury, which he fortified with a motte-and-bailey castle at Hendomen, near the Severn. A second castle succeeded this one in about 1095; it passed into the hands of Baldwin de Boulers, from whom the town's Welsh name, Baldwin's Town (Trefaldwyn), is derived.

The castle whose ruins still stand on a steep cliff above the town is a third fortress, built in 1223–7 by Henry III of England, and refortified by Edward I during his vast Welsh castle-building programme of 1276–96. The town's first charter and the town walls, of which only the bank and ditch now remain, also date from the thirteenth century.

To the modern visitor, the castle's most interesting associations are concerned with a rather later period of history. In the early sixteenth century it had passed into the hands of the Herbert family; and in the castle were born the sons of Richard Herbert of Montgomery. Two of the five sons were to earn a place in English letters: Edward (b. 1583), better known as Lord Herbert of Chirbury, and George (b. 1593), one of our finest religious poets. George Herbert spent only his early childhood at Montgomery, under the care of his mother, the learned patroness of another poet, John Donne. Edward, philosopher and poet, after an adventurous time in France (see his *Autobiography*), returned to the castle at the outbreak of the Civil War. In 1644 he was besieged there by a Parliamentary force, and surrendered the castle in exchange, it is said, for the preservation of his library in London. Sir Thomas Myddleton garrisoned the castle for Parliament and held the town after a decisive battle. Lord Herbert died impoverished in London; his Parliamentary pension had soon fallen into arrears. The year after his death, the King was executed, and Montgomery Castle ordered to be demolished.

The remains of the castle have not yet been fully excavated. It consisted of a keep, surrounded by a series of wards, and was protected on the northern side by a sheer cliff face. In the middle ward are remnants of a sizeable house built by Lord Herbert of Chirbury in the second quarter of the seventeenth century. From the castle, which is a stiff climb from the town, there are magnificent views over the English border.

Further relics of the Herbert family may be found in St Nicholas's church, a well-restored thirteenth-century building with a wealth of interesting features. The different styles of the roof should be noted: the western part of the nave has a superb hammer-beam roof in oak, with panelling and tracery; the eastern has a wagon-roof with colourful painted bosses. The chancel roof is modern, but that of the south transept is of sixteenth-century date or Jacobean. The elaborate rood-screen is also in two portions, with carved Elizabethan gates and fifteenth-century figures holding shields. The western side is the original screen of the church, though the oak panels at the bottom are of later date. The eastern side, the ornate rood-loft, the stall-work, and the misericords are thought to have been brought here from Chirbury Priory at the Dissolution. The misericords are, unfortunately, severely time-worn.

In the south transept lie two effigies, the smaller of which has been conjectured to be that of Sir Edmund Mortimer, son-in-law of Owain Glyndwr (Shakespeare's Glendower), who served as Constable of Montgomery Castle. The other is an early Herbert, possibly George Herbert's great grandfather, who died in 1534. The reddish paint has been added to give uniformity after a nineteenth-century restoration. It is, however, the splendid tomb of Richard and Magdalen Herbert that dominates this transept. Under a colourful and highly decorated canopy, the figures of the couple lie in elaborate costume. Behind them kneel their eight children; below, a shrouded corpse is a *memento mori*, repeated in the skull-and-crossbones motif of the upper storey. The coats of arms and fine dress emphasize the worldly status of the couple; the corpse recalls the vanity of such matters. The designer of this tomb is thought to have been Walter Hancock of Much Wenlock, who built the old Market Hall at Shrewsbury. The effigies do not necessarily mean a burial. After Richard Herbert's death in 1596 his wife married again; she was buried in Chelsea in 1627, with a funeral sermon preached by John Donne, the Dean of St Paul's.

From Montgomery, excursions can be made on foot into the Kerry Hills or along the Long Mountain track. There is a good stretch of Offa's Dyke visible not far from the town, on the Bishop's Castle side, while in the opposite direction, at the Severn, the ford of Rhydwiman was for centuries a place for negotiation of treaties between Welsh and Saxon. At Hendomen, the visible remains of a pre-Norman field system, one of very few known in Britain, have been recommended for schedule as an ancient monument.

Morriston (Treforys) W. Glam. 10C2
Not a very pretty town, Morriston is, however, unusual among the industrial towns of South Wales. A rare example of early town-planning, it owes that distinction to the enlightenment of its founder, Sir John Morris. Morris owned extensive copper-works and collieries in the area around Swansea. In 1750 he built a 'lofty castellated mansion' to house forty or so families of workers. This was the first example of workers' flats in Wales and one of the earliest in the country. In the nineteenth century it was already derelict. Forty years later, Morris began to build a new town, to the plan drawn up by his superintendent of construction at the copper-works, William Edwards (builder of the famous bridge at Pontypridd). Leases on small plots of land were granted, for three lives or fifty years, at an annual rent of seven shillings and sixpence. The houses were laid out on a gridiron plan, in straight lines, as in a North American town. Observers described the workers' dwellings as being 'of a very excellent and commodious construction'. Agents and other members of the works hierarchy had more elaborate homes. At its completion, Morriston housed about a thousand people. The original pattern can still be seen in the centre of the town, around the church.

Mumbles W. Glam. *see* **Swansea**

Myddfai Dyfed 6D5
The late-medieval church of this small village on the edge of the Black Mountain contains tombstones of the famous medical men who claimed descent from the fairy of Llyn-y-fan fach. Their medical lore is preserved in a medieval manuscript; the legend, which may well be much embroidered, was first written down early last century. There are, as usual, variations in the story, but the general outline remains much the same. A local farmer falls in love with a fairy he sees on the shore of the small lake known as Llyn-y-fan fach. She agrees to marry him, but warns that if he strikes her three times, she and all her fairy cattle will vanish again into the lake. They live happily together, and have three fine sons. Then, at a christening, the farmer hurries her along with a tap on the shoulder: the first blow is struck. Some time later, at a wedding, she weeps, and he pats her in sympathy: a second blow is struck. Finally, at a funeral, she laughs; he touches her once more, and she and all her flocks disappear as suddenly as they came. In another version, he strikes her thrice with iron; folk-lore specialists suggest that this reflects the difficult transition of early man from Bronze to Iron Age, and the continuing presence of non-iron-using societies in Britain long after that metal had been introduced. In any case, the fairy's medical secrets and herbal lore are passed on to her sons; a race of physicians is born, and lasts well into the eighteenth century, or even later.

The lake of Llyn-y-fan fach is an Ice Age formation, its waters dammed up in a hollow behind a moraine. The great reddish cliffs of the Black Mountain scarp tower over the lake, which has been made into a small reservoir without destroying its charm. It can best be reached from Llanddeusant. A Youth Hostel here is a centre for mountain walking.

Nanteos Dyfed *see* **Aberystwyth**

Nantyglo Gwent *see* **Abertillery**

Narberth (Arberth) Dyfed 8D4
From his court at 'Arberth', Pwyll Prince of Dyfed set out for the hunt where he was to meet the King of the Underworld and change places with him for a year. Here he first saw the beautiful Rhiannon, in her golden garment, riding past on a pure-white steed. So says the *Mabinogion*, the collection of medieval Welsh epic and romance. Pwyll's court may have been at Sentence Castle, now a mound, at Templeton, to the south. Narberth Castle, itself a ruin, was built in 1246 by Sir Andrew Perrott. It occupied a strategic position in Pembrokeshire, at the eastern end of the linguistic dividing-line, which begins at Roch, and south of which only English was spoken. Today Narberth is a charming market-town, full of pleasant old houses and pubs. The countryside around, with its hedges, cabins, and 'cars' (carts or traps), reminded Arthur Young, the late-eighteenth-century traveller and economist, of Ireland. The cottagers, he reported, live on 'bread and cheese, and milk, or water; no beer, nor meat, except on a Sunday'.

Blackpool Mill, about 6½km. away (turn left at Canaston Bridge off the main A40 to Haverfordwest), is an early-nineteenth-century water-driven corn-mill (1813), with much of the original wooden machinery. It is open to the public in the summer months.

Neath (Castell-nedd) W. Glam. 10D2
(*pop.* 28,568)
Neath is an industrial and market town of no great architectural distinction; it has, however, traces of a long history, and it lies conveniently near to the magnificent scenery of the upper Neath Valley.

It had long been known that the town was the Roman Nidum, but the exact site of the settlement was only revealed in 1948 when a new housing estate was built near what used to be the Neath Boys' Grammar School. The remains of two gates, of a stone fort dating from the early second century (the original fort was occupied from 75), are preserved near Roman Way (off the main Neath–Skewen road).

In the town centre are the fragments of Neath Castle, a stone fortress built around 1300 to replace an earlier, flimsier structure. The castle stood on the line of the Norman town wall. Its main gateway has a hooded arch linking two ruined drum towers; part of the curtain wall and a south-east tower that may have commanded the ford of the river are also visible. Both this castle and its predecessor were frequently attacked by the Welsh; indeed, Richard de Granville, Lord of Neath in the early twelfth century, is said to have retired to England,

finding the natives too much for him. Before leaving, however, he founded Neath Abbey.

The abbey at Neath, founded about 1129, was a daughter-house of the Abbey of Savigny in France, though, like other Savignac foundations, it joined the Cistercians, in 1147. It was one of the richest of the Welsh monasteries, and, according to Leland, writing in the sixteenth century, was the 'fairest abbey of all Wales'. It held extensive lands and property, from Glamorgan to Somerset; it had almost 5,000 sheep (in 1291), and horses and cattle; it owned a ship and a landing-place, worked mills, fisheries, and coal-mines. It suffered in the many skirmishes between Welsh and English or Normans: in the 1490s, for example, 'in the grete war between the men of Carmarthenshire and the lordship of Glamorgan'. It was visited by King John, and Edward I, and Edward II took refuge there, briefly, in 1284. In the early sixteenth century it was the home of the poet Lewis Morgannwg, who paid for his keep by spreading its fame as the 'resort of scholars', the 'lamp of France and Ireland'. By the 1530s, however, it had only eight monks left. At the Dissolution it went to Richard Williams, a nephew of Henry VIII's minister Thomas Cromwell. Since then, it has been in turn Jacobean mansion, iron foundry, and historic monument.

The ruins date mostly from the late thirteenth century, when the abbey church was rebuilt on a cruciform plan and in a more elaborate style than the earlier Cistercian doctrine of austerity would have countenanced. There are remains of conventual buildings, of lay brethren's quarters, and a portion of gatehouse, once a handsome two-storey structure, which stands on the opposite side of the main road. A carved stone hand-rail marks the night staircase, which led from the south transept of the church to the dormitory.

Today somewhat overpowered by neighbouring industries, Neath Abbey in the eighteenth century must have been a startling sight, its Gothic arches lit by the glare of copper-smelting furnaces set up within its very precinct. Early-nineteenth-century travellers found the ruins inhabited by pathetic bands of squatters who rushed out from their 'cells and holes' to demand coins from the visitor. George Borrow, in 1854, found a scene worthy of Hieronymus Bosch – a ruin of vast size, among 'grimy, diabolical-looking buildings', 'huge heaps of cinders and black rubbish', a pool as black as soot, and a swamp of a disgusting leaden colour.

Neath and its surroundings were very early industrialized. Copper was smelted here in the late sixteenth century, and by the mid eighteenth century, when the Rhondda Valley was still unspoiled, coal-mines and the workings of various metals had already begun to disfigure the landscape. Twentieth-century roads and housing have not done much to improve it since. However, the neighbourhood has much of interest. CADOXTON (Llangatwg) churchyard has its famous 'Murder Stone' calling for judgment on the soul of the

Neath Abbey: 'the fairest abbey of all Wales' (Leland)

slayer of Margaret Williams, twenty-six, who died on 14 July 1822. St Illtud's church on the opposite bank of the Neath River has an unusual D-shaped Norman font and a two-decker pulpit. At ABERDULAIS is a once-famous waterfall (vandalized by last century's industrialists and more recently by the Coal Board) and the remains of ancient furnaces. From Aberdulais, a minor road leads north to CILFREW (Cilffriw), where Idris Hale's Penscynor Bird Gardens, an amazing collection of exotic birds, are an unusual attraction.

Nevern (Nyfer) Dyfed 8C2

Nevern church, with its square, high-buttressed tower, is late-Perpendicular, but the dedication to St Brynach places it as an earlier, missionary settlement of the Celtic Age of Saints. Brynach, an Irishman, fled from a bad-tempered woman to the peaceful brook at Nevern. Here, according to legend, a voice told him to look for a white sow with piglets, and to build a church there. Two sixth-century stones, in the church, date from this same period. One is a pillar commemorating in Latin and Ogham a Welsh chieftain with Latin connexions, 'Vitalianus Emeretos'. Another now forms a window-sill; it reads, in Latin, '*Maglocuni fili Clutori*', and, in Ogham, '*Maglicunas maqi Clutari*' (i.e. Maglocunus son of Clutorius – *maqi* means 'son of', as in Scots and Irish surnames). Outside, in the churchyard, Nevern High Cross is a fine example of the vitality of early-Celtic culture. Like most of the Welsh crosses, and unlike the Irish ones, its superb carvings are geometrical, with no human figures. Its inscriptions have never been de-ciphered. Local tradition has it that on this cross the first cuckoo of spring alights and sings, each St Brynach's Day (7 April).

The Normans reached Nevern in about 1100. Robert FitzMartin ousted the local Welsh chieftain and built an

Early-Celtic High Cross, Nevern

unusual castle with bailey and double motte. Harassed by the Welsh, FitzMartin married his grandson William to the daughter of Rhys ap Gruffydd, one of the strongest of the native princes. In 1191 Rhys marched into Nevern and took the castle. The FitzMartins moved to Newport, a few km. distant, and established the lordship of Cemais there, building a stronger castle in stone.

Nevern is surrounded with prehistoric remains, not always easily distinguishable from the grey Preseli boulders. At Crugiau Cemais, beside the Cardigan road, and on a knoll above the Nevern Valley, is a large group of Bronze Age barrows. Towards Moylegrove (Trewyddel) are Trellyffont and Llechydribedd cromlechs, and at Caerau ('camps'), a concentric Iron Age fort of the second or first century BC. A large-scale map is essential for finding these remains.

Newbridge-on-Wye and **Disserth**   Powys 7E2
At Newbridge, on a beautiful stretch of the Wye, the old drovers' inn has been converted into an arts and crafts centre, Mid Wales House.

Disserth, just over 3km. away, has an ancient church with an embattled tower, a seventeenth-century three-decker pulpit, box pews (1666–1722), and a late-medieval font.

There is trout-fishing in the Ithon at Disserth, and there are salmon at Newbridge in the Wye.

Newcastle Emlyn (Castellnewydd Emlyn)   9E2
(*pop.* 654)
Roads from all sides converge on Newcastle Emlyn, a
surprisingly small but busy market-town on the Teifi,
which provides good fishing (salmon, sewin, and trout)
and was, until recently, the county boundary between
Carmarthenshire and Cardiganshire. Medieval Welsh
princes built the town's first castle, which only just survived the devastation of Glyndwr's revolt in the early
fifteenth century. Henry VII granted it to his supporter
in south-west Wales, Sir Rhys ap Thomas, who followed
the style of the times and rebuilt it more for elegance and
comfort than for security. During the Civil War, in 1645,
a Royalist force under the King's commander, Sir
Charles Gerard, took town and castle. When Parliament
eventually emerged victor, Newcastle was 'slighted',
that is, rendered incapable of causing any further
trouble. Very little now remains: part of the walls and a
ruined gatehouse on a grassy mound, with the loop of the
Teifi, its natural moat, close by.

Newcastle Emlyn's buildings are attractive but quiet.
There are a Victorian public hall and a nineteenth-
century church, which makes interesting use of local
Cilgerran slate. Near the Teifi bridge, a plaque commemorates the house where the first Welsh printing-
press was set up, in 1718, by Isaac Carter. The town's

most eventful period was probably the early 1840s,
when the 'Rebecca Riots', a protest against toll-gates
and other injustices affecting the countryside, spread
into this area.

Across the bridge, at ADPAR, 'Cilgwyn' (now a hotel)
is a Victorian Gothic mansion (1870) with a prize-
winning staircase brought from the Paris Exhibition
of 1867; the ballroom floor, laid on railway buffers, has
a rise and fall of 23cm.

Newport (Trefdraeth)   Dyfed 8C2
When the Norman William FitzMartin (with his Welsh
wife) was ousted from Nevern by his father-in-law, in
1191, he set up a rival castle at Newport. The small
coastal settlement became a borough, and the administrative centre of the lordship of Cemais. The remains of the Norman castle – thirteenth-century gateway, towers, vaulted crypt or dungeon – have been
incorporated into a modern residence (1859), now a
guesthouse.

Newport, still only a village, makes a good holiday
centre. There are good sea and river fishing, bathing,
and golf. Four km. or so away is Velindre, where the
Elizabethan building used as a school and later as a
court-house once belonged to the historian of Pembrokeshire, George Owen of Henllys. Near Velindre is

The ruined gatehouse of the castle at Newcastle Emlyn

Baldwin's Bridge, where Archbishop Baldwin preached the Crusade in 1188. The surrounding hills are rich in prehistoric remains. At Newport, in a field above the bridge, stands the cromlech known as Carreg Goetan Arthur; in Wales, as elsewhere in Britain, Arthur's name is often given to much earlier monuments. Cerrig-y-gof, in a field next to 'The Glen', was originally a circle of five standing stones. Both these are in fact burial sites. South of the town, on Carn Ingli Common (where St Brynach talked with angels), the traces of an Iron Age fort with enclosing wall and hut-circles are clearly visible. The most striking of all, however, is PENTRE IFAN, 5km. south-east, a Neolithic chambered tomb; it is one of the finest in Britain. Three uprights support an enormous capstone 2m. above the ground; in earlier times, as old pictures show, a horseman could ride beneath it. The mound, which contained the burial chamber, has been restored in its original outline. The stones, like those of Stonehenge, come from the Preseli Mountains. The form of Pentre Ifan, and the potsherds found in the area, have caused archaeologists to link this tomb with similar sites in Ireland, another instance of the very early colonization of south-west Wales by 'Irish' or Goidelic settlers.

Newport (Casnewydd-ar-Wysg)   Gwent   11G3
(*pop.* 112,048)
Newport in Gwent is essentially a nineteenth-century industrial port town, though its name and history go back much earlier, and it is at present undergoing some twentieth-century inner-city development. Its church, St Woolos, since 1921 the cathedral of the diocese of Monmouth, is said to be named after the Celtic ruler Gwynllyw. According to legend, this fifth-century man of violence was told in a dream to go to a certain hill where he would find a white ox with a black spot on its forehead. The next day he set out, found the beast, and was converted. The present church dates from the Normans; it has a fine Norman nave, and a Norman archway incorporating classical columns, perhaps brought here from Roman Caerleon.

Robert FitzHamon, the Norman responsible for the church, also, predictably, built a castle. This motte-and-bailey construction stood near Stow Hill until the

Pentre Ifan, 5km. SE of Newport, Dyfed

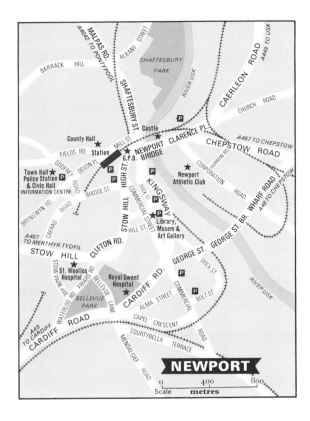

Like the valleys, Newport suffered from industrial unrest, born of over-rapid growth and inhuman working and living conditions. John Frost, a Newport tradesman, a guardian of the poor and Justice of the Peace, who had served as mayor of the town, was a prominent figure in the Chartist movement for reform. After the harsh sentences imposed on several Chartists at Llanidloes in 1839, the organization planned a large demonstration at Newport. Three divisions were to converge on the town, from Blackwood (led by Frost), from the upper Ebbw Valley (led by Zephaniah Williams), and from Pontypool. The last contingent was held up by storms and never arrived; the first two found the authorities were expecting them. Fighting broke out around the Westgate Hotel; the troops fired, and the mob fled, leaving several dead. The leaders, tried at Monmouth, were found guilty of High Treason and sentenced to be hanged and quartered. This was reluctantly commuted to transportation for life. Chartism in Wales received a death blow, though the struggle for reform continued. Bullet-holes can be seen in the porch of the old Westgate Inn, incorporated into its successor.

In John Frost Square – so do yesterday's traitors become today's martyrs – the Newport Museum and Art Gallery has collections relating to the Roman town at Caerleon and the Chartist Riots of 1839. A bust by Epstein commemorates one of the town's most famous sons, W. H. Davies, the super-tramp, born in the Church House, a tavern in Portland Street. Author of the lines 'What is this life, if, full of care, / We have no time to stand and stare' (which are to poetry what 1066 is to history), Davies did not spend much of his adult life in Newport.

For an interesting view of an urban and industrial landscape, the main catwalk along the top of the Transporter Bridge (towards the docks) is open to visitors for a small fee.

Between Newport and the 'Severn Sea', and on both sides of the Usk, there are curious fens or 'levels', reminiscent of the Low Countries, drained by ditches ('reens' as they are called, here and in Somerset) and protected by sea walls in a system that may date back to the Romans. The 'great flood' of 1606 is commemorated in several churches of the flat lands, including St Bride's, Wentlloog, and Redwick, which has a rood-loft. Magor's large church has a thirteenth-century tower and a two-storey fifteenth-century porch.

Inland and to the east lies Wentwood, an ancient royal forest still largely unspoilt. Near the A48, PENHOW castle is a Norman peel tower incorporated into a later farmhouse. Near here is said to grow the autumn crocus or meadow saffron, deadly to cattle, and brought by the Romans, who used it as a medicinal herb. PENCOED Castle, near LLANMARTIN, was a late-medieval or Tudor fortified mansion, with a fine gatehouse, a round tower, and some walls still remaining. Sir Nicholas Morgan, knight of Pencoed Castle in the reign of Henry VII,

1840s, when it disappeared under the debris from the railway-tunnel excavations. A later castle stands, however, on the muddy banks of the Usk. This was rebuilt in the fifteenth century after Owain Glyndwr had razed it – and much of the town – to the ground; it was destroyed once more in the Civil War. In its heyday, the castle was a large one. There remains a portion of wall with three towers; of these, the central one has a water-gate, with a chapel over it, while the bridge tower has notable Decorated windows.

Newport received its town charter in 1385. It remained, however, a small trading-port until the early nineteenth century and the expansion of the iron and coal industries in the South Wales valleys. Until 1834 it benefited from exemptions of duty on coal exported by way of the Monmouthshire Canal, and for a few years it was larger and more prosperous than Cardiff. From 1,100 in 1801, its population grew in a century to 70,000; before the Great War it was the chief iron port on the Bristol Channel.

OPPOSITE: *St Woolos cathedral church, Newport, Gwent: the Norman archway between the nave and the Galilee Chapel (the Classical columns perhaps came from Roman Caerleon). The S arcade of the nave is seen through the arch*

The Transporter Bridge, Newport, Gwent

yachting are excellent; lobster, mackerel, bass, pollack, and even shark may be taken, and fresh fish is on sale daily at the quayside. Pleasure-boats ply along the coast, where if you are lucky you may see basking seals, and if not there are still the amazing cliff formations and the colonies of sea-birds. From the cliffpath up and over New Quay Head to the next small beach, Cwm Tudu (8km. away), the view embraces the whole sweep of Cardigan Bay as far as Snowdonia.

At LLANINA, across the bay, the tiny church was re-built in 1850. The original building is marked only by an outcrop of rock, Cerrig Ina ('Ina's stones'), offshore. In the eighth century, it is said, a local fisherman and his daughter rescued some strangers from shipwreck. One of these was the English king Ina, who built a church as thanksgiving for his escape. The present church also seems perilously close to the sea. Inside, one of the beams, carved with a serpentine branch and oak-twigs, is the remnant of a medieval rood-screen. The lychgate contains stones from the previous church.

New Radnor (Maesyfed) and **Old Radnor** (Pencraig) Powys 7G2
A small picturesque village at the foot of Radnor Forest, New Radnor was 'new' in the thirteenth century, when its streets were laid out in a chessboard pattern beneath the castle. Here Rhys ap Gruffydd entertained Arch-bishop Baldwin and Gerald the Welshman as they set out into Wales, in 1188, to preach the Crusade. The castle was important enough to merit almost complete destruction at the hands of Owain Glyndwr during his rising, in 1401.

Old Radnor, about 4km. south-east, is an even smaller village on a hill, with magnificent views over Radnor Forest. Its castle has almost entirely disappeared but the church is particularly fine. It is largely fifteenth- to sixteenth-century Decorated, with some Perpendicular detail, including an elegant rood-screen. The organ case, with its linenfold panelling, is Tudor (the mechan-ism and pipes are of course much later). The font is thought to have been a Celtic altar-stone taken over for Christian ritual in the sixth or seventh century.

Newtown (Y Drenewydd) Powys 3G5
(*pop.* 6,122)
Like all the mid-Wales towns, this one surprises by its smallness: a few main shopping-streets, and a pleasant enough jumble of different styles and periods. There had been a market at Newtown since 1280, but the place saw its major growth (before the present one) in the first thirty years of last century. Then the expanding flannel-industry quadrupled the population. The flannel trade declined but somehow the town kept going. At present it is one of the central foci for the Mid-Wales New Town Development Corporation, set up to revitalize the region.

Newtown's air is unpretentious, and its numerous old

with his fourteen children, is vividly depicted in stone on a tomb in the chancel of Llanmartin church. To the north of Newport, in the lower Ebbw Valley, is the Ebbw Forest, partly a re-creation of the medieval Forest of Machen. From Cwmcarn there are scenic drives and walks in the forest, with views that stretch from the Brecon Beacons to the Bristol Channel.

New Quay (Ceinewydd) Dyfed 6A2 (*pop.* 747)
Narrow streets of sober Welsh terraces and lace-curtained cottages slant down to a sandy beach and a picturesque fishing-harbour. In winter, New Quay probably reverts to its own quiet life: this 'cliff-perched town at the far end of Wales' was, after all, one of the inspirations for Dylan Thomas's radio play *Under Milk Wood*. In sum-mer, it is one of west Wales' most popular resorts. New Quay has been likened to a Breton village – but the litter and the snacks are resolutely British. None the less, it repays a visit, and there is plenty of activity. Fishing and

inns and houses have largely escaped the pseudo-prettification meted out by more frequented tourist centres. With this goes, however, some unpicturesque dilapidation, as for example in the Georgian crescent at the Llanllwchaiarn end of the Long Bridge. And although it is unusual nowadays to have a functioning cinema in a town of this size, it seems a sad end for the neo-classical building (1832) that was successively Flannel Mart, Public Assembly Rooms, and Post Office.

Of the old parish church of Llanfair, by the Severn, there remain only a few walls and a thirteenth-century tower with timbered belfry. The churchyard, however, still has the elaborately chiselled tomb of Robert Owen. The church site was too vulnerable to flooding, and the 'new' parish church, St David's, stands well back from the river, in New Road. It is a striking and to some tastes perfectly hideous piece of Victorian Gothic (1847) in yellow brick. Inside, some woodwork comes from the ruins of Abbey Cwmhir and a reredos from the previous church, where it formed a screen. The town has the usual sturdy – and some impressive – chapels. The Roman Catholic church of the Holy Ghost is a lively conversion from an old warehouse. The old red-brick church at Llanllwchaiarn bears the date of Waterloo.

Some of Newtown's most interesting relics are last century's, the legacy of Victorian endeavour and of the squalid Industrial Revolution on which that was built. At Llanllwchaiarn, which adjoins Newtown on the opposite bank of the Severn, some of the grim rectangular tenements are still standing. The flannel weavers lived in nearby cottages, or on the lower floors of these factories, beneath the humming looms. One such building, in Commercial Street, has been transformed into a Textile Museum, with early machinery and other exhibits. Its entrance, through a narrow archway and cobbled courtyard, is evocative. Conditions were bad enough here at Newtown to inspire an (unsuccessful) Chartist riot in 1838–9.

Near the railway station, a towering red-brick building has survived almost a hundred years of trade. It is Pryce Jones's department store, formerly the Royal Welsh Warehouse, set up in 1879 as the first ever world-wide mail-order business. The wealth and optimism of the Victorians also refashioned the town centre. A new yellow-brick Market Hall was put up in 1870 (traces of the façade are still visible), and the neo-Byzantine Cross Buildings, which house a bank, were built in 1898–1903. W. H. Smith's, near the Market Hall, has recently restored its premises in the original 1920s style, as a contribution to European Architectural Heritage Year; it includes a separate 'ladies' bookstall'.

Another bank now stands on the site of a house where in 1771 Robert Owen, a pioneer of socialism and the cooperative movement, was born. Its upper floor has a small, interesting, if fusty, museum, and a darkly-furnished room that is said to be Owen's birthplace. Robert Owen spent only the first ten years of his life at Newtown. After a summary schooling, he was sent to Lincolnshire as a draper's apprentice. A selfmade man and a successful industrialist, Owen's radical experiments in social reform at New Lanark (Scotland) and New Harmony (Indiana), plus his voluminous writings, were to have enormous influence on the British working-class movement. Owen (strangely enough) returned to Newtown at the end of his long and active life, and died there in 1858. He was eighty-seven.

Present-day Newtown is endeavouring to stop being a place everyone moves out of. The development plans aim at doubling the population by the 1980s (though by 1990, it is envisaged, it will still only be 13,000, a not unmanageable size for a community). New industries have been encouraged; several new housing estates have been constructed, spreading the town out into its pleasant green countryside. There are a modern library, new bus station, and a small art gallery. One may regret perhaps that one chance of a good modern building has been muffed. The ancient and beautiful Newtown Hall (where Charles I slept, on his way from Naseby), unsound in structure, was replaced in 1965 by a 'Georgian' building, reminiscent of nothing so much as a building on a minor American college campus. It is not unattractive, but its red brick and white columns speak of timid conservatism.

Newtown has pleasant open spaces by the Severn (odd that this river, almost a trout-stream, will later flow greyish and swollen under the suspension bridge near Chepstow), and the Kerry Hills with their characteristic brand of sheep are in easy reach for walking. Near the town, two old buildings may be searched for. On the Milford Road side of town, Cwrt-yn-dre ('Court in the town') is a small building part stone, part half-timbering, which is said to have been one of Owain Glyndwr's Parliament Houses. It was brought here from Dolgellau in 1885. And on the top of the Bryn, Upper Bryn Farm was the seventeenth-century black-and-white half-timbered manor-house of the Baxters. An inscription on the gable-end reads 'Not we from kings, but kings from us' – a motto of some significance in an age that saw Charles I beheaded. Gregynog Hall, 6km. north-west of Newtown, belonged earlier this century to the Davies family of Llandinam. Gwendoline and Margaret Davies, sisters of the Welsh millionaire and philanthropist Lord Davies of Llandinam, moved there in 1919 and turned it into a centre of the arts. Festivals of music and poetry were held, and the Gregynog Press (1919–39) was renowned for its fine printings. Gregynog Hall was bequeathed to the University of Wales, and the Misses Davies' fine collection of paintings to the National Museum at Cardiff.

Offa's Dyke

Offa's Dyke is the most impressive of all the linear earthworks in Britain. It stands as a monument to the political supremacy of the Anglo-Saxon kingdom of

Offa's Dyke, nr Montgomery

Mercia in the eighth century AD. Within a hundred years the Mercian kings expanded their domain from north-western England to include the whole of England south of the Humber, with the exception of Wessex and Wales. King Offa (757–96), who now styled himself 'King of the English', waged a long and bitter struggle with the Welsh. He succeeded only in driving them back to their foothills. A frontier, more political than military, was needed, and Offa undertook this considerable task. A huge dyke was built, wherever the terrain required it, from the Dee at Prestatyn to the mouth of the Wye at Sedbury Cliffs. A hundred and thirty km. of earthwork were thrown up, in a long ridge, with a deep ditch on the west, or Welsh, side. Where there were natural obstacles – the Wye, for example, between Redbrook (near Monmouth) and a point about 8km. north of Hereford, or thick forest or scrub in the southern lowlands, or already existent fortifications, as at 'Wat's Dyke' – the line of the dyke is broken accordingly. Short lengths probably indicate clearings or crossings in the forest.

That the dyke was a negotiated frontier rather than a military line imposed by the Mercians is indicated by its course, which seems to favour both parties. Thus in the very south it left the Welsh the lower reaches of the Wye, which they used for transporting timber; even more vital, it left them the centuries-old ferry-crossing of the Severn at Beachley-Aust. As a frontier, it was for some years taken very seriously. In the Middle Ages anyone – Welsh or English – found on the wrong side of the dyke could lose their right hand as penalty. However, after the decline of Mercia, the Welsh returned to some parts of the land east of the dyke that they had occupied before Offa's day.

The dyke is by no means always clearly visible to the modern eye. In some places it looks like a large hedgerow or bank. It is at its best between Presteigne and Montgomery. There are impressive sections at Knighton, and at Discoed, near Presteigne, it is over 2m. high and 21m. wide. Its relation to the present border is a varied one.

In 1971 the Offa's Dyke long-distance footpath was opened, providing 269km. of walking through magnifi-

Ogmore Castle and the stepping-stones across the Ogmore River

cent country. Large-scale maps, a compass, and a special handbook are vital, for the footpath is not yet clearly posted throughout. The headquarters of the Offa's Dyke Association is at Knighton (Welsh, Tref-y-clawdd, 'town on the dyke'), which is the half-way point of the walk. Information can also be obtained from the Brecon Beacons National Park centre. The path passes through or close to Chepstow, Tintern Abbey, Monmouth, White Castle, Llanthony Priory, Hay-on-Wye, Knighton, Clun, Montgomery, Powis Castle, Chirk Castle, Valle Crucis Abbey, and Rhuddlan Castle.

Ogmore (Ogwr)   Mid Glam.   10D4
Ogmore is a castle and a few cottages near the mouth of the river of that name. Its fortress guarded the ford, now marked with stepping-stones, and, with Coity and Newcastle (Bridgend), formed a triangle of defences against attack on the fertile lands of the Vale of Glamorgan. The first fortifications here were the earthen banks and ditches, which are still visible. In the inner ward, the rectangular three-storey keep dates from the early

twelfth century, a time when stone had only recently begun to replace wood in the construction of castles. It may be the work of William de Londres, one of the Norman conquerors of Glamorgan, who died in about 1126, or of his son Maurice, who founded the priory at Ewenny. The stone curtain wall that surrounded the inner ward was put up in the early thirteenth century. Ogmore Castle remains are not extensive (the key may be obtained from the farmhouse opposite), but the tidal river, the sand-dunes, and the stepping-stones give them a considerable charm.

A few km. farther on, OGMORE-BY-SEA (Aberogwr) is a collection of bungalows and holiday homes set on a fine rocky shore-line. There are sandy beaches, but care is needed in bathing, especially near the river-mouth. From Ogmore-by-Sea, a clifftop road runs along to SOUTHERNDOWN, a village with an old pub and a Sunshine Home. A steep slope leads down to a small beach of sand and pebbles. On the headland opposite, the 'Witches' Nose', stood until fairly recently Dunraven Castle, a nineteenth-century Gothic mansion built on the site of a much earlier house or castle. From Dunraven Head, in the seventeenth century, the last of the infamous Vaughan family lured ships – so local legend has it – to their doom on the murderous Tusker Rock, visible only at low tide. The wrecker was rewarded by the death by drowning, on these rocks, of his own two small sons. While attempts were made to rescue them, the remaining child, a toddler, drowned in a pan of whey at home.

The whole of this coastline is of great interest to geologists. The cliffs are best seen from the flat terraces of lias limestone laid bare at low tide. (It should be remembered that landslips are fairly frequent.)

The names of two old inns in the district reflect the history of local landownership. At Southerndown, the 'Three Golden Cups' is a reference not to the effects of alcohol on vision but to the device of the Norman to whom was granted the lordship of Dunraven, Arnold le Boteler or Butler. Near Ogmore Castle, the 'Pelican' inn-sign refers to the Carne family of Ewenny. The pelican, in Christian symbolism, was said to feed its young on the flesh of its own breast; the Latin for 'with flesh' is *carne*.

Old Radnor   Powys   *see* **New Radnor**

Oystermouth   W. Glam.   *see* **Swansea**

Painscastle (Llanbedr Castell-paen)   Powys   7F3
The castle is named after Pain (Payn, Payen, 'Pagan') FitzJohn, the first Norman to fortify the spot. Its memories are, however, more closely connected with a later Marcher lord, the infamous William de Breos or Braose. William, the 'Ogre of Abergavenny', was noted for his cruelty. In 1176, at Abergavenny, he successfully carried out a 'night of the long knives' in which over seventy Welsh guests were murdered at supper by his men-at-arms. Then in the late 1190s he captured a Welsh leader, Trahaiarn Fychan (Traherne the Younger), and had him tied to a horse's tail and dragged through Brecon, before beheading him. Trahaiarn's cousin, Gwenwynwyn Prince of Powys, raised an army and marched to Painscastle to demand revenge. But William was able to use against him the endemic disunity of the Welsh ruling families. On 12 August 1198 William and the men of South Wales routed the men of Powys, slaughtering thousands.

De Breos, like all good villains, lived to see his luck run out: early in the next century King John confiscated his lands. While William died a beggar, his wife, Maud, and his eldest son were imprisoned in Corfe Castle (Dorset); Maud had rashly accused the King of murdering his nephew Arthur. After eleven days of starvation in Corfe's dungeons, both were found dead; the child's cheeks had been partially gnawed by the mother. The name of de Breos is kept alive in Wales in the names of pedigree cattle, the De Breos Maud and the De Breos

David, for example. Of their castle here, only an enormous mound and great ditches remain.

Painscastle today is a quiet village on no main road to anywhere. In earlier times it stood on one of the 'Drovers' roads' from the Welsh uplands to the markets of London and the South. Cattle were shod here for their long journey (*see* Abergwesyn). On the triangular village green is a well once used for watering the animals.

LLANBEDR church was a ruin when, in the late nineteenth century, Francis Kilvert the diarist visited its Vicar, an eccentric, solitary man living in a filthy cabin littered with dirty crockery and theological commentaries. There are fine walks over Llanbedr Hill and down towards Aberedw.

Parc-le-Breos   W. Glam.   *see* **Gower Peninsula**

Patrishow (Patrisio)   Powys   7G5
In the Grwyne Fawr Valley, a fold of the Black Mountains, Patrishow church is small and grey, with a double bell-turret. It has an eleventh-century font whose inscription refers to a local prince, Cynhyllin or Genillin, who ruled Ystradwy in 1056. An anchorite's cell, on the west side, is probably not earlier than the thirteenth century; it has its own consecrated altar. Inside the church are two more pre-Reformation altar-tables, and a wall-painting of Time and a skeleton, in red, on the west wall. The principal treasure, however, is the amazingly intricate rood-screen and loft, carved in Irish oak, and dating from the early Tudors. A curving vine grows from the mouth of a grotesque Welsh dragon. Here, for the few years between the screen's carving and the Reformation, hung the Cross or Holy Rood, focal point of worship.

Pembrey (Pen-bre)   Dyfed   9F5
Pembrey's old, thirteenth-century church has some interesting features, notably a sixteenth-century window in the south wall and a barrel-roof of similar date over nave and chancel. In the churchyard is buried a twelve-year-old niece of Josephine Bonaparte; the child was drowned in the wreck of the *Jeune Emma*, a French West Indiaman bound from Martinique to Havre-de-Grace with a cargo of sugar and rum; the vessel went down on the notorious Cefn Sidan sands, in November 1828. Outside the churchyard can be seen the village pound.

Pembrey village has been overtaken in size and importance by its younger neighbour, BURRY PORT, which developed as a coal port and a tin-plate manufacturing town. It has a somewhat bleak setting, on the edge of the sand-dunes, or 'burrows' as they are locally known. The presence of the old ordnance factory and the still active Pembrey Firing Range does not improve this atmosphere. There are sea-fishing, yachting, and a golf course.

Pembroke (Penfro)   Dyfed   8C5   (*pop.* 14,092)
Though its name is Welsh (from *Pen-fro*, 'land's end', or

Pen-broch, 'head of the inlet'), Pembroke, with its castle, walled town, and priory, is clearly a creation of the Normans. The castle dominates the townscape, as for centuries it dominated its history. The Normans' advance into south-west Wales was blocked for some years by a strong Welsh chieftain, Rhys ap Tewdwr. After his death, the conquerors poured down towards Pembroke, carving new lordships out of a more hospitable terrain than upland Wales. Arnulf de Montgomery arrived at Pembroke in 1093; he hurriedly fortified the rock with a temporary construction of staves and turves. Returning to England, he left the castle in the hands of Gerald de Windsor, who was confirmed as custodian by Henry I after Arnulf and his brothers had proved treacherous to the King. Gerald made his position doubly secure: he built the first stone castle on the site, and married, in a strategic move, a Welsh heiress, the daughter of Rhys ap Tewdwr. In 1138 the Earldom of Pembroke was created for Gilbert de Clare, also known as Strongbow. Gilbert enlarged the castle, which was used as a base by his son Richard Strongbow during the latter's incursions into Ireland.

What remains of the castle today is largely the work of the second Strongbow's son-in-law William Marshall, and of his immediate descendants. In about 1200 Marshall built the great round keep, the finest example of a circular stone keep in Wales. Round towers were developed to resist mining: their walls were much less vulnerable to collapse than square or rectangular structures. Marshall's keep is 22m. high, and still intact except for its floors. As with earlier square keeps, entrance is at first-floor level. From the domed roof (itself a feat of building) most of the ground outside and inside the castle walls could be kept under surveillance. Later earls made further additions. The male line of the Marshalls died out in 1245, fulfilling a curse put on William by the Bishop of Ferns in Ireland that all his sons should be childless. Pembroke Castle remained in English hands, however, throughout the medieval period. During the Glyndwr rebellion, which affected many of the neighbouring castles, the governor of Pembroke Castle raised a financial contribution for the Welsh, thus buying off the possibility of a siege.

Perhaps the castle's most illustrious occupant was the young Henry Tudor (Harri Tewdwr), who was born in a room on the first floor of the tower now known as the Henry VII Tower. His mother, Queen Katherine, had remarried, to Owain Tudor, a minor Welsh noble. Jasper Tudor, the offspring of this marriage, was created Earl of Pembroke in 1453, and it was to Pembroke that his elder brother, the Earl of Richmond, sent his young wife for protection while he fought in the Wars of the Roses. Here then, in 1456, Henry was born, two months after his father's death, and here he remained until 1471, when a Welsh revolt forced him to flee to Brittany. Henry returned in 1485, to Bosworth and the English crown. The Earldom of Pembroke he bestowed on his

son Henry, who in turn gave it to Anne Boleyn. Henry VIII later abolished the Palatinate of Pembroke; the castle remained Crown property until the reign of James I, when that king gave it to a private subject.

Nothing more is heard of Pembroke Castle until the Civil War. Then, under the influence of the Earl of Essex, whose seat was at Lamphey, and who had grievances against the King, Pembroke alone of the Welsh towns declared for Parliament. After six years on Cromwell's side, Poyer, the Mayor of Pembroke, and Rowland Laugharne (the local leaders of the Roundheads) defected to the Royalist cause, taking town and castle with them. Cromwell himself came to conduct the ensuing siege, eventually reducing the garrison by cutting the principal water supply. Poyer, Laugharne, and Powell drew lots for their lives; Poyer drew the blank, and was shot by firing-squad in Covent Garden in April 1649. Cromwell ordered the castle to be 'slighted'; most of the towers and part of the gatehouse were blown up at this time. Thereafter the castle fell into ruin, and remained so until 1880, when partial restoration took place. In 1928 large-scale repair work was undertaken.

The castle has much to offer the visitor, from the great gatehouse with its domed circular barbican tower (which resisted Cromwellian gunpowder) to the stupendous keep springing 22m. from the limestone rock. Equally spectacular is the 'Wogan', an immense natural cavern beneath the Northern and Norman Halls, and looking out onto the canal that led to the river. Its walls, coloured blood-red and seaweed-green by the damp of the atmosphere, have an eerie quality.

Castle, town, and priory – these new elements of life brought by the invaders displaced the earlier pattern of settlement and religion. Pembroke town grew up around the castle; like other Norman towns, Haverford, Kidwelly, Brecon, for example, it was given a borough charter in the reign of Henry I. The town not only served the needs of the garrison, but, since the burgesses, in early years at least, were exclusively non-Welsh, it provided the Norman lords with additional sources of support. The walls of Pembroke were fortified by William de Valence about 1265; they had three gates and a postern. Remains of Westgate can be seen on Monkton Hill, together with some medieval cottages. Stretches of the town walls overlook the mill-pond and the commons; Barnard Tower, recently restored, is where the townspeople of the east end took refuge in time of danger.

Monkton Priory, spiritual weapon of Norman domination, was founded, on the hill opposite, in 1098, only a few years after the first castle. Replacing an earlier Celtic church or monastery, the new priory was a daughter cell of the Benedictine house of Seez in Normandy. St Nicholas's church incorporates part of the priory, and Old Hall nearby (on Church Terrace) has a vaulted crypt that probably belonged to the priory guest house. Scraps of walls can also be seen behind the church, near Priory Farm (which is a late-seventeenth–early-eighteenth-century building). The other town churches are medieval – St Michael's and St Mary's – but are much restored.

Pembroke today is a quiet, attractive, rather grey town, its atmosphere composed of waterside walk (with swans) and early-nineteenth-century houses lining a long main street, which leads inevitably to the huge presence of the castle. The eighteenth-century town hall has acquired some rather unsuitable doors. There is an information centre adjoining the castle.

PEMBROKE DOCK. The Admiralty dockyard moved here from Milford Haven in 1813–14; it closed in the 1920s, and the harbour is now used mainly as a yachting centre. The town is laid out in a grid pattern, and there are some attractive early-nineteenth-century terraces from the days of prosperity. A small Motor Museum displays vintage cars (summer only) and other items of motoring history.

Penally Dyfed *see* **Tenby**

Penarth S. Glam. 11G4 (*pop.* 23,965)
Penarth has been a port since the Norman Conquest and perhaps before. Its present atmosphere, however, is that of a pleasant Victorian seaside resort and comfortable residential suburb of Cardiff. The pier was erected in the late nineteenth century, one of only four promenade piers in South Wales (the others are at Mumbles, Tenby, and Aberystwyth). Penarth offers ornamental gardens, cliff walks, pleasure-boating, and water-skiing. There are excellent possibilities for fossil hunters. Turner House, built by James Pyke Thompson in 1888, was given in 1921 to the National Museum of Wales as a branch art gallery. It has exhibitions of painting, period furniture, and porcelain. Llandaff House is now a residence hall for the University College at Cardiff; it began life as a Victorian female penitentiary.

From Penarth, the two islands visible in the Channel are FLAT HOLM and STEEP HOLM. Their Scandinavian names are due to the activities of the Norsemen on this South Wales coast. Flat Holm was used as a refuge by the Viking fleet that raided the country in 917. The island has since served as lighthouse, isolation hospital, and defensive outpost. Three Palmerstonian gun batteries, erected in the early nineteenth century against the threat of French invasion, have been recommended for scheduling as ancient monuments. In 1897 Marconi sent the first wireless message ever transmitted over water from Flat Holm to Lavernock Point, just south of Penarth. The words were 'Are you ready?'

Penclawdd W. Glam. *see* **Gower Peninsula**

Pencoed Mid Glam. *see* **Bridgend**

Pen-llin S. Glam. *see* **Cowbridge**

Penmark S. Glam. *see* **Barry**

Pennard W. Glam. *see* **Gower Peninsula**

Ponterwyd Dyfed 3E6
The George Borrow Hotel commemorates that indefatigable nineteenth-century traveller, who in *Wild Wales* describes how he walked from Machynlleth over the mountains and spent the night here on his way to Devil's Bridge. The landlord in those days was a pretentious and unpleasant fellow. However, Borrow found hospitable shepherds and had an interesting time visiting the Potosi Mining Company at nearby Esgyrn Hirion ('Long Bones'). A lead-miner described to him the eerie noises made by the spirits of the hill, who hoped to drive the miners out of their senses. Today the Llywernog silver-lead mine is open in summer as a folk museum. Above ground, Ponterwyd and its surroundings provide magnificent scenery and good fishing. Nant-y-moch is one of three reservoirs in an area formerly only accessible to the hiker. Those who like reservoirs will appreciate the fine landscaping of the viewing terrace on the Rheidol Valley lake.

Pontneddfechan W. Glam. 10D1
At Glyn Neath the main road curves round to the east towards Hirwaun. A minor road north to Ystradfellte and Sennybridge leads to the small hamlet of Pontneddfechan (Pont-Neath-Vaughan, in the Anglicized version; the name means, simply, 'bridge over the lesser Neath river'). On the edge of the Brecon Beacons National Park, the village is a convenient centre for exploring some of the most spectacular and least known river scenery in Britain. From the heights of Fforest Fawr, the headwaters of the Nedd – Nedd Fechan itself, Pyrddin, Mellte, Hepste, Sychryd – plunge down through wooded valleys; the erosion of damp centuries has left ledges of sandstone over which rush a series of falls and rapids, high threads of cataracts, wide, lacy waterfalls, dropping into pools. A good map, stout footwear, and several days of dry weather are essential. The simplest walk is probably to Scwd Gladys, a fall of the Pyrddin, which can be reached along a riverside path from the Angel Hotel. Scwd Einon Gam is only about 1km. further on but is much less accessible; it plunges 21m. over a high, wooded cliff. Of the dozen or so cascades, each with its own character, Scwd-yr-Eira ('fall of snow') is one of the finest, with, behind the falling curtain of water, a path wide enough for a flock of sheep to pass. Below Ystradfellte, the Mellte flows through Porth-yr-ogof, a limestone cavern, and out again over the three Clungwyn falls, 2km. or so further down. The Mellte joins the Sychryd beneath the huge limestone outcrop known as Craig-y-Dinas, one of several mountains in Wales in whose caverns King Arthur is said to be sleeping, waiting for the call to save his country.

Below Glyn Neath, which is a colliery township, the

VALE OF NEATH struck earlier travellers with its picturesque and romantic beauty: 'a very paradise of rock and
river, hill and valley', as one put it. Turner painted it;
Darwin's colleague Alfred Russell Wallace, who had
travelled the globe, thought it one of the most special of
all valleys for the fine scenery and the interest it contained in one small area. The vale remains impressive,
though its character has been changed, first by industry
and more recently by the Forestry Commission, which,
with good intentions, has replaced Welsh oakwoods with
regiments of Scandinavian conifers.

On the outskirts of Glyn Neath, standing up on the
hillside above the Neath road, Aberpergwm House is a
Tudor mansion extended in the nineteenth century. It
was the home of the Williams family, one of whose distant relatives was Oliver Cromwell. Near the hamlet of
Pentre-clwydau, on the same road, the poet Southey (in
1802) tried to rent a house from Squire Williams of
Aberpergwm. For some reason the deal failed, perhaps
because the Squire discovered Southey's dangerous
Radical views (which he shared at this time with
Coleridge and Wordsworth). Southey took, instead, a
house in the Lake District; his children became, as he
put it, 'Cumbrians not Cambrians', and a minor change
of emphasis was (possibly) the result for English poetry.

RESOLVEN also had collieries, most of which have
closed. New industries have replaced them to some extent. In the former Reading Room of the Miners' Wel-
fare Hall, now a club, hangs a $2\frac{1}{2}$m. panorama water-
colour of the Vale of Neath, painted by Thomas Hornor
in 1819. Below Resolven, one of the valley's finest falls
can be easily reached on foot from Melincourt. Scwd
Rhyd-yr-Hesg plunges nearly 24m. in one white sheaf of
water, past chapel burial-ground and the site of an early
ironworks. Turner drew this fall, and the one at Aberdulais, which in his day was still unpolluted.

Pontrhydfendigaid and Strata Florida
(Ystrad-fflur) Dyfed 6C2

This village – the name means 'bridge of the ford of the
Virgin' – consists largely of one long, main street, which
crosses the Teifi (here a small stream) by an old and
simple bridge. Arriving from Ffair Rhos in 1854, George
Borrow found the place unwelcoming and primitive:
'There was much mire in the street; immense swine lay
in the mire, who turned up their snouts at me as I passed'.
Today the village is cheerful enough, and once a year it
even bursts at the seams with the two-day *Eisteddfod* (a
festival of music and poetry), generously endowed with
prize-money and a spacious if utilitarian building by the
local-born London–Welsh millionaire Sir David James.

The fine Methodist chapel (1859) stands in the village,
while St Mary's church and the abbey of Strata Florida
lie about $1\frac{1}{2}$km. away down a narrow lane. The church
dates from 1700; it was restored in 1815 and 1961.
(Medieval congregations would have worshipped in a
special chapel within the monastery.) The pulpit (1724)

and the curved communion rails are survivals from the
eighteenth-century building. Like the village, church
and churchyard testify to the importance of the James
family: the 1961 Whitefriars windows inside, and a large
ugly monument without. The graveyard has other features of interest. One notices, for example, the number
of headstones bearing London addresses: Welshmen
brought back from Putney or Maida Vale to lie at last in
native soil. More dramatically, near the large yewtree,
there is the 'grave of a leg', that of Henry Hughes,
cooper, whose limb was amputated after a stagecoach
accident in 1756. The yew itself is said to mark the
burial-place of Wales' great medieval poet, Dafydd ap
Gwilym (fl. 1340–70); there is a memorial slab in his
honour, erected by the Honourable Society of Cymmro-
dorion, in the abbey grounds, and inscribed, appropriately, in Latin and Welsh, the two languages of the
educated medieval Welshman.

Strata Florida Abbey, a peaceful grey ruin, stands in
meadows near the river. The Latin name means 'valley
[or plain] of flowers' (as does the Welsh equivalent,
Ystrad-fflur), though another theory has it that the first
site of the abbey lay near the Fflur brook. Whichever
may be the case, Strata Florida's setting shows the
Cistercians, as usual, choosing a site that was at once
remote and convenient, in that it had good land, running water, and a wildness conducive to devotions.

The abbey at Strata Florida was an offshoot of Whitland Abbey, which was the earliest Cistercian foundation in Wales. A Norman baron, Robert FitzStephen, is
thought to have 'founded' the new house, that is, made
legal and financial provision for it, in 1164. But Robert's
lands in west Wales were very quickly reconquered by
the Welsh, and the actual construction of the abbey
must therefore be ascribed to a Welsh prince, Rhys ap
Gruffydd (or 'The Lord Rhys', as he is often known).
The abbey became, indeed, a centre of Welsh culture,
and a place of pilgrimage. Members of the Welsh royal
houses lie buried in the abbey. The medieval annals of
Welsh history, *Brut y Tywysogion*, may have been com-
piled there. And place-names on the approach-roads –
Yspytty Ystwyth, for example – denote hostels and stop-
ping-places for pilgrims who came to see the abbey's
treasured relic, a chalice popularly thought to be the
Holy Grail.

The Cistercian Rule had begun as a return to piety
and austerity within the religious life. But it proved impossible for the White Monks to remain withdrawn from
the world. For one thing, the times were troubled ones,
especially in Wales. In 1401, after the revolt of Owain
Glyndwr, only the walls of the church remained standing. In October that year Henry IV and the Prince of
Wales occupied the abbey and drove out the monks,
who had sided with Glyndwr. The next year it was given
into the custody of the Earl of Worcester, and in 1407 and
1415 it became a military post housing several hundred
men-at-arms and archers. Their task was to defend the

abbey from the Welsh 'rebels' and to use it as a base for sorties into North and South Wales.

Even the abbots were violent and lawless at times. The Abbot of Aberconwy raided Strata Florida in 1428; he imprisoned some of the monks in Aberystwyth Castle, stole their treasure, and drove away stock. In 1534 the Abbot of Strata Florida had two men put in irons for counterfeiting money at the monastery, but he himself was accused by his own monks of clipping and coining. Natural disasters added to the abbey's troubles. A great fire in 1284 burned almost the whole of the abbey church, except for the presbytery, which was miraculously preserved (according to one chronicle) because the Body of Our Lord was kept there, on the altar, under lock and key.

The Cistercians' economic enterprises also interfered with their spiritual concerns. They were huge landowners, and vigorous and successful farmers. Strata Florida owned over 1,000 sheep as well as cattle, horses, and pigs. Their pastures stretched from the sea at Cardigan Bay to Rhayader. They held their own fairs and courts, and may have had their own port for shipping, at Aberarth. In 1534 they had a public house selling their own brew within the abbey precinct. They had fish-ponds nearby, and sea-fishing at Aberarth and Penwedic (officially, they ate no meat). They cleared large areas of woodland, which, among other things, provided fuel for smelting the lead that they mined at Cwm Ystwyth. Indeed, in 1278 they were ordered by the English King to cut down their woods, to prevent shelter being given to criminals and rebels.

The remains of the abbey buildings date from a number of successive periods of construction, destruction, and repair. Stones from the abbey have probably found their way into local farms, such as the one still standing on the site of the south side and the frater. There is not a great deal left, but three items are of particular interest. One is the series of graves on the east side of the south transept, two of which are decorated with Celtic ornament. Also worth looking for are the medieval floor-tiles, plain and patterned, in the transept and presbytery. Of the building itself, the west door remains, a fine Norman arch, with five slender capitals and mouldings ending in the spiral of a shepherd's crook. This archway has the elegance and austerity of the best Cistercian work. There are carvings and other relics in a small museum at the entrance booth.

Pontrhydygroes Dyfed 6C1

In the magnificently wooded Ystwyth Valley, Pontrhydygroes ('bridge of the ford of the Cross') is a place that has returned to a peaceful nonentity. The leadmines, once prosperous, are now derelict. Hafod House, still marked on maps, is gone; this, had it survived, would have been one of the most interesting relics of the not-so-distant past. Here, in the late eighteenth century, Thomas Johnes devoted many years to the creation of an ideal house and estate. In line with the fashionable theory of the Picturesque, Johnes commissioned the Bath architect Thomas Baldwin to design a Gothic mansion. The church was built by James Wyatt (in 1803) and decorated by Fuseli. Johnes brought farmers from Scotland to improve agricultural methods on his estate; he planted over 2 million trees. His plans were fraught with ill luck. In 1807 the house burned down, destroying a priceless collection of books and a library designed by Nash: 'burning rafters mixed with flaming books were hurled high above the summits of the hills', as George Borrow describes it. Johnes started again, replacing his lost treasures with articles bought at the sale of 'Fonthill', another Gothic mansion and the creation of William Beckford, the eccentric and outrageous author of *Vathek*. Five years later, tragedy put an end to Johnes's endeavours. His beloved and only daughter died, and he lost interest in the place, retiring to Dawlish where he lived on for only a few more years. Borrow describes the second Hafod as it was in 1854: 'A truly fairy place it looked, beautiful but fantastic. . . . At the southern end was a Gothic tower; at the northern an Indian pagoda; the middle part had much the appearance of a Grecian villa. The walls were of resplendent whiteness, and the windows, which were numerous shone with beautiful gilding'. This curious monument to nineteenth-century architectural fantasy was destroyed in 1950. The church, with Chantrey's famous monument to Johnes's daughter, was burned out in 1932; it has been well restored as Eglwys Newydd (New Church).

Hafod is now a caravan site. Of Johnes's efforts, there remain some fine trees and the well-known Jubilee Arch, a stone archway set up to celebrate the Jubilee of George III. It stands across the mountain road (B4574) between Devil's Bridge and Cwm Ystwyth. Elizabeth Inglis-Jones's *Peacocks in Paradise* (1950) tells the story of Hafod House.

Pontypool (Pont-y-pŵl) Gwent 11G2
(*pop.* 37,014)

Pontypool lies in the most easterly of the Gwent valleys, that of the Afon Lwyd, and on the very perimeter of industrial South Wales. It is one of the oldest industrial towns in the Principality. Forges existed here in the Middle Ages and possibly in the time of the Romans. In the mid sixteenth century a London banker named Capel Hanbury established furnaces for smelting iron ore, on a site that is now the town's municipal park. In the early eighteenth century a descendant of his, John Hanbury, elaborated a method of rolling iron plates, and by 1782 the tinplate industry was launched. Decorated tin-plated ironware, known as Japan ware from its resemblance to Japanese lacquer-work, was one of the town's major products; it remained very popular well into the nineteenth century.

Coxe describes the town in 1801 as a 'large straggling place, containing 250 houses and 1500 souls. Several neat habitations, and numerous shops, present an appearance of thriving prosperity, notwithstanding the dusky aspect of the town, occasioned by the adjacent forges'. At this time one of the most notable features of the town was already the weekly market, held for the 'hardy mountaineers', all Welsh-speaking, whose women wore the tall Welsh hats, which for Coxe gave an 'arch and lively air to the younger part of the sex'. By the end of the century the boom in coal and iron had increased the population to over 27,000; to the 250 houses of 1801 had been added the innumerable long terraces characteristic of the valley towns. The population reached a peak of 44,000 between the Wars; since the Depression, however, it has fallen, with a natural emigration to the south of the industrial belt, where most of South Wales' heavy industries are now situated.

BLAENAVON, in a cul-de-sac of mountains at the head of the valley, is also an industrial settlement with a long history. The Blaenavon Iron Works opened in 1789; the last furnace closed in 1938. Here, in 1877–8, Sidney Gilchrist Thomas and Percy Gilchrist tested their new formula for manufacturing steel from phosphorous iron ores. The formula was purchased by Andrew Carnegie and used extensively in America and Germany. St Peter's church (1806), built by the ironmasters, has, appropriately, an iron font and iron tomb-covers in the churchyard. Next to it stands the school, also in neo-Gothic style (1816, with later wings), built by Sarah Hopkins as a memorial to her brother, one of the local ironmasters.

Until fairly recent times, this sort of area – scarred by industry, with hardly a country house, medieval church, or thatched cottage in sight – was dismissed as of no interest to anyone. The historian has, however, become more democratic, more discerning, less of a snob and an aesthete. Now, for example, instead of repudiating its industrial past, Pontypool (or Torfaen, as the borough is now called) has decided to embrace it. An exciting new development is taking place that will eventually, and without spoiling it, 'decipher' the whole of the valley for the intelligent tourist. The centre of operations is to be a new museum (opening in 1978) housed in the early-nineteenth-century stable-block of Pontypool Park House. The 'trail', which runs from Newport to Blaenafon, will take in villages and farmhouses, early coal-mines and ironworks, canals and tramroads, nineteenth-century chapels in Greek or Gothic style. At Pontypool itself are the 1850s Town Hall, the Art Deco Cooperative store, and Pontypool Park House (c. 1830, with later, unfortunate, additions), which has surviving original ice-houses and a small, circular Grotto. Other sides of this open-air museum will include the early-nineteenth-century stone-built engine-houses at Glyn Pits; the pre-1820 pit-head gear at Cwmbyrgwm; Forge Row at Cwmafon, a well-preserved example of early industrial housing (1804); and at Blaenafon, the Workmen's Hall and Institute (1894), Horeb Chapel (1862), St Peter's church and school, and the eighteenth-century Old Ironworks, which are being restored by the D.O.E.

Pontypridd Mid Glam. 11F3 (*pop.* 34,465)
This industrial town has a certain liveliness, partly due to its position at the converging-point of the Taff and Rhondda valleys. It has a market well known in this part of Wales. Its name means 'bridge by the earthen house', for in 1755, when the place consisted of a few 'neat cottages' set in picturesque woods, hills, and fields, William Edwards, a local, self-taught genius, succeeded in spanning the Taff with his graceful bridge. At the time, it was considered to be the largest single-arched bridge in the world; it remained the most ambitious in Britain until 1831. It can be seen at close quarters from the modern road-bridge, which masks its effect.

Pontypridd is essentially a nineteenth-century town, though it has recently acquired new shopping areas and new roads. It has two connexions with the revival of Welsh national consciousness that began in the late eighteenth century. On the Common above the town, a large block of sandstone is known as the 'Rocking Stone'. This, according to the eccentric patriot and scholarly legend-maker Iolo Morgannwg, was the site of the only true ancient *Gorsedd* or Assembly of Bards. Somewhat later, the equally eccentric Dr Price of Llantrisant performed druidical rites here. He also erected two follies, at Glyn Taff (Craig-yr-Helfa Road): these are the Round Houses, a pair of three-storey towers with octagonal slate roofs. Price intended them as part of a scheme for a druidic museum and palace, which was to be erected at the Rocking Stone.

The second connexion is commemorated in a fine, large park in the town centre. Two statues by William Goscombe John depict Evan and James James, father and son, both weavers, who composed the words and music of 'Land of my Fathers', adopted as the Welsh National Anthem in 1856.

Pontypridd prospered on coal and iron until the Depression, when its population began to decline. New industries are now centred at the Treforest Industrial Estate, while the scars left by extinct ones are being gradually erased. Slag-heaps have been reseeded, and a stretch of the Glamorgan Canal, which once carried valley coal and iron down to Cardiff, is being excavated and landscaped. The Glamorgan Naturalists' Trust publishes a leaflet for a nature ramble around the edges of the town. Those unfamiliar with the Welsh valleys may be surprised to find how close to industry lies a rich variety of natural life.

Port Einon W. Glam. *see* **Gower Peninsula**

Porthcawl Mid Glam. 10D4 (*pop.* 14,065)
Porthcawl seems so typical a small seaside resort that it is difficult now to imagine its several decades of existence as a nineteenth-century coal-port. In the 1820s a horse-

drawn tramroad was constructed to run from Maesteg in the Llynfi Valley to a new harbour built here for the export of coal. When the railway came, in 1865, the inner dock became the terminus of the Llynfi and Ogmore Valley railroads. By 1873 165,000 tons of coal were being shipped out yearly. Then, with the opening of new docks at Barry and Port Talbot, trade declined. The dock closed in 1907, and the inner harbour was filled in after the Great War. The small tidal basin, the breakwater, and the lighthouse remain, for the use only of pleasure-craft.

After 1860 Porthcawl had in any case found a new vocation. John Street and Mary Street commemorate members of the Brogden family who were responsible for much of its development as a seaside town. It became, and has remained, a favourite resort for the population of the industrial valleys; now, however, day-tripping and caravanning have largely replaced the traditional boarding-house holiday. Like many seaside towns, it also caters for retirement.

Like others, too, it has its class distinctions, expressed as 'ends' of the town. At the eastern end, Coney Beach is a large funfair overlooking the harbour and a long, sandy beach. Further away from the town centre in the same direction lies Trecco Bay, a gigantic caravan park – larger than many a Welsh village – with its own sands. West of centre, and a stiff walk past the 'Grand Pavilion' and the Seabank Hotel and numerous respectable sea-front villas, Rest Bay is unspoilt, with rocks and sands and large stretches of springy common. Further on this way lies the Royal Porthcawl Golf Course and eventually, on a rocky coast, Sker Point. Sker House, a Tudor farmhouse standing a little way back from the sea, was the setting for R. D. Blackmore's popular novel *The Maid of Sker*.

On the outskirts of Porthcawl, Nottage Court (on the South Cornelly road) is a Tudor manor-house complete with priest-hole. Blackmore stayed there with his family. Nottage parish church is at Newton Nottage (Drenewydd yn Notais), to the east of the town. It has a carved fifteenth-century pulpit, pre-Reformation altar, and an octagonal font. Outside, on the eastern wall of its fortress-like tower, note the stone projections. In medieval times these supported a 'hourd' or covered gallery, from which defenders could command the area below. The gallery has, of course, gone, but the doorway leading to it can still be seen in the wall. Across the village green, the tidal spring of St John's Well was a wonder to early antiquaries.

Port Talbot (Aberafan) W. Glam. 10D3
(*pop.* 50,658)

Between the coast of Swansea Bay and the bare mountains that rise dramatically behind it are sandwiched a giant steel works – the largest strip mill in Europe – and the straggly town of Port Talbot, a good example of how Industrial Man can despoil a fine setting. A recently-built motorway runs along the hillside and above roof-level of the town, giving spectacular views over a Welsh urban landscape: docks, derricks, steel and chemical works, churches, chapels, park, and rugby-ground.

Originally a small Norman borough, with a castle (now disappeared) to protect the crossing of the Afan River, Aberavon was officially renamed Port Talbot in 1836, in honour of the Talbot family of Margam Castle, who owned most of the land on which town and docks were built. As a modern port, the town's development dates from 1898 with the opening of a new dock to serve the coalfields; it is now the largest deep-water harbour in Britain, and serves the enormous Abbey steel works, on which the town largely depends. Much of the town centre, Late-Victorian and Edwardian, has recently been torn down and replaced by modern building. A few old landmarks survive: St Mary's church (rebuilt 1860), where the martyr of the 1831 Merthyr Riots, 'Dic Penderyn', was buried, and St Joseph's Roman Catholic church, both in a maze of motorway approach roads.

Aberavon Beach is a good 3km. stretch of sands, safe for bathing, backed by a somewhat featureless modern promenade with funfair, putting greens, paddling pool, and so on. The Afan Lido has an Olympic-size indoor swimming-pool, a bar, and a restaurant; international sports events of various kinds are held there. Behind the beach is the Sandfields Estate, a large housing development built on sand-dunes; in its early days it attracted much attention from town-planners and sociologists.

BAGLAN, 3km. west, is now a suburb of Port Talbot. According to nineteenth-century travellers, its beautiful setting and splendid views over Swansea Bay gave it a higher than usual proportion of 'gentlemen's seats'. One of these was Baglan House (now demolished), where the poets Gray and Mason were visitors. St Catherine's is a notable Victorian church sometimes referred to as the 'Alabaster Church' from the Penarth alabaster much in evidence within. The east window is a fine piece by Burne-Jones and represents a beardless Christ crucified on an unhewn tree. The church contains a ninth- or tenth-century carved and ornamented cross slab, with the inscription '*Brancu*'.

MARGAM, at the opposite end of the town, has a long history. There in 1147, on the site of an earlier, Celtic religious house, Robert of Gloucester, natural son of Henry I, founded a Cistercian abbey. The original grant of land, which lay between the Afan and Kenfig rivers, was about 7,200ha.; by the Dissolution Margam owned about 20,000. It was one of the richest of Welsh monastic houses, with estates in the Vale of Glamorgan and as far afield as Bristol. Grangetown in Cardiff was one of its granges. It had over 5,000 sheep (in 1291), and cattle and horses; it exported wool to Flanders. Its ships traded with Bristol and the West Country; it owned mills, fisheries, and coal-mines. It had right of wreck of sea along the marshy coast: in 1333 seven people were drowned nearby, and the abbey salvaged the boat (worth forty

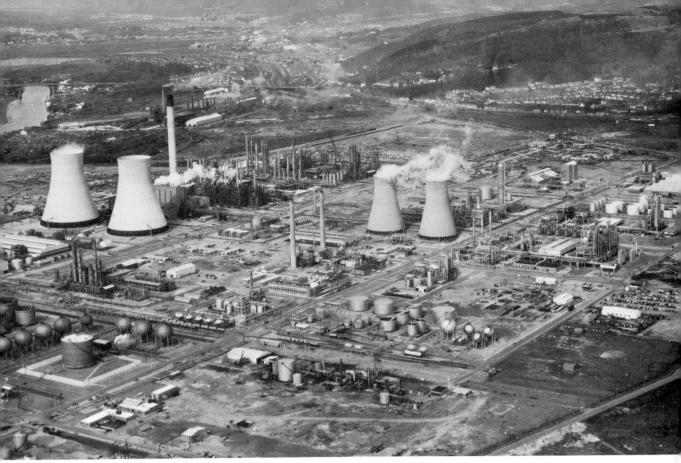

The industrial landscape at Briton Ferry, nr Port Talbot

shillings), three bales of wool (sixty shillings), a small coffer, and a cask worth eightpence.

Like other Welsh abbeys, Margam was by no means always a peaceful haven from the world. It suffered from the violence of its times and from natural disasters such as fire, flood, plague, and sandstorms. In 1384 old age and the 'horrid intemperance' of the coastal winds were blamed for the partial collapse of the monastery buildings. Kings, and men rich and poor, demanded hospitality, while the monks themselves engaged in lengthy litigation over lands and pastures. In 1206 the *conversi* (lay-brethren), who did most of the manual work, rose in revolt, 'attacked and pursued the abbot . . . barricaded themselves in their dormitories, refusing to provide the monks with the wherewithal to live'. In spite of all this, the abbey gained some reputation as a centre of learning; among its manuscripts was the copy of Domesday Book now held by the British Museum. Margam Annals are the only contemporary authority to accuse King John of the murder of his nephew Arthur.

Margam Abbey parish church occupies most of the nave of the original abbey church; like all Cistercian churches, it was dedicated to St Mary. It is one of only three Cistercian churches still in use in Britain, and the only one in Wales. The west front was much restored in the early nineteenth century (when the Italianate 'pepperpots' were added), but the doorway and three windows above it are late-Norman (*c.* 1175–80). Inside, the original nave has been reduced from 81½m. to 34½m. by the addition of an east wall. The six bays with their rectangular piers are the original Norman work. The west windows are the work of William Morris, the visionary poet-artist. There are numerous elaborate tombs and effigies of the Mansel and Talbot families. Theodore Talbot (d. 1876) brought Tractarian influence to Margam, and this is still evident in its rituals and vestments.

The remainder of the ruins are not normally open to the public. They include parts of the rest of the church, with doorway and piscina in the south wall of the choir. South of the chancel, a cloister led to the exquisite chapter-house, twelve-sided without and circular within. In the time of the Mansels and Talbots it deteriorated badly; it was used as a coal-house, while in 1799 the roof collapsed after a storm felled the elegant central column. The circular window beneath the easternmost of the nine lancets was inserted after the Dissolution and may have come from the east wall of the abbey church. South of the chapter-house, an isolated vaulted building may have been part of the Infirmary. All these fragments are Early English in style, dating from *c.* 1200.

To the north of Margam churchyard, a small building, once the old village school and one of the earliest

The Margam Stones Museum

church schools in Wales, is now a museum housing a fascinating collection of ancient stones. Most have been found on the abbey site or on the surrounding hills. (Casts may be seen in the National Museum at Cardiff.) The Pumpeius stone, a pillar that stood on the verge of the road between Margam and Kenfig, has Latin and Ogham inscriptions. The important Cross of Cynfelyn is a late-ninth- or early-tenth-century wheel-cross decorated with intertwining Celtic ornament and with human figures. Other exhibits include carved medieval grave slabs, one of which commemorates Abbot Robert of Rievaulx (Yorks), who must have died *en visite*.

Margam Castle, a large neo-Tudor mansion, was built in 1830–5 for C. R. M. Talbot. It suffered damage during the Second World War when British and American troops were housed there, and is now falling into decay. Its beautifully-laid-out park contained some fine trees, including a huge Aleppo pine, the largest in the country. Its glory, however, is the Orangery, built in 1787–90 for an earlier Talbot. Unique in Wales, this 98m.-long classical structure faces south, its tall windows looking out onto formal gardens and fountains. At the east and west ends, pavilions once housed statuary and books. (The original collection of citrus trees is said to have been a present from the King of Spain – or Portugal – to the English royal family; wrecked on the South Wales coast, the cargo was claimed by the local lord of the manor.) The local council have recently acquired the Park and Orangery and plan to restore them for public use.

A local landmark at Margam, the 'Round Chapel', has recently been bodily moved to make way for a motorway extension. The chapel, which is in fact octagonal, was built in 1838 on land given by the Talbots of Margam on condition it was built in that form (and not 'to keep the devil out of the corners', as local tradition had it). It is unique in South Wales, though English Wesleyan Methodist chapels up to about 1790 were frequently octagonal. It now stands on a piece of ground known as 'Banana Island', near the Twelve Knights Hotel.

In the Afan Valley, north-east of Port Talbot and near the former mining township of Cymer, the Afan Argoed Country Park combines industrial history with woodland and riverside walks in a fine setting. Its trails, exhibits, and displays will eventually form the South Wales Miners' Museum, the first phase of which is already complete.

Preseli Mts. (Mynydd Presely)   Dyfed   8C3/D3
Mynydd Presely, 'Prescelly Mountain', is a ridge of smooth, rounded hills, largely treeless, made up of open moorland, heath, and bog. Heather, gorse, and bilberry grow in profusion; lark and curlew are common; huge boulders strewn by the Ice Age are as grey as the sheep. The highest point of Preseli is Foel Cwm Cerwyn, or Prescelly Top (528m.), which lies a little to the east of the B4329, the old coaching-road from Cardigan to Haverfordwest. At Bwlch Gwynt, between Foel Cwm

Cerwyn and Foel Eryr (460m.), the B4329 crosses the Flemings Way, a prehistoric track that ran along the top of the ridge. (The Flemings came to Pembrokeshire centuries later, in the Middle Ages.) From here, on a clear day, you can see the West Country, Ireland, and Snowdonia.

Mysterious and ancient, these hills have attracted myth and legend. King Arthur, in the Old Welsh collection of tales, the *Mabinogion*, hunted the legendary boar Twrch Trwyth across these summits. The Roman Emperor Magnus Maximus, who married the Welsh princess 'Helen of the roads' (many Roman roads in Wales are known as *Sarn Helen*), also hunted here and left his name to the summit of Y Freni Fawr: Cadair Fachsen, 'Macsen's Chair' (near Crymmych). Certainly in prehistoric times and for whatever reason, Preseli seems to have been a place of special sanctity. From its igneous outcrops (Carn Menyn is the largest) came the 'bluestones' used in the building of the circles of Stonehenge. More than eighty of these boulders, weighing about 250 tonnes, were transported over 288km. by land and sea, probably via the Flemings Way to the Cleddau at Milford Haven. Stone axes of spotted dolerite and of rhyolitic tuff were produced here in some quantity, and distributed along trade routes far afield in the Neolithic world.

Prehistoric monuments from a variety of periods have been found on Preseli. Near Mynachlog-ddu, Gors Fawr is a stone circle of sixteen uprights with a diameter of some 21m. Two outlying stones, about 132m. north-east, clearly have some relation to the circle. Moel Drygarn,

Gors Fawr stone circle, nr Mynachlog-ddu, Preseli Mts.

near Crymmych, is the site of a huge Iron Age hill-fort, which has three sizeable Bronze Age cairns within its great stone ramparts. It was occupied by a large population during the first century BC. Carn Alw, a little to its west, has the remains of another prehistoric fortified site, one of only seven known in Britain to make use of *chevaux-de-frise* (a system of defence provided by setting low, pointed stones on end and at an angle in the ground – a serious obstacle to the advance of foot-soldiers or cavalry). Further standing stones and burial chambers can be seen near Maenclochog.

CRYMMYCH itself (8D2) is a market-centre that grew up almost entirely as a result of the railway, which has now vanished. MAENCLOCHOG (8C3) is a small village standing round a church and village-green. At ROSEBUSH (8C3) Lord Macaulay's nephew planned a holiday resort. In the 1870s he laid out gardens, dug lakes, and built a small hotel. Railway-lines were extended from Fishguard and Clunderwen to bring tourists in and carry slates from the local quarries out. The scheme came to nothing.

Presteigne (Llanandras) Powys 7G2
(*pop.* 1,214)

East of Offa's Dyke, the Lugg River is a quiet boundary between Wales and England. Presteigne, on its banks, was until very recently the small county town of the most sparsely populated county in England and Wales. (Radnorshire, now part of Powys, had in 1971 a population of only 18,262.) The town has Georgian houses, and the half-timbered cottages typical of the Border country. Of the numerous public houses, the Duke's Arms may be medieval, while the Radnorshire Arms is of sixteenth- and seventeenth-century date and has a priest-hole above the Tudor doorway. St Andrew's church, Perpendicular, contains a Flemish Renaissance tapestry, one of a set woven for Canterbury Cathedral; the others were sold to the cathedral at Aix-en-Provence during the Commonwealth period.

The town makes a peaceful base for walking or pony-trekking. Stapleton Castle, in ruins, lies just over the border, in Herefordshire. Westwards are the bleak hills of Radnor Forest and the Lugg Valley. About 6km. north-west, on Pilleth Hill, were ploughed up about a hundred years ago large quantities of human bones and other relics. It seems that this was the site of a terrible battle (1401) in which Owain Glyndwr and the Welsh slaughtered the forces sent to subdue them by the Earl of Mortimer. Many of the latter's troops are thought to have deserted to the Welsh during the encounter. Mortimer, taken prisoner, was forced not only to recognize Glyndwr as ruler of Wales but also to marry his daughter. (*See* Shakespeare's *Henry IV.*)

Glyndwr, or Glendower, was not the only man in this neighbourhood to be able to 'call spirits from the vasty deeps'. Maxwell Fraser in her book *Border Country* tells of a seventeenth-century exorcism that took place at Hergest Court, near Kington (just over the border). The evil spirit of Black Vaughan of Hergest was reduced to nothing more frightful than a common bluebottle. And at CASCOB, about 8km. east of Presteigne and deep in Radnor Forest, the ancient church (itself of great interest) contains a charm known as the Abracadabra (1700). It is a jumble of Christian and pagan elements: for example, 'Pater pater pater noster noster noster ave ave ave Maria in secula seculorum [part of the old Latin Mass] X On X Adonay X Tetragrammaton . . . in the name of the Holy Trinity and of Hubert . . . Grant that this holy charm Abracadabra may cure thy survent Elizabeth Loyd from all evil sprites'.

Pumsaint Dyfed 6C4

The village name means 'five saints', for the quintuplets born to Cynnyr Farfdrwch ap Gwron ap Cunedda – Gwyn, Gwynno, Gwynoro, Ceitho, and Cynfelyn – all achieved sanctity in the Celtic Church. This curious legend reflects the wonder with which primitive societies regarded multiple births and other natural freaks; the dark side of the same coin meant that a deformed or misshapen child might be considered the work of the devil, and left to die on the church steps.

Traces of a Roman fort and civil settlement have been recently revealed by excavations at Pumsaint village. The reason for the Romans' interest in this area lies nearby at DOLAUCOTHI (between Pumsaint and Caio). As the only known Roman gold-mine in Britain, and the second largest in the Empire, this site is unique. That gold could be found in the Carmarthenshire hills was probably known to the Romans, for there is evidence that the mines were worked before their time. Certainly they lost no time in taking over: it has been calculated that they were already exploiting the mines only five years or so after the 'conquest' of Wales in 75. Under Roman law all mineral rights belonged to the Emperor (and the Romans worked lead and silver in Flintshire, and copper in Anglesey, Caernarvonshire, and Montgomeryshire). In the case of gold, it was the Army that was made responsible for supervising production. The techniques used at Dolaucothi were sophisticated ones. Gold-bearing pyrites were extracted by means of open-cast workings and of underground galleries that reached a depth of $43\frac{1}{2}$m. The galleries were drained by a timber waterwheel, a fragment of which is preserved in the National Museum at Cardiff. Large quantities of water, used to remove debris, and perhaps also to treat the ore, were brought by three aqueducts cut into the hillside.

The remains are not easily traced without the help of an explanatory leaflet (on sale at the site). Remains of the aqueduct system and reservoirs are visible; entrances to shafts can be clearly distinguished but should not of course be entered. The gold extracted here may have been exported, to the imperial mint at Lyons, or even to Rome itself. The mines may have been worked again in medieval times, for Talley Abbey, whose

Roman gold-mine – the Empire's second largest – at Dolaucothi, nr Pumsaint

monks mined lead within their grounds, lies only 6½km. south. They were opened again in the nineteenth century and in the 1930s, but proved disappointing. The land is NT property, and there are signposted trails starting at Ogofan Lodge on the minor road to Cwrt-y-cadno.

Raglan (Rhaglan)   Gwent   11H1
The imposing, angular ruins of Raglan are of later date than most other castles of the Marcher lordships.

Although the layout of the site makes it likely that an earlier castle stood here, perhaps in the eleventh century, soon after the Conquest, no trace of it survives. The building as we see it today was begun by Sir William ap Thomas, Steward of the lordship of Usk and Caerleon, in the years preceding the Wars of the Roses. Sir William was as aggressive as any of his contemporaries: his method of ensuring the appointment of a new prior, for example, was (in 1441) to carry off the rival candidate and throw him into chains in Usk Castle. At Raglan, Sir William's

Raglan Castle

main work was the 'Yellow Tower of Gwent' (1432–45), a formidable moated keep of hexagonal shape, in which his family could feel secure, even against their own retinue.

William Herbert, his son, supported the Yorkist cause, and made his fortunes as a result. From Chief Justice and Chamberlain of South Wales, he was raised by Edward IV to the peerage, and was eventually created Earl of Pembroke in 1468. At Raglan, his main seat, he continued the enlargement of the castle, adding, notably, the Fountain Court buildings, the Kitchen Tower, the Closet Tower, and the Great Gate. At about this time, too, Raglan was made an independent lord-ship, with rights to a weekly market and two annual fairs.

The Earl of Pembroke lost his head in 1469 after his defeat at the Battle of Edgecote. The next set of major alterations to the castle was not begun until the middle of the following century. Then, in Elizabeth's reign, William Somerset, Earl of Worcester, extensively re-modelled the Hall and the buildings in the Pitched Stone Court. He also provided a Long Gallery, a typical feature of Elizabethan great houses, and built upper storeys onto several parts of the castle. William's son Edward, Master of the Horse under Elizabeth and James I, was a patron of Spenser and of William Byrd. In his time

(£40,000, while his aid to the King was said to have been nearly a million). Two gates were added – the White and the Red – and earthworks were thrown up near Castle Farm. A large powder magazine was brought from Caerleon.

The siege of Raglan in 1646 was one of the most important of the Civil War. Worcester, with his garrison of 800, held out against a besieging force almost double that number. After the fall of Oxford in June the number of attackers was increased to 3,500. In August Cromwell's Commander-in-Chief, Sir Thomas Fairfax, came in person to direct the siege. Eventually, on 19 August, Raglan surrendered; the garrison marched out with flying colours. Parliament ordered a day of general thanksgiving; the first Civil War was effectively won.

Cromwellian gunpowder had not succeeded in destroying the castle; this was left to the deliberate 'slighting', the usual policy designed to ensure that a fortress could not be used again. The Great Tower was mined and partly fell; many of the other buildings were badly damaged, the woods cut down, and the lead and timber taken to Bristol to rebuild a bridge. The Somerset family, later Dukes of Beaufort, soon built a new seat at Badminton, which has some relics (including a fine chimney-piece) from Raglan. Only in the early nineteenth century did the castle re-emerge from obscurity, when travellers were attracted by the newly fashionable 'romantic' ruins. Some neo-Gothic restoration took place at that time. In 1938 the castle came into the care of the State.

The Great, or Yellow, Tower of Gwent should perhaps be looked at first, since this was the nucleus of the fifteenth-century castle. On its north-west face can be clearly seen the remains of the elaborate drawbridge system. There were originally two separate drawbridges here, a wide one for ceremonial entry, and a narrower one for everyday use. In the second phase of the fifteenth-century reshaping additional gateways elsewhere in the castle made it possible for these wooden bridges to be replaced by a permanent two-decker stone bridge, which entered the tower at first-floor level and below. The hexagonal tower was in itself an extraordinary structure. Higher by one storey and battlements than the present ruin, it was a self-contained residence as well as a powerful fort. Inside there are garderobes, fireplaces, and a well, plus arrowslits and gunports. There are splendid views from the upper staircase.

Of the later buildings, the Great Hall is the best preserved. Unfortunately, the Irish oak roof with its cupola, and the heraldic glass proclaiming the noble descent of the owner, have long disappeared. There remain the mullioned windows, the great fireplace, the roof corbels, and the time-eaten plaque on the dais wall bearing the arms of the third Earl of Worcester as Knight of the Garter (1570). Elsewhere in the castle are fine traceried windows and ornamental fireplaces in English Renaissance style. Pitched Stone Court has original cobbles and

(1589–1628) were probably added the brick gazebos, or summer-houses, and the niches along the moat-walk, which held statues of Roman emperors. The interior also received sumptuous additions.

Raglan, it would seem, was turning into a richly comfortable residence, expressive of the power and wealth of its owners, whose lives now centred on the Court rather than on the battlefield. But its days as a fortress were by no means over. The Earls of Worcester of the following century were prominent Catholics and Royalists, and Raglan itself, in the Civil War, the centre of the Royalist cause in the West. Worcester's enormous fortune now went into the garrisoning of the castle

drainage channels. Fountain Court has unfortunately lost its marble fountain, which was known as the White Horse.

Ramsey Island (Ynys Dewi) Dyfed 8A3/A4
Like most of the Pembrokeshire islands, Ramsey was named by the Vikings. The botanist John Ray, however, had a charming if fanciful theory: Ramsey was named, according to this seventeenth-century authority, after the quantity of ramsons that grew there. (Ramson – *Allium ursinum* – has long broad leaves like a lily-of-the-valley, and white star-like flowers in a single cluster. The leaves smell strongly of onions if trampled.) Ramsey certainly has a profusion of wild flowers. Its magnificent cliffs are also a major breeding-ground of the grey Atlantic seal. The island is privately owned, and managed as a Nature Reserve by the Royal Society for the Protection of Birds. Visitors may take boats to or around the island, from Porth Stinan, which is reached via a minor road out of St David's.

The scatter of rocks further out to sea from Ramsey are known as the Bishop and Clerks.

Resolven W. Glam. *see* **Pontneddfechan**

Reynoldston W. Glam. *see* **Gower Peninsula**

Rhayader (Rhaeadr Gwy) Powys 7E2
This small mid-Wales market-town on the Wye consists largely of two main streets with a clock-tower War Memorial at the cross-roads. Numerous public-houses and inns, many of them centuries old, testify to the importance of the town as a market-centre and, in former days, as a stopping-place on the coach road to Aberystwyth. Near the cattle-market, St Clement's church contains an early font with primitive carvings of human heads. Across the tumbling Wye (the town's name is an Anglicization of the Welsh for 'waterfall', *rhaeadr*) is Cwmdeuddwr, a village in its own right, with church, Tudor inn, and some ancient cottages.

BELOW: *Claerwen Reservoir, Elan Valley, nr Rhayader*　　　OPPOSITE: *The Claerwen Dam*

Public transport here is deplorable, but pony-trekking is well organized, and there is excellent walking in magnificent and varied countryside. Each road out of Rhayader leads into mountains. (It was on the road between Rhayader and Builth that, according to Kilvert, Wordsworth met the original of his poem 'Peter Bell'.)

Only a few km. from Rhayader are the ELAN VALLEY reservoirs, which have become a major scenic attraction. The road to the dams leaves Rhadayer behind in a bowl of hills and climbs up past Elan Village with its picnic-places and small white-painted iron suspension bridge. The four Elan Valley lakes were begun in 1894, and opened by Edward VII in 1904; 2,000 workmen were brought into the area to construct the dams. The fifth and largest, Claerwen, was completed in 1952 and holds 45 thousand million litres.

For those who like reservoirs, these are certainly fine examples, well landscaped into the hills and new pine-forests. For the Welsh, though, they are a sore point, for while Welsh farmland and valleys are drowned for an English city's (Birmingham's) water-supply, water rates in Wales are higher than in many English towns. The reaction can be a strong one; R. S. Thomas, Anglo-Welsh poet and Vicar of an upland parish near Machynlleth, expresses the uneasiness the reservoirs inspire:

> There are places in Wales I don't go:
> Reservoirs that are the subconscious
> Of a people, troubled far down
> With gravestones, chapels, villages even;
> The serenity of their expression
> Revolts me, it is a pose
> For strangers.

Under the waters of the Elan lakes lie several farms, an old church, a Baptist chapel, a school-house, and eighteen cottages. Elan Village was constructed as compensation by the Birmingham City Corporation, and designed by the architect of Cadbury village. Two of the drowned farms are connected with the poet Shelley, who was himself to die by drowning, in Italy, in 1822. In 1811 Shelley spent a few weeks at Cwm Elan, an estate that belonged to his cousin Thomas Grove, after he had been sent down from Oxford for expressing dangerous ideas. The following year he returned, to Nant Gwyllt, a neighbouring farm, with his new wife Harriet (who drowned herself in the Serpentine in 1816); they intended to farm the land, but were fairly quickly evicted. When the waters are low, during a dry summer, the garden walls of Nant Gwyllt appear in the mud about 1½km. from Garreg Ddu bridge.

As incidental reading for the Elan Valley and Rhayader, Francis Brett Young's novel *The House under the Water* is a fictional account of Nant Gwyllt and the flooding of the valley. Elizabeth Clarke's very readable memoir, *The Valley* (1969), gives a good picture of life on the farms around Rhayader in the early years of this century.

Rhondda Mid Glam.   11 E2   (*pop.* 88,924)
'The Rhondda' is in reality two adjoining valleys, that of the Rhondda Fawr (Great Rhondda), which runs down from Blaenrhondda through Treherbert, Treorci, and Tonypandy to Pontypridd, and that of the Rhondda Fach (Little Rhondda), which rises above Maerdy and comes down through Ferndale and Tylorstown to join the main valley at Porth. These are, in the minds of many, the archetypal South Wales valleys.

Only 150 years ago the extraordinary beauty and solitude of these valleys struck travellers such as Malkin: 'Hereabouts, and for some miles to come, there is a degree of luxuriance in the valley, infinitely beyond what my entrance on this district led me to expect. The contrast of the meadows, rich and verdant, with mountains the most wild and romantic, surrounding them on every side, is in the highest degree picturesque'. Development, in fact, came late to the Rhondda; it was not until the 1860s that the steam-coal, which lay deeper here than in any of the other valleys, began to be extracted. After that, growth was an explosion.

From less than 1,000 in 1851, the population rose to 163,000 in 1931. But by 1935 the dream was over. An anonymous satire (by Dr Thomas Jones) entitled *What's wrong with South Wales?* suggested that the whole region be scheduled as a Grand National Ruin: 'For the Rhondda and Merthyr area we urge that the First Commissioner issue an irrevocable Standing Order, once all human beings have been evacuated to the Hounslow–Dagenham green belt. The Office of Works should then proceed to protect the approaches from souvenir hunters and should invite His Majesty to declare the area an open Museum or Exhibition to illustrate the Industrial Revolution of the nineteenth century. We claim this as an original suggestion. The march of science is such that old landmarks are constantly being removed or blotted out, and if we are not alert we shall have few traces left of what nineteenth century industrialism and individualism combined were able to achieve'.

Since the Depression there has indeed been a considerable drop in population, as the centres of industry in South Wales shift more and more to the coastal belt. On a grey or rainy day, when the slate roofs slant endlessly against the grey hillsides, it is hard to believe that anything but frustration could flourish here. Yet these were vigorous communities, with a thriving musical, religious, political life of their own making. Nor has industry entirely succeeded in destroying the environment. The Glamorgan Naturalists' Trust publishes *Three walks in the coalfield*, a leaflet that gives an excellent guide to the unexpected variety and interest of these valleys. From Blaenrhondda, for example, one can explore the falls of the Rhondda headwaters, find remains of prehistoric hut-circles and Dark Age dykes, look out for buzzards and snow buntings, foxes and rare butterflies.

On the mountain above Ferndale, LLANWONNO's

isolated church has the curious grave of a famous Welsh runner, Guto Nyth Bran (Griffith Morgan, 1700–37), who could run twelve miles (19km.) in less than an hour – or from Porth to Llantrisant in the time his mother took to boil the kettle.

A little to the west of the Rhondda Fawr Valley, GILFACH GOCH has a small valley to itself. This was the first 'garden village' in South Wales; founded in March 1910, it was the creation of the Welsh Garden Cities Ltd of Cardiff. It is now the setting for another important reclamation scheme.

Rhosili   W. Glam.   *see* **Gower Peninsula**

Roch (Y Garn)   Dyfed 8B4
Roch Castle, high on its crag, was the most westerly of the line of Norman castles built to contain the Welsh behind an imaginary line – and real linguistic boundary – running between north and south Pembrokeshire, 'Welshry' and 'Englishry'. Built in the thirteenth century, Roch (from the French, *roche*, a rock) commanded an imposing view over a hostile countryside. Legend suggests another reason for its siting on this outcrop: Adam de la Roche had been told by a witch that he would die of a serpent's bite unless he could pass the year in safety. Locked in an upper room of this castle, he survived 364 days; on the 365th day a servant brought in a basket of firewood, out of which wriggled an adder.

Since 1420, when the last male de la Roche died, the castle has passed through numerous hands. In 1601 it was bought by William Walter, a gentleman of the neighbourhood, and ancestor of the Lucy Walter who became Charles I's mistress and mother of the Duke of Monmouth. Elizabeth Goudge's novel *The Child from the Sea* is a version of Lucy's story, and contains many local references. In 1965 the castle was purchased by an American, and cannot now be visited.

In the village, the parish church is modern but its circular enclosure is evidence of an ancient religious site. At LLANGWM (8C5) on the Cleddau, the fourteenth-century Roch Chapel in the church has effigies that may represent knights and ladies of the Roch family.

St Clears (Sanclêr)   Dyfed 9E4
Only the mound of its Norman castle remains at this small agricultural centre, which stood until recently on the very edge of Carmarthenshire. The ancient church, however, is the remnant of a priory, one of only two in Wales founded by the Cluniac Order (the other was at Malpas, Gwent). Henry V dissolved all 'alien' priories in his kingdom, and Henry VI is said to have given the possessions of St Clears to the Warden and Fellows of All Souls, Oxford. The present church has a very fine Norman chancel arch with carvings, and a Norman font.

Arthur Young, the traveller and economist, visited St Clears in the 1770s and admired the scenery. He found a number of iron furnaces working in the neighbourhood; these have now all disappeared. The poor spun wool; weavers earned a shilling a day. Young continues, 'The poor live on barley-bread, cheese, and butter; not one in ten have either cows or pigs, fare very poorly and rarely touch meat. Their little gardens they plant with cabbages, carrots, leeks, and potatoes. Rent of a cottage and garden, 10s. to 20s. Building a mud cabin costs 10 l.' Young then gives a list of food prices, which it is interesting to compare with the weavers' wage given earlier: 'Beef, 3d. per lb. Pork, 2½d. to 3d. Mutton, 3¼d. Butter, 7d. 20 ounces. . . . Chickens, 3d. to 3½d. Turkies, 1s. 3d. . . . Wild ducks, 9d. to 10d. a couple. Teal, 1s. a couple. Widgeon, 6d. to 10d. a couple. Salmon, 1½d. per lb.'

In the following century agricultural unrest erupted around St Clears into the Rebecca Riots. Bands of young farmers and labourers, on horseback, with blackened faces and women's clothing, swooped down at night to destroy the hated toll gates. Their nickname, 'Rebecca', was taken from *Genesis* XXIV, 60. Hugh Williams, a leader of the Chartists, had settled in St Clears; while he was opposed to the violence of Rebecca, he drafted her petitions and helped to defend those of her followers who were captured. Eventually, the riots brought results. In 1844 the ringleaders were transported, but the turnpike system was reformed, bringing some measure of relief to the countryside.

The church at LLANDDOWROR, a village just over 3km. south-west, has the square embattled tower typical of south-west Wales. This was the parish of Griffith Jones (1683–1761), who is famous in Wales for his 'circulating schools'. In 1731 Jones wrote to the SPCK, suggesting the establishment of a new type of school that would alleviate 'the extremely miserable blindness' of his country. In the countryside at this time men were dying in an epidemic, and Jones believed that eternal damnation lay in store for those who died in ignorance of Christ. He proposed to teach reading, not only to children, but also to men and women of all ages, with the primary purpose of reading the Bible. Jones's work soon extended beyond the bounds of his own parish. Teachers were sent out for periods of about three months in each place, long enough to teach elementary reading without interfering with the seasonal labours of the farm. Lessons were conducted in Welsh; reading and the catechism were the only subjects on the curriculum.

Griffith Jones's achievement far transcended his religious aims. Over 150,000 pupils passed through his schools, as well as the many thousands of adults who came to night-classes. Not only was the Nonconformist cause strengthened, but a potential reading-public was formed, and the Welsh language helped to survive. Thomas Charles, another pioneer of Welsh popular education, was also born near Llanddowror, six years before the death of Griffith Jones.

St David's (Tŷddewi)   Dyfed   8A3

On the windy Land's End of Wales, and about a km. from the shore, St David's Cathedral has grown over the centuries, each age adding the visible marks of its faith or its neglect. Its Welsh name, Tŷddewi, 'David's house', reflects its earliest origins as a semi-monastic religious settlement founded by the sixth-century missionary saint. The Celtic Churches in Wales, Ireland, and Scotland had developed their own traditions of rite and doctrine, which survived the Roman retreat and the Saxon invasion. St David's, in its sheltered hollow, outlasted the Viking raids as well, and was a flourishing community when the Normans came. For the latter, a church was almost as much of a threat as a castle. They set about reorganizing the Celtic communities, imposing their own pattern of cathedral and diocese, importing a new form of monasticism from France. At St David's a royal official was quickly appointed bishop; he rebuilt the church and consecrated it as a cathedral in 1131.

Forcibly reconnected to the Roman Church, St David's acquired a new fame and valuable financial support. Henry II, *en route* to Ireland, visited the church as a pilgrim, in the hope of pacifying public opinion after the murder of Thomas à Becket. (The nearest village on the coast road north of the city is called Rhodiad-y-brenin – 'King's walk' – for an English king is said to have dismounted there to finish his pilgrimage on foot.) Two journeys to St David's were equal in value to one pilgrimage to Rome, though this piece of spiritual accountancy reflects the state of the Welsh roads as much as the holiness of the relics. Soon, the cathedral was rich, and the Chapter planned a new building that would do justice to the shrine.

This new church was begun by Bishop Peter de Leia not long after his appointment in 1178. De Leia's craftsmen used the grey and purple Cambrian sandstone from local quarries, hewing the church out of the very materials of its landscape. The building was cross-shaped, with a squat central tower. Of this twelfth-century work, the round-headed arches of the nave and the richly complex arcading of the clerestories are impressive survivals.

De Leia's tower collapsed in 1220, a fairly common occurrence in medieval churches. Three of the crossing arches were rebuilt with it. At this time, too, the Chapel of St Thomas of Canterbury was added to the north transept; of this chapel, only the beautiful double piscina now remains. The thirteenth and fourteenth centuries saw further chapels tacked on to the main structure: in particular, the Lady Chapel at the east end, which testifies to the growing cult of the Virgin Mary during the later Middle Ages. Meanwhile, around the expanding cathedral, an increasing number of clerical residences were now protected by a city wall complete with gatehouse.

In 1328 Henry Gower was appointed bishop and set about vigorous reconstruction. For example, he raised the walls of the aisles, replacing the Norman windows with much larger ones in Decorated style and giving the church its characteristic light interior. He added the south porch, put an extra storey on the tower, and had the Lady Chapel and St Thomas's Chapel vaulted in stone (the latter still surviving). Gower's finest work – apart from the Bishop's Palace – was the rood-screen or pulpitum that separated nave from sanctuary. This unique asymetrical screen houses Bishop Gower's own tomb.

Gower's successors continued to embellish the cathedral. In the late fourteenth century a college of chantry priests was founded by Bishop Houghton and provided with a set of buildings on the river side of the church. Of these, St Mary's Chapel remains, with the traces of the cloister still visible on its outside wall. Then, in the fifteenth century (a time of religious revival), a number of projects gave the cathedral some of its most magnificent features. The Norman roof, unsafe, was replaced by the glorious oak ceiling that adorns the nave. Choir stalls were added, with a fine carved parapet and twenty-eight inventive misericords. The bishop's throne, with stone canopy, dates from about 1500. The seats for the priests celebrating Mass, on the south side of the sanctuary, are of typical Perpendicular complexity; they are rare examples of pre-Reformation wooden sedilia.

Bishop Vaughan (1509–23) was not to be outdone. He completed the nave ceiling and gave the tower its final storey. The Holy Trinity Chapel, where he lies buried, is also his work, in honey-coloured West-of-England limestone. At its entrance is a fine late-Perpendicular screen. The chapel's delicate, soaring fan-vaulting seems to represent the final tranquil flowering of medieval forms before the upheavals of Reformation and Renaissance.

The cathedral itself escaped almost intact from the Dissolution of the monasteries. Indeed, it was entrusted with the tomb of the grandsire of the new Defender of the Faith, Edmund Tudor, who had lain till then in the Grey Friars' in Carmarthen. However, the outlying buildings – Bishop's Palace, chantry college, chapels – were allowed to fall into decay. The cathedral kept up its struggle against time and weather as best it could on the reduced resources of the diocese. By 1793 the west front needed restoration. This task was given to John Nash, but his work proved unsound and had to be undertaken anew in the following century by Sir George Gilbert Scott. This time the job was better done, though Scott in his usual way insisted on 'purifying' some of the existing features, replacing, for example, the sixteenth-century upper window of the sanctuary by a set of four

LEFT: *St David's Cathedral : looking up into the tower*

ABOVE: *St David's Cathedral: the nave*

BELOW, LEFT and RIGHT: *St David's Cathedral: misericords*

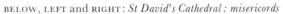

ABOVE, CENTRE: *The Bishop's Palace: the arcaded parapets of the great hall, from the courtyard*

ABOVE, RIGHT: *St David's Cathedral: from the NW*

ABOVE: *Arthur's Quoit, St David's Head*   OPPOSITE: *St Non's Bay, nr St David's, looking E*

small lancets. Later restoration has been carried out this century by W. D. Caroe and Alban Caroe. The most recent has been the conversion of the ruined St Mary's Chapel into an assembly hall.

The tombs and monuments are a record of Welsh history. The bones of St David, hidden from the iconoclasm of the Reformation, now rest behind the high altar. A modern statue of the saint shows a dove on his shoulder, a reference to the legend of his eloquence at Llanddewi Brefi, at the synod held to confute the Pelagian heresy. In the wall of the south transept, an eleventh-century tombstone has a Celtic motif that reminds us of the church's origins; it commemorates the sons of Bishop Abraham (Celtic priests were not necessarily celibate), killed by the Norsemen in 1080. As well as the tomb of Edmund Tudor, father of Henry VII and the Tudor dynasty, there are effigies of the Lord Rhys, one of South Wales' last and strongest princes, and of Gerald the Welshman, Giraldus Cambrensis, the twelfth-century churchman and writer, born at Manorbier, whose ambition to become Bishop of St David's and make that see independent of Canterbury went unfulfilled.

Gerald's feelings about the alien bishops of this Welsh see were not unfounded. According to an anecdote recounted in James Brome's eighteenth-century tour of Britain and ascribed by him to Rudburn's Annals of the Church of Winchester, Bishop Peter de Leia went in about 1190 to Rhys King of Wales to ask him to disturb no longer the peace of the Church nor make the King of England his enemy by his invasions. Rhys, not surprisingly, answered very rudely and had the Bishop beaten up in bed. De Leia retaliated by excommuni-

cating the King and his sons, and placing an interdict upon his kingdom. Eventually the King's son Gruffydd, being 'of a milder Temper than his father', came with his brothers and friends, meekly begging pardon and promising 'all due Obedience and Subjection to the king of England'. Brome continues: 'Upon this, the Bishop being fully satisfied with his Submission, orders the Corps of his dead father, tho' then sufficiently stinking, to be taken up, and whipp'd, and having order'd likewise as many Stripes for the Sons, as he thought fit, he then absolv'd both Dead and Living, and all that Land . . . from the dreadful Sentence of Excommunication'. True or not, this story illustrates clearly the way in which the Norman bishops made their religion a political tool in Wales.

West of the cathedral, the Bishop's Palace is a building magnificent even in ruin. A series of distinguished incumbents, from 1280 to 1350 (with some sixteenth-century additions), took a hand in its making. Chiefly, however, the Palace is the work of Bishop Gower (1328–47), whose characteristic arcaded parapets can here be seen at their best. Notice too the rose-windows, the barrel vaulting, the doorway to the Great Hall, and the piscina in the chapel. Bishop Barlow, at the Reformation, is said to have removed the roof, selling the lead to provide dowries for his five daughters.

St David's village – it has, of course, the right to call itself a city – is unprepossessing, as Wesley remarked in 1781. The peninsula, a triangle of ancient rock that juts out further westward than any other tip of Wales, has spectacular cliff scenery and scattered traces of early man. This was Ptolemy's Octapitarum, shown on ancient maps. There are Neolithic chambered tombs at

Carn Llidi and Coetan Arthur, and an Iron Age promontory fort on St David's Head. In nearer but legendary times, St Patrick set out for Ireland from WHITESAND BAY, while at ST NON'S, on the coast, and about a km. from the cathedral, a ruined chapel and holy well are named after David's mother (the earliest remains here may date from the seventh or eighth century). Both prehistoric sites and Celtic missionary shrines have clear connexions with Ireland, a reminder of the long centuries when the Celtic lands – Wales, Ireland, Scotland, Brittany, and Spain – were linked by the western sea-routes, sending from one to another their settlers, traders, and saints.

At CAERFAI, to the south-west, the sandstone for the cathedral was quarried; in 1382 four men were paid sixpence a day between them for working the windlass that lifted the stones to the clifftop. PORTHCLAIS, directly south, was the harbour where Irish timber for the cathedral scaffolding was landed. SOLVA (Solfach), east, a charming village at the head of a drowned river-valley, was a busy port up to the late nineteenth century. Ships traded as near as Bristol and as far as New York. The present Smalls lighthouse, put there by Trinity House in 1861, replaced an earlier one in wood that had been designed in 1773 by a Liverpool musical-instrument maker. Solva today is a harbour for yachtsmen and fishermen.

St Dogmaels (Llandudoch)   Dyfed   8D2
The Norsemen on one of their tenth-century coastal raids sacked the original Welsh religious foundation that stood here. After the Norman conquest Robert FitzMartin, Lord of Cemais, brought Benedictine monks from Tiron in France, and re-established the abbey (1115), which was rededicated to St Mary the Virgin. The north and west walls of the nave are still standing; the north door has very fine fourteenth-century moulding. Notice in the north transept the carved corbels: an angel (for St Matthew), a lion (for St Mark), and the Archangel Michael.

The parish church of St Thomas the Martyr (1847) contains the Sagranus Stone. This early-Christian monument has inscriptions in both Latin and Ogham, or Ogam, an alphabet of Irish or Goidelic origin consisting of strokes of varying lengths marked on each side of a line or edge. The inscription, which reads '*Sagrani fili Cunotami*' ('stone of Sagranus son of Cunotamus'), provided the key to the Ogham script, which was deciphered in 1848.

St Donat's (Sain Dunwyd)   S. Glam.   11E4
The castle on the coast at St Donat's has been in continuous occupation since the fourteenth century. For much of that time it was in the hands of the Stradling family, who claimed descent from the first Norman conquerors of Glamorgan. In the Middle Ages the Stradlings reputedly engaged in piracy and smuggling,

Tinkinswood, c. 2500 BC, one of the best-preserved chambered tombs in Britain

setting out to sea from the small inlet conveniently placed just below the castle. In the reign of Mary Tudor Sir Thomas Stradling was an ardent Catholic, active in suppressing heresy. When the Protestant Queen Elizabeth came to the throne he kept rather quiet. But two years later he was imprisoned because of the publicity surrounding St Donat's through the discovery in the trunk of a tree, brought down by a storm, of a figure of the Cross. He spent two years in jail for this ill-timed miracle. In the Civil War the Stradlings were vigorously Royalist; Sir Edward was wounded at the Battle of Edgehill.

Numerous tales and legends have gathered round the castle. In the early eighteenth century, for example, it is

the proceeds went in lawyers' fees; Tyrrwhit's heirs were granted the castle, but the baronetcy remained in the Stradling family.

This sort of grisly history, plus the ghosts, of which there are supposedly several, and the castle's secluded position on a beautiful and unfrequented coast, naturally attracted the American newspaper magnate William Randolph Hearst, who bought it early this century and filled it with medieval antiquities. Since the last War it has been turned into an international Sixth Form institution, Atlantic College (opened in 1962). The beach is used for life-saving practice. The castle, which has medieval and Tudor features, is not normally open to the public. Below the castle, St Donat's church is an eleventh-century building with a fourteenth-century tower; its fine fifteenth-century churchyard cross has carvings of the Crucifixion and of the Virgin crowned.

The villages along this rocky coast lie away from the sea, which forms no part of their economy. MARCROSS, about 1½km. west, is a ribbon village. Its small Norman church has an unusual chancel arch with chevron ornament. The valley runs down through woodlands to NASH POINT, whose two lighthouses are well-known landmarks on a perilous coast. Somewhere in the parish there was once a holy well renowned for its cures. A local rhyme ran: 'For the itch and the stitch, / Rheumatic and the gout, / If the devil isn't in you, / The well will take it out'.

The name of MONKNASH (Yr As Fawr), about 3km. north-west of Marcross, reflects its medieval origins as a grange of Neath Abbey; ruins of the grange are still visible in the village. The Cistercian monks reputedly had over 400ha. under the plough in this fertile region. St Mary's church is Norman; its roof timbers were claimed to be salvaged from wrecks of the Spanish Armada, but they may well be even older. A wooded valley, Cwm Nash, leads to the sea.

St Fagan's S. Glam. *see* **Cardiff**

St Hilary S. Glam. *see* **Cowbridge**

St Lythan's (Llwyneliddon) and **Tinkinswood**
S. Glam. 11F4
Turn off the A48 Cowbridge–Cardiff road at St Nicholas for two impressive Neolithic burial chambers lying conveniently close to one another. The houses of the dead are the only permanent architectural remains left by the pastoral societies that inhabited Britain from about 4000 BC. The forms and construction of these communal tombs vary according to cultural and geographical links. In Wales, the type known as 'Irish Channel', that is, long, chambered cairns, often with evidence of cremation, are found in the west, and are related to the tombs of northern Ireland, south-west Scotland, and some of the long barrows of lowland England. The two chambers here in the Vale of Glamorgan

said that the Stradling heir planned to make the Grand Tour of Europe with a friend named Tyrrwhit. Before setting out they signed a pact that if either died, the other would inherit his property. On 27 September 1738 Stradling was killed in a duel at Montpellier, and his body was brought back to St Donat's for burial. Suspicion naturally fell upon Tyrrwhit, who stood to gain from the death. An old nurse, sitting up with the body, opened the coffin: to her horror she found that whereas the true Sir Thomas had had one finger bitten off by a donkey, this corpse's hands were perfect. It was long expected that the real heir would reappear. Eventually, after fifty years of lawsuits, during which Tyrrwhit himself died, the estates were settled. Most of

St Lythan's burial chamber

are of the type known as 'Cotswold–Severn'; their builders were part of, or influenced by, a culture centred in the Cotswold hills. The special features that distinguish Cotswold–Severn cairns are the wedge shape, with funnel-shaped forecourt; the chamber approached by a short passage; the dry-stone walling; and the practice of burial rather than cremation. The entrance and forecourt often face due east.

Tinkinswood, *c.* 2500 BC, is one of the largest and best preserved chambered tombs in the whole of Britain. The cairn, 39m. long, is contained by a dry-stone revetment wall. The entrance, at the east, with its 'horns' formed by the curve of the wall, has been reconstructed (as can be seen from the herring-bone pattern of the masonry), and may originally have been more rounded. Inside, a trapezoid chamber is formed by three large upright slabs and a capstone weighing about 40 tonnes: all the large stones are Triassic mudstone, locally quarried. Here were found the bones of about fifty people, an unusually large number, probably all members of one family or clan group. Pottery of a somewhat later date found in the tomb suggests that it was reopened several centuries later. A 3m.-wide pit, inside the cairn, may have had some ritual purpose.

At St Lythan's, the long cairn (about 30m. long) has been almost entirely removed, leaving the chamber exposed. The plan is similar to that of Tinkinswood, on a smaller scale. Three uprights and a massive capstone remain, but the entrance passage, if there was one, has gone. The monument has never been fully excavated.

Dyffryn House, between St Nicholas and St Lythan's, was built in 1883 for John Cory, whose heir, Reginald Cory, a well-known horticulturalist, created magnificent ornamental gardens. The house belongs to the County Council and is used for courses and conferences, but the gardens are open to the public in summer.

Saundersfoot Dyfed *see* **Tenby**

Sennybridge Powys *see* **Defynnog**

Seven Sisters (Blaendulais) W. Glam. 10D1
The Dulais River runs down past disused collieries and forestry plantations to meet the Nedd at Aberdulais (where Turner painted the mill and falls). The small hamlet of Blaendulais on its banks was renamed Seven Sisters in honour of the seven daughters of David Bevan. It was the eldest, Isabella, who in March 1872 cut the

Skomer Island seen from the Dyfed coast

first sod of her father's new coal-mine, to the accompanying fanfares of the Seventeenth Glamorgan Volunteers band. On the same day the first load of coal was sent down from Brynteg colliery at Crynant on the newly-opened Neath and Brecon Railway. Of the dozen or so pits that were worked in the valley, most have now closed.

On the eastern mountain, which separates the Dulais Valley from the Vale of Neath, there are traces of the Roman road that ran from Nidum (Neath) to Brecon; it was still used as a trackway for centuries after the Romans had left. Celtic artefacts, dating from about AD 100, were found at Seven Sisters late in the nineteenth century; they included horse trappings, tankard handles, and bells, and may represent the remains of a chariot burial.

The peregrine falcon may occasionally be sighted on these hillsides.

Skenfrith (Ynysgynwraidd)   Gwent   7H5
On the Welsh bank of the Monnow, Skenfrith is the smallest of the three Norman fortresses – Grosmont and White Castle are the others – known as the Trilateral. This triangle of castles was an important element of Norman strategy in the borderlands; it controlled a vital route between Wales and England.

Originally a motte-and-bailey castle with the usual timber defences, Skenfrith, like its two neighbours, was later refortified in stone. Hubert de Burgh, Royal Justiciar, was responsible for these reconstructions, which probably took place between 1228 and 1232. The ground-plan at Skenfrith is essentially rectangular, but, in accordance with the latest developments in fortifications, the motte was crowned with a fine round keep and the bailey enclosed by a curtain wall with D-shaped towers at its angles. Round towers resisted mining much better than did square ones; projecting round towers also enabled defenders to pick off besiegers who moved in too close to the moat and curtain wall. The keep was evidently intended more for defence than for comfortable residence. As at Pembroke, entrance was at first-floor level; the external staircase here was made of timber. The tower was at least provided with a fireplace and a privy. In the western range can also be seen a finely carved fireplace and doorway.

Skenfrith, with its old inns, slanting bridge, and green river-meadows, is a delightful village. St Bridget's church has an attractive tiled and slatted lantern-tower (a silhouette not common in the 'interior' of Wales), and a minstrels' gallery. The Skenfrith Cope, a pre-Reformation vestment, was for years used as an altar-covering. At the altar, the tomb is that of John ap Philip Morgan (d. 1557), Receiver of the Duchy of Lancaster, and farmer of the Three Castles, which had been given to the Earls of Lancaster by Henry III in 1267.

GARWAY, on the Hereford and Worcester side of the Monnow, has a remarkable church, which belonged in turn to the Knights Templar and the Knights Hospitaller; it has a dovecote and a detached, fortified tower.

Skokholm Island and Skomer Island   Dyfed   8A5

Skokholm and Skomer, two Norse-named islands, lie off the peninsula that forms the southern arm of St Bride's Bay. Both are part of the Pembrokeshire Coast National Park. Skokholm, 97ha., is composed of Old Red Sandstone. The author and naturalist R. M. Lockley began farming it in the late 1920s, and in 1933 established the first bird observatory in Britain. This still exists, but is now run by the Field Studies Council; there are no day visits.

Skomer, much larger (288ha.), is a grey volcanic rock, once inhabited by a large population of Iron Age farmers. The ancient fields and remains of stone-built scattered beehive huts are of especial interest to archaeologists, for the settlement, apart from a small promontory fort on the Neck, appears to have been undefended. Skomer was farmed until fairly recently. In 1958 it too became a nature reserve. Wild flowers carpet the island; rabbits are everywhere, and there is a subspecies of the common bank vole that is peculiar to the island. Seals breed, producing fifty or more pups each autumn. Seabirds, however, are the chief attraction, for here nest great colonies of Manx shearwater, some thousands of guillemots, razorbills, puffins, and gulls, numbers of oystercatchers, shags, cormorants, fulmar petrels, and stormy petrels or Mother Carey's chickens. Owls and other land-birds such as wheatears and meadow-pipits also live on the island. Skomer is in the care of the West Wales Naturalists' Trust and has a resident warden. Day trips may be made in summer, by boat from Martins Haven (at the end of the road from Marloes).

GRASSHOLM, about 8km. west of Skomer, has no fresh water, and is inhabited almost exclusively by an immense colony of gannets, 15,000 of them, who appear to

boatmen as one great white mass covering the rocks. Puffins once nested here, also in vast numbers, but they have moved to Skokholm, apparently after the collapse of the vegetation that sheltered their burrows. Grey seals are also common.

Strata Florida   Dyfed   *see* **Pontrhydfendigaid**

Swansea (Abertawe)   W. Glam.   10C2
(*pop.* 172,566)

Swansea began as a Danish land-grab (the name is 'Sweyns-ey', Sweyn's island); it is now the most attractive of all the large industrial towns of South Wales. It inspires attachments that are out of all proportion to its architectural merits and that are only partly explained by its setting, which is, indeed, magnificent. 'That streak of black along the most beautiful coast in the universe will never succeed in rendering me indifferent to Swansea', wrote Walter Savage Landor from Italy. 'An ugly, lovely town', according to Dylan Thomas, who grew up in it, 'crawling, sprawling, slummed, unplanned, jerry-villa'd, and smug-suburbed by the side of a long and splendid-curving shore'. Perhaps it was its copper, tinplate, and nickel works, and its docks, that saved Swansea from becoming Bognor Regis, just as the sea, and the hills, and the Gower Peninsula saved it from the fate of Merthyr Tydfil.

As a town, Swansea dates back to the Normans, whose castle here was the political centre of the lordship of Gower. The present ruins known as Swansea Castle (in Castle Square) are the remains of an early-fourteenth-century fortified manor-house, whose fine arcaded parapet marks it out as the work of Bishop Henry Gower of St David's. These fragments managed to survive the air-raid of 1941, which flattened much of the surrounding area.

Industry came early to Swansea. Because of its navigable river and its easily accessible coal deposits it had already by the mid eighteenth century become an important copper-smelting centre. By 1860 seventeen of the eighteen copper works in Britain were located in the Swansea area. Collieries had been opened at nearby Llansamlet in the eighteenth century. And as the copper industry declined, new metallurgical enterprises took its place: zinc, tinplate, nickel, and steel.

The cost of these industries, in terms of the environment, was a high one. In 1848 an estimated 92,000 tons of sulphurous acid were being discharged into the atmosphere by the copper works. The woods of native sessile oak and birch, the grass, and the heather disappeared from Kilvey Hill; the topsoil was washed away, leaving hideous gullies. Much of the lower Swansea Valley became a desert, a landscape of the moon, whose craters and spoil-tips have only begun to be reclaimed since 1960. The entry to Swansea from the east, by railway, was until recently a horrifying experience.

While industry despoiled the town to the north-east,

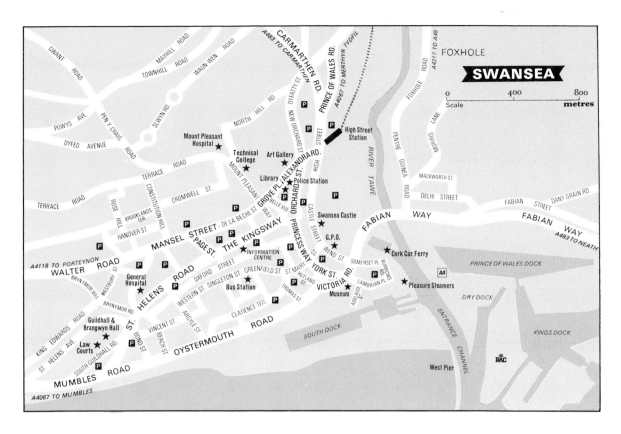

on its south and west comfortable suburbs spread along the high ground overlooking the bay. This end of the town aspired, in the nineteenth century, to the status of fashionable watering-place: a 'gay resort of fashion', as the *Cambrian* newspaper said in 1804. This was after all the birthplace of Beau Nash, the creator of Bath. Here 'Ann of Swansea', poet and novelist, sister of Sarah Siddons, kept a Bathing House (she was being paid £90 a year to reside more than 150 miles from London). It was this Swansea that so attracted Landor that he longed, even from Italy, to spend the rest of his days between 'that place and the Mumbles'.

The centre of Swansea, with its main shopping streets, has been largely rebuilt since the War, when bombing destroyed 16ha. of familiar landmarks. The modern buildings are, as usual, convenient, somewhat feature-less, lacking visual excitement. There has been some pleasant landscaping between the predictable chain-stores. The church of St Mary was reconstructed in 1955; it had already been rebuilt in 1745 and in 1898. According to one tradition, the first church fell down on a Sunday morning in 1739; the vicar, delayed by his barber, arrived late for service, so that only two people were killed. There is a good fifteenth-century memorial brass in the sanctuary floor.

Swansea Market, still the largest in Wales, has also been rehoused. Cockle-women may be seen there, and stalls sell laver-bread, a delicacy made from seaweed and eaten fried with bacon. Near the centre of town, too, are the Royal Institution of South Wales (1835), a building in Greek Revival style, the 'museum which should have been in a museum' (Dylan Thomas), which has geo-logical, historical, and archaeological collections, and the Industrial Museum of South Wales nearby. The Glynn Vivian Art Gallery in Alexandra Road has paint-ings and sculpture, and special collections of Swansea and Nantgarw pottery and porcelain. A new Industrial and Maritime Museum is being built on the South Dock and its first phase should be completed by 1977.

From the town centre, Mount Pleasant Road climbs up Town Hill and turns off west into Terrace Road, which leads to the 'Uplands' where confident Victorian villas look out over the sea. Dylan Thomas was born in 5 Cwmdonkin Drive (not a Victorian house); nearby is Cwmdonkin Park, which makes several appearances in his poetry and radio prose and now houses his memorial.

St Helen's Road, or Oystermouth Road (nearer the shore), also lead west, passing the 1934 Guildhall with its white clock tower and sixteen exuberant murals by Frank Brangwyn. These depict the people, animals, and flowers of the British Empire; they were rejected by the House of Lords, which had commissioned them. The

Oystermouth Castle : the gatehouse, seen from the courtyard

Brangwyn Hall in the Guildhall is the setting for the concerts of the Swansea Music Festival, which takes place annually in October. Further along the road, the modern buildings of the University College, founded in 1920, stand in Singleton Park.

Between the Mumbles road and the shore can be seen the disused track of a railway. This was the famous Mumbles Railway, opened in 1804, and claimed to be the first ever passenger rail-road. Horse-drawn in its earliest days, it ran for about 8km., from Swansea to Oystermouth, carrying coals and limestone, and drawing a regular passenger car of sixteen or eighteen persons. In 1877 it progressed to steam and in 1928 to electricity; its double-decker, open cars were a familiar and well-loved sight. It was closed down in 1960 with great lamenting. Older cricket-fans may remember that it featured in John Arlott's cricket commentaries from the Glamorgan cricket ground at nearby St Helen's.

OYSTERMOUTH (Ystumllwynarth), on the curve of the bay, and the MUMBLES are also officially parts of Swansea. The attractive, angular, and substantial remains of Oystermouth Castle stand above the coast road on a patch of green. This is a late-thirteenth-century fortress erected by the notorious de Breos family to replace an earlier structure, which the Welsh had probably destroyed. The castle buildings are arranged around a single courtyard with one main gateway; the latter's flanking drum-towers have disappeared, but the portcullis has been reconstructed. A rectangular keep contains domestic apartments, including a banqueting hall on the second floor, with fine Early English windows. The chapel, adjoining, and on a floor above the kitchen, has a piscina, and elaborate windows that contrast with the arrow-slits of the lower storey.

Oystermouth church, largely restored, has the low, embattled tower typical of this part of Wales. Its three bells came from the burned cathedral of Santiago in Chile. The font is a thirteenth-century feature and the aisle contains fragments of Roman pavement found nearby. Dr Thomas Bowdler of Bath, who expurgated Shakespeare, is buried in the churchyard.

The name of Oystermouth is a reminder that a flourishing oyster fishery on this shore once employed as many as 400 men during an eight-month season. The name of Mumbles is, on the contrary, a mystery. 'The Mumbles' are two small peaked islands, one with a lighthouse, that close off this end of Swansea Bay. On the Swansea side is Mumbles Pier (1898), where anglers for bass sit and ignore the idle promenaders. Mumbles has excellent yachting facilities; there is good surfing at times, and there is swimming at Bracelet Bay just around the Head.

Talgarth Powys 7F4 (*pop.* 1,500)
This small town in the shadow of the Black Mountains stood on the direct line of the Norman advance into Wales under Bernard of Newmarch in the late eleventh century. The area is rich in defensive mounds or mottes; and the square tower on the town bridge, now part of a house, shows that this strategic importance still held good as late as the fourteenth century.

In St Gwendoline's church, medieval but restored in 1873, is buried Howel Harris, little known outside Wales, but one of the most creative figures of the eighteenth-century religious revival. After hearing a Palm Sunday sermon preached at Talgarth in 1735, Harris, then aged twenty-two, experienced a powerful religious conversion. In conjunction with Griffith Jones and other Welsh leaders, Harris spent years preaching, travelling the length and breadth of Wales, and often speaking two or more times daily. By spiritual affiliation a Methodist, Harris refused to leave the Church of England, and some of his later doctrines, influenced by Moravian thought, alienated the Welsh Methodists. In 1752 he returned to his birthplace, Trefecca (Trefeca) (3km. south of Talgarth), and bought a tract of land. There he set up a religious commune, which had over a hundred members. All property was sold, and the proceeds shared between everyone. Three religious services were held daily, and four on Sundays. The members worked at rural trades, grew flax and hemp, and set up their own printing press. Harris was progressive in his ideas, introducing new farming methods and machinery; he was one of the founder members of the Brecknockshire Agricultural Society. No pacifist, Harris equipped five men and sent them to serve against the French in Canada; with twenty-four others, he personally formed the county militia as an aid to the war effort. Harris and the Welsh Methodists were eventually reconciled, and in 1768 Lady Huntingdon founded a college for ministers at Trefecca so that students could learn from Harris's inspiring presence. After his death in 1773 the community did not survive long, though the college continued for many years. The chapel at Trefecca (1873) houses a small museum devoted to Harris and his work.

Within a few km. of Talgarth, the churches at Llanelieu (Llaneleu) (3km. east), Llanfilo (west), and Llandefalle (3km. west of Bronllys, on a minor road) all have fine carved medieval screens. Beside the road south to Crickhowell, Castell Dinas stands 443m. above the valley it guards. This now fragmentary Norman castle was built on the remains of an Iron Age hill-fort some fifteen centuries older.

Talley (Talyllychau) Dyfed 9G2
The fragmentary remains of Talley Abbey lie in the

Llanelieu church, nr Talgarth

heart of rural Carmarthenshire. In the late twelfth century the Welsh prince Rhys ap Gruffydd, emulating Norman patronage, founded a House of Premonstratensian Canons. This order, also called Norbertine, took its name from the abbey at Prémontré, near Laon, France, which dated from 1120. Like the Cistercians, these canons' rule was austere, and included abstinence from

Talley Abbey: the crossing

cian abbey at Whitland. A new parish church was erected in 1773, using some materials from the ruins. This too has been rebuilt. One of the two small lakes where the monks used to fish (*Talyllychau* means 'head of the lakes') almost laps the churchyard.

Edwinsford, north of the lakes, and now in decay, was a seat of the Drummonds, descendants of Drummond of Hawthornden, the seventeenth-century Scots poet.

Talybont Dyfed 2D5
Once an important centre of lead-mining and of the woollen industry, Talybont is now just a village of small stone cottages, a hotel or two, and a chapel. Only one of its mills is still in operation, the Lerri, named after its small river; the hand-loom machinery is original and dates from 1809. From Talybont, minor roads climb up east into Pumlumon.

TRE'R DDOL lies north of Talybont on the main Machynlleth road. The 'Old Chapel', opened in 1845, was the starting-point of the 1859 religious revival, led by the Wesleyan Methodist Revd Humphrey R. Jones, who had returned from America. The stern classical building now houses a local museum, with special collections relating to Methodism, and some contemporary paintings.

From Talybont, or Tre'r Ddol, or Tre Taliesin (which lies between the two), a climb of 2 or 3km. brings you to Bedd Taliesin, 'Taliesin's Grave'. Motorists can take the road out of Talybont towards Pen-sarn. This curious and somewhat neglected-looking ancient monument, which is thought to be a Bronze Age burial site, consists of a large stone slab on a cairn. Most of its other stones have been removed over the centuries by farmers in search of gateposts or Methodists on the hunt for pagan superstition. The figure of Taliesin, like that of King Arthur, whose name is also very frequently given to much earlier monuments, such as standing stones, is part history, part legend. The 'real' Taliesin was a sixth-century court poet who wrote eulogies and elegies for his patrons, men such as Cynan King of Powys, and Urien Rheged. The other, legendary, Taliesin is a character in a collection of medieval Welsh stories, and may be better known to English readers from Thomas Love Peacock's *Misfortunes of Elphin*. Gwion Bach is swallowed by the witch Ceridwen and reborn as a child with a beautiful brow (*taliesin*). He is sewn up in a skin bag, or a coracle, and thrown into the sea. Washed up on the shore somewhere near Borth, the child is taken in by Prince Elphin, and becomes the hero of many an adventure.

The village of Tre Taliesin was renamed in the 1820s. Its previous name, Cwmins-y-dafarn-fach, meant 'commons of the little tavern' and thus offended the strict observances of the local devout.

Between the A487 and the Dovey Estuary, an expanse of marshy peat-bog known as the Cors Fochno has been partly reclaimed as farmland and partly retained as a National Nature Reserve. Not only has it a rich and

meat. Talley, which was dedicated to the Virgin Mary and John the Baptist, was an offshoot of St John at Amiens; it was the only house of this order in Wales.

Well endowed by the Lord Rhys, Talley suffered in the risings and revolts of the later Middle Ages in Wales. In the late thirteenth century, and after his punitive incursions into Wales, Edward I of England took the abbey under his protection. Probably hoping to use it as a centre of influence (for Welsh monastic houses were often hotbeds of patriotism, or treachery, depending on your point of view), he placed it in the care of various English sister-houses. By 1410, after the rebellion of Owain Glyndwr, Talley was 'despoiled, burned and almost destroyed'. At the Dissolution only eight canons remained; but this was not unusual.

Stones from the abbey must have found their way into many a local farmhouse or barn, for little is left on the site except low walls and a portion of church tower with high pointed arches and lancet windows. This church was, it seems, never completed, perhaps because of a long drawn-out dispute between Talley and the Cister-

West Gate, or Five Arches, c. 1300, Tenby

unusual flora and fauna, but the pollen-grains preserved in its peat make it of special interest to historians of vegetation and climate. Permits are needed to enter the reserve area, and, in any case, the bog can be dangerous for the unwary. (The Great Toad, which dwelt in Cors Fochno, was consulted as an oracle in medieval Welsh story.)

LLANGYNFELYN, in the marsh, has a circular churchyard, though the church itself is a fourteenth-century building that has been restored. It is dedicated to Cynfelyn, a Celtic missionary saint whose name has obvious connexions with Cunobelinus, or, in Shakespeare's language, Cymbeline.

This whole area – the flat, reedy estuary, the North Wales mountains high and bare behind it, the scattered cottages austere as Puritans – has its own peculiar beauty.

Tenby (Dinbych-y-pysgod) Dyfed 8D5
(*pop.* 4,985)

'The most agreeable town on all the sea coast of South Wales, except Pembroke', wrote Daniel Defoe, and though Tenby has changed since the days of *Robinson Crusoe*, it is not difficult to accept his verdict. Its sea and sands, harbours and islands, historic, colourful, and often elegant buildings make it a popular and sometimes crowded resort.

An early Welsh poem praises the 'fortress on the shore' where the poetry and merriment of the bards drowned the noise of the waves beating below. Of this first settlement, nothing remains except the town's Welsh name, Dinbych-y-pysgod, 'little fort of the fishes'.

The Tudor Merchant's House, Tenby

When the Normans arrived they built a stone castle on the headland and attached the town to the Earldom of Pembroke. The present castle ruins date from the thirteenth century: a gate-tower with later barbican, a double tower, and some domestic buildings. The best thing about these fragments is their splendid setting; more substantial medieval remains are those of the town walls, of which considerable portions survive almost intact. These defences were built by about 1300, and consist of a high curtain wall with projecting towers and four gates. West Gate, or Five Arches, in excellent condition, can be seen at the end of St George's Street; its

position shows how small was the medieval town, which lay almost entirely between South Parade and Castle Hill. In 1588 the walls were repaired to face the threat of the Spanish Armada.

Medieval Tenby, a Norman borough with the usual trading privileges, became a prosperous little port. The Tudor Merchant's House, an NT property and museum, gives a good idea of how a wealthy burgher lived and how a late-medieval house was constructed (though they were not commonly made of stone). A fascinating discovery in recent years has been the original wall decoration, a floral pattern painted directly on to the wall surface and later covered over with further coats of lime.

Tenby's prosperity in the fifteenth century can be clearly seen from St Mary's church, which more than doubled its size in those hundred years. To the old, probably thirteenth-century, church was now added a north aisle and numerous chapels; the chancel was reconstructed, with a raised sanctuary and a chantry loft (the latter has not survived). The wagon roof of the chancel, one of the church's finest features, dates from this period, while the arcade on the south side of the nave shows West Country influence.

St Mary's church is an exceptionally large and fine parish church. Its exterior is imposing, and the 46m. spire, out of keeping from a strictly stylistic point of view, makes a striking landmark from the North Beach. Inside, the fifteenth-century chancel roof has the original carved bosses, picked out in gold and coloured paints, where gargoyle-faced mermaids are set side by side with Evangelists or Symbols of the Passion. A fine Jacobean octagonal pulpit (1634) has recently been restored. There are fascinating tombs and memorials from a variety of periods. Near the north door lie two effigies, one a fourteenth-century lady and the other a cleric of the fifteenth century, depicted as a shrouded skeleton. In St Thomas Chapel are two fine tombs of wealthy local merchants, both Mayors of Tenby, in their robes. Margaret Mercer (d. 1610) has an impressive monument; above her reclining figure, in its starched ruff, her husband Thomas ap Rees kneels between heraldic shields. Below are the seven surviving children, also on their knees. Margaret was thirty at her death; she had been married twelve years and had borne ten children. An interesting curiosity, much later in date, is the wall tablet near the west window that commemorates Peggy Davies, who died in 1809 after forty-two years as bathing-woman to the ladies of Tenby.

Tenby's first Rector was the cleric and writer Gerald the Welshman (1210–23), who was born at Manorbier on this same coastline. Queen Elizabeth gave the living to the famous scientist and astrologer John Dee, while a tablet in the church recalls that Robert Recorde,

mathematician and Royal physician, who invented the sign of equality and the plus and minus signs, was born in the town in 1510.

The seventeenth century saw a decline in Tenby as a trading port, and although in the following century Defoe comments on a 'great fishery for herring' and a 'great colliery, or rather export of coals', other evidence suggests that there was considerable poverty. A new industry, however, was soon to change all that. By the turn of the century Tenby was becoming a fashionable resort for the delicate in search of health and the rich in search of amusement. Nelson and Lady Hamilton paid a visit. Fine Georgian houses were built, in the Norton, the Croft, St Julian Street, and others. The new sea-water baths were built by S. P. Cockerell for Sir William Paxton of Carmarthen, in 1811; the Greek inscription, from Euripides, reads: 'The sea washes away all the ills of mankind'. A traveller described the scene on the beach in 1861: 'Beneath, on the hard sands, were troops of laughing children, tripping ladies . . . and gentlemen with telescopes, or opera-glasses, phaetons, and horses, "promenading". The sands are alive with company; the bathing-machines, like overgrown bandboxes, are drawn up on the shingle, while the "washed-out" bathing-women sit in the sun. . . . Presently a steamer comes in sight, and all the glasses are directed to her; the gentlemen, and some of the ladies, rush off, some round the Castle Hill, others through the town, to see the strangers disembark at the pier, by the baths – that is, the sheltered and west end of the quaint little town'.

The Victorian era brought the railway, and more tourists, and the icy statue of the Prince Regent, 'Albert Dda' (Albert the Good), was unveiled on Castle Hill to the sounds of massed brass bands. Inner Tenby has not changed much, in some ways, since those times; modern developments have mostly taken place outside the walls and beyond the railway station.

As well as its bathing and boating, Tenby now offers angling, deep-sea fishing, water-skiing, and courses in aqualung diving. St Catherine's Island (cut off only at high tide) is a nineteenth-century fort made into a small zoo. On Castle Hill, Tenby Museum occupies part of the Norman fortress. It has archaeological and local-history exhibits, railway relics, some postal history, including a collection of Great War postcards, which make poignant reading. There are paintings of Tenby by the early-nineteenth-century local artist Charles Norris, and some rather better work by Paul Sandby. Augustus John, whose portrait of Richard Hughes hangs in the gallery, was born in Tenby, and spent childhood holidays nearby at Bugelly.

Tenby's surroundings are increasingly invaded by dreary modern housing, and caravans. PENALLY, now almost a suburb, has a thirteenth-century church dedicated to St Teilo, who, according to one tradition, was born in this parish. Inside the church is a sculptured Celtic cross and a thirteenth-century wall tomb of a

OPPOSITE: *St Mary's church, Tenby*

French merchant and his wife. St Lawrence's at GUM-FRESTON has a pre-Reformation sanctus bell and wall-paintings that may represent the saint martyred on his grid. Three warm springs behind the church are reputed to have healing properties.

SAUNDERSFOOT, a popular resort on the coast just north of Tenby, seems the very antithesis of a coal town. But on the beach itself an exposed anticline (a geological curiosity) reveals the coal measures whose folded strata provided a high-quality anthracite, shipped from Saundersfoot in the nineteenth century. There are a sandy beach and a good sheltered harbour.

Tinkinswood S. Glam. *see* **St Lythan's**

Tintern (Tyndyrn) Gwent 12A2
Tintern is one of the loveliest and most complete of all the ruined British monasteries; it is also, thanks to Wordsworth's lines, one of the best known. It stands on the Welsh bank of the Wye, yet its connexions were largely English, and it escaped much of the damage suffered by the other Welsh houses during the Middle Ages.

Among the earliest Cistercian houses in Wales, Tintern was founded directly from Normandy, by monks from L'Aumône, who came in 1131 at the request of the Norman lord of Chepstow, Walter FitzRichard. (The other Cistercian houses in South Wales were mostly offshoots from Whitland in Dyfed.) The site chosen was wild and remote, in accordance with the ideal of

austerity these reformed monks set themselves; it also provided good fishing, for they ate no meat. The early buildings, too, were small, and simpler than the ruins that can be seen today.

The house at Tintern soon prospered. In 1139 its monks founded a daughter-house at Kingswood in Gloucestershire. Another offshoot was Tintern Minor or De Voto ('by the vow'), so called from a vow made by William Marshall (Lord of Chepstow and one of the Norman conquerors of Ireland) while in danger of shipwreck in the Irish Sea. In 1220 work began on rebuilding Tintern itself. A new and larger refectory was the first task, followed by a much enlarged and more elaborate church, built between 1270 and 1301. The abbot's hall was completed in the fourteenth century and in the fifteenth the infirmary was divided up into separate cubicles with fireplaces, an obvious decline from the early ideal of austerity.

Tintern was the wealthiest of the Welsh abbeys, though it was not rich compared with the monasteries of England, especially those of the Benedictines. Alone of the Welsh houses, too, it appears to have retained through troubled times the thirteen professed monks considered as minimum strength for a regular monastery. Its money came partly from donors, some of whom, of course, required spiritual returns. For example, Rogerstone Grange was given to the abbey in about 1219, on condition that the monks kept a lamp perpetually lit at the tomb of the grantor's mother, Isabel, Countess of

BELOW: *Tintern Abbey*

OPPOSITE: *Tintern Abbey: the nave*

Pembroke. Other wealth came from extensive agricultural activities, carried on with the help of lay-brothers. Thus Tintern had about a dozen 'granges' and manors, in places as near as Gloucestershire and as far away as Norfolk. These estates were carefully run; special courts of justice tried offenders against the regulations. At Porthcaseg manor in the fifteenth century these regulations included the clauses: 'No beggar or minstrel shall enter the lordship (Penalty ten shillings). . . . No one is to play at dice or cards. . . . No one is to play at hand ball within the gate of the abbey (Penalty ¾d.)'. A reaper was paid 2d. a day with food, and 4d. a day without.

Here as elsewhere, the monks were enterprising in their use of natural resources. They had over 3,000 sheep, as well as cattle, horses, and pigs, and exported wool of the highest quality to England and the Continent. The abbey held town property in Bristol, Monmouth, and Chepstow, and had free right of passage on the Aust–Beachley ferry. From the Forests (Dean, Wentwood, and the park of Trelleck), the monks took wood for fuel and for their iron forges. They had rights of venison in Wentwood from 1301, ostensibly for the sick brethren, and, in the park of Trelleck, 'both shoulders from all deer'. Their fishing-rights in Wye and Severn brought them good salmon. They had, it is thought, their own ships – there is a water-gate still visible near the Anchor Hotel – and they brewed and sold their own beer.

At the Dissolution Tintern's monks were dispersed, and the Earl of Worcester, the abbey's patron, received the site and buildings. The Earl removed the lead from the roofs and melted it down, together with the abbey bells, for use at his castles at Raglan and Chepstow. The outbuildings fell into disrepair, and gradually cottages sprang up within the original 11ha. abbey precinct. The great church, however, remained remarkably intact, at least as far as the basic stonework is concerned. Its west window and doorway are particularly fine, while the slender soaring columns and the four arches of the crossing still give some flavour of the church's original grace and elegance. Its strict division – by means of stone screens – into monks' quire and lay-brothers' quire, so that worship of the two groups was almost totally separate, is no longer easily apparent.

The cloister at Tintern was built to the north of the church and not to the south as was usual; it is thought that drainage problems may have been responsible for this departure from tradition. In the east walk of the cloister, note the twelfth-century recesses for books, and a fine fourteenth-century doorway, which leads into a special book-room and vestry. On the side of the cloister opposite the church, the 25m.-long monks' frater or dining-hall has recesses near the doorway, one for washing hands and another for towels. Also still partly visible are the stairs that led to a pulpit where a brother would read aloud during meals. The western

range of buildings was traditionally reserved for the lay-brothers; this was the section nearest the entrance gate and the outside world. (East is also the direction faced by the priest at the altar; west is the least sacred part of the abbey.) Lay-brothers were from the start an essential element in the Cistercian economy; after the Black Death, however, they became almost impossible to recruit. To the east lay the infirmary for sick and aged monks, a notably large building with its own cloister and kitchen. Late in the fifteenth century, as we have seen, the infirmary was made a lot more comfortable by the addition of partitions and fireplaces. To the north, the abbot's hall and camera probably also gained in luxury in the latter years, before the Reformation. A small museum in the grounds has exhibits dealing with the life of the abbey, together with some prehistoric and Roman remains (flints, bones, coins, tiles) that belong to the earlier history of the site.

Tintern in summer is often thronged with visitors. Fewer, however, will take the footpath that from a point about 3km. down river climbs almost 240m. to the summit of Wynd Cliff. The view over the Wye and its valley is unbeatable.

Trecastle (Trecastell)   Powys   6D5
Only earthworks now remain of the Norman castle that gave a name to the village. Trecastle lies in one of those valleys that provide a natural line of penetration through the empty uplands and into west Wales. The village's large coaching inns testify to the importance of this route.

In earlier times, however, the valleys were thickly forested. The Romans, here as elsewhere, chose to march on the drier and less encumbered terrain of the higher ground. About 6km. from the present village, at Y Pigwn ('the beacon'), on the summit of Trecastle Mountain, remains of Roman marching-camps are clearly visible. (Take the minor road, which runs roughly parallel to the A40, over Trecastle Mt. Beware of firing ranges.)

Marching-camps were temporary fortified sites set up by the Roman army on march. A rampart of earth about 1½m. high would be thrown up, with a ditch surrounding it and a palisade of stakes on top. The soldiers carried stakes in their kitbags; their leather tents were transported by mules. Y Pigwn has remains of two separate marching-camps, one of about 10ha., one of about 15ha., which are thought to date back to the earliest, first-century, advance into Wales, under Ostorius Scapula, the Roman governor of Britain. Lead-workings have destroyed the southern ramparts. On the other three sides, however, entrances can be detected, with their characteristic defences – curved extensions of the rampart, known as *claviculae*.

Llywel, just outside Trecastle on the main Llandovery road, has an interesting church with a fifteenth-century tower. It is dedicated to the three great Celtic missionary saints of Wales: David, Padarn, and Teilo, not usually found in trinity. The David dedications in South Wales can be traced from St David's in Dyfed through mid Wales and into the Border Country almost to Hereford; their line seems to follow the Roman roads, as here, where Y Pigwn marks the Roman way from Brecon to Llandovery. Inside the church are two Ogham stones: the Taricora stone, and a cast of the Llywel stone, which bears sixth- and seventh-century inscriptions (the original is now in the British Museum). The village stocks are also kept here, and a colony of Natterer's bats was discovered in the church in 1962.

Tredegar Gwent 11F1 (*pop.* 17,976)
Tredegar lies at the top of the industrialized Sirhowy Valley and just south of the impressive new Heads of the Valleys road. Like the other valley towns of Glamorgan and what was west Monmouthshire, Tredegar was a creation of the Industrial Revolution. From a village of 513 people in 1801, it grew in fifty years to a huge, unplanned conurbation of 15,424. Men poured in, from west Wales (where there was an agricultural recession), from Ireland, and from England. Coal and iron were pre-eminent: the iron clock-tower in the centre of Tredegar, put up in 1858, was an appropriate monument. Conditions in the valley towns (the 'Black Domain') were appalling in many ways. Housing was poor, overcrowded, and unhygienic, work was dangerous and unpleasant, shops were company – or 'truck' – shops, which exercised a virtual monopoly and whose vouchers frequently replaced money wages. It is not surprising, then, that Tredegar became a centre of early industrial unrest. In 1816 there were riots. In the 1820s there were the 'Scotch Cattle', bands of workmen who formed what was almost a secret society. In times of recession, when wages fell and men were laid off, the Scotch Cattle held their mass meetings and went into action. At night, on the hillsides above the ribbons of terraces, drums and horns could be heard, and the sound of gunshots. Threatening letters were sent, signed in blood; visits were made, at night, by men in disguise, who beat up their victims and smashed their furniture. The victims were generally those who threatened the unity that was the only hope of resistance against the coal- and iron-masters: blacklegs, agents, contractors ('doggies', who subcontracted workers), shopkeepers, and landlords. Though physical violence and looting took place, they were not the principal purpose. That was, rather, intimidation, the attempt to weld forcibly together a disparate workforce, any part of which the iron-masters would exploit against the rest. Out of this crude political activity there emerged in the following decades a support for Chartism, and, later, a strong Trades Union movement. Indeed, Tredegar's best-known citizen, this century, has been Aneurin Bevan.

No coal-mines now operate in Tredegar, and the Tredegar Iron and Coal Company, once the foremost in the region, has also closed. Efforts are being made to attract new industry and revivify the town, most of whose population now work in Ebbw Vale.

Tregaron Dyfed 6C2
Tregaron's buildings have an almost harsh simplicity, which seems well in keeping with the hills and moors that surround the town. In the eighteenth century this was one of the places where the drovers assembled their herds of cattle for the long trek over the mountains, through Abergwesyn, to Hereford and the South. At that time, too, it was famous for its stocking-fairs, the product of a cottage industry, by which farmers' wives made some little extra money in these infertile uplands. Of recent years, the only expanding industry has been tourism: the country is ideal for pony-trekking.

The church of St Caron, an Irish saint who is said to be buried on the site, stands in a rounded churchyard, probable indication of an earlier place of worship. The church itself is restored, but the battlemented tower is a fourteenth-century structure. St Caron's fair, three days long, was once one of the most important in Wales. Among the numerous inns, a sign of a town's vitality as a market-centre, is the early-nineteenth-century Talbot Arms, on the main square; George Borrow stayed there on his journey through 'Wild Wales', and had 'an excellent supper and a very comfortable bed'.

The market-place is dominated by the bronze statue of Henry Richard (1812–88), the son of a local minister, who became successively a draper's apprentice, a Nonconformist minister, and a politician of international stature. Richard was a pioneer and champion of all the major Welsh causes of his time: Disestablishment of the Welsh Church, a Welsh university, the use of Welsh in schools, the working conditions of Welsh miners. Member of Parliament for Merthyr Tydfil from 1868, he was one of the earliest advocates of arbitration as a method for settling international disputes. Through his efforts, a peace congress along such lines was opened in Paris in 1849, under the presidency of Victor Hugo. After the Crimean War, Richard went with Sturge and Hindley to the peace talks in Paris; as a result, for the first time in Europe, a declaration in favour of arbitration was written into a major peace treaty. A library named after Henry Richard is available, near the Houses of Parliament, for the use of Members.

Twm Shon Catti, also born in Tregaron, was more sinner than saint, and his exploits are as famous in Wales as those of Robin Hood in England. Twm has the native cunning of all folk heroes of this sort. He goes, for example, to buy a saucepan in Llandovery. 'There's a hole in this saucepan', says Twm to the ironmonger. 'I don't see it', replies the latter. 'Here', says Twm, jamming the pot down over the man's head. 'If there weren't a hole in it, how could you get your head in it?' – making his escape with the rest of the goods. Like any

sensible rogue, Twm marries a rich widow, and, as a result of this new wealth, he is made Justice of the Peace. He makes a huge success of this: 'he said that as he himself could not have a finger in the pie, he would take care no-one else should'. George Borrow, who made this last remark, also points out rightly that the tales told of Twm are told of all rogues from Ireland to Russia. That Twm is alive in the collective folk unconscious rather than in the Welsh hill country of the sixteenth century need neither surprise us nor spoil our enjoyment.

Directly north of the town, Cors Goch Glan Teifi, the 'Red Bog of Tregaron', is a National Nature Reserve of about 800ha., managed by the Nature Conservancy. It is a fine example of a raised peat-bog, formed by the draining, during the post-glacial period, of two lakes dammed up by a glacial moraine. The Teifi River cuts through the centre. Entrance is by permit only. Naturalists will find a great variety of bog plants, some of them rare, polecat, otter, badger, and fox, and a wealth of bird life.

Trelleck (Trellech) Gwent 12A1
This village takes its name from the three huge standing stones that can be seen near the crossroads. These leaning monoliths, 3m. high, may, like Stonehenge, have formed part of a system in which precise calculation of the positions of the heavenly bodies was closely connected with the seasonal work and rituals of the tribe. Certainly they have nothing to do with Harold of England, though one of their traditional names is Harold's Stones. In Trelleck church, the great sundial of 1689 is decorated with crude carvings of these stones and of the village's other 'wonders': the Virtuous Well, in a meadow, protècted by a low stone wall with recesses for offerings, and for centuries a place of pilgrimage; and the Terret Tump, an artificial mound near the church, also connected with Harold but more probably the remains of a Norman motte-and-bailey castle.

Tretower (Tretŵr) Powys 7G5
This 'small village on a little brook', as Leland described it in 1540, has two buildings that between them span nearly six centuries of British architecture. They exemplify, too, an important change in the whole way of life of the rural aristocracy. Picard's Tower, whose earliest features date from the late eleventh century, was built for defence, with a few concessions to comfort; Tretower Court, which received its last major additions in 1630, was built for comfortable living, with a few prudent concessions to defence.

Picard's Tower was one of a number of motte-and-bailey castles thrown up by the Normans as they advanced along the Wye Valley and the Usk into Wales. In its earliest form, it consisted of a small motte or

LEFT: *The sundial (1689) in Trelleck church*

Harold's Stones, Trelleck: represented in relief on Trelleck's sundial (see opposite page)

mound with wooden buildings, and a roughly four-sided bailey defended by a timber palisade. Marshy ground and ditches made access difficult on three sides. The motte itself was given a revetment of stone, presumably to offset the extremely soft nature of the soil. In the twelfth century, as usual, the wooden defences were replaced by stone throughout. A shell keep was constructed on the top of the motte (this is a good example), and stone walls joined the keep to the curtain wall now surrounding the bailey. Within the keep, a hall, solar, and kitchen were also constructed, in stone; the remains of fireplaces and windows with some mouldings can still be seen.

In the following century, and in line with the latest developments in the science of fortifications, further changes were made. The domestic buildings were gutted, and a large circular keep (a feature of the Welsh Border castles) was erected within the shell. The three-storey tower, 6½m. in diameter, was high enough to enable defenders to shoot over the top of the curtain wall. Inside, there was a well, and there were windows and ornamented fireplaces on each level. By the early fourteenth century this keep was probably only used as a last resort, in times of extreme danger. The family had certainly moved to the nearby Tretower Court by the time of the Glyndwr revolt in 1403. An extension built between the round keep and the shell wall was perhaps intended as a garrison or store-house building.

From the castle, it is only a few hundred metres' walk to its successor. Tretower is a rare and fine example of a medieval manor-house. To the road it presents a sturdy, walled front, embellished by arched doorways and a simple row of corbels marking the upper storey. Through the gatehouse, one enters a courtyard; the hall is directly opposite, and the solar or private parlour to its right. The family apartments on the upper floor of the north range look out onto a fifteenth-century gallery. The basic plan, similar to that of Oxford colleges of the

Picard's Tower, Tretower : C12 shell with C13 round keep

same period, affords a generous share of daylight and privacy as well as easy access to a central meeting area and a reasonable security from the outside world.

This arrangement of buildings around a central courtyard was the result not of one original design but of a series of enlargements made by several generations of a family that was increasing its wealth and local prestige. The fourteenth-century house (the present north range) was in fact a small one. Its central feature was a large hall the whole height of the building, with small private bedchambers on the upper floors to east and west. In the early fifteenth century Sir Roger Vaughan added several rooms to this section and transferred the main living quarters to the upper floor. Shortly after 1450 he had a new west range built, with a new hall, solar, and a separate mess-room for armed retainers. This new section is more elaborate in design and more elegant in its detail than the earlier building. Towards the end of the century Sir Thomas Vaughan added several features, including the gatehouse and the large oriel window (now restored) on the west range.

Later alterations brought the manor-house to its present-day appearance. In the sixteenth century a long mullioned window was pierced at the gable end of the north range, overlooking the road; this, together with the windows and tall chimneys added to the west front in 1630, clearly show to what extent considerations of elegance and comfort had by this time replaced those of defence.

The Vaughan family lived here from the fifteenth century to the eighteenth. A younger son of the family acquired by marriage the estate of Newton Scethrog, in Llansantffraed parish. Henry Vaughan the Silurist was one of twins born in 1621 at Newton; he is buried in Llansantffraed churchyard (*see* Llansantffraed).

Usk (Brynbuga) Gwent 11H2 (*pop.* 2,028)
Usk is named after its river, which itself (Usk or Wysg) is named, not surprisingly, 'water' – Scotsmen and philologists will know that the first element of the word whisky means the same. The town stands on the site of what is now known to have been a very large Roman legionary base, more extensive and earlier than that of Caerleon. BURRIUM, founded before 60, formed an essential link in the military frontier that ran from Chester through Wroxeter to the mouth of the Usk. The Romans made their largely unsuccessful sorties into the mountainous centre of Wales from such forts.

The Normans, ten centuries later, left as usual a castle and a church. Usk Castle (privately owned) stands in ruins above the main town square. An original wooden fortress was replaced by stone buildings in the twelfth century, at a time when the lands around Usk were under the control of the de Clare or Strongbow family. Further additions took place down to the fourteenth century. The castle suffered badly in the Glyndwr rebellion; it was near Usk, in 1403, that the Welsh

under Glyndwr's son lost 1,500 men in a battle with Henry Prince of Wales. After the Civil War the castle was 'slighted', on the orders of Cromwell.

Richard de Clare, son of Strongbow, founded a Benedictine priory of nuns some time before 1135, when the Welsh put a violent end to his charities. Of this foundation, a gatehouse remains (in private hands) and the church of St Mary, which has retained some Norman features. One of its treasures is a brass plaque with an inscription (the earliest in Welsh on brass) commemorating Adam of Usk, a fourteenth-century priest, lawyer, and writer of chronicles. The fine screen is Perpendicular, and dates from the Tudors. The organ was brought from the cathedral at Llandaff.

Usk has been a borough since 1324, but its growth has been gentle. Long a market-town, as the shape of Twyn Square with its ancient inns attests, it shared for over a century the manufacture of 'Japan ware', centred at Pontypool. This industry died in the mid nineteenth century, and Usk remains as a centre for fishermen and farmers. It provides a good base for exploring the Usk Valley both up- and down-stream, Wentwood, and the little-known rural scenery between Usk and Wye. Among nearby villages, LLANGWM church has a remarkable medieval rood-screen; there are others at Betws Newydd, Gwernesney, and Llangeview (all within about 5km. radius). TREDUNNOCK (Tredynog) church, lower down the Usk Valley, has a Roman memorial stone inscribed to a soldier of the Second Augustan Legion, which was based at Caerleon.

Vale of Glamorgan S. Glam. *see* **Cowbridge**

Vale of Neath W. Glam. *see* **Pontneddfechan**

Vaynor Mid Glam. *see* **Merthyr Tydfil**

Whitland (Hendy-gwyn) Dyfed 8D4
Now a large milk-marketing centre, Whitland is more noted in Wales for its past than its present. It was here in 930, at Tŷ Gwyn ar Daf ('white house on the Taf'), that the Welsh king Hywel Dda, 'Howell the Good', called an assembly of wise men. The purpose was to approve Hywel's codification of Welsh law, that is, a setting in writing of the legal customs already existing in Wales. Hywel's laws throw a fascinating light on life in Wales before the Norman Conquest – their provisos regarding women show that that country was already highly civilized – and are an impressive contribution to medieval thought.

Hywel's 'white house' may well have been the site chosen two centuries later for the Cistercian abbey of Whitland or Alba Landa, 1½km. north of the present town. Almost nothing remains of this religious house, founded in 1140, the earliest Cistercian monastery in Wales outside the Norman lordships. Whitland gave rise to no less than seven daughter-houses, including

Strata Florida and Abbey Cwmhir. Like these two, it was built in a site fit for religious seclusion: Leland describes it as 'standing in a vast wood as in a wilderness'. It had, like other Cistercian houses, extensive agricultural interests; it had fishing-rights at Haverfordwest every Friday (the day of special abstinence); it also had corn mills, and the ruins of one have been found at Cwm-felin-mynach ('valley of the monk's mill'), a village about 8km. north, in the Gronw Valley.

Ysbytty Cynfyn Dyfed 6C1
This is the nearest village to Parsons Bridge, a famous beauty spot where an iron bridge spans the Rheidol. *Ysbytty* means 'hostel' or 'hospice', and it seems likely that this was a stopping-point on the pilgrims' way to Strata Florida Abbey, at Pontrhydfendigaid. The church of St John the Baptist is an early-nineteenth-century building, but its circular enclosure suggests the existence of some prehistoric place of worship, possibly pre-Christian. Notice inside the church the Commandments, Creed, and Lord's Prayer in Welsh, gold letters on a black background (1836), a not uncommon sight in the churches of west Wales.

Ystradfellte Powys 7E6
The hamlet of Ystradfellte has an ancient, restored church and churchyard yews that are said to be eight centuries old. North-east of the village stands Mellte Castle, a red ruin of uncertain antiquity. To the south, the Mellte and other headwaters of the Nedd River flow through wooded valleys and over cliffs and ledges in an unrivalled series of rapids and falls (*see* Pontneddfechan).

Ystrad Meurig Dyfed 6C2
Ystrad Meurig, a small settlement on the moorland road west of Pontrhydfendigaid, is famous in west Wales for its eighteenth-century grammar school, founded by Edward Richard, a local innkeeper's son and its first master. Here began the career of a more famous Welsh teacher, described by Sir Walter Scott as 'the best schoolmaster in Europe'. John Williams (1792–1858) was a pupil at Ystrad Meurig. A fine Classical and Celtic scholar, he became Vicar of Lampeter and, from 1820, headmaster of the Grammar School there. It was because of Williams's reputation for learning that Scott sent his son Charles to be educated at Lampeter, and later invited Williams to be first Rector of the new Edinburgh Academy. Williams was the inspiration for Scott's novel *The Betrothed*. In 1851 he returned to Wales to become first Warden of the newly founded boys' college at Llandovery.

A few mounds remain of the Norman castle at Ystrad Meurig, dismantled as early as 1208.

Conversion Tables for Weights and Measures

The figures in bold type can be
used to represent either measure
for the purposes of conversion,
eg 1in. = 2·540cm., 1cm. =
0·394in.

kilometres		miles
1·609	**1**	0·621
3·219	**2**	1·243
4·828	**3**	1·864
6·437	**4**	2·485
8·047	**5**	3·107
9·656	**6**	3·728
11·265	**7**	4·350
12·875	**8**	4·971
14·484	**9**	5·592
16·093	**10**	6·214
32·187	**20**	12·427
48·280	**30**	18·641
64·374	**40**	24·855
80·467	**50**	31·069
96·561	**60**	37·282
112·654	**70**	43·496
128·748	**80**	49·710
144·841	**90**	55·923
160·934	**100**	62·137

centimetres		inches
2·540	**1**	0·394
5·080	**2**	0·787
7·620	**3**	1·181
10·160	**4**	1·575
12·700	**5**	1·969
15·240	**6**	2·362
17·780	**7**	2·756
20·320	**8**	3·150
22·860	**9**	3·543
25·400	**10**	3·937
50·800	**20**	7·874
76·200	**30**	11·811
101·600	**40**	15·748
127·000	**50**	19·685
152·400	**60**	23·622
177·800	**70**	27·559
203·200	**80**	31·496
228·600	**90**	35·433
254·000	**100**	39·370

hectares		acres
0·405	**1**	2·471
0·809	**2**	4·942
1·214	**3**	7·413
1·619	**4**	9·884
2·023	**5**	12·355
2·428	**6**	14·826
2·833	**7**	17·297
3·237	**8**	19·769
3·642	**9**	22·240
4·047	**10**	24·711
8·094	**20**	49·421
12·140	**30**	74·132
16·187	**40**	98·842
20·234	**50**	123·553
24·281	**60**	148.263
28·328	**70**	172·974
32·375	**80**	197·684
36·422	**90**	222·395
40·469	**100**	247·105

metres		yards
0·914	**1**	1·094
1·829	**2**	2·187
2·743	**3**	3·281
3·658	**4**	4·374
4·572	**5**	5·468
5·486	**6**	6·562
6·401	**7**	7·655
7·315	**8**	8·749
8·230	**9**	9·843
9·144	**10**	10·936
18·288	**20**	21·872
27·432	**30**	32·808
36·576	**40**	43·745
45·720	**50**	54·681
54·864	**60**	65·617
64·008	**70**	76·553
73·152	**80**	87·489
82·296	**90**	98·425
91·440	**100**	109·361

kilograms		av. pounds
0·454	**1**	2·205
0·907	**2**	4·409
1·361	**3**	6·614
1·814	**4**	8·819
2·268	**5**	11·023
2·722	**6**	13·228
3·175	**7**	15·432
3·629	**8**	17·637
4·082	**9**	19·842
4·536	**10**	22·046
9·072	**20**	44·092
13·608	**30**	66·139
18·144	**40**	88·185
22·680	**50**	110·231
27·216	**60**	132·277
31·752	**70**	154·324
36·287	**80**	176·370
40·823	**90**	198·416
45·350	**100**	220·462

Glossary

The glossary that follows gives the English equivalents for some of the commoner Welsh place-names. Many of these are in fact a combination of several elements, e.g. Aberystwyth = Mouth of the Ystwyth, Pontrhydygroes = Bridge of the ford of the Cross, Llanfair = Church of St Mary. Often the original Welsh name has been transformed out of all recognition, so that it is hard to find Llanymddyfri in 'Llandovery', or Dinbych in 'Tenby'. This may be the result of Anglicization, especially in the Border Country and in Pembrokeshire, but it may also be due merely to the passage of time (as in the party game where a message whispered from ear to ear turns out at the end quite different from the way it started). There is also the question of 'mutation'. In a number of circumstances too complicated to explain here, Welsh words change their initial sound and letter. The mutations that most affect place-names are a) the change in the feminine noun after the definite article, e.g. *Ban*, a peak, becomes *y fan* (as in *Llyn-y-fan*); and b) the change in the adjective when used with a feminine noun, e.g. *Castell Coch*, but *Carn Goch*. These changes are noted below where appropriate.

A note on pronunciation

ch	is pronounced as in *loch*
dd	is a soft *th* as in *the*
f	is pronounced as *v*
ff	is pronounced as *f* in *forest*
ll	silently put the front of the tongue to the roof of the mouth as if to make *l*, then blow out gently
u	is pronounced 'ee', e.g. *du* = 'dee'
w	i) as a consonant, is pronounced as in English, e.g. *Wyn* = 'win'
	ii) as a vowel, is pronounced as a short 'oo', e.g. *betws* = 'bett-oos'
	iii) with *y*, it can form a different sound, pronounced 'oy', e.g. *lwyd* = Lloyd. This does not apply after *g*: *Gwyn* = 'gwin'
y	i) 'er' as in *under* (without the *r*), e.g. *y bont* = 'er bont'
	ii) a short 'ee', or 'i' as in *it*, e.g. *bryn* = 'brin' Some words contain both sounds, e.g. *ynys* = 'unn-iss', *dyffryn* = 'duff-rin'.

Welsh words are most frequently stressed on the penultimate syllable, but where a place-name is a combination of several words, the stress follows the original sense, e.g. Péntrebách = Pentre-bach; Péncóed = Pen-coed; Áberfán = Aber-fan.

Abaty Abbey
Aber River mouth, confluence
Aderyn (*pl.* **adar**) Bird
Afanc Beaver
Afon River

Allt Hill-side, hill, slope, wood
Amgueddfa Museum
Ap, ab Son of
Ar On, upon, over, by
Arth *see* **Garth**

Bach, fach (*adj.*) Small, little, lesser
Bach, y fach (*n.*) (*pl.* **bachau**) Nook, corner, bend
Ban, y fan (*pl.* **bannau**) Peak, crest, bare hill, beacon, high place
Banc Bank, hill, slope
Bangor Consecrated land or monastery within a wattled fence
Bardd Bard, poet
Bedd (*pl.* **beddau**) Grave
Bedwen, y fedwen (*pl.* **bedw**) Birch
Betws Oratory, chapel; birchgrove
Blaen (*pl.* **blaenau**) Head, end, source of river, upland
Bod Abode, dwelling
Bont *see* **Pont**
Braich, y fraich Arm, ridge, spur
Brân Crow; also a Welsh mythical hero
Bras, fras Rich, large
Brenin King
Bro Region, lowland, vale
Bron, y fron Hill-breast, hill-side
Bryn (*pl.* **bryniau**) Hill
Bugail Shepherd
Bwlch Pass, gap
Bychan, fechan Little, small, lesser

Cadair, y gadair Chair, seat, stronghold
Cadno Fox

GLOSSARY

Cae (*pl.* **caeau**) Field, enclosure
Caer, y gaer (*pl.* **caerau**) Fort, camp, stronghold
Cain, gain Fine, elegant
Calch Lime, chalk
Cam (*n.*) step
Cam, gam (*adj.*) crooked
Canol Middle
Cant Hundred
Cantref A hundred (division of land)
Capel Chapel, meeting house
Carn, y garn (*pl.* **carnau**) Cairn, rock, mountain
Carnedd, y garnedd (*pl.* **carneddau**) Cairn, barrow, tumulus, mountain
Carreg, y garreg (*pl.* **cerrig**) Stone, rock
Castell Castle
Ceffyl Horse
Cefn Ridge
Cei Quay
Celli, y gelli Grove, copse
Celyn Holly
Cemais (*pl.* of **camas, y gamas**) River bends
Cenedlaethol, genedlaethol National
Cerrig *see* **Carreg**
Ceunant Ravine, gorge, brook
Cil (*pl.* **ciliau**) Corner, retreat, nook
Cilfach, y gilfach Cove, creek, corner
Cistfaen, y gistfaen Prehistoric grave
Clas Cloister, 'mother-church'
Clawdd Dyke, embankment, hedge, ditch
Cledd (*pl.* **cleddau**) sword
Clogwyn Precipice, crag
Clun Meadow, brake, moor, thicket
Clwyd, y glwyd Gate
Cnwc Hillock, knoll
Cob Embankment
Coch, goch Red
Coed Trees, wood, forest
Coetre, coety Woodland dwelling
Collen Hazel
Cors, y gors Bog, fen
Corwg Coracle
Craig, y graig (*pl.* **creigiau**) Rock, crag
Crib Narrow ridge, crest, summit
Croes, y groes Cross, cross-roads
Croesffordd, croeslon Cross-roads
Crug (*pl.* **crugiau**) Mound, knoll
Cwch Boat
Cwm Valley, combe
Cwrt Court, yard
Cwt Shed, hut, cottage
Cymer (*pl.* **cymerau**) Confluence
Cymraeg Welsh
Cymro Welshman

Da, dda Good
Dafad, y ddafad (*pl.* **defaid**) Sheep
Dan Under, below

Dâr (*pl.* **deri**) Oak
Darren *see* **Tarren**
Dau, dwy Two
Derwen, y dderwen (*pl.* **derw**) Oak
Dewi David
Din Hill fortress
Dinas, y ddinas Fort, city, hill fortress
Diserth Hermitage, wilderness, retreat
Dôl, y ddôl (*pl.* **dolau, dolydd**) Meadow, water-meadow
Domen *see* **Tomen**
Draen, y ddraen Thorn
Dre *see* **Tre**
Drum *see* **Trum**
Drwg, ddrwg Evil, bad
Drws Door, gap, pass
Du, ddu Black, dark
Dwfr, dwr Water
Dwy *see* **Dau**
Dyffryn Valley
Dyn (*pl.* **dynion**) Man

Efail *see* **Gefail**
Eglwys Church
Eisteddfod Competitive festival of music and poetry
Eithin Furze, gorse
Elegug Guillemot
Eos Nightingale
Erw Acre
Esgair Long ridge, hill spur

Fach *see* **Bach**
Faenor *see* **Maenor**
Fan *see* **Ban**
Faerdref *see* **Maerdref**
Fawr *see* **Mawr**
Felin *see* **Melin**
Ffair Fair
Ffin Boundary
Fflur Flowers
Fforch Bifurcation, Fork
Ffordd Road, way
Ffos Ditch, trench
Ffridd (*pl.* **ffriddoedd**) Mountain-pasture, sheep-walk
Ffrwd (*pl.* **ffrydiau**) Stream, torrent
Ffynnon (*pl.* **ffynhonnau**) Spring, well
Foel *see* **Moel**
Fron *see* **Bron**

Gaer *see* **Caer**
Gafr, yr afr Goat
Gallt, yr allt Hill, slope, wood
Garn *see* **Carn**
Garnedd *see* **Carnedd**
Garreg *see* **Carreg**
Garth, yr arth Hill, height, enclosure, ridge, garden

Garw, arw   Rough, coarse
Gefail, yr efail   Smithy
Gelli   *see* **Celli**
Ger   Near, by
Gilfach   *see* **Cilfach**
Glan, lan (*adj.*)   Clean, holy, fair, beautiful
Glân, y lân (*n.*)   Bank, shore
Glas, las   Green, blue
Glas, glais (as in Dulas, Dulais)   Brook, stream
Glo   Coal
Glyn   Glen, deep valley
Goch   *see* **Coch**
Goetre   *see* **Coetre**
Gors   *see* **Cors**
Gorsaf   Station
Gorsedd   Throne, bardic order
Graig   *see* **Craig**
Grib   *see* **Crib**
Groes   *see* **Croes**
Grug   Heather
Gwastad   Plain, flat
Gwaun, y waun   Meadow, moor
Gwely   Bed
Gwern, y wern   Swamp, place where alders grow
Gwig, y wig   Wood
Gwylan, y wylan   Seagull
Gwyllt, wyllt   Wild
Gwyn, wen   White
Gwynt   Wind
Gwyrdd, werdd   Green

Hafod, hafoty   Summer dwelling, shieling
Haidd   Barley
Haul   Sun
Helygen (*pl.* **helyg**)   Willow
Hen   Old
Hendre(f)   Winter dwelling, established settlement
Heol, hewl   Road
Hir   Long
Hiraeth   Yearning, nostalgia
Hwyl   Mood, inspiration

Is   Below
Isaf   Lowest, lower
Isel   Low

Las   *see* **Glas**
Llain (*pl.* **lleiniau**)   Narrow strip of land
Llam   Leap
Llan   Church, originally the enclosure of a Celtic religious community
Llannerch   Clearing, glade
Llawr   Floor, flat valley bottom
Llech   Slate, slab, stone, rock
Llechwedd   Hillside, slope
Llethr   Slope, steep
Llety   Small house, shelter, lodging

Lluest   Hut, cottage, shieling
Llwch (*pl.* **llychau**)   Lake
Llwybr   Path
Llwyd, lwyd   Grey, brown
Llwyn   Grove, bush
Llyfrgell   Library
Llyn   Lake
Llys   Court, hall
Llythyrdy   Post Office (*lit.* 'letter-house')
Lwyd   *see* **Llwyd**

Mab (*pl.* **meibion**)   Son
Maen (*pl.* **meini**)   Stone
Maenol, maenor, y faenor   Manor, residence of district chief
Maerdre(f)   Hamlet attached to chief's court, lord's demesne, 'royal village'
Maes (*pl.* **meysydd**)   Field, plain
Mair   Mary
Mam, y fam   Mother
Mawn   Peat
Mawr, fawr   Big, great
Meini   *see* **Maen**
Melin, y felin   Mill
Melindre(f)   Mill village
Merthyr   Saint's grave, place commemorating a martyr
Melyn, felyn   Yellow
Mign, y fign (*pl.* **mignedd**)   Bog, quagmire
Min   Edge, brink
Mochyn (*pl.* **moch**)   Pig
Moel, y foel   Bare, rounded hill-top
Môr   Sea
Morfa   Bog, sea-marsh, fen
Mur (*pl.* **muriau**)   Wall
Mwyn   Ore, mine
Mynach   Monk
Mynachlog, y fynachlog   Monastery
Mynydd   Mountain

Nant (*pl.* **nentydd, nannau**)   Stream, brook
Neuadd   Hall
Newydd   New
Nos   Night

Oen   Lamb
Oer   Cold
Ogof   Cave
Olaf   Last
Onnen (*pl.* **onn, ynn**)   Ash tree

Pandy   Fulling-mill
Pant   Valley, hollow
Parc   Park, field
Pen   Top, head
Penrhyn   Promontory
Pentre(f)   Village, homestead

GLOSSARY

Pigwn Cone
Pistyll Spout, waterfall
Plaid, y blaid Party
Plas Hall, mansion
Pont, y bont Bridge
Porth Port, gateway, harbour
Prifysgol, y brifysgol University
Pump, pum Five
Pwll Pool, pit
Pysgodyn (*pl.* **pysgod**) Fish

Rhaeadr Waterfall
Rhedyn Bracken
Rhiw Hill, slope
Rhos (*pl.* **rhosydd**) Moorland, plain
Rhyd Ford

Saesneg English language
Sain, sant, saint Saint
Sarn (*pl.* **sarnau**) Causeway
Sgwd Waterfall
Sir County
Swyddfa Office
Sych Dry

Tad Father
Tafarn (*pl.* **tafarnau**) Tavern
Tair *see* **Tri**
Tâl End, forehead, front
Tan Below, under
Taran, y daran Thunder
Tarren, y darren Rocky height, precipice
Tarw Bull
Teg, deg Fair, pretty
Tir Land, territory

Tomen, y domen Mound
Ton Grassland, lea
Traeth Strand, beach, shore
Traws Across, cross, transverse; direction, district
Tre(f), y dre(f) Homestead, hamlet, town
Tri, tair Three
Troed Foot
Tros Across, over
Trum, y drum Ridge
Trwyn Point, cape (*lit.* nose)
Twll Hole
Twyn Hillock, knoll
Tŷ (*pl.* **tai**) House
Tyddyn, ty'n Small farm, holding
Tylwyth Teg The 'fair family', the fairies

Uchaf Higher, highest, upper
Uchel High
Undeb Union, religious denomination
Uwch Above, over, higher

Waen, Waun *see* **Gwaun**
Wen *see* **Gwyn**
Wern *see* **Gwern**

Y, yr, 'r The, of the
Ych Ox
Yn In, at
Ynys Island, water-meadow
Ysbryd Spirit, ghost
Ysbyty Hospital, hospice
Ysgol School
Ysgubor Barn
Ystrad Vale, valley floor, strath
Ystum Bend (in river)

Further Reading

General

Davies, Margaret. *Looking at Wales* (1968).

Evans, Gwynfor. *Land of my Fathers* (1974).

Fishlock, Trevor. *Wales and the Welsh* (1972).

Fraser, Maxwell. *West of Offa's Dyke. South Wales* (1958).

Humphrys, Graham. *Industrial Britain: South Wales* (1972).

Jones, R. Brinley (ed.). *Anatomy of Wales* (1972).

Lewis, Eiluned and Peter. *The Land of Wales* (2nd edit. 1945).

Lockley, R. M. *Wales* (1966).

Rees, Vyvyan. *Shell Guide to Mid Western Wales: Cardiganshire and Merioneth* (1971), *Shell Guide to South-West Wales: Carmarthenshire and Pembrokeshire* (revised edit. 1976).

Verey, David. *Shell Guide to Mid Wales* (1960).

The Wales Year Book (annual publ.).

Geology, geography, natural history, and landscape

Carter, Harold. *The towns of Wales: a study in urban geography* (1965).

Earp, J. R. and Hains, B. A. *British Regional Geology: the Welsh Borderland* (3rd edit. 1971).

Emery, F. V. *The world's landscapes. 2. Wales* (1969).

George, T. Neville. *British Regional Geology: South Wales* (3rd edit. 1970).

Hilling, J. B. *Cardiff and the Valleys: architecture in townscape* (1973).

Hyde, H. A. and Wade, A. E. *Welsh Flowering Plants* (1957).

Jones, Anthony. *Chapel architecture in Merthyr Tydfil, Glamorgan* (1962).

Lockley, R. M. *The Naturalist in Wales* (1970).

Peate, Iorwerth. *The Welsh House* (2nd edit. 1944).

Saunders, David. *A guide to the Birds of Wales* (1974).

Sylvester, Dorothy. *The Rural Landscape of the Welsh Borderland* (1969).

Trueman, A. E. *Geology and Scenery in England and Wales* (revised edit. 1974).

Williams, Moelwyn. *The Making of the South Wales Landscape* (1975).

Archaeology and history

Alderson, Frederick. *The inland resorts and spas of Britain* (1973).

Chadwick, Nora. *The Celts* (1970).

Chadwick, Nora and Dillon, Myles. *The Celtic Realms* (1967).

Collingwood, R. G. *Archaeology of Roman Britain* (1930) (new edition, with Sir Ian Richmond, 1969).

Cornforth, John. *Country houses in Britain – can they survive?* (1974).

Dodd, A. H. *Life in Wales* (1972).

Evans, C. J. O. *Glamorgan, its history and topography* (2nd edit. 1953).

Foster, I. Ll. and Daniel, G. E. *Prehistoric and early Wales* (1965).

Fox, C. F. *Regional guides to ancient monuments, Vol. IV, South Wales* (1954).

Girouard, Mark. *The Victorian Country House* (1971).

Grimes, W. F. and Savory, H. N. *The Prehistory of Wales* (2nd edit. 1951).

Houlder, Christopher. *Wales: an archaeological guide* (1974).

Jones, David J. V. *Before Rebecca. Popular protests in Wales 1793–1835* (1973).

Jones, Francis. *The Holy Wells of Wales* (1954).

Knowles, D. and Hadcock, R. N. *Medieval religious houses, England and Wales* (2nd edit. 1971).

Liversidge, Joan. *Britain in the Roman Empire* (1968).

Nash-Williams, V. E. *Early Christian Inscriptions in Wales* (1950).

North, F. J. *Sunken Cities: some legends of the coast and lakes of Wales* (1957).

Rees, D. Morgan. *Mines, mills and furnaces* (1969).

Rees, William. *Cardiff. A history of the city* (2nd edit. 1969), *An historical atlas of Wales* (1951).

Reid, Alan. *Castles of Wales* (1975).

Roderick, A. J. *Wales through the Ages* (2 vols.) (1959–60).

Smith, Peter. *Houses of the Welsh Countryside: a Study in Historical Geography* (1975).

Strong, Roy et al. *The Destruction of the Country House (1875–1974)* (1975).

Stuart-Jones, E. H. *The last invasion of Britain* (1950).

Williams, David. *A History of Modern Wales* (1950), *The Rebecca Riots* (1955).

Williams, David H. *The Welsh Cistercians. Aspects of their economic history* (1969).

Williams, Glanmor (ed.). *Merthyr Politics: the making of a working-class tradition* (1966), *The Welsh Church from Conquest to Reformation* (1962).

Wilson, Roger J. A. *A Guide to the Roman Remains in Britain* (1975).

Literature

A Book of Wales (ed. D. M. and E. M. Lloyd) (1965).

A Celtic Miscellany (translations from the Celtic literatures by Kenneth Hurlstone Jackson) (revised edit. 1971).

The Lilting House (ed. J. S. Williams and Meic Stephens) (1969) (anthology of Anglo-Welsh poetry).

The Mabinogion (translated by Gwyn Jones and Thomas Jones: 1949) (translated by Jeffrey Gantz: 1976).

Parry, Thomas. *History of Welsh Literature* (translated by H. Idris Bell) (1955).

The Penguin Book of Welsh Verse (translated by Anthony Conran) (1967).

The Penguin Book of Welsh Short Stories (ed. Alun Richards) (1976).

Twenty-five Welsh Short Stories (selected by Gwyn Jones and Islwyn Ffowc Elis) (1971).

Welsh Short Stories (selected by Gwyn Jones) (1956).

Welsh Voices (ed. Bryn Griffiths) (1967).

Welsh life, early tours, etc.

Borrow, George. *Wild Wales* (1862) (edit. 1955).

Bradley, A. G. *Highways and Byways in South Wales* (1903).

Clarke, Elizabeth. *The Valley* (1969).

Defoe, Daniel. *A Tour through England and Wales* (1724–6) (edit. 1971).

Fitzgibbon, Theodora. *A Taste of Wales* (1973).

FURTHER READING

Giraldus Cambrensis ('Gerald the Welshman'). *Description of Wales* (1194), *Itinerary of Wales* (1188) (edit. 1906).

Hall, Mr and Mrs S. C. *The Book of South Wales, the Wye and the Coast* (1861).

Jones, T. Gwynn. *Welsh folk lore and folk custom* (1930).

Kilvert, Francis. *Kilvert's Diary* (ed. William Plomer, 3 vols., 1938–40) (selections, in one vol., 1944).

Leland, John. *The Itinerary in Wales (1536–1539)* (ed. L. T. Smith 1906).

Lewis, Samuel. *A Topographical Dictionary of Wales* (1833).

Malkin, Benjamin Heath. *The Scenery, Antiquities and Biography of South Wales* (1804).

Morgan, Gerald. *The Dragon's Tongue: the Fortunes of the Welsh Language* (1966).

Owen, Trefor M. *Welsh folk customs* (1959).

Parry-Jones, D. *A Welsh Country Upbringing* (1948).

Rhys, Sir John. *Celtic folklore* (2 vols.) (1901).

Rhys, Sir John and Jones, D. Brynmor. *The Welsh people* (1900).

Roberts, H. A. E. *Legends and folklore of South Wales* (1931).

Stephens, Meic (ed.). *The Welsh Language Today* (1973).

Thomas, Ned. *The Welsh Extremist* (1971).

Williams, Raymond. *Border Country* (a novel) (1960).

See also the publications of the Wales Tourist Board, Her Majesty's Stationery Office (particularly the guide-books to the National Parks), and the Department of the Environment's guides to separate monuments.

Photograph and Map Credits

PHOTOGRAPH AND MAP CREDITS

Index

Map Section

GEOLOGY OF SOUTH WALES

km.

0   10   20   30

KEY

Jurassic

LIAS AND RHAETIC: *Marine shales and marly limestones*

Triassic

KEUPER MARL: *Continental mudstones*

Carboniferous

COAL MEASURES: *Rhythmic sequences of shales, sandstones, and coals*

MILLSTONE GRIT: *Coarse sandstones*

CARBONIFEROUS LIMESTONE SERIES

Devonian (OLD RED SANDSTONE SERIES)

Sandstone, siltstone, and marls

Siluria

S

Ordov

S

Cambr

S

Igneou

E

I

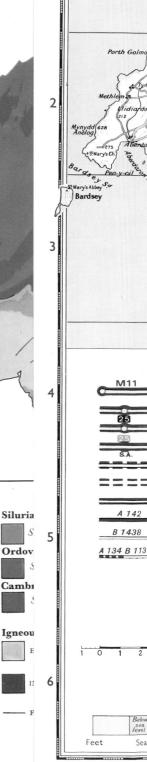

A

I

Penllech
Porth Golmon   Llan
Tyhen   Rhos-hirwaun
Methlem   406
Uidiardou   212
Mynydd   628
Anelog   B 4413
275   Aberdaron   Llo
St Mary's Ch.   Aberdaron B.
Bardsey Sd.   Pen-y-cil
St Mary's Abbey   Bardsey

C

M11   Moto
Inte
25   Lim
25   Ser
S.A.   Unc
Pro
Dual
A 142   'A' Ro
B 1438   'B' Ro
A 134 B 113   Single

STATUT

1   0   1   2   3   4

Below
sea
level

Feet   Sea Level

2

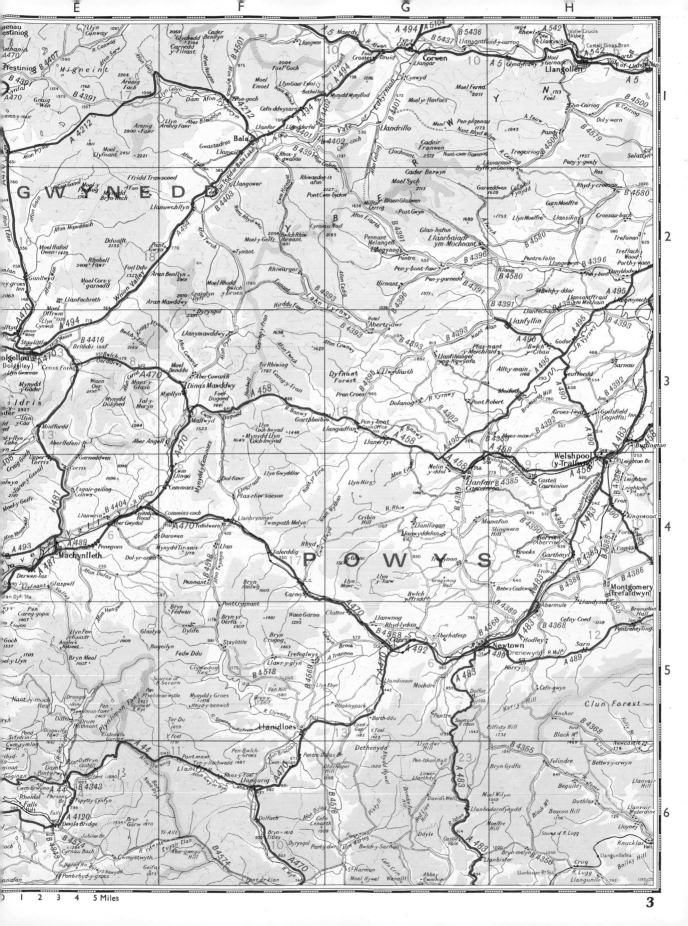

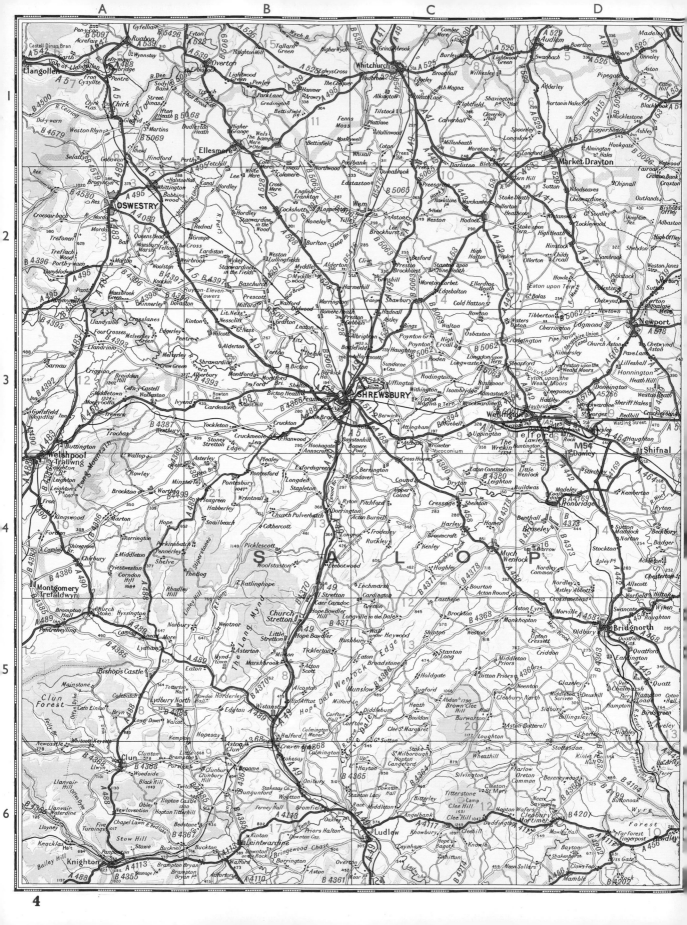

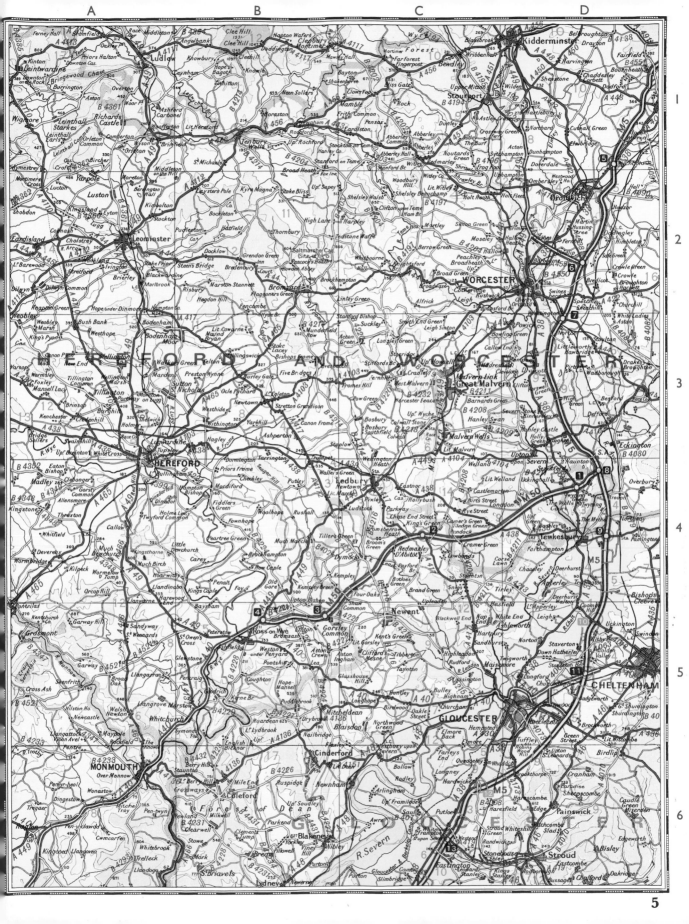

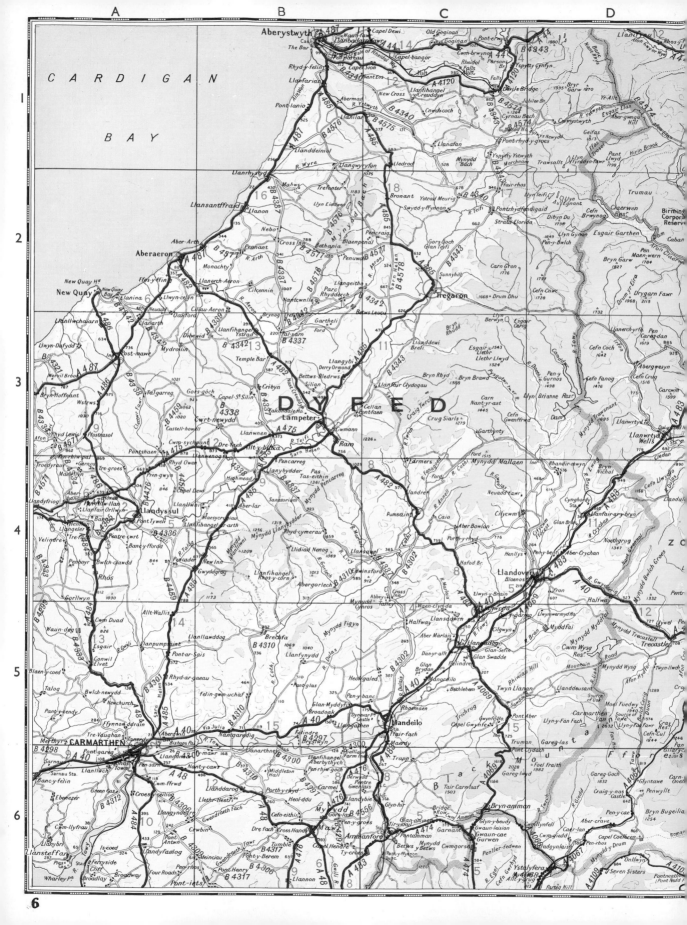

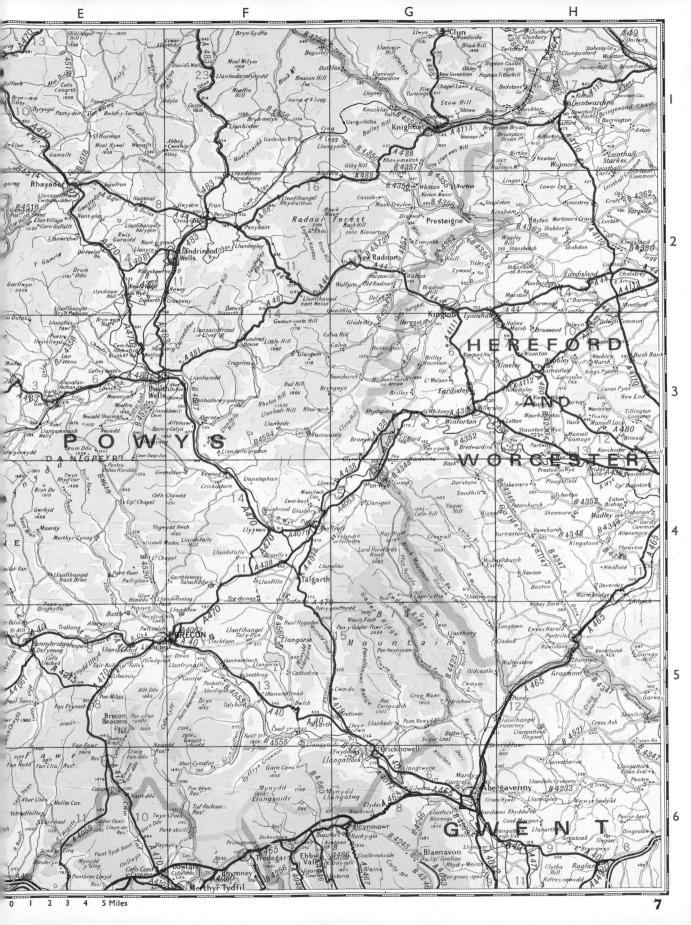

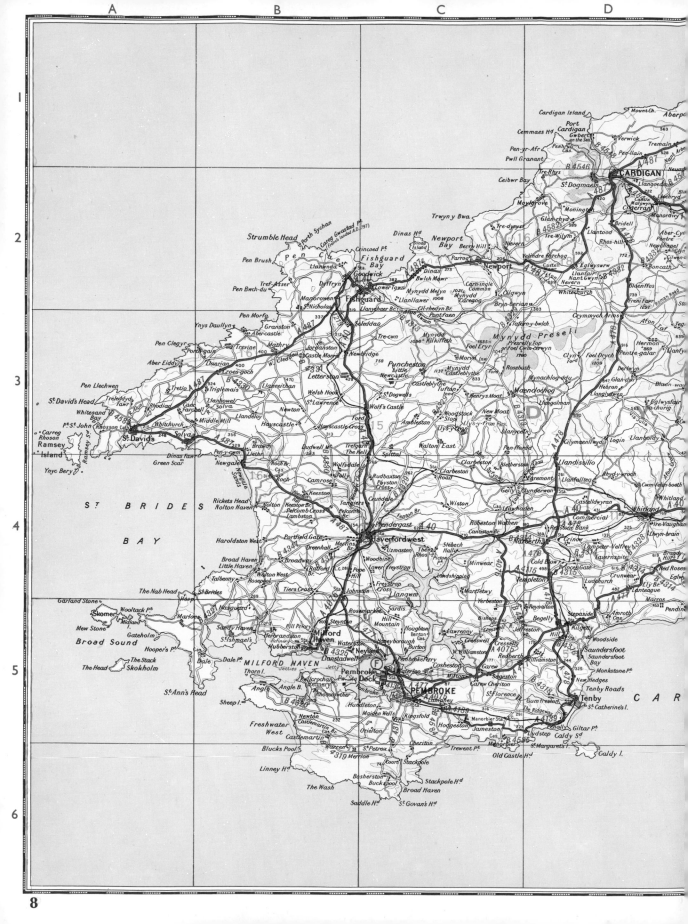

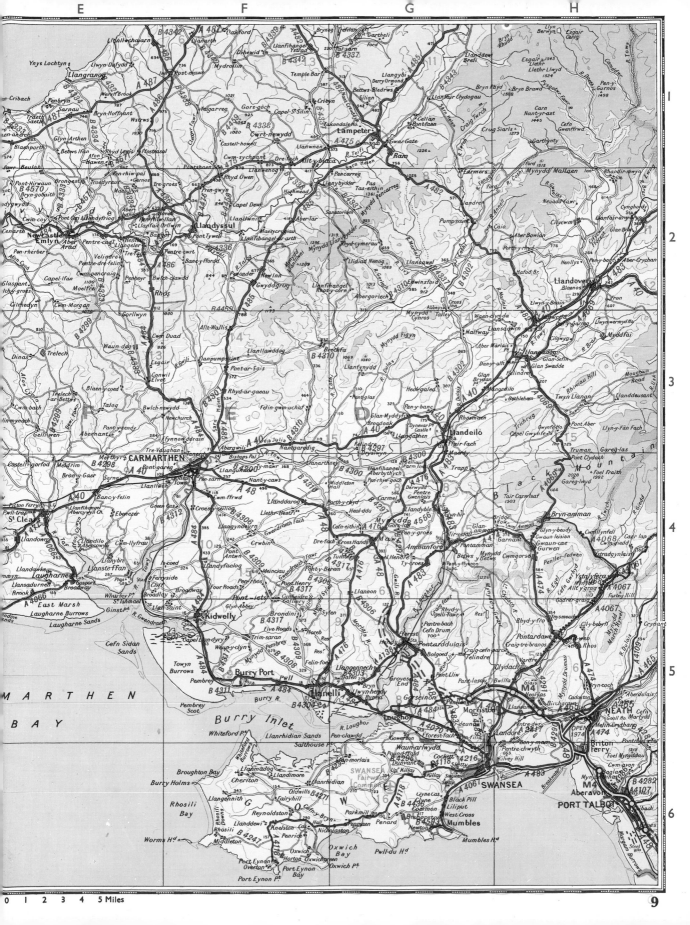

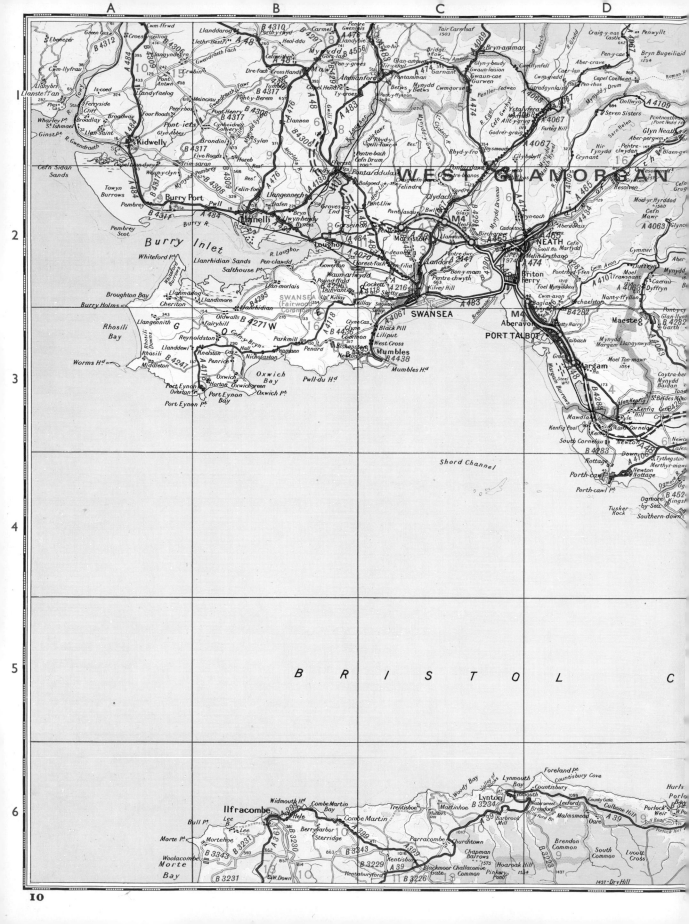